Highland Indians and the State in Modern Ecuador

PITT LATIN AMERICAN SERIES

HIGHLAND INDIANS AND THE STATE IN MODERN ECUADOR

Edited by

A. Kim Clark *and*

Marc Becker

UNIVERSITY OF PITTSBURGH PRESS

Published by the University of Pittsburgh Press, Pittsburgh, PA 15260

Manufactured in the United States of America
Printed on acid-free paper
10 9 8 7 6 5 4 3 2 1

Library of Congress Cataloging-in-Publication Data

Highland Indians and the state in modern Ecuador / edited by A. Kim Clark and Marc Becker.
p. cm. — (Pitt Latin American series)
Includes bibliographical references and index.
ISBN-13: 978-0-8229-4336-5 (cloth : alk. paper)
ISBN-10: 0-8229-4336-0 (cloth : alk. paper)
1. Indians of South America—Ecuador—Sierra—History. 2. Indians, Treatment of—Ecuador—Sierra—History. 3. Indians of South America—Ecuador—Sierra—Government relations. 4. Sierra (Ecuador)—Politics and government. 5. Sierra (Ecuador)—Race relations. I. Clark, A. Kim, 1964– II. Becker, Marc.
F3721.1.S54H55 2007
986.6'00498—dc22

2007016271

Contents

Acknowledgments

We first began planning this volume in the year 2000; one measure of how long it has been in the works is that it takes two hands to count the number of children who have been born to the authors, collectively, during the period this book was in preparation. Our first thanks must go to all of the authors whose work is included in this volume, some of whom have been involved from the very beginning and who have shown remarkable patience as the volume took form and changed shape several times over the years. We equally thank authors who joined us relatively late in this process, sometimes on fairly short notice, to fill slots vacated by authors who moved on to other projects. We are also grateful to those who at different moments were involved in some way with this volume but who do not appear in the final product, or who were unable to participate although they expressed support. These include Rudi Colloredo-Mansfeld, Guillermo de la Peña, Andrés Guerrero, Tanya Korovkin, Brooke Larson, David Nugent, Galo Ramón, Susana Sawyer, Carol Smith, and Steve Striffler. Their ideas and insights have significantly improved the quality of the final product. We are especially grateful to Lyman Johnson, who carefully looked over the manuscript and suggested ways to rethink the book's structure. Peter Kracht and Deborah Meade at the University of Pittsburgh Press have shown sustained enthusiasm for the project, and our thanks go to Peter, Deborah, and their colleagues at the Press, as well as to the anonymous readers who offered provocative comments and suggestions that helped make this a much better book.

Abbreviations

ANIPA	Asamblea Nacional Indígena por la Autonomía (National Indian Assembly in Support of Autonomy; Mexico)
CIDOB	Confederación de Pueblos Indígenas de Bolivia (Confederation of Indigenous Peoples of Eastern Bolivia)
CNC	Confederación Nacional Campesina (National Peasant Confederation; Mexico)
CNI	Congreso Nacional Indígena (National Indian Congress; Mexico)
CODENPE	Consejo de Desarrollo de las Nacionalidades y Pueblos del Ecuador (Council for the Development of Nationalities and Peoples of Ecuador)
CONACAMI	Confederación Nacional de Comunidades del Peru Afectadas por la Minera (Confederation of Communities Affected by Mining Industries)
CONAIE	Confederación de Nacionalidades Indígenas del Ecuador (Confederation of Indigenous Nationalities of Ecuador)
CONAMAQ	Consejo Nacional de Ayllus y Markas del Qollasuyo (Confederation of Ayllus and Markas of Qollasuyo; Bolivia)
CONFENIAE	Confederación de Nacionalidades Indígenas de la Amazonía Ecuatoriana (Confederation of Indigenious Nationalities of the Ecuadorian Amazon)
COPPIP	Conferencia Permanente de los Pueblos Indígenas del Perú (Conference of the Indigenous Peoples of Peru)
CSUTCB	Confederación Sindical Única de Trabajadores Campesinos de Bolivia (Unified Confederation of Rural Laborers of Bolivia)
DINEIB	Dirección Nacional de Educación Intercultural Bilingüe (Directorate of Bilingual Education; Ecuador)
ECUARUNARI	Ecuador Runacunapac Riccharimui (Awakening of the Ecuadorian Indians)

EZLN	Ejército Zapatista de Liberación Nacional (Zapatista Army of National Liberation; Mexico)
FEI	Federación Ecuatoriana de Indios (Ecuadorian Federation of Indians)
FEINE	Consejo de Pueblos y Organizaciones Indígenas Evangélicas del Ecuador (Council of Indigenous Evangelical Peoples)
FENOC	Federación Nacional de Organizaciones Campesinas (National Federation of Peasant Organizations; Ecuador)
FENOCIN	Confederación Nacional de Organizaciones Campesinas, Indígenas y Negras (Federation of Peasant, Indigenous, and Black Organizations; Ecuador)
FEPOCAN	Federación Provincial de Organizaciones Campesinas de Napo (Provincial Federation of Peasant Organizations of Napo; Ecuador)
FOIN	Federación de Organizaciones Indígenas del Napo (Federation of Indigenous Organizations of Napo; Ecuador)
FTAA	Free Trade Area of the Americas
IERAC	Instituto Ecuatoriano de Reforma Agraria y Colonización (Ecuadorian Institute of Agrarian Reform and Colonization)
ILO	International Labor Organization
INCAYAC	Instituto de Culturas Aborígenes y Acción Comunitaria (Institute of Aboriginal Cultures and Community Action; Ecuador)
INI	Instituto Nacional Indigenista (National Indigenist Institute; Mexico)
JCAP	Junta Central de Asistencia Pública (Social Welfare Board; Ecuador)
MUPP	Movimiento Unidad Plurinacional Pachakutik (Pachakutik Plurinational United Movement; Ecuador)
NAFTA	North American Free Trade Agreement
OPIP	Organización de Pueblos Indígenas de Pastaza (Organization of Indigenous Peoples of Pastaza; Ecuador)
PRD	Partido de la Revolución Democrática (Party of the Democratic Revolution; Mexico)
PRI	Partido Revolucionario Institucional (Institutional Revolutionary Party; Mexico)
PRODEPINE	Proyecto de Desarrollo para Pueblos Indígenas y Negros del Ecuador (Development of Indigenous and Afro-Ecuadorian Peoples)

Highland Indians and the State in Modern Ecuador

COLOMBIA
PACIFIC OCEAN
Esmeraldas
Carchi
Imbabura
Otavalo
Nueva Loja
Sucumbíos
Cayambe
Pichincha
Quito
Manabi
Napo
Puerto Francisco de Oreliana
Orellana
Tigua
Latacunga
Cotopaxi
Tungurahua
Guaranda
Los Rìos
Bolìvar
Riobamba
Pastaza
Milagro
Chimborazo
Guayas
Guayaquil
Cañar
Morona-Santiago
Cuenca
Azuay
El Oro
Zamora-Chinchipe
Loja
PERU

1

Indigenous Peoples and State Formation in Modern Ecuador

A. KIM CLARK AND MARC BECKER

The formal political system is in crisis in Ecuador: the twentieth century ended with a four-year period that saw six different governments. Indeed, between 1997 and 2005, four of nine presidents in Latin America who were removed through irregular procedures were in Ecuador.[1] Sociologist Leon Zamosc calls Ecuador "one of the most, if not *the* most, unstable country in Latin America."[2] At the same time, the Ecuadorian Indian movement made important gains in the last decade of the twentieth century, and for at least some sectors of society, at the turn of the twenty-first century had more prestige than traditional politicians did. The fact that Ecuador has a national level indigenous organization sets it apart from other Latin American countries. National and international attention was drawn to this movement in June 1990, when an impressive indigenous uprising paralyzed the country for several weeks. Grassroots members of the Confederación de Nacionalidades Indígenas del Ecuador (CONAIE, Confederation of Indigenous Nationalities of Ecuador) marched on provincial capitals and on Quito, kept their agricultural produce off the market, and blocked the Pan-American Highway, the country's main north-south artery. The mobilization was organized to draw attention to land disputes in the Ecuadorian Amazon (Oriente) and highlands (Sierra), and ended when the government agreed to negotiate a 16-point agenda presented by CONAIE.[3]

Since 1990, Ecuadorian Indians have become increasingly involved in national politics, not just through "uprising politics," but also through

Pachakutik, an electoral movement representing an alliance of indigenous organizations with other social movements that has elected several indigenous members to congress. In January 2000 Indians participated directly in a change of government when they joined with disaffected military officers to oust President Jamil Mahuad in a context of economic crisis and political corruption. When one of the leaders of those events, retired Colonel Lucio Gutiérrez, was elected president in November 2002 with indigenous support, one of his first acts was to name two indigenous intellectuals and activists to important cabinet posts. Despite subsequent disillusionment and a break with the Gutiérrez government, Ecuadorian Indians are widely recognized as important political actors on the national scene.

Much has been written in recent years about the Ecuadorian Indian movement, notably the 1990 uprising and subsequent political mobilizations in 1992, 1994, and 2000, among other events. The image of erudite Indians, in indigenous dress, negotiating directly with the national government—particularly during the 1994 negotiations over proposed changes to the agrarian law, parts of which were widely televised in Ecuador—is a potent symbol of the changing relationship between Indians and the Ecuadorian state. However, for many Ecuadorians, including many scholars, when the Indian movement burst onto the national political scene in 1990, it seemed to emerge out of thin air. A study frequently cited in the 1980s, for instance, noted that in the 1970s Indians in an area of Chimborazo Province, when asked the meaning of *la patria* (fatherland or nation), identified it as the name of an interprovincial bus company.[4] This has fed into images of highland indigenous peasants as isolated and disengaged from the Ecuadorian nation or state. Those who have conducted archival research, however, were not surprised by the growing indigenous activism, given the deliberate and strategic way in which at least some Indians, in some circumstances, have engaged the Ecuadorian state since the early nineteenth century. One purpose of this book is to demonstrate the deep historical roots of the relation between Indians and the state in highland Ecuador and to counteract the impression that this relationship barely existed until quite recently.

Another reason for undertaking this book is that Ecuador is often ignored in discussions of state formation or Indian-state relations in Latin America. This is no doubt because among Andean nations Ecuador is clearly the poor cousin of Peru and Bolivia in terms of research undertaken on relations between Indians and the state. Moreover, some of the research that has been carried out has not reached a wider audience. The relative lack of scholarly interest in Ecuador may result from the many historical differences between Ecuador and its neighbors. Unlike Peru and Bolivia, Ecuador did not experience spectacular indigenous rebellions during the late colonial period. Nor were Ecuadorian Indians important participants in international or civil wars in the late nineteenth century, such as the War of the Pacific in Peru or the Federal War in Bolivia, where Indians had clearly stated autonomous political projects. Perhaps there was less large-scale indigenous resistance in Ecuador in this period because rapid expansion of export production occurred primarily in the more sparsely populated and less indigenous coastal region, rather than in the indigenous heartland. In the second half of the twentieth century, there were no large-scale revolutions or civil wars involving the indigenous peasants in Ecuador, comparable to those in Peru, Guatemala, and elsewhere. In other words, in nineteenth- and twentieth-century Ecuador there were fewer violent conflicts between the state and indigenous peoples.

Many of these differences may be partly explained by the preponderance of the hacienda in highland Ecuador. Unlike Peru and Bolivia, where mining was the focal point of the colonial economy, Ecuador emphasized hacienda production, leading to a fusing of economic and political power in the hands of highland landowners who directly controlled Indian labor. As a result, there were proportionately fewer autonomous Indian communities in Ecuador than in Bolivia or Peru; in contrast, there appears to have been a subterranean process of concentration of indigenous population in the highest altitude zones *within* haciendas in the early twentieth century.[5] Another important contrast between Peru and Ecuador is that in the agrarian reform period, Peru focused on creating state cooperatives that micromanaged agricultural production (dissatisfaction with which provided an opening for the Shining Path guerrillas in the 1980s), while in the same era Ecuadorian peasants seized upon a community model of development, drawing on 1937 legislation regulating the indigenous community. Paradoxically, there are more opportunities for building bonds of local cooperation in the communal model than in the top-down cooperative model as developed in Peru.[6] To restate these points, in Ecuador the state historically has not intervened in indigenous life on a day-to-day basis, representing a primary source of the lived experience of oppression. State agents and institutions have at times acted instead as distant interlocutors in local conflicts. Certainly, the emergence of such a strong indigenous movement within the bounds of civil society, rather than outside it, suggests that something interesting and unusual occurred in Ecuador.

At various moments it has been possible for Ecuadorian Indians to pursue some of their interests *within* the bounds of state policies. This was not a result of the kindness of government authorities, but of conflicts among various elite groups or state institutions in which Indians were enlisted—often in purely rhetorical terms—as components of these struggles. Regardless of the reason for the importance of the "Indian problem" at different times, Indians were able to use these political openings to press their own concerns. As they did so, their organizational experience and capacity also increased. In short, highland Indians have been central to the processes of Ecuadorian state formation, rather than simply the recipients of state policy. At times, their actions led to the generation of new laws or government orders, and their political strategies sometimes affected state policy by stretching the meaning of government discourse, and in the process, transforming it.

We explore three interlocking dimensions of state formation in Ecuador.[7] First are specific projects of moral regulation conceived and carried out by the state. Regarding state projects imposed "from above," we examine how governments sought to impose on Indians a common discursive framework that set the terms in which contention could take place. (This follows Roseberry's reading of Gramsci.)[8] Second, we consider how state formation was enabled "from below," such as when indigenous groups might view state building as advantageous and thus embrace those efforts, helping to bring the state into being in new social arenas.[9] David Nugent's work on Peru provides fine examples, since the isolation of the zone he studied led subordinate groups there to conclude that it was the *absence* of the state that caused some of their most pressing problems, leading them to "invite the state in" to intervene in local social relations.[10] Third, we view the state itself as fragmented and internally contradictory, sometimes loosely grouping together institutions and representatives with divergent and contradictory interests. Although Steve Striffler does not write about Indian-state relations in the highlands, some of his comments about the Ecuadorian state in a discussion of how the United Fruit Company gained access to land in Ecuador's southern coast in the 1930s are also relevant here. He writes,

> This minor set of disputes, involving a major multinational, a pseudo-capitalist, an Ecuadorian senator, members of Congress, the Cabinet, the president, a former U.S. ambassador, and various state institutions/agencies not only suggests that the Ecuadorian state was highly divided, extremely biased, and easily influenced by a range of interested actors. It indicates that the state can in no way be seen as a discrete policy-making actor that stands above or apart from entities called "society" and "economy." It is worth remembering that Senator Navarro was negotiating a contract between (his) Congress and (his) Pacific Fruit Company in which the latter would purchase bananas from entrepreneurs/congressmen who could obtain financing through

> the *State* Mortgage Bank, which was partially funded by the Pacific Fruit Company. This complex collusion between members of the Ecuadorian government and the emerging banana industry contradicts the notion of a sharp distinction between state and society/economy.[11]

The point here is that the state is shot through with internal contradictions that can sometimes be exploited by social groups—including subordinate ones. To develop this perspective, we drew on Philip Abrams's discussion of the state as including a state system and a state idea. As Abrams described it, a state system is "a palpable nexus of practice and institutional structure centered in government and more or less extensive, unified and dominant in any given society"; here we take the phrase "more or less" as a research question. Equally important, Abrams argues that there is also an *idea* of the state that is "projected, purveyed and variously believed in different societies at different times."[12] Thus we should not confuse the actual functioning of the state system with the claims made in state discourse; nonetheless, how the state represents itself can end up constraining the actions of specific state institutions or authorities when subaltern groups, through political struggles, pressure the state to live up to its own self-image.

The research cited above has much to offer to an analysis of relations between subordinate groups and the state, and much of the most interesting recent work on the state is similarly informed by situating itself in the space between Gramsci's insights and those of Foucault. For instance, the essays in Thomas Blom Hansen and Finn Stepputat's edited volume, *States of Imagination: Ethnographic Explorations of the Postcolonial State,* develop a number of points that parallel our findings here: the state should not be seen ahistorically and should be denaturalized; the state is not the same everywhere, but involves distinct characters and different historical trajectories; both the myth of the state and its everyday practices should be examined; the state should not be seen as a monolithic "social actor"; and the state should be seen as shot through with ambiguities and contradictions.[13] Unlike Hansen and Stepputat's collection, however, we bring these notions together to examine state formation in relation to the indigenous population in a single country. While the case studies presented here cover different parts of the Ecuadorian highlands, at different times, and with rather different emphases, they build an image of the Ecuadorian state as permeable, tension-ridden, full of contradictions, and thus susceptible to the active and creative responses of subordinate groups. The Ecuadorian state is seen here as a historically specific configuration of practices and ideas.

The concept of the state that emerges from these studies is one in which many conflicting interests and projects coexist. Because some of the most serious problems for Indians at the local level were created precisely by local authorities who either contravened superior orders or used their positions to pursue their own economic interests, in some cases it was the absence of strong central state control over its own officials that subordinate groups saw as a problem. (David Nugent sees the same dynamic in Peru.) One strategy Indians used was to seek the intervention of higher state authorities to resolve local disputes. Such appeals to the central state further legitimized the state, although often by undermining the authority of local officials. This dynamic was surprisingly common in Ecuador, but whether this indicates a weak state or strong state is open to debate—or perhaps, the terms "weak" or "strong" simply do not adequately capture the complexity of the matter.

One aspect of this dynamic is explained by Ecuador's dual system of political power: elected officials work side by side with authorities appointed by the central state. Elected officials include mayors and municipal councils, provincial assemblies, members of the national congress and senate (different constitutions mandated a unicameral or bicameral legislative branch), and the national president and vice president. Appointed officials in turn include political lieutenants (*tenientes políticos*) at the parish (*parroquia*) level, political administrators (*jefes políticos*) at the cantonal (*cantón*) level, provincial governors, and national cabinet ministers. While one might expect elected officials to be more closely linked to local interests (although perhaps merely to those of local elites) and appointed officials to be more closely associated with central state priorities, even appointed officials at the more local levels were often so deeply immersed in local social relations that national projects were jeopardized. This led to a process whereby indigenous social actors played off appointed and elected officials at different levels of the state in the pursuit of subaltern projects, as well as playing off state rhetoric against the reality of state rule.

Regionalism and Ethnicity in Ecuador

Ecuador is composed of four zones: the tropical Pacific coastal lowlands, the temperate Sierra highlands, the eastern upper Amazon basin, often called the Oriente, and the Galápagos archipelago 780 kilometers west of the mainland. These geographic divisions obscure even deeper and more persistent political and cultural divisions. Historically, these were manifested in the highland capital, Quito, which declared its independence from Spain in 1809 in an action separate from the coastal port of Guayaquil, which proclaimed its independence in 1820. When Spanish forces were defeated outside Quito at the Battle of Pichincha on May 24, 1822, Quiteños watched while foreigners and Guayaquileños fought under the leadership of Antonio José de Sucre. When Ecuador separated from Gran Colombia in 1830, its constitution defined the new country as a weak federation of Guayas on the coast, Azuay in the southern highlands, and Quito in the northern highlands. Three decades later, this regionalism had clearly not been overcome. The country was nearly dissolved as four governments claimed to rule the national territory from the highland capital of Quito, from the port of Guayaquil, and from the two southern cities of Cuenca and Loja. This crisis was resolved by the strongly centralizing project of the government of Gabriel García Moreno, who came to power in 1860. Regionalism nonetheless continues to be a central feature of Ecuadorian politics, with Guayaquil still petitioning for more autonomy from the rest of the country.

Until well into the twentieth century, economically and demographically the highlands dominated the rest of the country. This emphasis dates to before the Spanish conquest, with the Inkas focusing their imperial efforts in the highlands largely to the exclusion of the coastal and Amazonian regions, where their civilizing project achieved much less success. In 1780 under Spanish colonial rule, 90 percent of the population in what is modern-day Ecuador lived in the highlands, with only 7 percent on the coast and 3 percent in the Oriente.[14] In the last decades of the eighteenth century, rural workers from the central Sierra began to migrate to the coast in search of work on plantations, thereby causing a population shift to the coast. At the beginning of the twentieth century, only 20 percent of the population lived on the coast, but by 1950 this figure had risen to 40 percent. By the 1970s, more people lived on the coast than in the highlands, with less than 4 percent living in the eastern Amazon. Simultaneously, there was a shift from rural to urban areas. Ecuador's first national census, in 1950, determined that 71 percent of the population still lived in rural areas, and it was not until the 1980s that the urban population surpassed that of the rural population.[15]

Similarly, ethnic divisions have also had a notable impact on Indian-state relations and political developments in general. Scholars have divided Ecuador's population (somewhat simplistically) into four groups: whites, mestizos, Indians, and Afro-Ecuadorians.[16] This rubric tends to gloss over a much more complex ethnographic landscape and ignores the variations that have occurred over time. In particular, the homogenous category of *Indian* incorporates many groups. In "The Historic Tribes of Ecuador" in the *Handbook of South American Indians*, John Murra lists the following ethnic groups at the time of the Inka and Spanish conquests: the Esmeralda, Manta, Huancavilca, and Puná on the coast, and in the highlands the Pasto (near the Colombian border), Cara (in the current province of Imbabura), Panzaleo (near Quito), Puruhá (around Riobamba), and Cañari and Palta (in the southern highlands). "The tribal entities these names represent," Murra writes, "have been disorganized and are completely obliterated. Their different, mutually unintelligible languages are gone and lost; no written documents have been preserved and the last speakers died in the 18th century."[17] To this list may be added the "forest tribes": the Jívaro (Shuar), Záparo (Zápara), Cofán (A'I), and Quichua (Kichwa) in the eastern Amazon.[18] Undoubtedly, before the Inka and Spanish conquests, many more indigenous groups existed in Ecuador than survive today. José Alcina Franch describes what has occurred as "ethnocide," as the number of indigenous groups dropped from twenty-four before the Inka conquest to ten in the 1980s, including a drop from twelve to four on the coast.[19]

Spanish colonial administration attempted to simplify this ethnic landscape by dividing the population into two "republics," one for the white Spaniards and another for the Indians. This division proved to be highly problematic, partly because of entrenched class divisions within both the indigenous and the Spanish societies. Elite Spaniards with access to economic resources or prestigious administrative posts enjoyed more rights and privileges than artisans or women.[20] Likewise, the survival of indigenous elites into the colonial period meant that not all Indians were equally subject to abusive and exploitative labor drafts, and in fact indigenous elites facilitated white dominance in the Americas.[21] In addition, indigenous migration fostered economic and social inequalities, as not all Indians were subject to the same labor and taxation demands.[22] Furthermore, divisions between European-born (*peninsular*) and American-born (*criollo*) whites led to cleavages within elite society that eventually resulted in Ecuador's independence in the early nineteenth century. In addition, the proliferation of mestizo groups in the interstices of colonial society further undermined the neat bipartite division that the Spanish crown hoped to maintain.

The Spanish colonial administration treated Indians as wards of the state and considered them legally inferior to white and mestizo inhabitants of the Americas. Along with this status came the crown's paternalistic policies that defended the Indians from some of the worst abuses at the hands of the colonial elite. With independence from Spain, liberal ideals flourished that did away with special privileges and obligations for certain groups of people while at the same time retaining aspects of Spanish colonial legislation and institutions that ensured the continued subjugation of Indians. All Ecuadorians (including Indians) were constitutionally declared to be equal, but racial discrimination (including African slavery) continued. Indians still faced debtors' prison, laws against begging and vagrancy, demands for tithes and tribute, forced labor, and loss of land. Andrés Guerrero notes that until the abolition of obligatory tribute payments in 1857, Indians were objects of "ethnic administration," with the government defining them as "miserable people" who were incapable of exercising or defending their own rights. Continuing colonial traditions, the republican government still legislated for, represented, and protected the interests of the Indians.[23]

The 1830 constitution established requirements for citizenship that included being married or at least 22 years of age, ownership of property worth at least 300 pesos or engagement in an independent "useful" profession or industry (this explicitly excluded domestic servants and day laborers), and the ability to read and write. Although this constitution declared the government to be "popular, representative, alternative, and responsible," only the 2,825 people (0.3 percent of the population) who met the stringent citizenship requirements selected the government that ruled over the rest of the country.[24] As Guillermo O'Donnell observes, although "equality before the law" was a liberal value, its reality was effectively skirted because the masses were excluded from the discourse of citizenship.[25] Nevertheless, liberal assimilationalist ideas persisted. For example, General Guillermo Rodríguez Lara, who came to power following the 1972 military coup, stated, "There is no more Indian problem. We all become white men when we accept the goals of the national culture."[26]

In 1857, with the merging of interests of large landowners, manufacturers, and merchants from both the highlands and coast, tribute payments that "weighed exclusively on the most miserable class in society" were finally and definitively abolished.[27] This did not mean the extension of universal citizenship rights to Indians, and much less the termination of racism. After this act, the word "indigenous" virtually disappeared from public and legal discourse, and the government's ethnic administration of Indians ended. Similar to what Mark Thurner describes for neighboring Peru, Ecuador experienced a transition from two separate sets of laws governing white and Indian society to one set of laws that hid a deeply fractured and contradictory society.[28] Eloy Alfaro's 1895 Liberal Revolution led to a return to legislation that attempted to address the "Indian problem." Casting himself as the protector of the "indigenous race," Alfaro established a minimum wage, prohibited unpaid services, and gave peons the right to pay off their debts and leave haciendas. He declared that "public power must be used to alleviate the unfortunate state of the indigenous race."[29] The most extensive and significant liberal legislation to address indigenous issues was the 1918 Reforma de la Ley de Jornaleros

(Reform of the Day Laborer Law) that instituted an eight-hour workday, outlawed debt prison, and abolished the inheritance of a parent's debts. Reformers believed that freeing Indians from feudal economic relations and forcing them into a free wage labor system would help modernize the Ecuadorian economy. Notably, this occurred along with the growing importance of the coastal sugar elite, who required a steady supply of migrant labor. Nevertheless, land tenure and service tenancy patterns that ensured hacienda owners a large labor supply while holding wages down survived well into the twentieth century. Xavier Albó dismisses these changes as "a rhetorical modernization of Indian exploitation,"[30] and, indeed, the hacienda system survived until the 1964 agrarian reform. Nonetheless, changes in law did affect the political resources available to indigenous peasants.

It is difficult to estimate the ethnic composition of Ecuador's population, largely because of the fluidity of ethnic categories and a lack of reliable statistical data.[31] Furthermore, as Jorge León and Joanne Rappaport note, "It is not always in one's interest to identify [oneself] as indigenous to a census-taker: hence many of the discrepancies in census figures."[32] A study from 1942 estimated that about 40 percent of the population was indigenous, with another 40 percent mestizo, 10 percent white, 5 percent black and mulatto, and 5 percent "other."[33] The majority of Indians live in the highlands and are often grouped under the global category of "Quichua" (or Kichwa). They are part of the larger ethnolinguistic Quechua group, the largest surviving indigenous language in the Americas that stretches across the Andean highlands from Colombia to Chile and includes between eight and twelve million speakers.[34] Regional divisions, however, are significant, and identity remains overwhelmingly local.

In the highlands, indigenous populations have become integrated into national society through their economic roles. The Saraguro Indians of Ecuador's southern Loja Province have earned a degree of economic independence through cattle production on large ranches, which sometimes puts them at odds with the rest of the Indian movement, which is largely composed of poor people chronically short of land. The Cañar people, on the other hand, began manufacturing Panama hats in the late nineteenth century as a way to cope with increasing poverty caused by the fragmentation and erosion of their land base. Ironically, in 1532 the Cañaris were one of the groups that considered the Spanish invaders as their liberators from Inka tyranny, but now they have assumed an Inka identity as a strategy of adaptation to cultural imperialism and economic exploitation.[35] The central highland province of Chimborazo has the highest concentration of Indians in Ecuador. They have gained a reputation as Ecuador's most rebellious Indians, a legacy of Fernando Daquilema's 1871 rebellion against taxes demanded by the church and the state.[36] Both the Salasacas of the central highland province of Tungurahua and Otavalos from Imbabura in the north have become integrated into the dominant economy through their weaving. The Otavalos in particular have achieved international renown as one of the most celebrated and prosperous indigenous groups in the Americas for their textile production and Saturday tourist market. Over the past fifty years, developments in the textile trade have led to the creation of a middle class of increasingly urbanized and Westernized Indian entrepreneurs, who exploit the labor of more traditional weavers and artisans in outlying villages. This has led to a process of social stratification whereby an indigenous elite controls the best locations in the Saturday Indian textile market to the exclusion of poorer members of society. This further challenges the perception of a homogenous indigenous population with common and undisputed interests.[37]

Eight different indigenous groups survive today in Ecuador's Amazon region, the largest being various groups of Kichwa speakers. Even though these Indians share a language similar to that spoken by the highland Kichwas, their forest culture is quite different from that found in the Sierra.[38] Michael Harner characterizes the Shuar, the second largest and one of the most studied Amazonian groups, as the only indigenous group in the Americas "to have successfully revolted against the empire of Spain and to have thwarted all subsequent attempts by the Spaniards to reconquer them."[39] In 1964, with support from Salesian missionaries, the Shuar founded the first ethnic federation in the Ecuadorian Amazon. The Shuar used radio programs, a printing press, and other means to defend and revitalize their culture.

Related to the Shuar are the Achuar. Nearby are the Zápara, the smallest surviving group in the Amazon. In the northeastern Amazon live the Sionas, Secoyas, and Cofán (A'I), who have been devastated in recent decades by outside forces, particularly intensive petroleum exploitation and the accompanying influx of colonists. In November 1993, the Sionas and Secoyas fought back by suing Texaco for more than one billion dollars for a variety of environmental abuses, including dumping more than three thousand gallons of oil a day into their lagoons.[40] The Huaorani (sometimes called Aucas, a Kichwa word meaning "savages," by outsiders) have faced similar problems. They are perhaps best known for spearing five North American missionaries in 1956. David Stoll credits the Huaorani with defying "the world market like few others" by defending 7 percent of Ecuador's valuable jungle territory against those who wish to exploit the area for its natural resources and economic potential.[41] To defend their interests in the face of outside intrusion (including oil companies, missionaries, environmental groups, and sometimes also threats from the larger neighboring Kichwa and Shuar), all of these groups have formed indigenous organizations with varying degrees of success. Nevertheless, as Blanca Muratorio observes, "The process of conquest and initial evangelization brought about an 'ethnocidal simplification' of the Amazon's rich ethnic variety."[42]

The four indigenous ethnic groups that survive on the coast are the Awa, Chachi, Epera, and Tsáchila. Each of these groups is small and has struggled to preserve its ethnic identity. The Chachi (traditionally called "Cayapas") often clash over limited resources with the Afro-Ecuadorians who occupy the same region. Best known of the coastal groups are the Tsáchila, who are often called Colorados because of their red body paint. Their first sustained contact with the dominant culture was as a tourist curiosity. A road in the 1950s brought colonists into their territory, and now they have been integrated into the export-oriented agricultural economy. On the rest of the coast, indigenous ethnic groups have either died out or have disappeared into the mestizo culture, frequently through the economic influence of export-oriented agribusiness, which has resulted in the formation of a rural proletariat. This large group of lower-class mestizo peasants on the coast are known as *montuvios*, with traditional interpretations placing their biological makeup "scientifically" at 60 percent Indian, 30 percent African, and 10 percent European.[43]

For most of its history, Ecuador has been primarily an agricultural country built on the manual labor of Indians. On the coast, Ecuadorian agricultural production has been oriented toward an export economy since the eighteenth century, whereas in the highlands agriculture served a domestic market. In the highlands, large haciendas owned by white elites functioned side by side with *minifundia* (small landholdings) cultivated by Indian peasants. *Terratenientes* (large landowners) were notorious for neglecting fertile land on their large estates. In contrast, on neighboring minifundia limited land resources were used intensively and continuously, often to their eventual degradation. Neither system provided an efficient or sustainable form of production.

The largest and most extensive estates emerged in the late nineteenth century in the central and northern highland provinces of Chimborazo, Pichincha, and Imbabura, which were also the areas of highest indigenous concentration. While the earlier part of the century saw the coexistence of large properties with numerous small ones in the north-central highlands, after 1870 the consolidation of large haciendas began. This was partly a response to the incentive offered by new possibilities of the internal market, associated with improved transportation links effected during the government of García Moreno. In the north-central highlands, a growing emphasis on livestock production required large tracts of land and stimulated the land market. The consolidation of livestock production coincided with a crisis of artisanal production, generating labor migrations toward the coastal region, where cacao production was expanding.

Landowners were not always private individuals; religious orders became some of the largest hacienda owners. They acquired land through a variety of mechanisms, including donations and outright purchase. The religious orders were no more kind or generous with their land and labor dealings than private landowners and were often much more aggressive. In the aftermath of the 1895 Liberal Revolution, General Eloy Alfaro sought to turn back the power of the Catholic Church in Ecuador. This led to the 1904 Ley de Cultos (Law of Worship) that confiscated church lands and a subsequent 1908 Ley de Beneficencia (Law of Charity) that created *Juntas de Beneficencia* (welfare boards) to administer the previously church-owned haciendas, now in state hands.[44] The government rented these estates to private individuals on limited term contracts, using the proceeds to fund social programs in urban areas. Since the rental system did not favor the limited relations of mutual constraint that existed on private estates,[45] these state-owned haciendas became the theater of some of the most militant peasant-indigenous movements in the twentieth century and were often converted to cooperatives after the 1964 agrarian reform.[46]

In 1954, Ecuador conducted its first agricultural census, which revealed that 19,665 *huasipungueros* (service tenants who worked the estates in exchange for a hut and a plot of subsistence land) and their families comprised 22 percent of Ecuador's rural population. The majority of these (12,795) lived in only three provinces: Chimborazo, Cotopaxi, and Pichincha. Conversely, few huasipungueros lived in the southern provinces of Azuay, Cañar, and Loja, which had a much higher percentage of free Indians. Altogether, in 1954 elites owned about 700 estates larger than 500 hectares, comprising about half of Ecuador's agricultural land. Just over 1 percent of the population possessed estates larger than 100 hectares, which totaled almost two-thirds of the tillable land in the Sierra. Meanwhile, 2,500 peasant households farmed plots smaller than 50 hectares, which comprised less than one-third of Ecuador's tillable land. Eighty-two percent of the agricultural production units had access to only 14.4 percent of the tillable land, whereas 0.66 percent of agricultural estates controlled 54.4 percent of the land. Only 15 percent of the land on large estates was under permanent cultivation, whereas on the small estates this proportion could reach as high as 90 percent.[47]

Regional differences reflect differentiation in the resources available for agricultural and livestock production.[48] The northern highlands (Carchi,

Imbabura, Pichincha, and Cotopaxi provinces) have the most fertile and productive lands, with valleys, a broad sub-Andean belt, and vast extensions of high-altitude *páramo* grasslands. The central highland provinces (Tungurahua, Chimborazo, and Bolívar) have similar characteristics, but with smaller agricultural and livestock zones than the north. Finally, the southern provinces (Cañar, Azuay, and Loja) have less fertile, more volcanic soil, with fewer possibilities for agricultural development. Where agriculture was undertaken in the south, an intense process of soil erosion occurred, which resulted in the disintegration of the haciendas and the emergence of *minifundista* peasants.

Explorations of Ecuadorian Indian-State Relations

From independence in the early nineteenth century through the beginning of the twenty-first century, this book examines how Indians approached the state in local contexts and how they attempted to navigate the political spaces created by conflicts among state officials at different levels. It challenges dominant ideologies about Indians in their gendered and racial dimensions, critiques political debates over the position of Indians in the national polity, and analyzes Indian-state relations in contexts that include agrarian reform, bilingual education programs, and military conscription. The concluding chapters explore indigenous organizing in the late twentieth and early twenty-first centuries.

Aleezé Sattar introduces the idea of a bifurcated state, a concept that applies both to the distinction between citizens and Indians, and to the divide between the central and local exercise of state power. The distinction between citizens and Indians was based primarily on the survival of a colonial institution, Indian tribute, well into the nineteenth century. By paying tribute, members of indigenous communities were exempted from paying most other taxes (with the exception of *diezmos*, an ecclesiastical tax that also provided some state revenues). The collection procedures legitimated the existence of traditional authorities (caciques) within indigenous communities, as well as the preservation of community lands. It was only after the "personal contribution" (as tribute was euphemistically called after the 1820s) was eliminated in 1857 that the ethnically based *legal* distinction between Indians and citizens was dissolved. Sattar shows how the state conceived of this distinction and how Indians themselves used their different status to protect their interests. Because tribute was the basis for certain rights and this distinction could be used to appeal to the central state for other forms of protection when local officials were abusive, Indians in Chimborazo Province protested when tribute was abolished. Sattar's discussion of the bifurcation of the state itself in its local and central instances of power is particularly important to this book's argument. Indians were able to maneuver between central state and municipal authorities, which also indicates how the interests of the state varied at different levels. Since local elites sometimes competed among themselves for access to Indian taxes, land, and labor, these issues become more complex. Finally, because the other tax assessed on Indians, the diezmo, was farmed out for collection by quasi-state officials, this created yet another dynamic by which different local instances of state power were sometimes at odds.

Derek Williams's chapter moves north to Imbabura Province, home of the Otavalo Indians, regarded since the nineteenth century as model Indians for their industrious artisan production. Williams examines the shifting triangular relationship linking the state, large landowners, and Indians, during the transition from the era of popular liberalism under Urvina to a new period of conservative-Catholic rule under García Moreno. His emphasis is on how Indians figured into the relationship between the state and landowners. Locally based and national state actors had differing views of progress and therefore different approaches to governing Otavalo Indians. García Moreno's centralizing project was to subordinate local government and landlord interests to national imperatives, and, since one important way to achieve this was by constructing large-scale infrastructure, Indian labor figured centrally in this project.

Erin O'Connor focuses on a view of Indians "from above," examining state attempts at moral regulation that reflected gendered images of the Indian population.[49] Basing her analysis on newspaper writings and judicial documents, O'Connor shows how the dominant gender ideologies of late nineteenth-century Ecuador affected not only all women, but Indian men as well. State discourse constructed images of Indian men alternately as helpless children and undeserving patriarchs—images with real implications for people's lives when developed and applied in court cases. Ultimately, the failure of Indian men to serve as good fathers suggested that they were unworthy of becoming members of the political nation. Given the virtual disappearance of references to Indians and explicit concerns with race in nineteenth-century political discourse after the 1857 abolition of tribute, gender becomes an analytical window onto notions of inherited bases of inequality. Like Sattar, O'Connor bases her analysis on research in Chimborazo Province.

Michiel Baud takes us south to Cuenca, focusing on the period after the 1895 Liberal Revolution. He examines the nature of *indigenista* liberal rhetoric and the extent to which indigenous peoples used it to improve their lot. Indeed, the reappearance of the Indian in public discourse is notable in the liberal period, after the submergence of this topic after 1857. This is likely for three reasons: the Liberal Revolution included some elements of an authentic popular mobilization (although we know little about what the subaltern followers of Eloy Alfaro might have been seeking through their participation); the liberals tried to distance themselves from the poor treatment of Indians under previous republican and colonial governments; and, related to this, labor issues were central to liberal concerns as they sought to undermine conservative highland landowners and promote labor migrations to the agro-export enterprises of the coast, whose owners tended to be liberals. Baud shows that the rhetoric of the liberal state helped Indians to resist the abuses of local landowners, as they selectively incorporated elements of liberal *indigenismo* into their struggles. The mere existence of national laws to which Indians could appeal changed their political strategies and their expectations. When peasants appealed successfully to the central state, this legitimated the state; however, the state's failure to meet these rising expectations was likely one of the causes of the increased radicalization of indigenous social actors in the 1920s. Baud notes that it is equally important to examine how the state incorporated certain aspects of subaltern projects into its own project and how Indians incorporated state discourse into their political strategies. In other words, state and popular discourse are mutually constitutive.

In examining labor issues in Chimborazo and Pichincha provinces, Kim Clark takes up some of the issues raised by Baud, extending the analysis from 1895 through 1950. Clark focuses on how Indians used deference as a strategy of negotiation with state officials at various levels. The deference offered to some officials (or acceptance of their paternalism) was clearly linked to a withdrawal of deference from others. The nature of indigenous discourse and strategies of resistance changed over time, as Indians incorporated new aspects of state rhetoric and dominant ideology into their appeals to state officials. Crucial to this dynamic were the fissures in the state system—differing interests among authorities at various levels or in diverse state institutions—that allowed Indians to appeal to some officials who were willing to undermine the authority of others. Ultimately, this may indicate a strength, not weakness, since it led to the legitimization of the central state and channeled indigenous resistance in particular ways. These strategies often allowed indigenous peasants to deal quite effectively with pressing everyday problems.

Marc Becker examines debates in the Constituent Assembly convoked after the Glorious Revolution of May 1944 that returned Ecuadorian populist José María Velasco Ibarra to power for the second of his five terms. For a brief period, it seemed possible to rethink the relationship between Indians and the state, as well as the structure of state-society relations more generally. The

1944–1945 Constituent Assembly saw heated debates regarding citizenship rights, suffrage, representation, and language. Delegates engaged fundamental issues of how state structures were designed and who controlled them. For the first time, indigenous organizations had an indirect voice through the presence of Communist leader Ricardo Paredes as the functional representation of the "indigenous race." Indians were among the many groups disappointed a year later when Velasco Ibarra revoked the new constitution and declared himself dictator. In the meantime, Indians had taken advantage of the general political climate to establish their first organization, the Federación Ecuatoriana de Indios (FEI, Ecuadorian Federation of Indians). Ultimately, the frustration with the political process begun in 1944 demonstrated to Indians the limitations of trying to participate in formal politics while literacy requirements excluded them from voting or running for office. When Ecuadorian Indians emerged as important actors in formal politics in the 1990s, it was on the basis of significant gains in education. Nevertheless, whether to engage the state in the electoral realm or to organize as a social movement remained an issue that indigenous activists would debate for years to come.

William Waters's chapter examines Indian-state relations in the context of agrarian reform in Cotopaxi Province. Even before the formation of the contemporary indigenous movement, Indian communities had emerged as actors engaged in struggles with local elites and the state. Indeed, the agrarian reform laws of 1964 and 1973 were only one component of a complex process in which both peasants and landowners sought to protect their own interests. Indigenous communities' ability to negotiate with landowners, often through technocratic state agencies, led to a profound transformation of rural areas in the 1960s and 1970s. As Waters shows, this process was uneven, and depending on the availability and quality of land, some indigenous communities benefited more than others. However, the overall changes were crucial to the appearance of indigenous organizations. Autonomous peasant communities arose from among a sector that had been largely a dependent labor force living within or subject to haciendas. These communities gained the power to negotiate directly with state agencies: in many cases, they first gained experience negotiating with IERAC, the agrarian reform agency, and increasingly with other state agencies providing water or other basic services. Whereas most Latin American agrarian reform initiatives have had only partial success in improving the economic well-being of peasants, perhaps in the long run the political repercussions of these processes may be just as important.

Amalia Pallares examines the Ecuadorian indigenous movement of the 1980s and 1990s. Following the military regimes of the 1970s, the return to democracy in 1979 saw new attempts to incorporate Indians into the nation-state. In the 1980s, these policies focused on cultural issues, especially on developing bilingual and bicultural educational programs. While indigenous organizations struggled for a greater voice in decision making over these programs at the national level, their success in controlling local programs and curricula gave an important impetus to their organizational capacity. It also stimulated broad discussions about what might be considered indigenous content in these programs. In the 1980s, Indians were frustrated in their attempt to move beyond sometimes narrowly defined "cultural" issues to economic issues in negotiations with the government. Following the 1990 indigenous uprising, however, the national government was more willing to address economic issues, including the resolution of land disputes; yet it often refused to negotiate over political autonomy. Indigenous organizations took up the state model of pluriculturalism in the 1980s but gave it different meanings. By the early 1990s, the indigenous movement began to speak of plurinationalism, which led the state and many other social groups to reject indigenous claims, arguing that the movement threatened the integrity of the Ecuadorian nation-state. Since then, indigenous groups have returned to some extent to concepts of pluriculturalism but have stretched this language to include their plurinational projects. Overall, the Indian movement has gained in organizational capacity over two decades, as state discourse and indigenous projects have evolved and have influenced each other. Moving beyond its traditional concern with the situation of Ecuador's indigenous population, the Indian movement today is involved in national debates over issues of citizenship and inclusion that affect all Ecuadorians.

Brian Selmeski explores Indian-state relations in a quite different arena: the experience of Indian military conscripts. Military conscription is one of the clearest settings in which state projects to forge citizens are carried to fruition for a significant proportion of the Ecuadorian population. As with bilingual education, the military has also developed a pluricultural model of the nation that is inclusive enough to embrace Indians, rather than insisting on *mestizaje* (cultural or racial mixing), as earlier notions of Ecuadorian citizenship often did. Conscription promotes "personal formation," which quite explicitly involves learning to become well-formed (but still Indian) citizens. The military has a rather different history in Ecuador than in many other Latin American countries: while armed force has sometimes been used to repress popular movements, in the twentieth century military governments of one kind or another have also passed some of Ecuador's more progressive legislation. Currently, the institution is involved in development initiatives within indigenous communities; it also gives Indians a central role in Ecuador's history in classes offered to conscripts. Selmeski suggests that Indians are attracted to military service (which they could evade if they so desired) and the opportunities it affords to form themselves into national citizens. Many would also like to become professional soldiers, but few can satisfy the basic educational requirements. Clearly, in this arena, the state is successful in drawing Indians into a national project and in carrying out moral regulation. Selmeski attributes part of this success to the gendered and family ideologies promoted by the military.

The research materials available for these analyses of Indian-state relations in Ecuador vary with the era under study. For the earlier periods, documents produced by various state officials can reveal fissures in the state itself. These include court records inscribed by judges and officials at various levels and correspondence among assorted state officials and institutions. The often muffled voices of Indians can also be heard—in their petitions and complaints to the state (often written by cultural brokers), in their testimony in court (often translated, sometimes presented by their lawyers), in the record of their actions (often interpreted by others). Newspaper accounts and other published sources are also drawn upon for an understanding of both indigenous actions and of dominant ideologies toward them. Debates from the 1944–1945 Constituent Assembly also reveal the multiplicity of views of the "Indian problem," although they reflect less of the reality of Indian life.

For the twentieth century, oral histories and interviews become increasingly important, allowing for rich analyses of indigenous views and experiences. While the archival sources for the nineteenth and early twentieth centuries are not ideal, they can be mined for understanding many aspects of indigenous life. As Florencia Mallon pointed out some time ago, the difficulty of analyzing subaltern practices and discourses does not mean we should not try, even if our results are always partial.[50] We can draw some conclusions about indigenous political strategies, if not their intentions and experiences at a deeper level. This is a key point, since it is actual practices that subordinate groups and the state engage in that create and transform social relations. As Talal Asad observes about hegemony, "What is shared in such situations is not 'belief' as an interior state of mind but cultural discourses that constitute objective social conditions and thus define forms of behavior appropriate to them."[51]

Four comparative chapters place the processes occurring in the Ecuadorian highlands in a larger Latin American context. All are concerned with the recent history of Ecuadorian indigenous organizations, since the emergence of a unified movement is the most visible sign of Ecuador's distinctiveness. Juliet Erazo looks east of the Andes to examine how Indian-state relations in the Ecuadorian Amazon (the Oriente) contrast with those in the highlands. In reviewing the history of Indian-state relations in the Oriente, Erazo emphasizes the importance of religious missions, which took on a quasi-state role in governing the indigenous population. Another factor was resource extraction in the region, which informed rather different approaches to labor in contrast to the settled agriculture in the highlands. Labor policies in the Oriente differed, too, because Indian laborers could flee into inaccessible territories if exploitation became too intense. Finally, indigenous organizing in the Ecuadorian Amazon eventually led to the emergence of a national organization linking highland and lowland confederations.

Shannon Mattiace compares Indian-state relations in twentieth-century Mexico and Ecuador, and finds important differences between the two countries. Indigenismo in Mexico arose from a revolutionary context, and in Ecuador from a liberal one. These nationalist ideologies, and the policies they informed, provided an important early frame for relations between Indians and the state. The last decades of the twentieth century saw a shift from indigenista-inspired assimilation to multiculturalism, in the context of economic liberalization and electoral democracy, as well as a changing international order. Mattiace discusses important differences between indigenous organizing in Ecuador and Mexico in organizing tactics, the state institutions and climate they confront, the articulation of these movements with formal politics, and the scale of their activities.

Like Mexico, Bolivia has not produced an umbrella indigenous organization with the strength of Ecuador's CONAIE. José Antonio Lucero compares the sequence, style, and structure of indigenous organizing in the two Andean countries. While in Ecuador, Amazonian groups (using a language of ethnicity) emerged "early," before or contemporaneous with the main highland organizations (who initially developed a language of class), in Bolivia lowland groups emerged "late," as lowland groups had to confront strong local elites. This sequence in Ecuador resulted in a strong lowland presence when the two regional federations joined together, which facilitated the adoption of a flexible language of nationalities by CONAIE, which was capable of encompassing many different indigenous groups and local organizations in a single national movement. The style of the Ecuadorian and Bolivian movements also differ substantially, with an emphasis on pre-Columbian and corporatist imaginaries in Bolivia that do not carry similar weight in Ecuador. Finally, the two movements have been confronted by rather different neoliberal economic policies; such policies managed to fragment indigenous politics in Bolivia, while they might be said to have strengthened indigenous mobilizing in Ecuador.

In the final chapter, José Antonio Lucero and María Elena García question common assumptions about the indigenous movements in Peru and in Ecuador. Peru stands out for the absence of a strong indigenous movement, especially when compared to its neighbor to the north. However, in light of García's ethnographic research on local Peruvian organizing efforts in pursuit of bilingual education, perhaps the problem is not that there is no indigenous movement in Peru, but that we cannot recognize where such a movement might exist. In particular, we must rethink evolutionary assumptions about scale, whereby a national movement is regarded as more "advanced" than local organizing. Lucero and Garcia emphasize the importance of recognizing in both the Ecuadorian and Peruvian contexts that indigenous identities are "plural, contested, and constructed in dialogue with a great number of actors." Finally, while the mobilizing tactics of Peruvian and Ecuadorian Indians differ significantly, we should avoid attributing more importance to mass mobilizations than to local resistance and organization; perhaps the successes of the Ecuadorian movement are not as great as some think, while the failures of the Peruvian movement are not so grave as others have assumed.

Together, these studies build an argument about how Indians in highland Ecuador gained political and organizational experience over the better part of two centuries, and how those gains are manifested in contemporary relations between Indians and the Ecuadorian state. This book provides a historical framework for understanding the politicization of ethnic identities and offers Ecuador as a particularly important case for understanding the range of historical alternatives in subaltern-state relations.

2

¿Indígena o Ciudadano?

Republican Laws and Highland Indian Communities in Ecuador, 1820–1857

ALEEZÉ SATTAR

The history of early nineteenth-century Ecuador, between independence in the 1820s and the abolition of Indian tribute in 1857, proves that state formation is not simply a project of moral regulation in which elites attempt to impose on subaltern groups a dominant discourse that defines their role in society. Indigenous communities and other groups selected and appropriated those aspects of state legislation and state ideology that coincided with their interests and their vision of society. State and indigenous discourse in early nineteenth-century Ecuador reveals multiple discursive frameworks that operated simultaneously. A focus on the different coexisting discourses and imaginations about the state and about state-Indian relations, as conceived by both state builders and Indians, shows that contradictions and "noncoherence" are very much integral aspects of state formation and the "negotiation of rule."[1] Given that states are necessarily fragmented and contradictory, the more important objective is to examine the *specific historical contexts* within which these contradictions and incoherencies take on significance. The context is the uneven and problematic transition from colony to republic, a transition in which the status of Indians posed one of the core dilemmas for postcolonial Ecuadorian state formation.

One of the key contradictions of early Ecuadorian state formation was that the colonial corporatist legacy of a separate republic of tribute-paying Indians became Ecuador's most viable resource, in the form of fiscal revenue and labor, even as it undermined the project of building a liberal nation and creating citizens. Since Indians continued to pay tribute, a central and unresolved issue for the early postcolonial state was whether Indians were *indígenas* (Indians) or *ciudadanos* (citizens). Focusing on Chimborazo Province, I examine this dilemma by studying different state and local indigenous discourses, combining views from above and below, a process that illustrates the peculiarly hybrid nature of the early Ecuadorian state. The state was "bifurcated" both in the distinction between citizens and Indians and in the divide between the central and local levels of state power.

A close reading of archival documents reveals that even as Indians embraced their colonial-appointed identity as the "miserable race" and legal minors, they were actually far from minors in their shrewd use of state laws and legislative procedures. They exploited the state's fragmentation and internal contradictions and often successfully used the gaps between the local and central instances of the state in their struggles to defend their lands, their communities, and their vision of Indian-state relations.

The Problem of Persistence

As Jeremy Adelman states, the notion of persistence is a powerful organizing frame for understanding particular historical processes.[2] In Ecuador, colonial institutions and relations—the corporate Indian community, Indian tribute, Indian caciques, and Indian protectors—endured after independence. However, Ecuador's "colonial legacy" was not "the dead weight of the past." Following William Roseberry and Raymond Williams, one can see these institutions as a bundle of residual institutions with an *active* force that played an inherently political role in shaping the nineteenth-century state.[3] Although I denote certain institutions and relations as "colonial" and others "republican," these were linked by interconnected and dynamic historical processes. The transformation from colony to republic involved the creation of new expressions of cultural difference as well as the redefinition of old ones.

Ecuador's Indian communities were shaped in the colonial period through their complex engagement with the colonial state. As subjects of the crown, Indians had to be assigned a particular status within society, but this entailed a struggle among different colonial factions with different interests and different ideas about the structure of colonial society. The eventual status assigned to Indians was that of the corporate collective: the República de los Indios. All Indians belonged to this separate "Indian republic," in opposition to the "Spanish republic," each governed and administered by a distinct set of laws and regulations. One major legacy of the colonial period was that Indians entered the republican nation with a distinct political culture because of their membership in their separate "republic," their complex engagement with the colonial legal system, and their strategic use of the special privileges and exemptions granted to them.[4]

Theoretically, Latin American independence from the Spanish monarchy implied a transformation from the colonial system, founded on caste-based hierarchies, to a system based on social classes whose members were equal before the law and unequal only socially and economically. The republican state attempted to abolish ethnic forms of community and to introduce a state community of individual citizens with private property. However, despite the state builders' attempts to distance themselves from the colonial past, they could not realize this transformation for fiscal and political reasons.

Between 1820 and 1830, when the departments of Quito, Guayaquil, and Cuenca constituted the Distrito del Sur—the Southern District of Gran Colombia—Simón Bolívar attempted unsuccessfully to abolish Indian tribute and to make Indians into citizens. In 1821 he attempted to eradicate tribute and erase a separate "Indian" identity by abolishing the tax that was imposed only on Indians. The traditional indigenous forms of authority (the *cacicazgos*) were also to be eradicated, and Article 181 of the Law of 1821 stipulated that all honorific titles (such as that of cacique and cacique governors) granted by the Spanish government were to be eliminated. All Indians would henceforth be citizens and equal before the law.

According to the Law of 1821, Indian communal lands were to be distributed to the heads of Indian families, a portion reserved for common use, and the *sobrantes*, or surplus lands, were to be publicly auctioned. Bolívar, arguing that education was the key to "civilizing" Indians and converting them into citizens, ordered that the proceeds were to be used to construct parochial schools for Indian children. However, by 1828 Bolívar was forced for fiscal and political reasons to reinstate Indian tribute, which he euphemistically renamed the "personal contribution of Indians." With the reinstitution of tribute, Indian communities, under their traditional caciques, the colonial institution of the Indian *cabildo* (with its elected officials), the intermediary body of bureaucrats (to administer and protect the Indians), and Indian communal landholdings regained their former status. This return to the dual structure of the colonial period was partially justified by claims that Indians themselves wanted to pay only this "personal contribution" and remain exempt from all other obligations of citizenship (such as indirect taxes and military conscription).[5] Indians actually supported this antirepublican model because it legally recognized their separateness. Processes of republican state formation that sought to homogenize the population and convert Indians into citizens threatened the survival of their separate cultural identity and productive autonomy. Thus, the bankrupt nation's fiscal needs and Indians' political aspirations coincided and were furthered by the reinstatement of tribute payments. Indians regained their former privileges and exemptions and their former status as a corporate entity with a distinct legal standing.

When the Southern District separated from Gran Colombia and the independent Republic of Ecuador was established, Indian tribute was a significant source of revenue for the debt-ridden young republic. Ecuador inherited 21.5 percent (7,122,896 pesos) of the debt contracted by Gran Colombia during the wars of independence.[6] In 1830, annual tribute obligations were set at three pesos, and tribute paid by all adult Indian males accounted for 28–35 percent of government revenue.[7] Indians made up more than 66 percent of the population, and the majority lived in the highlands.[8] All Indian males of the highland communities between the ages of 21 and 50 were obliged to pay the personal contribution, although women and men over 50 who owned property were also supposed to pay tribute. Indians who became indebted peons on highland estates did not have to pay; hacendados were supposed to pay the tribute for the Indians living on their property.

In addition to tribute, Indians also paid another direct tax, the *diezmo*, a tithe on production. Although the diezmo was an ecclesiastical tax, it was collected by the state, which retained a portion of the revenue. Indians were exempt from all other indirect taxes (such as the sales or property tax), legal fees, and military conscription. Certain Indians were exempt from tribute payments. They included the Indian governors and caciques, initially all caciques but later only those who were responsible for the collection of tribute. Also exempt were Indians working in the postal service, those pursuing an education (during their schooling, or permanently if they obtained a degree), those who served as primary school teachers, and those who were lay clergy or held other religious offices.

Until the 1857 abolition of tribute, Indians continued to belong to a separate republic within the state. They were denied citizenship rights and were legally defined as minors. Both state and Indian discourse defined Indians as the "raza miserable" in need of state protection. Indians pushed for the legal recognition of their difference and for a paternalistic state that guaranteed the protection of their communal lands in exchange for tribute and other services provided to the state.

The Bifurcated State

Mahmood Mamdani's notion of the bifurcated state is useful for understanding the peculiar incorporation of Indians into the republican Ecuadorian state.[9] Mamdani describes how direct and indirect forms of rule evolved into complementary forms of native control in colonial and early postcolonial Africa. The notion of the bifurcated state highlights distinctions between Indians and non-Indians as well as among different types of Indians (caciques and commoners, for instance) that go to the heart of the problem of nineteenth-century state formation. Because it needed to perpetuate Indian tribute, the Ecuadorian state, like the states in colonial and early postcolonial Africa, separated its population into citizens on the one hand, Indian subjects on the other.[10] Thus the bifurcated state combined under a single authority two distinct forms of rule.[11] Despite the republican impulse to dissolve the Andean ethnic communities and to convert males into propertied citizen taxpayers, the state reproduced selected aspects of colonial administrative structures. The continuation of tribute meant the prolongation of one of the institutional pillars of the colonial state: the "Indian republic" and the dual classification of the population. The Ecuadorian republican state was forced to perpetuate the colonial bifurcation of the two "republics," each governed according to its own laws and regulations and by distinct machineries of the state.

In "Governmentality," Michel Foucault traces a very complex transformation through which the modern state shifts from being a "stratum" to a "modality," from being one strata of society to a more abstract mode of organization.[12] The modern state does not stand apart from society, but becomes instead a mode of organizing society. One implication of a bifurcated state in early Ecuador is that society was organized and governed according to two very different modes. One was the "colonial" mode of governance, through which the republican state related to its Indian population, and which organized society along a stratification of different estates and corporate entities, each with legally entrenched privileges and disabilities. The other was the "republican" mode, based on the notion of citizenship, in which all citizens were equal before the law and unequal only socially and economically. According to this mode, national society was a collection of individuals who owed their primary loyalty to the "imagined community" of the nation.[13] Therefore, two modes of governance coexisted during the first few decades after independence and the postcolonial state had two distinct (imaginary) classificatory schemes. In one, every Ecuadorian was equal before the law; in the other, each individual was assigned a position within the "two republics," and in all government and court documents each was identified as either ciudadano or indígena.

The two republics were articulated through tribute collection. Caciques, as the chiefs and representatives of the Indian communities, occupied an ambiguous intermediate position. Within the communities, caciques ensured order and stability by mediating disputes, allocating communal lands to the families, distributing labor assignments, arranging marriages, regulating markets, and maintaining local security. Their primary responsibility to the republican state—as to the colonial state—was to collect the "personal contribution" of the Indians in their communities. Negotiating the disjuncture between republican rhetoric and reality was difficult for the caciques, as their roles as mediators between opposed forms of governance involved them in a complex web of conflicting expectations, both from above and below.

Indian tribute, the most important structural axis of the colonial economy and society, continued in the republican period to be an essential source of government revenue. Tribute was tied with the spheres of circulation (including the circulation of labor) and mercantile production, and was economically essential to the Hispanic and Creole minority. Tribute was also the symbolic element that ordered the classificatory schemes of the social and political hierarchy. The problem for the republican state was that Indian tribute involved a whole system of social, economic, and political structures that harked back to the colonial past, challenging the very possibility of hegemony for the republican state and obstructing any attempt to construct "a regime of citizenship."[14]

State builders recognized that to deny citizenship to the majority of the population contradicted one of the foundations of republican liberalism. One response was to assert that Indians were not yet prepared for citizenship, but needed further guidance and education. Thus, state discourse suggested that under the care of an enlightened citizenry, Indians would eventually attain maturity and become full citizens capable of representing themselves. They had been reduced to this state of misery by centuries of colonial abuse but had potential that could be released through the civilizing impact of republican laws. Since for the moment Indians were "miserable peoples," exploited and depressed, not yet prepared for the responsibilities of citizenship, they needed protection. All Indians (including caciques and cacique-governors) were considered legal minors who could not enter into contracts with non-Indians or appear in court without a protector or an intermediary who had to be a citizen—that is, white-mestizo, male, literate, and property-owning.[15]

From its inception, the republican state legally regulated the administration of its Indian population. In September 1833, Ecuador's first president, the Venezuelan military general Juan José Flores, promulgated the following decree: "Considering the better civilization of Indians, it is important to check the abuses that they continue to experience and which maintain them in the same oppression of the colonial system."[16] According to early republican rhetoric, Indians were unable to escape from ignorance and misery to which they had been reduced because they continued to be abused and exploited. Preventing these abuses would make it easier to "civilize" Indians. Since "for now" the tribute imposed on the "indigenous class" was necessary, laws should protect them from excessive vexations in the exaction of the tribute. Such measures included banning corporal punishment, arbitrary imprisonment, and confiscation of animals or other property of those who were delinquent in tribute payments, as well as forcing widows and children to pay the debts of a deceased tributary.

State mandates to reduce the abuses experienced by Indians at the hands of local elites were not particularly effective. In 1835 the government of Vicente Rocafuerte passed a decree which addressed this issue: "Despite the municipal laws that protect the indígenas, they continue to be abused. It is absolutely crucial that these abuses be stopped, so that this class with a potential to contribute to society not be oppressed in any way, and that they enjoy the same rights and guarantees that the constitution dispenses to *all* Ecuadorians."[17]

Central state discourse blamed local elites for the continued misery of its Indian population. What was needed was to implement the laws that already existed against the abuses committed by parish priests, landlords, tax collectors, and even local state officials. The *diezmeros* (tithe collectors) were seen as particularly problematic. By law, diezmos were only supposed to be a tenth of all crops actually cultivated and Indians were not to be forced to pay them before the harvest. Further, laws prohibited the use of physical force to exact tithes and tributes from the Indians. Local elites, whether hacendados, priests, or state officials, were forbidden to force Indians to provide personal services against their will. However, as the above decree indicates, and as is amply evidenced in archival documentation, these abuses were the most common: excessive collection of tribute and tithes, the use of violence to enforce greater tax payments, and the conscription of Indians to provide personal services to priests, tax collectors, and local officials.

Two cases in which Indian communities accused diezmeros of abuse will serve as examples. The state farmed out Indian tax collection (for both tribute and diezmos) to individuals who bid for the position. Diezmeros, who were contracted by the state and were thus quasi-state officials, were particularly aggressive in their collection procedures. The examples below demonstrate that the state was fractured and internally contradictory, and that Indians were not passive victims but were able to use the state's legal procedures to attempt to redress their grievances.

In 1836, an Indian community from the parish of Cajabamba filed a criminal complaint against the diezmero, Sr. Joaquin Osaeta, for excessive collection, unjust fines, and physical abuse. They testified that, for no good reason, the diezmero had physically assaulted a number of Indians in the village. At that point, some went to fetch the *teniente*, the political lieutenant of their parish. According to Indian witnesses at the trial, when the teniente arrived and asked why he was committing these excesses, Sr. Osaeta responded, "No diezmero is subject to the authority of tenientes."[18] Diezmeros, Osaeta claimed, were independent agents who answered only to the highest authorities. Neither the judge nor any of the lawyers addressed Osaeta's alleged statement about the relative authority of diezmeros and tenientes. The judge found in favor of Osaeta, stating that the Indians' testimony could not be trusted. He even fined the Indians for their "bad faith."

The second case concerns a dispute in 1844 between the Indian community of the parish of Yaruquíes and the diezmero, Sr. Rafael Astudillo, who was accused by the Indians of collecting amounts far in excess of their appropriate contribution. Instead of waiting for the harvest, Sr. Astudillo had arbitrarily assigned in his tax registers the amount owed by each Indian, which did not correspond to amounts actually cultivated. Sr. Astudillo's lawyer argued that the practice of "anticipating" the diezmos was necessary because "it was a general custom among the Indians to begin to consume their crops before they had matured."[19] The Indians' protector argued that even if this were the case, Indians did so because of their poverty and hunger, and that the tax collectors should still be able to collect the correct amounts after the harvest through careful supervision of the Indians' fields. He added that since Indians were legally minors, the allegedly voluntary contract that they entered into with the diezmero when they were registered in the tax rolls could not be legal. The protector invoked the Law of September 2, 1835, which prohibited the collection of diezmos in advance of the harvest. Sr. Astudillo's lawyer retorted that the measures recommended by the protector to avoid the "frauds" committed by the Indian taxpayers were impossible to implement since "they would require a multitude of agents for surveillance, to watch over the premature consumption of crops."[20]

The judge agreed that because Indians were "personas miserables," they could not legally enter into contracts without a protector or citizen judicially appointed to represent them. He nullified the contract between Astudillo and the Indians. Sr. Astudillo appealed, asking why "Indians could freely enter into trade and commerce with their fruits and crops, and yet they were suddenly miserable persons who needed the protector when it came time to pay the miserable quantity of the diezmos and primicias."[21] Astudillo argued further that Indians were engaged in trade and were hardly minors in their commercial relationships. He claimed that they hid behind the Indian protectorate only to avoid paying these taxes. The appellate judge reversed the decision and required the Indians to pay the amounts set by Astudillo.

These examples illustrate the large gap between central state laws and their implementation at the local level. These laws, though good on paper, were unable to curb the abuses committed by local tax collectors. While the municipal judges usually favored local elites, the supreme court often ruled in favor of Indians. These cases reveal the bifurcation of the nineteenth-century state: a wide chasm separated the central state and its policies regarding Indians from the local instances of power. Local and provincial elites, officials as well as judges, were not only unclear about laws and decrees coming from Quito, but quite often their interests were at odds with those of the central state. Local elites competed in their efforts to control Indians and to reap the benefits of Indian taxes, Indian labor, and Indian lands. Despite the central state's inability to implement its laws, Indians in their litigious contentions with those who sought to control and exploit them at the local level continued to appeal to the central state and its protective laws. In doing so, they legitimated the state's power. These examples also show how the state was fragmented, with local state officials making claims that diverged from the proclamations of central state legislators.[22]

Within the central state's discursive frameworks there was plenty of confusion regarding the status of Indians. In the above-cited 1835 decree, President Rocafuerte had asserted, "Indians were to enjoy all the rights and guarantees that the Constitution granted to *all* Ecuadorians." Yet in this period, Indians were clearly different in their juridical, political, and social status from other Ecuadorians. They were indígenas and not ciudadanos. Prior to 1857, this paradox governed republican sensibility regarding Indians and how they fit into the nation. On the one hand, liberal republican principles demanded that all Ecuadorians were equal under the law. On the other hand, fiscal and political realities fueled the contrary view that some members of the population—Indians—were distinct from other Ecuadorians and had to be regulated by a different set of (paternalistic) laws. This paradox is most apparent in the postcolonial state's dealings with the Indian caciques.

State Discourse on Caciques

In 1847, Mariano Pacheco, an Indian from the parish of Punín, claiming to be a descendant of the deceased cacique Don Pablo Duchinachay y Sañay, solicited the government to legitimate his hereditary title of cacique. Through his defender, Mariano Pacheco asserted that his grandfather's brother, Don Pablo Duchinachay y Sañay, had been granted the title by a royal provision in

1780. Don Pablo left no heirs, so the cacicazgo had passed to his brother, Don Francicso Duchinachay y Sañay. Don Francisco's daughter, Doña Maria Concepcion Sañay, had inherited the cacicazgo upon her father's death. She married Don Pascual Pacheco, and of this marriage was born Mariano Pacheco the supplicant, who argued that the cacicazgo now belonged to him. The mayor of Riobamba, Dr. Larrea y Checa, responded: "The solicitation by Mariano Pacheco is *opposed and contrary to our system of government.* The cacicazgos and other prerogatives predating our political emancipation disappeared with the independence of America from Spain."[23]

Dr. Larrea was referring to Bolívar's Law of 1821, which stipulated that "the titles of honor granted by the Spanish government are henceforth suppressed." In the mayor's view, emancipation from Spain implied a complete break with colonial institutions, including the cacicazgos. Although the mayor's view prevailed in the lower court, it was at odds with central state policy. The Supreme Court in Quito, as well as certain local courts such as that of Otavalo, had already established the necessity of reinstitutionalizing the positions of the caciques and cacique governors.[24]

Mariano Pacheco's defender appealed to the Supreme Court, and relying on the court's earlier decisions, argued that the mayor's judgment suffered from serious errors in reasoning. He showed that after the 1828 reinstatement of tribute, the Law of Civil Procedure clearly stipulated that the Recompilation of the Laws of the Indies should continue to be observed. And according to those laws, the rights of the institution of cacicazgos were to be strictly maintained. His appeal declared: "The cacicazgo is a very important institution and to deny it would be to afflict the 'miserable indigenous class' who so adhere to their customs that in the presence of the caciques they find a sort of consolation and moral guidance."[25]

The lawyer added that caciques were important not only for tribute collection, but also because only they could obtain the resources and services (tribute and Indian labor) required of Indian communities by the parish priests and state officials. He claimed that the mayor's opinion of the rupture with colonial institutions was an ideal not yet realized. The mayor had asserted that the eradication of cacicazgos was decisive because "the collection of tribute is today practiced by individuals deemed trustworthy by the collector, a practice that was not the case during the Spanish government. During the latter, it was the caciques who were called to collect the tribute, in exchange for certain exclusive privileges granted to them."[26]

In response, Pacheco's lawyer correctly observed that caciques were still important in the collection of tribute, a fact that had not gone unnoticed by the local state functionaries. For example, when in 1848 the cacique governor of the community of Licto, Don Felix Llimayco, was imprisoned on the accusations of a citizen (motivated by personal animosity), the teniente of the parish of Licto wrote to the mayor asking for the cacique's release. The teniente argued that the presence of the Indian governor Llimayco was "absolutely essential for the collection of the 'personal contribution' of Indians for the parish, which in the present year had not taken place due to the absence of Llimayco, with enormous damage to the fiscal revenue."[27]

In Mariano Pacheco's case, the position argued in 1847 by the municipal authority clearly contradicted the position of the central state. In 1846, the Ministry of the Interior under the government of Vicente Rocafuerte had delivered a decree to all provincial governors regarding the situation of Indians. The circular stated:

> Since the first days after its installation, the new Congress has seen as one of its primary objects of attention the means to improve the situation of the indígenas: to correct their customs and to restrain those who abuse their simplicity in order to maintain them in a state of ignorance, idleness, and misery, which damages public wealth and morality. However, after much meditation the Congress is convinced that the stagnant and even worsening situation of the indígenas has its cause in the *lack of implementation of already existing laws*. The problem is not at the level of legislation since *our code of laws, since the Law of the Indies,* has included special dispositions favoring the indígenas.[28]

The sentiment expressed in the circular was clearly that the republican state was willing to prolong certain colonial institutions, including the cacicazgos. However, as the mayor's statement indicates, municipal officials were more likely to assert that the current system of governance was quite distinct from the colonial system. Colonial institutions such as the cacicazgos were considered "opposed and contrary" to the current system of government. There were two very different approaches to the Indian problem at the different levels of the state. The central state—given its reliance on Indian tribute—professed to be concerned with the protection of Indians, maintenance of a "reciprocal pact," and the continuation of colonial structures. The municipal government, on the other hand, was more willing to assert a clean rupture with the colonial past and thus erase the special situation of the Indian population and the privileged position of caciques and cacique governors.

Given the contradictions between the institutions of tribute and the corporate structure of Indian communities on the one hand, and the liberal republican ideal of propertied individual citizens on the other, the Ecuadorian state was unable to imagine, let alone create, a common discursive framework.[29] While Creole "liberators" since Simón Bolívar had sought their American identity in breaking with the colonial past, at certain moments republican Ecuadorian statesmen were forced to assert a clear continuity of law from the colonial period, and hence the phrase, "*our* code of laws, since the Law of the Indies." The contradiction for Ecuadorian state formation lay in the fact that Indians were a part of *all* Ecuadorians and yet distinct and separate from other Ecuadorians.

Indians, Central State, Local State

We can read the protective laws passed by the central state regarding Indians as evidence of an attempt to correct the egregious conditions under which Indians were forced to live. But we can also read them as evidence of systematic abuse, exploitation, and domination of the Indian population by elite groups. Even though the central executive branches of the state passed laws ad nauseam, these laws had uneven effects at the local level, especially because many municipal state officials and functionaries—many of whom were large landowners—were the very people abusing and exploiting the indigenous communities under their authority. Since colonial times, Indians had recognized this chasm between the central and local instances of state power and were adept at appropriating the discourse of the central state in their struggles against local elites.

A civil case involving pasturelands between a powerful landowner and neighboring Indian communities of the parish of Calpi in northern Chimborazo provides a specific example of Indians appealing to the central state in their struggle with a hacendado, Sr. Carlos Zambrano. This hacendado was extremely influential within local institutions, including the municipal courts. His father, Don Estanislao Zambrano, had been a colonial official, and one of his brothers was the governor of the province during the early republican period. Yet another brother was a municipal mayor. Like other family members, Carlos Zambrano owned numerous haciendas throughout the province, and later he himself became the *jefe político* of the cantón of Riobamba.[30]

Throughout the mid-nineteenth century, the Zambrano family was frequently embroiled in legal disputes with Indian communities over land. In this case, the Indian communities, locked in a protracted civil dispute with Carlos Zambrano over grazing lands, appealed again and again to the Supreme Court in Quito, complaining that they could find no justice within the municipal courts. They stated: "Sr. Carlos Zambrano is so powerful that nobody, not even the judges can restrain him, attesting to the *hierarchy of power over justice*. Such behavior demands another legal decision from the Superior Tribunal to correct such abuses, and to protect us *infelices* as set down by the laws."[31]

Just as the Indians complained of the "hierarchy of power over justice" and referred to themselves as miserable, they called the Supreme Court their "father" and proclaimed their faith in the constitution. Being "infelices," they appealed to a paternalistic state that was supposed to protect them. However, the republican state owed them protection also because they had "always and willingly provided [their] services to the Republic."[32] This strategy of invoking the special laws meant to protect Indians could succeed, if only as a delaying tactic, even when their foes were powerful local officials. Later Carlos Zambrano protested, "The facility and ease that Indians have for fraud is well known, as are the excesses and exaggeration of those who claim to act in their defense."[33] In a similar dispute, another landowner exclaimed that not only were the Indians protected by unfair special laws, but that "many an otherwise intelligent and impartial judge goes too far in applying these misunderstood laws that protect the Indians, even giving them what does not belong to them."[34]

This is just one example from among hundreds of cases in which Indians turned to the central state in their struggle with hacendados and other local elites and officials. Indians recognized the gap between the local and central instances of power and appropriated the discourse of the central state in local struggles, and thus were able to shape aspects of the "state system" and to maneuver between different institutions of power.

The Abolition of Indian Tribute

By the 1850s, official rhetoric regarding Indians began to change drastically and protectionist policies were slowly replaced. A decisive moment came in 1854 with a circular stating that the institution of Indian protectors was no longer sustainable, as it was "clearly in contradiction to democratic ideals."[35] The Indian protectorate was eliminated and adult Indians were proclaimed to have the same legal capacity as other Ecuadorians. They could henceforth represent themselves in court and sign contracts. After this moment, a new state discourse proclaimed that Indians remained "backward" because of the continuation of outdated colonial institutions.

The abolition of tribute finally became feasible as other sources of government revenue became more important: the cacao boom provided an alternate source of financing that supplanted tribute as the largest source of national income. By the mid-1850s, the customs tax (from cacao exports) accounted for 49 percent of national revenue, while tribute represented a mere 12.6 percent.[36] In 1857 the Ecuadorian parliament passed a law that stated: "In the Republic the tax known as the personal contribution of Indians is abolished, and individuals of this class are now equal to the rest of Ecuadorians in terms of obligations and rights imposed and granted by the fundamental charter."[37]

President Flores had made a similar attempt to abolish tribute in 1843, but in the face of powerful opposition was forced to reinstate it. In the 1857 vote for abolition there was a wide consensus in a parliament that still predominantly represented highland landlords. Abolishing tribute freed hacendados from the obligation to pay the tribute of indigenous workers living on the hacienda. A circular of 1854 had stated that revenues from Indian tribute had been diminishing for a number of years primarily because hacendados had not been paying the tribute they owed for their Indian *conciertos* (debt peons).[38] By this time, the hacendados had already consolidated their own ways of recruiting, maintaining, and reproducing the indigenous labor force.

The abolition of tribute was, however, perceived as a major threat by many indigenous communities. Indians of Chimborazo protested violently against the abolition. In the parish of Calpi, more than 300 Indians rebelled. Distraught over the loss of their former exemptions and privileges, Indians demanded that officials reinstate tribute.[39] The local priest who had tried to pacify the Indians reported: "The Indians were irritated by the suppression of tribute, which in their lamentable ignorance they believe is a dishonor to them, and moreover they are exasperated because they now have to pay municipal taxes on their *chicha* [corn beer]. These Indians have declared that they have agreed with the Indians of Cajabamba, Licto, and Guamote to proceed collectively with their hostilities until tribute is reestablished, even if it is of a higher amount."[40]

Despite Indian resistance, tribute was abolished and the two republics finally became one. The abolition of tribute dissolved once and for all the "Indian republic," and Indians became, at least theoretically, free and equal to other Ecuadorian citizens. Yet formal equality concealed substantive inequality. As Corrigan and Sayer state, "In a materially unequal society, the assertion of formal equality can be violently oppressive, [indeed] it is itself a form of rule."[41]

The dissolution of Indian tribute and other legal changes regarding Indian communities and their lands undermined the bases of Indian peasant autonomy in Ecuador's highland provinces. It also meant that Indians had to fulfill obligations from which they had been exempt. Their "personal contribution" was replaced by the "contribución subsidiaria" and the "trabajo subsidiario," monetary and labor obligations that theoretically applied to all Ecuadorians but whose burden fell disproportionately on Indians. Moreover, the abolition of tribute left Indian communal lands much more vulnerable to expropriation by outsiders as Indians lost their justification for state protection of these lands.[42]

Clear parallels emerge in the state's relations with Indians between this early period and the period following the 1895 Liberal Revolution. The liberal state once again presented itself as the protector of indigenous rights, using this as a pretext to curb the power of local landowners. In the liberal period, Indians continued to present themselves as "timid," "ignorant," and "miserable" and argued that they therefore deserved protection from the central state. Throughout the nineteenth century, Indians appropriated and utilized law and state discourse, thus participating in the creation of particular government decrees, and by extension the construction of discursive frameworks. Indians were always active, though never equal, participants in processes of state formation.

3

Administering the Otavalan Indian and Centralizing Governance in Ecuador, 1851–1875

DEREK WILLIAMS

The year 1859 brought to a close the era of popular liberalism under President José María Urvina (1851–1858) and ushered in a new period of conservative-Catholic rule under Gabriel García Moreno (1860–1865, 1869–1875). When Urvina went into exile a year later, his ventures in anticlericalism and anti-landlordism were banished as well, not to return to national politics until the 1890s.[1] Replacing the central government's tenuous alliance with coastal elites and popular sectors was a political pact that García Moreno built with landlords and clergy, one that positioned ultramontane Catholicism as the basis for nationalism. During the 1859 civil war, highland elites in large part rejected the Urvinista project that had openly favored popular sectors through a discourse of equality and had actively sought to centralize state power.[2] The abolition of slavery (1854), the end of Indian tribute (1857), and the implementation of centralized legislation facilitating rural labor mobility, had encouraged subaltern groups to claim their rights and bolstered the central government's authority as the supreme arbiter of class and ethnic conflict.[3] When national consensus was reestablished by García Moreno under the constitution of 1861, political decision making was initially decentralized and democratized.[4] The central government's retirement from its paternal tutelage over the rural masses, however, was to be short lived. The Garcian regime quickly conceived a universalizing and centralizing project of ultramontane progress, one that necessitated an activist state presence in administering the indigenous population.

Urvina and García Moreno square quite comfortably with their respective liberal and conservative typologies, neatly illustrating two extremes of nineteenth-century approaches to postindependence nation building in Latin America. The two caudillos embodied divergent understandings of "republicanism": one pluralist and class-based, the other monist and corporatist.[5] However, the Urvinista and Garcian administrations faced the same postcolonial challenges to state building and nation making. Both ambitiously sought to define and disseminate state-led projects of "progress" but were obliged to filter their visions of republicanism through the neocolonial reality of Ecuadorian society—a situation marked by sharp political regionalism, formidable clerical influence, structures of economic dependence, and systems of unfree labor. They also were troubled by the country's nonwhite racial composition, in particular an indigenous majority that was judged to be "miserable"—stuck at the margins of political and economic life. The urgency to incorporate, or at least use productively, "the *indígena*" fundamentally shaped both governments' strategies for building a national community and extending state power.

Indeed, the "Indian problem"—as it was later labeled—was a nexus both for state formation and nationalism in nineteenth-century Ecuador. The mid-century anti-landlord project elevated the issue of the unequal treatment of indígenas to an issue of national import; similarly, the redemption of the "miserable" Indian formed a defining trope of the Garcian project. Urvinista ideals of republic rested upon notions of socioeconomic equality. The Garcian government countered with an inclusive (but hierarchical) ideal of a "Catholic republic," a country of pious, moral, and industrious members, open to all races and to every class.[6] Yet while each would define the Indian problem differently, both governments recognized the political utility of speaking on behalf of the indígena. Both understood that the administration of Ecuador's highland Indian population was central to fortifying state paternalism and legitimacy. Governing strategies with regard to the indigenous population were seldom about eroding corporate identities to establish a direct relationship between state and citizen. Rather, they were about reshaping and centralizing the existing relations of dependence—borrowing Lomnitz's useful conception—between strong and weak citizens (or between "full" and "embryonic" citizens).[7] To this end, the central government directed much energy toward consolidating the institutional authority of church, hacienda, *municipio*, and Indian *comunidad*, whose hierarchical networks had long mediated the governance of the indígena.[8] Thus, to investigate the central government's administration of the indigenous class is necessarily to study the state's conflicted relationship with local structures and rationalities of rule.

The centralization of governance in Ecuador's northern highlands between 1851 and 1875 was an uneven process. The discourses and practices of the state toward its indigenous population reveal how state activities organized society and defined legitimate expressions of identity.[9] By tracing the implementation of two "national" projects in the *cantón* of Otavalo, we can observe the "official" discourses of state elites and the institutions and mechanisms through which the central government sought to establish "national" objectives. In particular, the state sought to subordinate municipal government and landlord interests to national imperatives, infusing local cultures and institutions with state-centered understandings about progress and nation.

Studying Ecuador's nineteenth-century state is not a matter of unmasking or demystifying the idea of the state. To be sure, the central government sought to reify itself as the "*supremo gobierno*"—a superordinate, moral, and independent entity.[10] However, this was an uneven and conflicted process whose success was far from inevitable. Rather, this turbulent political period saw various attempts by a state-in-formation to construct such a mask—to normalize its interests and the hierarchies of region, gender, class, and race that underwrote them. As the ideological project of the state intersected with the institutional practices of governance, the central government's discourse on the Indian question bolstered the identity of the state as a supreme moral authority vis-à-vis decentralized and private governing strategies.

The Otavalan Indian and Midcentury Liberalism

Although imagined as national initiatives, both the liberal project under Urvina and the Garcian project of Catholic modernization were implemented unevenly across Ecuador's territory. Some of Urvina's initiatives, such as emancipation of the slaves, resonated more strongly in coastal regions. The Garcian government favored the upper Amazon region by regenerating missionary settlements. In the Sierra, the influence of government objectives under both regimes was far from uniform. One highland area that received considerable state attention during both periods was the northern province of Imbabura, and particularly the cantón of Otavalo. Indeed, the valley of Otavalo emerged as a sort of showcase for Urvina's anti-landlord liberalism and, later, García Moreno's Catholic modernity. Various features explain the region's attractiveness for the central government. Its proximity to Quito—

only an overnight journey away—meant that its regional elites and identity overlapped with Quiteña society and that local political decision making was more open to influence by state agents. The region was also positioned strategically at the crossroads of highland markets of the north-central highlands and a long-dreamed-of roadway from the capital to the Pacific port of Esmeraldas. The central government had other reasons to be optimistic about the transformative potential of its policies in Otavalo: within Ecuador's densely indigenous highlands, Otavalan Indians were judged to be most promising in their capacity for progress and civilization.

The Indian peoples of the Otavalo region had long been identified as exceptional. As skilled weavers, they had enjoyed special privileges during the early colonial period in the crown *obrajes* (textile manufactories), and by independence were renowned for their industry and relative prosperity.[11] By the mid-nineteenth century, the extraordinary character of the Otavalans was widely acknowledged, although usually to prove the rule of more general Indian backwardness. Visitors routinely found them to be "cleaner and whiter" than other Indians, and more intelligent and hardworking.[12] In *Geografía de la República del Ecuador* (1858), Manuel Villavicencio deemed the *Imbabureño* ethnic group (to which the Otavalans belonged) to be the "whitest" and most "European" of Ecuador's indigenous groups, "naturally disposed" to civilization.[13] In the eyes of state policy makers dedicated to the radical transformation of Indian society, the Otavalo region seemed the point of least resistance. It was judged to be especially ready for progressive change, a promising model for emulation by other indigenous regions.

The liberal political project between 1851 and 1858 echoed decidedly "Anglo-American" principles in calling for egalitarianism and civil rights for all Ecuadorians.[14] Under the strongman José María Urvina, liberals forwarded a republican model of social and economic equality—a politics that could transcend class interests and remove the ideological basis for Catholic-conservative authority. The central government sought to position itself as the legitimate mediator in class and regional conflicts. African slavery was abolished, suffrage requirements were loosened, and popular electoral participation expanded. Beginning in 1854, the Urvinista government committed itself to bettering the condition of the indígena class, promising to raise their status relative to the rest of the population. At the center of the popular liberal experiment, the Urvinistas put forth an ambitious, if ultimately ambiguous, reconfiguration of state-Indian relations. Eschewing the classically liberal advocacy for a race-blind bond between the citizen and the state, the Urvinistas sought to reinvigorate the colonial state-Indian covenant at the expense of the power of landlords and the church. A more temperate application of Enlightenment ideas, Urvina's Indian policy was decidedly neocolonial and far from ethnocidal.[15] Some efforts were made toward weakening the colonial structures of caste obligation and privilege. The onerous *contribución de indígenas* (Indian tribute) was gradually phased out after 1845 and definitively abolished in 1857.[16] A 1854 law ended the colonial institution of the *protecturía de indígenas* (legal tutelage), which had made Indians dependent on local officials for legal representation. Urvinista educational policy campaigned to liberate Indians from "misery, ignorance, and dejection." However, the sum effect of Urvinista policy was not to erase Indian caste identity but to reinforce indigenous collective rights and community structures. More radically, the state attempted to regulate and ameliorate rural labor servitude by facilitating labor mobility and empowering "free" Indian communities against the demands and abuses of highland landlords.[17]

Within the logic of the Urvinista liberal project, the Otavalan Indian was held up as proof of the degenerating effect of the hacienda-*concertaje* (debt peonage) system on the Indian and as a reason for optimism regarding the potential of all Ecuadorian Indians. Such arguments appear in Villavicencio's *Geografía*, in which highland Indians were viewed as the direct descendants of a once great pre-Hispanic Quitus civilization, and their present lamentable social situation the consequence of centuries of descent from civilization. He saw this deterioration expressed unevenly, with wide variations depending on whether Indians were formally under the service of haciendas. *Indios sueltos* (literally Indians "unattached" to a hacienda or patron) remained closer to an authentic Quitus character, whereas the *indios conciertos* (debt peons) resident in haciendas had deteriorated further from their earlier civilized state.

What is most remarkable about Villavicencio's interpretation is that he considered the "free Indian" to be racially distinct from (and superior to) his hacienda counterpart. Compared to the concierto who was "almost black in color," the suelto had "better" (lighter) features. He contended that Indians that were free from servitude were "so white, and [had] such agreeable features, that if dressed as Europeans they would be distinguished from them with difficulty."[18] To support his claim, he offered the evidence that the "expressive" and white-as-European Otavalan Indian hailed from a region where the hacienda-concertaje complex was relatively weak. The quasi-European Otavalan with his "natural dispositions" toward civilization and "special talents" in the manual arts allowed anti-landlord liberals such as Villavicencio to imagine that the entire "Quitus race," if released from the degenerating impact of an unfree labor system, would "differ very little from the European

[race]."[19] Thus, while recognizing the lamentable condition of the country's highland Indian population, the Urvinistas deemed this to be a superficial phenomenon, the result of racial deterioration, not biological inferiority. A selective rendering of the Otavalan Indian allowed midcentury liberals to argue that with a politics promoting socioeconomic equality the state could harness the Ecuadorian Indian's strong and perfectible character.

There is considerable, if shadowy, evidence that the rhetorical and legislative trappings of the Urvinista government economically empowered Ecuador's highland indigenous population, although with wide regional variation. This was particularly true in regions such as Otavalo and Loja, where landlord power was customarily less formidable than elsewhere in the highlands, and workers were better positioned to benefit from the pro-Indian attitude of the central government. In Otavalo, landlords and obraje owners faced a tradition of strong autonomous communities and growing competition for labor from sugarcane estates to the north. Moreover, obrajes required well-trained weavers, giving skilled textile workers considerable leverage to transfer their services to another estate or to move entirely outside the concertaje system. The relative resilience of Otavalo's colonial Indian community structure further hampered estate owners' capacity to combat Indian labor mobility. Indeed, many Indian peons were able to work the system of debt peonage to their advantage, freely moving from hacienda to hacienda in search of better working conditions. To be sure, the ability to shed one's concierto status was exceptional; that is, the freedoms fought for and partially won by Otavalo's peons were generally within the concertaje system. Still, from the perspective of conciertos, the right to "vary their servitude" was an important weapon in their everyday struggles to improve living and working conditions. Indeed, mobility rights in Otavalo seem to have made up part of a generally favorable climate for the district's Indians in negotiating terms of service with haciendas.[20]

Indian engagement with state discourse in Otavalo during the 1850s and early 1860s entailed a selective assertion of both citizenship rights and neocolonial corporate rights as indígenas. Within the pro-Indian climate forwarded by the Urvinistas at midcentury, indígenas across highland Ecuador were able to defend their rights both as individual citizens and as a protected "class." In Otavalo, this political potential became a substantial, if temporary, resource for certain Indians in their prosaic conflicts with local landlords. From the perspective of the central government, its anti-landlord policies fortified the state's image vis-à-vis the highland Indian population. By exposing the customarily private negotiation between peon and patron to public scrutiny, Urvinismo broadened the space for Otavalo's peons to pursue their legal rights. Peons had well-founded reasons to see the central government as a benevolent ally in legal claims for new amenities or in challenges to unjust changes to customary labor practices. These legal conflicts over economic issues and, more broadly, over the terms and meaning of the contractual bond between Indian and landlord involved the state as a mediator through its laws and network of local officials.

Central-Local Conflict in Otavalo, 1861–1869

The political crisis of 1859, from which García Moreno eventually emerged as president, was a resolute rejection of Urvinista state centralization and its anti-landlord and pro-Indian rhetoric. Indeed, during the brief balkanization of Ecuador into four "republics" in 1859, regional power holders sent a double barreled message to those who sought to govern the nation: decentralize political decision making and rescind the state's role as paternal tutor of the rural masses.[21] The 1861–1868 period was characterized by a general harmony between government and landlords, one that restored political autonomy to local authorities and terminated the state's legal favoritism toward the popular classes. The strongly decentralized constitution of 1861, and resulting legislation, gave *municipios* an unprecedented jurisdiction and autonomy.[22] Across the highlands, municipal labor codes were passed to reverse the "disorderly" impact of liberal legislation on agricultural production. More generally, local elites tried to assert local visions of progress over central initiatives. In Otavalo, as elsewhere, the municipio sought to reestablish its authority and interests over what they saw as top-down national policies that empowered "disorderly" rural classes.

The Garcian era (1861–1875) is correctly remembered as a period when the central government pursued national policies of schooling, policing, moralization, and public works, part of its ambitious project of "Catholic modernity." However, achievements in these areas came overwhelmingly after 1869, only after the implementation of a highly authoritarian constitution changed the balance of power from municipalities to the central government. Between 1861 and 1868, the Garcian government lacked the political wherewithal to overcome regional resistance and was often compelled to tolerate local customs, practices, and decision making. Still, despite his government's political debility, García Moreno was an activist in trying to promote his national agenda. As such, the 1860s was marked by conflict between local and national understandings of progress. In Otavalo, as in other highland districts, intergovernmental conflict centered on a cluster of issues: public works taxes, the expansion of rural schooling, and the administration of *baldíos* ("vacant" lands). The question of governing the indigenous population often underlay and informed the debate. In part this was a struggle for Indian labor and land, scarce and valuable commodities in an impoverished Ecuador. But friction over the administration of indígenas was also about broader issues of governmentality, about who had the legitimate right "to structure the possible field of action of others."[23] While engaging national initiatives, Otavalo's landed elites articulated an alternative understanding of progress and of the place of the indígena in local society.

In the 1860s, the Garcian government embarked on a grand project to connect Quito to Guayaquil with a modern roadway. As with the rhetoric of railways a generation later, the highland-to-coast road promised to unify the nation, integrate regional markets, and symbolize Ecuador's potential as a progressive country.[24] To fund the project, the state sought to centralize various locally administered revenue streams. One major move was to consolidate the locally collected *contribución subsidiaria* (a public works labor tax) and the local mobilization of Indian labor gangs for road construction. The Ministry of the Interior also sought to increase existing "national" revenues from the sale of baldíos and in 1863 crafted new legislation in this regard. The law defined baldíos, as was customary, to be all lands not already belonging to "individuals, corporations or communities." However, in unprecedented fashion, it also sanctioned the inclusion of *sobrantes* ("excess" lands) in Indian *pueblos* not "destined for the communal or individual use."[25] The novel addition of sobrantes was an affront to the customary prerogative of local government to profit from the repartition of the community lands. The 1863 law was equally distasteful to local government in that it potentially threatened municipally owned *ejidos* (common lands), placing the onus on local officials to demonstrate that such lands did not belong to "the nation."[26]

A second aspect of local-central land disputes was the criteria by which sobrantes were determined. Since independence, executive-appointed provincial governors had been empowered to distinguish between what were "necessary" versus "excessive" Indian lands.[27] As the beneficiaries of sobrante revenues, local governments advocated a narrow definition of Indian needs and actively tried to influence government officials charged with the survey of community possessions. After fending off the central government's bid to reclassify sobrantes as national lands, local elites stepped up their attempts to maximize *resguardo* expropriations. In the province of Pichincha, for instance, local government sought to extend the designation of sobrantes and tacitly legitimated white-mestizo settlers who squatted on Indian lands.[28] In the southern province of Loja, where large estates were the exception and Indian communities were well established, the municipal council also advocated having large expanses classified as excessive.[29]

The central government tried to counteract municipal ambitions by exercising its legal right to determine sobrantes. It routinely intervened, for instance, when municipios sought to bypass the provincial governor's office and unilaterally annex Indian common lands.[30] It sought as well to defend the customary possession rights of the *comuneros* (community-based indígenas), insisting that these indígenas remain in full control of their lands "whatever their extension."[31] In response to petitions, provincial governors frequently intervened on behalf of indígenas, resolving claims of illegal renting of individual property and of incursions of municipal renters onto community lands.[32] The central government was equally vigilant in ensuring that any revenues from legally rented ejido lands were being invested in benefit of rural schooling—another national priority—and not other local public works projects.[33] Yet, in its efforts to centrally administer Indian lands, the Interior Ministry found itself on unstable legal and political footing. Bereft of legitimate jurisdiction and possessing little on-the-ground presence in the provinces, the central government was obliged to cede much authority to local officials. In a much-publicized dispute with the Pichincha Council, for example, the Ministry of the Interior was forced to back off its claim to municipal lands, recognizing the local government's prerogative to "remedy its financial needs."[34]

Disputes between central and local government over the administration of Indian land and labor were clearly influenced by material considerations, as both bodies competed over scarce resources. Yet a strictly economic interpretation is not enough.[35] Considerable political and cultural tensions also informed these conflicts. In particular, local and national elites struggled over what legitimately constituted progress. In judging sobrantes as national "vacant lands," the central government looked to boost revenues for nationally scaled development, particularly its education projects and transcordillera highway projects. Municipalities, for their part, sought to label sobrantes as saleable ejido lands, hoping to invest the resulting revenues in projects of cantón-level development, such as local waterworks, roads, and municipal offices. These disputes were about who had the legitimate moral authority to determine the shape and scale that "progress" would take. Thus, the rhetorical and legal wrangling of the early Garcian era sharpened the boundaries between an increasingly defined ethic of "national" development and a diversity of local conceptions of progress.

Prior to 1869, the Garcian government had achieved little toward establishing an administrative foundation to implement its blueprint of national progress. In its efforts to overcome the intransigence of local elites, however, the central government was more successful in its efforts to portray itself as a moral and independent entity. Central to this "state idea" was an articulation of its unique relationship with the nation's Indian population. To curb municipal power in administering Indian lands, for instance, it depicted the state as the paternal protector of the "clase de indígenas."[36] In a universalizing pro-Indian discourse, it questioned whether local elites possessed sufficient compassion toward this "miserable class."[37] It challenged local governments to respect all Indian property as evidence of their commitment to "better the lot of the Indian race."[38] It further highlighted its paternalism by attacking the unenlightened, self-interested, parochial governance of local authority. The central government frequently contrasted its benevolence and good works with local government's inability or unwillingness to intervene on behalf of the comuneros.

For the central state, such rhetorical (and juridical) support of indígenas served the useful function of advancing its political legitimacy relative to local government. After abolishing tribute and legal tutelage of the indígena class, the state sought to rebuild a neocolonial pact with the nation's Indian comunero population. Its frequent intervention on behalf of comuneros was vital to the self-presentation of the "supreme government" as a legitimate—and more emphatically, the supreme—authority for Indian communities. Of course, refashioning a colonial paternalist relation with the indigenous population would no longer bring the economic reward of lucrative tribute revenues. Yet the fledgling García Moreno government had a strong incentive to position itself above the fray of "parochial" and "abusive" local officials. By maintaining its supreme authority, it hoped to harness the organizational and labor power of the indígenas in pursuing its ambitious projects of road building, moral improvement, and education.

Otavalo's municipal elites were understandably reluctant to embrace the universalizing Indian policy of the early Garcian state. While never openly eschewing their "humanitarian" obligations to protect Indian rights, the local council was less than willing to accept such a broadly applicable Indian policy. Rather, it pushed for a more restricted application of philanthropy and compassion toward the Indians, echoing the arguments of its constituent "landlord class."[39] Municipios expected that under the decentralist 1861 constitution they would expand their domain of authority, multiply sources of income, and pursue locally defined development projects. This vision was in part based in a reinterpretation of the rights and obligations of the indígena class. Since the end of tribute in 1857, local government had hoped for an abrupt end to Indian privileges and exemptions, giving the council a freer hand to exploit Indian land, wealth, and labor. For most local authorities—judges, tax collectors, military recruiters—the abolition was understood in a strict liberal sense: if the indígena now enjoyed equal rights, he should be responsible for his obligations as a citizen.

Given these expectations, municipal governments forwarded their own understandings of Indian rights and the state-Indian covenant. In advocating for a broad determination of excess Indian territory, municipios forwarded their own ideas of how much land Indian comuneros merited in post-tribute Ecuador. Humanitarian and philanthropic gestures toward the indígena, as advocated by the central government, were applicable only to the poor, those lacking the means for subsistence. The broader colonial notion protecting the entire indígena class could no longer be justified, as it unfairly favored wealthy Indian communities.

Such sentiments were especially relevant in regions where indigenous communities had managed to maintain significant control over land. In Loja, for example, officials complained that indígenas possessed more common pasturelands than were "necessary for their subsistence." They questioned the legitimacy of community possession, noting the "very scarce number of live stock" found grazing on Indian common lands. Local leaders suggested that if these same lands were placed in "more intelligent hands," livestock breeding would dramatically increase in productivity. Why "must this kind of possession be respected?" they asked the central government, when the Indians' common lands could be greatly reduced and still be "sufficient for their necessities."[40]

In Otavalo, the local government forwarded a similar interpretation of Indian rights and obligations in the early post-tribute period. In 1863, to increase its income from tribute, the Otavalo council proposed a requirement that indígenas pay six reales instead of the customary four.[41] While the proposal never became law, the council's justification for the modification reveals the commonsense attitude among Otavalo's governing elites about the Indian population. First, it revealed a fundamental dichotomy in their paternal and humanitarian responsibilities toward the indígena class. That is, local government advocated protection and benevolence primarily for the Indian concierto, while largely ignoring the comunero. In lobbying for approval to restructure the tax, the council experienced no pangs of conscience in increasing the tax obligations of the comunero population. Rather, it complained about the damaging local implications of reverse discrimination in the national legal system: one that taxed indígenas the same as whites, while allowing them to enjoy "a thousand guarantees," to possess lands "without paying for them," and to avoid military service to the "fatherland."[42] Otavalo's councilmen questioned the fairness of a legal system that gave Indians the best of both colonial and republican rights without the full obligations of either.

More remarkable, however, was the council's contention that a higher tax would not be harmful to the comunero given his "limited necessities." Not only did comuneros have the means to pay a higher tax (a plausible assertion perhaps, given the relative well-being of many of Otavalo's landholding, manufacturing communities), but also the councilmen drew on commonsense notions of indígenas as feeble consumers.[43] With the Indians' limited spending habits, indígena wealth was deemed superfluous and, as such, fair game for an "impoverished" municipal treasury. Such views indicate a general hardening of the national association of Indians with poverty. Indeed, the Otavalo case appears to be but one salient instance of a broader pan-Andean trend that exclusively linked special treatment for indígenas to their impoverished economic status.[44] However, the council's position also marked an early example of what became in the twentieth century a common feature of Otavalan politics: local disgruntlement toward indígenas who achieved prosperity but continued to enjoy special ethnic, "class" rights.

National Road Building and State-Indian-Hacienda Relations, 1869–1875

Throughout the Garcian era, the central government pursued a bold Indian policy, based on a strikingly neocolonial interpretation of the Indian problem. Like the Urvinista administration before it, the Garcian state understood the importance of creating a national culture of inclusion vis-à-vis the Indian population. In part, the government prioritized the spiritual conquest of the indígenas of the upper Amazon, renewing Jesuit missionary activity in the region. It believed that Christianizing and acculturating the Amazon Indians would foster economic progress and patriotism, creating a hardworking and manageable labor force while shoring up Ecuador's tenuous territorial claims.[45] Rhetorical optimism for transforming the Oriente, however, was facilitated by an idealized representation of the more "civilized" provinces of the Sierra, whose "hardworking villages" of indígenas were to be a model for their Amazonian brethren.[46] As an 1874 article in the official newspaper claimed, in regions where they had not been "neglected," Indians were "very religious, sober, industrious, and display[ed] an artistic disposition."[47]

Such references to "industrious" and "artistic" characteristics were inspired by (if they did not allude to) the indígenas of Otavalo, whose productive and high-quality cottage textile industry was much esteemed. More remarkable, however, is the unprecedented association of the Otavalan with piety and temperance. For conservative Catholics, the Otavalan Indians were clearly seen as the leading edge of indigenous civilization, on the verge of embodying the national ethic of hard work, progress, and religious devotion as inseparable. To be sure, the idealized discourse of the morally upright and hardworking Otavalan ran counter to much of the reality of Indian conduct.[48] Still, this selective rendering of the Otavalan became a key discursive piece within the Garcian Indian policy, heartening Catholic conservatives as to the universal potential of the highland indígena. Thus, while local authorities and European travelers continued to decry Indian idleness and laziness, the central government used the idealized Otavalan to emphasize the productive and disciplined potential of the Indian "class" in agriculture, manual arts, and road building.[49]

Not surprisingly, Otavalo emerged as a principal site for state-led moralizing and modernizing initiatives after 1869. When the government contracted the Christian Brothers to establish a normal school to train indigenous teachers, for instance, many of the youths recruited for the school came from Otavalo.[50] The central government believed that these Indians could be trained to be "intelligent and moral teachers" who, in turn, would "propagate the ideas of enlightenment and progress" throughout the most remote villages.[51] Perceptions of an Otavalan ethic of industriousness similarly buoyed hopes for cooperation in the state's most ambitious road-building project of the 1870s, from Quito to the fledgling northern port of Esmeraldas, and the transoceanic economic opportunities beyond. The Esmeraldas road project was to run through the region of Otavalo and promised to boost the agricultural and industrial potential of the north-central highlands. It formed part of a long-standing dream to overcome the Sierra's economic dependence on Guayaquil and to establish a national development axis directed by Quiteños.[52] However, despite the enormous material and political resources devoted to the project between 1870 and 1875, the roadway was never completed; a provisional thoroughfare was opened briefly in 1874, only to be abandoned shortly thereafter. Unlike the pride and optimism generated by Quito-Riobamba highway construction in the 1860s, the half-finished mule path to Esmeraldas was a source of government frustration and disappointment.

Although the ambitious highway project never met its grand nation-building expectations, the process by which it was implemented had a substantial impact—both deepening the central government's authority and reshaping state-Indian relations. Indeed, the construction project itself was a formidable expression of the central government's capacity to establish an on-the-ground institutional structure. It demonstrated the state's ability to conceive, direct, and implement public works projects of national scale. For half a decade, the project dominated the resources and politics of Otavalo. It epitomized the broader Garcian strategy of development that sought to reconfigure local power constellations to direct capital and labor resources to national projects. At the center of both the state's moralizing and modernizing projects in Otavalo was a broader political struggle over the administration of the region's Indian population—a complex conflict among agents of the central state and municipal government, landlords, the church, and Indian communities. In unprecedented fashion, the central government channeled existing clientelisms of municipal, landlord, church, and Indian-community authority to the ends of national development.

The Esmeraldas road project began in late 1870 with much enthusiasm from volunteer workers, who showed up on site with their own axes and shovels. Attracted by a high daily wage of up to two reales, brigades of several hundred men began carving the road out of Otavalo and westward up into the *páramo* (dry highland plateau). However, as construction began to descend into the *monte* (humid woodlands), the project ran into difficulties. Beleaguered by malaria and mudslides, the volunteer system quickly collapsed.[53] After just a few months, the project became entirely dependent on labor recruitment by local authorities. *Tenientes* (political lieutenants) of each parish, directly appointed by the central government, were officially responsible for recruiting between 30 and 50 peons each week, rotating among different communities.[54] However, despite a veneer of a centralized state administration, in practice recruitment was subcontracted outside the formal state apparatus to community-based authority structures and clientelisms. These included both state-appointed Indian *cabildo* members (*gobernadores de indígenas* and Indian *alcaldes*) and community authorities (caciques and *curagas*).[55]

By late 1871, the imperfections of the rotation system were coming to light. Given the high numbers of comuneros and sueltos in the province, it had seemed feasible to government administrators that a 500-man force could be raised and renewed with minimal coercion. However, the early gangs of volunteers disguised the fact that peons were not being recruited evenly from the province's rural labor pool; in addition to being uniformly indígena, road peons arrived from only a handful of parishes. In fact, while some workers were being repeatedly sent into the monte, other indígenas, or even whole communities, avoided the labor drafts altogether. The recruiting imbalances among the comunero population are explained primarily by the fact that sueltos could avoid the road work by changing their "unattached" status for an alliance with a hacendado or other patron. As the road work became more arduous, increasing numbers of indígenas entered into concertaje arrangements with local landlords or migrated to estates outside the region.[56] Others negotiated less formal alliances as sharecroppers or service tenants. Suspicious state officials considered both types of arrangements as "fictitious" and increasingly blamed the hacienda system as the principal impediment to labor recruitment. Combating these alliances of convenience and other resistance by landlords to national road projects quickly became the focus of state recruiting strategies.

Collectively, the implications of migrations and status changes by sueltos were grave for recruiters. As early as January 1871, local state agents began calling for the central government to "dictate strong measures" against landlords to counteract dubious relationships between free indígenas and haciendas.[57] And while the Garcian government generally supported the principle of landlords' prerogative over their labor force, it was not willing to watch idly as haciendas became safe zones for Indians looking to dodge their public works obligations. To discourage potential road laborers from seeking alliances of convenience, it openly challenged the haciendas' privilege and paternal power. Beginning in mid-1871, the central government began to strike back systematically at recent contractual arrangements between indígenas and landlords. First, it acted to combat the scarcity of workers caused by the massive emigrations, issuing a provincewide ban on contracting conciertos from the district of Otavalo.[58] Interjurisdictional efforts were organized to bring back draft-dodging peons who had entered into these contracts of convenience or were hiding in haciendas or towns in the neighboring cantón of Ibarra.[59] Second, within the Otavalo district itself, the government annulled all individual concertaje contracts that had been made after the start of the road project in 1870. It authorized petty officials to enter local haciendas to take custody (by force if necessary) of free peons deemed to be "fictitious conciertos" or those simply taking refuge on hacienda property.[60]

In October 1871, a Treasury Ministry decree authorized a novel system whereby local state officials could get access to the Indian labor in haciendas.[61] In an unprecedented move, it extended the 30-day road work obligation to all conciertos of the cantons of Ibarra, Otavalo, and neighboring Cotacachi. Each estate was required to release two of every ten laborers of its workforce on a rotating basis over a five-month period, until all had served. By ensuring landowners four-fifths of their workforce, the decree acknowledged the hacendados' assertions that public works obligations damaged estate agricultural production. Yet it insisted that traditional exemptions needed to be harmonized with the state's labor needs. Thus, the legislation was a formidable attack on the paternal power of the landlord class, undercutting one of the essential guarantees that a patron customarily offered his peons. By late 1871, a contract with a patron was no longer sufficient for exemption from public works labor. Equally intrusive, local governments could gain legal access to hacienda ledgers and could create lists of conciertos to determine the required contribution of each estate.[62] These lists gave state recruiters valuable knowledge and facilitated the institutionalization of the hacienda obligation. By mid-1873, the state had independent recruiting records for all indígenas in haciendas, and parish tenientes had standing orders to take conciertos from the estates in their jurisdiction.[63]

The success of this initiative, to be sure, had mixed results for the advancement of the Esmeraldas road and never solved the problem of labor scarcity. However, as a sustained government challenge to hacienda privilege, its implications in Imbabura were more clear-cut. For the centralizing Garcian government, the collection of accurate statistics of hacienda laborers not only enabled it to combat fraud and underreporting of laborers but also challenged customary landlord autonomy and demonstrated government authority within local society. Indeed, by going after contracted conciertos, the government made an important incursion into the private sphere, bringing landlord privilege in line with the "public good." Landlords and their administrators were confronted by state officials on their own turf, obliged to concede real and symbolic lines of customary power. Reminiscent of the overt anti-landlord politics of the 1850s, Otavalo's landlords faced a substantial threat from the conservative Garcian regime to their long-standing monopoly control over their contracted labor force.

State demands on estate labor also corresponded with broader nationwide attempts to subordinate local landlord autonomy to the interests of central government. Although its agenda was distinct from the midcentury liberal government, the Garcian administration built on many of these earlier interventions into landlord privilege and power. The central government continued to regulate and enforce working conditions within estates, fielding concierto complaints and publicly overseeing adjustments or liquidations of debt peon accounts.[64] Police chiefs routinely investigated complaints of hacienda punishment, increasingly intruding on a patron's ability to privately implement the *ley del patio*.[65] Imbabura's landlords were obligated to collaborate with state national guard recruiters as well; even though conciertos were exempt from military service, the government collected data on each resident's age, race, and vocation.[66]

After 1869, central authorities justified intervention into the private sphere of the hacienda not only through nationalist discourse, but also by asserting the superior morality of its interests. Landlords faced criticism when they did not actively support the government's education and moralizing initiatives. The president grew impatient, for instance, with the lack of primary schools in estates, which he hoped would provide an example for Indian education throughout the Sierra.[67] The government also complained of a lack of landlord commitment to its campaign to reestablish the sanctity of the Sabbath and chastised landlords for routinely demanding *faenas* (unpaid labor obligations) on Sundays and holidays. As in the effort to end Sunday markets, García Moreno abolished these "irreligious" labor practices, authorizing criminal punishment for violators.[68] Thus, government challenges to customary hacienda labor exemptions comprised part of a more ambitious project of asserting national imperatives above customary landlord privileges. State-hacienda relations, it seemed, had deteriorated considerably since the happy alliance under the highly decentralized 1861 constitution. While not displaying the overt anti-landlord sentiment of the 1850s, the 1870s central government was similarly intrusive in hacienda affairs. Indeed, the Garcian state boldly sought to reorient material and human resources to a national plan of development. Whether protecting conciertos from abusive administrators, promoting their moral education, or including them in public works brigades, government intervention struck at the heart of landlords' legitimacy and paternal authority. Moreover, by regulating patron behavior and formalizing hacienda obligations, the government opened the way for a more unmediated relationship between state and Indian peons. Implementing its national vision of progress, after all, required a national system of administration (and domination) of the Indian population. By attacking landlord privilege, the central government sought to supplant traditional forms of domination and to gain a more direct access to both hacienda—and community—indígenas.

State and Society in Nineteenth-Century Highland Ecuador

The "Indian problem" in nineteenth-century Latin America is sometimes described as the state's dilemma over how to "turn Indians into citizens." Such shorthand has a certain utility as it neatly captures the imperative among would-be nation builders to erase corporate and caste identities and to replace them with individual, state-centered ones. After independence, citizenship remained as the primary official language for communication between a country's inhabitants and the state. This was solidified after the definitive abolition of Indian tribute, removing the fiscal underpinnings of the colonial "pact" between the Indian class and the state.[69] However, as is well documented, full citizenship was seldom on the table for Latin America's indigenous people in the nineteenth century.[70] Colonial structures of caste and corporatism continued to mark the governance of indigenous populations. As Guerrero demonstrates for the Ecuadorian case, indígenas remained governed by the de facto reality of ethnic segregation, existing as Indian subjects of the republican state "concealed beneath the body of the citizenry."[71]

Guerrero also argues that after the abolition of tribute in 1857, the central state withdrew from "Indian administration" in rural highland zones. In these "regional backstages," the indígena class was increasingly left to fend for itself in the institutions, practices, and norms of "private and everyday administrative power."[72] Such a conception is particularly helpful for understanding the political utility of the "Indian" to discourses of power and the construction of racial identities in Ecuador. It is less revealing, however, about the shifting nature of state-Indian relationships and the broader process of state formation in highland Ecuador in the nineteenth century.

First, it is far from clear how the 1857 abolition of tribute exacerbated the central government's reliance on private and local "institutions" for governance in highland regions. The state had long depended on corporative entities that functioned partially within that state, but with considerable autonomy.[73] As elsewhere in early republican Latin America, Ecuador's early postindependence governments were incapable of centrally coordinating tasks such as tax collection, juridical punishment, and military defense. Particularly in rural, indigenous zones, such functions were formally or tacitly delegated to the semiautonomous governing structures of the municipio, hacienda (and its semi-institutionalized clientelisms), *comunidad de indígenas* (and its authority structures), and the Catholic Church. Each performed certain "state functions"—varyingly exercising executive, judicial, fiscal, military, and in some cases legislative roles—and maintained its own hierarchy and substantial independence from the central government.

Second, the conception of a post-1857 withdrawal of the central government from Indian governance tends to overstate the abolition of tribute as a turning point in state-Indian relations. Midcentury liberal reformism in Ecuador was weak by Latin American standards and left an ambiguous balance between individual and corporate rights.[74] Just as before the abolition of the head tax, when Indians found themselves "astride two codes of state recognition, the tributary and the citizen," post-1857 indígenas maintained a dual status.[75] From the state's perspective, far from removing itself from the governance of the highland Indian population, the Garcian government continued to maintain a direct relationship with the indígena. Both its moral initiatives (such as education) and modernization programs (such as road building) depended on a disciplined and cooperative Indian population, and the central government directed much attention and considerable economic resources to this class. It clearly had much to gain from maintaining a paternal relationship with the indígena. Positioning itself as the ultimate arbiter between Indians and non-Indians, the state forcefully asserted its identity as a moral and autonomous entity. At the same time, state power in Ecuador was bolstered in its capacity to permeate existing networks of civil society and to coordinate them under its own infrastructure.[76] The process of state formation in nineteenth-century Ecuador centered less on attempts to reclaim state functions from private and local corporative entities than on efforts to subordinate and centralize them under the central government.[77] This is especially salient with regard to the municipio and hacienda, but is equally relevant for understanding state-comunidad and state-church relations.[78]

Expanding the state's administrative scope was of course an uneven and imperfect process, even when substantial inroads were made, as during the Urvina and Garcian eras. Thus, throughout the period, the state-Indian relationship remained highly mediated by private and local forms of authority. Yet, rather than highlighting 1857 as a definitive break in the state-Indian relationship (only to be restored by the liberal governments after 1895), we might fruitfully look at how the central government sought to reconfigure this longstanding pact. Indeed, the history of the Ecuadorian state in the indigenous highlands can be further illuminated by studying the shifts and continuities within the "bonds of dependence" between full citizens and embryonic citizens.[79] It was this articulation between strong and weak citizens, between the promise of citizenship and some broader (and hierarchical) notion of political membership that gave the state-Indian relationship its character. As indígenas and the state in Ecuador engaged one another through existing institutions and corporations of colonial origin, they reconfigured not only their own identities, but also the nature of the institutions themselves.

4

Helpless Children or Undeserving Patriarchs?

Gender Ideologies, the State, and Indian Men in Late Nineteenth-Century Ecuador

ERIN O'CONNOR

Ideas about gender disguised deepening racial inequalities in late nineteenth-century Ecuadorian politics and society, assisting the state in its "triumph of concealment" at a time when the central government refused to recognize its own role in racial oppression.[1] As Philip Corrigan and Derek Sayer contend, patriarchy is a critical means through which state power is exercised, and therefore any moral conscience emanating from the state "is always that of the dominant class, gender, race, delineating and idealizing its conditions of rule."[2] In late nineteenth-century Ecuador, the state manipulated particular gender ideas to reflect and defend its paradoxical relations with Indians. At the core of state-sanctioned gender ideologies were Catholic morality and the doctrine of separate spheres for males and females, both of which stressed the husband's duty to protect and provide for his dependents and to control himself in his personal habits. These patriarchal ideas served as a "moral conscience" that classified Indian men as inadequate father figures, either childlike and themselves in need of paternal guidance, or abusive patriarchs lacking in self-discipline. Because they did not measure up to the state's patriarchal ideals, Indian men were deemed unworthy of becoming part of the political nation. This is similar to Derek Williams's discussion of the relationship between the central state and hacendados, whereby state officials justified their anti-landlord policies by arguing that estate owners fell short of their patriarchal responsibilities toward Indians. The purpose of such judgments was, however, different between the two groups: state officials sought to subordinate hacendados to central state objectives, whereas with Indians they were concerned with justifying racial inequalities and state policies of exclusion. Examining the intersection of racism and patriarchy at a particular point in the process of Ecuadorian state formation advances gender along with class, race, and region as a means of scrutinizing the uneven development of Indian-state relations.

In Latin America, multilayered interethnic paternalism was central to both the colonial and early republican political systems. For the newly independent nations, political power was strongly associated with paternalism, as the colonial system of two republics left lingering images of Indians as *niños con barbas* (children with beards) who, although physically mature, lacked intellectual or moral maturity and therefore required European rulers to father them.[3] Additionally, the European states that republican leaders sought to emulate were deeply patriarchal themselves.[4] Patriarchal politics was therefore doubly reinforced in nineteenth-century Ecuador; the continuation of the tribute system perpetuated paternalism as a central component of Indian-state relations in the early republic. Noting that tribute kept Indian men subservient to non-Indians in Ecuador, champions of abolition proposed ending the tribute system to liberate Indians from this legally enforced perpetual childhood. They also conjured up images of Indian men as well-intentioned heads of households who, despite their best efforts, were unable to provide for their families because of their tribute requirements; termination of the tax would enable them to fulfill their responsibilities. Statesmen who demanded the end of the tribute system following independence thus alluded to the need to make Indian males into capable men and potential citizens rather than perpetual children and subjects.[5]

By justifying and shaping Indian-state relations, attitudes about gender were crucial to the development of the state idea in nineteenth-century Ecuador. Developing the nation-state depended on bolstering the idea of equality before the law, in contrast with colonial practices that distinguished one's rights and obligations according to corporate identities, including racial ones. In practice, both central state policies and local authorities upheld racial differences; the state's goal was not really to make Indians into full citizens, but rather to reshape and centralize bonds of dependence. Such a goal, however, failed to offer a coherent idea that could serve as the foundation for the nation-state. This is where gender came into play: revitalized patriarchal discourses helped to render the state "cohesive despite its contradictions," with patriarchal concepts smoothing over the contradictions inherent in state formation.[6]

The abolition of tribute set the scene for antagonistic Indian-state relations in the late nineteenth century. Though legislators claimed that its abolition made Indians equal to other Ecuadorians before the law, it instead intensified racial oppression by eliminating Indians' previous privileges, burdening them with obligations to the state, and undermining their cultural autonomy. Whenever racial inequalities were apparent, politicians and judges needed ways to mask them in order to reaffirm that all Ecuadorians were equal before the law. Gender was an important tool—though certainly not the only one—that helped to smooth over the contradictions of Indian-state relations.[7] Using gender arguments to justify racial inequality was of course not new; this was precisely the purpose of the paternalistic practices of the colonial and early nineteenth-century state. Yet the context of Indian-state relations had changed with the abolition of tribute, since Indians were now technically equal to non-Indians before the law. As a result, the Indian problem went from being the first major topic of congressional debate to an issue that was officially ignored and denied. Similarly, the purposes of gender ideologies shifted, and they were now used not only to justify interethnic oppression but also to blame Indians themselves for the gap between the state's equalizing rhetoric and oppressive reality.[8]

In addition to highlighting the multifaceted images the state used to defend racial oppression, gender also illuminates the relatively scarce central government documentation pertaining to Indians from the period. Since the central state refused to acknowledge racial differences, relations with the Indians were left, by default, in the hands of local administrators. This prolonged ethnic divisions and the marginalization of Indians in Ecuadorian politics and society, and as a result there are few records of the links between state formation and interethnic relations.[9] Laws, government decrees and communications, criminal court cases, and scholarly writings seldom addressed the Indian problem, but when they did they often used patriarchal principles to evaluate Indians and declare Indian men to be lacking in the ideal qualities for citizens of the emerging nation. The central state therefore identified Indian men, in Garfield's terms, as "raw material rather than finished products of nation building" who had to be refashioned by the state.[10] Though official government declarations regarding Indians were infrequent, the late nineteenth century was an important phase in the development of modern Indian-state relations, as the first wave of state centralization occurred under President Gabriel García Moreno. Patterns of gendered interethnic relations established in this period reached beyond the fifteen years dominated by García Moreno (1860–1875), establishing the basis for Indian-state relations for the remainder of the century. Garcianismo also provided liberal politicians with both a foundation for and a useful antithesis to their own state-building project beginning in 1895.

García Moreno and the Politics of Patriarchy

Gabriel García Moreno controlled the central government with a combination of classic nineteenth-century notions of progress and Catholic conservatism to unite the country into *una sola familia*, a single family. The patriarchal tenets of family identified good women as dependent but useful members of the private sphere, and good men as responsible members of the public sphere who protected their women. Laws and political (or judicial) declarations show the centrality of patriarchy to conservative state formation. Catholic doctrine provided the foundation for state morality and Garcian political ideology. García Moreno acknowledged this when he described his goals as president: "To reestablish moral authority without which order is no more than suspension or weariness, and outside of which liberty is deceit and fantasy; to moralize a country in the bloody battle of good against evil, of honorable men against perverse ones, which has endured for half a century, and to moralize it through the energetic and efficient repression of crime and through solid religious education of new generations."[11]

Perhaps the ultimate symbol of the church-state link during this period was García Moreno's 1866 concordat with Rome. Along with submitting to the Catholic Church through this agreement, García Moreno clearly gained by it: he could use religion as a tool for social control, to augment state power (and his own), and to justify political repression. He could also bring in foreign priests and nuns to serve as the backbone of his educational project, expelling many Ecuadorian religious officials from their posts. Thus he gained firmer control over church members, as the new religious officials were indebted to him for their positions.[12] Using Catholicism as the cultural basis for state formation had numerous legal implications, particularly in the later years of Garcian rule, from 1869 to 1875. State ritual itself was affected by the church-state connection, as was evident when Vice President Mariano Cueva ordered state officials to participate in religious festivals and gave priority to certain religious holidays. Such practices were crucial to the central government's control over both its own officials in the provinces and over the Ecuadorian public more generally.[13] Individual actions and rights were also legally limited by Catholic morality: sexual behavior that García Moreno deemed aberrant was illegal, excessive alcohol consumption was discouraged, and the 1869 constitution made Catholic faith a requirement for Ecuadorian citizenship.

The state identified women—and some women identified themselves—as pivotal actors in maintaining national morality. As a Catholic women's group in the city of Ambato asserted: "Woman has her duties, as well as her intimate joys, in the domestic sphere"; she is therefore interested in "all things related to religion, the fatherland, and her own family, of which she is the core and principal center."[14] Domestic tranquility and feminine morality paralleled and reinforced the progressive agenda for economic development through exports (mainly cacao), and nation building through political centralization and developing infrastructure. As a scholar of the era put it: "Woman has become the handsome mosaic of the national edifice: at the side of piety, economic industry; at the side of modesty, delightful instruction; all in the proper proportions."[15]

If women were important to state building, however, they were limited in their public behavior. Not only were women denied the right to vote until 1929, but the 1860 civil code identified married women as legal dependents, giving the control of all marital goods, and responsibility for presenting women's civil and financial interests, to husbands. A wife could act directly on her own behalf only with her husband's—or, in his absence, a judge's—authorization, which could be revoked at any time. The explanation for limiting female rights was that "the husband is the master of conjugal society, and as such he freely administers his wife's worldly goods."[16] In this vision of patriarchy, women could uphold the culture of the state while they were simultaneously outside the political nation; they therefore helped to define and augment their husbands' status and legal rights.[17] Men's public roles, in the economy and politics, were based in large part on their responsibilities as heads of households, as husbands and fathers who acted in their dependents' interests. Women were to be obedient and protected, and while they remained firmly in the private sphere, their presence in the home was consequential in public matters.

Marriage was at the center of these patriarchal state ideas during the Garcian period because it was both a civil contract and a sacrament; as such, it helped to maintain social order.[18] Given its importance to the moral mission of the state, the sanctity of marriage had to be legally secured and the proper roles of husband and wife upheld. While the state did not allow the dissolution of marital bonds, couples with certain marital problems could seek a *divorcio* (permanent separation) from the church and use civil courts to separate their goods. Both processes reinforced state- and church-sanctioned gender ideas. First, there were specific grounds for such separations, such as routine mistreatment that put a wife or children in jeopardy, a husband's failure to provide food and clothing for his family, habitual drunkenness, or adultery.[19] Separations were largely a female prerogative since accepted grounds focused on women's need to be provided for and protected. Moreover, the 1860 civil code noted that a husband was still required to support his wife after they were granted a divorcio, although he could retain control of his wife's goods if her infidelity was the cause.[20] Husbands involved in divorcios lost their manly rights to financial administration owing to their own irresponsibility in the home, unless their wives had displayed unfeminine, immoral qualities by having an affair. Again, both requirements reinforced images of the male provider and the female homemaker.

García Moreno used his presidential power to protect the sanctity of marriage when he declared concubinage illegal on May 5, 1869. Because the penal code had to address offenses that "destroy public morality," the decree established punishments of up to two months' imprisonment and two years of exile for men and women who lived together outside of marriage. If both parties were able to marry and did so even after a sentence was submitted, they would not be punished.[21] This decree placed the central government squarely in the innermost sanctum of private life, the bedroom. State intervention in illicit relationships blurred the line between public and private spheres, especially because the law itself was concerned with the impact of concubinage on the wider society. Accordingly, most concubinage cases that reached the Supreme Court in Quito focused specifically on public aspects of alleged affairs: accused couples were convicted if witnesses testified that they lived together openly, acquitted if this was denied; if witnesses' testimonies were mixed, the case could be decided either way.[22] Evidence of a man's good reputation in business and other public transactions could at best only lessen his time spent in prison, while references to a defendant's ignorance or rusticity rarely reduced a guilty sentence.[23]

Making concubinage a crime punishable by the state heightened the public and scandalous aspect of these relationships. Elias Laso, prosecuting attorney for the state, sometimes mentioned the shame that extramarital affairs brought upon innocent wives. In one case, he reinforced his argument for a conviction by referring to the tears shed by the defendant's wife; in another he called for leniency to minimize the suffering of the defendant's wife.[24] The image of the long-suffering wife, whether used to increase or lighten a defendant's penalty, was an especially powerful tool because it played upon the patriarchal concepts of female vulnerability and male responsibility that were central to García Moreno's moral agenda. Concubinage charges could bring disgrace upon a family, particularly a family of high status, even if unfounded. Once the accusation was made, this public scandal could be alleviated only publicly, as when an edition of the national newspaper in March 1870 noted that the Supreme Court had dropped concubinage charges against Modesto Velástegui and Paula Cisneros.[25] From all angles, the decree making concubinage illegal was an important facet of the state's social control that publicized its commitment to eradicate immorality, whether or not cases were vehemently pursued in practice.[26]

In addition to anything he deemed aberrant sexual behavior, García Moreno was also greatly preoccupied with alcohol abuse. A telling piece of political literature was an eight-segment opinion piece in the official *El Nacional* newspaper in 1875 entitled "El Demonio Alcohol," which stated that those who drink to excess "frequently lose the ability to reason and ordinarily remain in a violent and dangerous state."[27] Alcohol abusers were supposedly prone to criminal behavior, and one drunken murderer was depicted as having "a savage appearance, his eyes gleaming, his hair standing on end, his gestures menacing, his teeth gnashing; he spit on the faces of those present," after which the author concluded, "alcoholic insanity is characterized by absolute brutality, and by stupidity."[28] In sum, alcohol abuse eliminated natural moral inclinations to such an extent that even the drinker's humanity was lost and the alcoholic had the "repulsive appearance of a filthy animal."[29] The association between drink and brutality helped to justify special taxes on alcohol and a higher drinking age. García Moreno himself, when calling for a tax increase on alcoholic beverages in 1869, referred several times to the moral depravity caused by alcohol to justify higher levies.[30]

A frequently discussed moral problem in "El Demonio Alcohol" was the dissolution of the family and, more precisely, the drunken husband's failure to uphold his patriarchal duties. Rather than providing for his wife and children, he spent his money on alcohol, and "his wife, suffering much as a consequence of this detestable custom, often [left] her domicile to seek refuge in her parents' house."[31] Rather than protect his wife and children, he beat them: "A certain individual, once he submitted to liquor . . . habitually abused his wife and son . . . [and] his family came to live in misery, which is ordinarily what happens when the head of the household surrenders to drunkenness."[32] This disdain for patriarchal responsibilities could result in even more formidable consequences, as when a drunken husband murdered his wife because he mistakenly suspected her of infidelity.[33]

Whether the issue was marriage, sexuality, or alcohol consumption, the moral mission associated with Garcian state formation was founded on patriarchal concepts. Men's and women's proper roles were clearly defined, and straying from them had serious legal and social consequences. Men's public powers stemmed from their duties as responsible patriarchs of their homes; women's exclusion from public life was an extension of patriarchal protection. García Moreno was, of course, the ultimate father figure for the national family he was creating. In short, patriarchy was the glue that held the Garcian state idea together.

Though presented as universal, these gender concepts were far from racially neutral. Indian women in particular were rendered invisible in the gendered politics of nation making. For one thing, some of the policies ostensibly issued to benefit women were irrelevant to Indian women's lives, such as allowances for formal marital separations that were costly and therefore unattainable, or laws regulating concubinage, which was rarely a cause of scandal in indigenous communities. In general, state-sanctioned gender ideas did not reflect Indian women's experiences or needs: the public and private spheres were not as neatly divided in indigenous communities as for upper-class whites and mestizos, and Indian women were often more concerned with class or cultural oppression than with gender issues alone.[34] Indian men shared some of these experiences, but their position in the Ecuadorian national family was distinct. Though ignored most of the time, Indian men sometimes drew state officials' attention for falling short of the prescribed archetype. When this happened, descriptions of Indian men waffled between discussions of their childlike humility and vulnerability and assertions of their brutal savagery.

Indian Men as Helpless Children

Political and scholarly generalizations of Indian qualities in late nineteenth-century Ecuador frequently emphasized that Indians were naturally submissive, particularly in their relations with whites and mestizos. Juan León Mera, author of Ecuador's first novel and supporter of Gabriel García Moreno's conservative regime in the 1860s and 1870s, wrote a school text depicting Ecuadorian law, society, and history in which he claimed, "Among Indians, humiliation, timidity, and guile are predominant [traits], acquired in their long and perverse servitude, from which also comes their notable air of sadness . . . but they are [also] hardworking, active, long-suffering, and constant."[35] If Mera did not openly criticize indigenous attributes, he did not view Indians as equal to whites and mestizos in Ecuadorian society. Europeans, he asserted, were by nature "religious, honorable, generous, and lovers of their independence and liberty." Mestizos supposedly fell between the indigenous and European extremes, but "as they become more civilized they continue to mold themselves more and more toward [European traits]."[36] He used similar distinctions in his discussion of Ecuadorian customs: Indians "exceed extreme simplicity in their rural [or coarse] character, and superstition holds great influence over them; those of European descent maintain Spanish customs . . . [and] mestizos have less uncultured customs than the Indians, but different from the Europeans."[37] Mera thus constructed "a world replete with social and hierarchical distinctions" to justify racially based social inequalities.[38]

Mera used this text and its racial profiles to construct a vision of the nation that outlined the relative value of various components of society. By asserting that mestizos were becoming more civilized by adopting European traits and discarding indigenous customs, he reinforced nineteenth-century notions of progress. European culture represented civilization and progress, and Indian (and other non-European) cultures represented barbarism and backwardness. The so-called progressive elites hoped that by emulating European culture and embracing export-oriented economics they could duplicate European economic success and political stability.[39] Ecuador's Indians, maintaining their own language and customs, farming small subsistence plots or toiling begrudgingly as peons on large estates, inhibited both cultural and economic progress. The traits Mera catalogued under each ethnic group suggested how they could be most useful to national development. As honorable men and lovers of liberty, those of European descent were best suited to lead the nation, while Indians, timid but hardworking and constant, had the potential to serve as the backbone of labor in the search for national economic success. Mestizos, given their mixed qualities, could be either leaders or laborers.

Indians' submissiveness not only made them unlike whites and mestizos, but also created a problem. Indians' humility, combined with accusations of inherent dishonesty, could be used to justify the cruel treatment that many Indian servants received from their employers. James Orton's travel account elaborates: "Always humble and submissive to your face . . . [the Indian] will do nothing unless he is treated as a slave. Treat him kindly, and you make him a thief; whip him, and he will rise up to thank you and be your humble servant. A certain curate could never trust his Indian to carry important letters until he had given him 25 lashes."[40] In essence, Indians were figurative children who needed patriarchal discipline lest their dishonest tendencies get the better of them. Likewise, Indians' childlike ignorance and dishonesty supposedly made them unreliable witnesses in court. As one defense attorney asserted, "If an obraje Indian overheard [a discussion of] geology . . . he wouldn't know what they meant . . . and would [simply] repeat what he had heard."[41] The lawyer's point was that no Indian could be trusted as a witness because he did not understand what he had heard or observed, and in particular had no concept of how the law functioned. Unmanly humility also left Indian men defenseless, as Pedro Fermín Cevallos explained when he claimed that their "cowardice and humility are such that [Indians] allow themselves to be dominated even by the lowliest members of the other castes."[42] Even in his vulnerability, the Indian man was not described as a victim, since his own shortcomings were to blame for how he was treated.

Given that Indians' (presumably inherent) timidity left them susceptible to mistreatment, the central government sometimes defined Indians as a social sector in need of protection and guidance. In an 1870 letter to provincial governors, the minister of the interior remarked that local political and judicial officials often abused their power by "compelling Indians to labor on private construction work against their will, and this scandal is so extreme that the aforementioned authorities oblige [Indians] to contracts that supply them with peons." In response, García Moreno declared that any authority discovered doing this would be subject to removal from office and potentially face criminal charges.[43] Most important, these orders were carefully worded so that they could not be taken to call for special treatment or protections for Indians, a critical point in the post-tribute era when the central state insisted that Indians were legally equal to whites and mestizos.

Another dubious attribute that state officials frequently associated with Indians was their supposed idleness or laziness, and most often they proposed educational initiatives to eradicate this problem. Gabriel García Moreno suggested this in his 1869 message to congress when he stated: "It is not, therefore, strange that ignorance and lack of honor are so frequently transmitted like a fatal inheritance, which perpetuates *the lazy idleness with which we justly find fault*, and as a result of which the indigenous race, especially in the interior provinces, continues to be wretched, depraved, and miserable."[44] The solution was to found new primary schools that would help Indians to raise themselves out of their abject condition. Literacy would also change Indian men's political status by making them eligible to vote; it was only illiteracy that officially kept most Indian men from suffrage. The educational initiative did not proceed easily or smoothly, however. Just two years before García Moreno declared a need for primary schools, the minister of the interior admitted that "public education has advanced only slowly . . . [in part because of] the idleness of our villages. . . . [Rural schoolchildren] deserve to be called crowds of wretched beings who grow in indolence without having their sublime destiny in the land known to them."[45] The submissive timidity attributed to Indians therefore placed indigenous peoples in the childlike role of needing guidance and protection as they advanced toward true civilization.

Just as the state identified submissiveness and vulnerability with women, their descriptions of Indian timidity identified all Indians with a trait considered naturally feminine. This was evident in an 1892 statue depicting Sucre, an independence hero in Ecuador, standing protectively over an Indian woman.[46] Identifying Indian women as passive followed general ideas about intrinsic gender traits, but classifying Indian men as passive meant that they lacked true manliness. This in turn helped to justify their political and social marginalization, as the assumption quietly condoned the patriarchal behavior of employers and state officials. After all, if men were the proper authorities within the family, and Ecuador was una sola familia, it followed that the national family needed reliable patriarchs. Considering Indian men to be passive and ignorant, white and mestizo men had to take charge of the Ecuadorian household, sternly but fairly ruling over all women and Indians.

Indian Men as Undeserving Patriarchs

Though politicians and scholars of late nineteenth-century Ecuador considered highland Indians submissive on many, if not most, occasions, they also attributed darker, more violent characteristics to Indians, mainly regarding how Indian men treated their families and peers. A Supreme Court case from 1874 offers an excellent example. Asencio López, an Indian from the central highland province of Chimborazo, was charged with beating his wife, María Aguagallo, and his mother-in-law, Rosa Aguagallo. Both the prosecution and defense used the trial as a platform on which to argue over Indians' place in the Ecuadorian nation.

Defense attorney Alejandro Rivadeneira admitted that López committed the crimes of which he was accused. He maintained, however, that domestic violence was a natural, and therefore unchangeable, part of indigenous life. He requested the minimum sentence because of "López's coarseness (rural character) . . . which is *congenital*, with very few exceptions, to the indigenous class to which he belongs; . . . there is a deep-seated custom between the poor Indians, in which a wife *requires* a dozen monthly blows from her husband as a token of his affection for her: a peculiar way to show love!; but . . . when a husband . . . beats [his wife], he is driven by love, rather than by hate and vengeance."[47]

Rivadeneira also called upon racial stereotypes in his plea for leniency when he insisted that his client failed to understand the severity of the crime he had committed. By presenting domestic violence as an inborn trait of this ethnically distinct group within Ecuadorian society, he could claim that such brutal displays of so-called affection, while horrifying to non-Indians, should not be severely punished. Furthermore, he argued that López could not understand the brutality of his actions owing to his limited intelligence and his drunken state at the time.[48] In short, the barbaric Indian could not be held responsible for his actions because his very nature was contrary to civilized behavior. In this analysis, the Indian man was as much, if not more, of a victim than the Indian woman, because his wife instigated the crime by requiring violence as a sign of affection.

Prosecutor Elias Laso maintained similar ideas about white civilization versus Indian barbarism, but he interpreted them differently:

> The judge should use all means at his disposal to contain the *savage* custom which unfortunately exists among our lower orders . . . of mistreating wives without taking into account the consideration that a man should have for a woman, not only because of religious or family obligations, but also *because it is characteristic of the rational mind. In a . . . free republic born in the century of enlightenment and in a culture which guarantees individual rights to all within its territory* . . . it is not impertinent to . . . request that you weigh heavily these *offenses which deface the customs of a faithful people, renowned through other qualities for their gentle character.*[49]

Like Rivadeneira, Laso identified domestic violence as endemic within Indian societies; however, he did not recognize this as an inherent trait that absolved the Indian man from responsibility. Yet even within this interpretation, the Indian woman was not the true victim. Instead, the more significant threat was that this example of barbaric behavior would reflect badly on the nation as a whole, and on civilized ("white") society in particular. Laso firmly declared that the government had to forcibly obliterate Indian domestic violence by severely punishing Indian men charged with the crime.

The conflicts and continuities in the attorneys' arguments not only related to their roles in this case, but also reflected broader ideas about European civilization and Indian barbarism. Here, however, barbarism had a tangible consequence with the disruption of the core unit of society, the family. This may explain why both the prosecutor and the defense attorney in Asencio López's case were relatively unconcerned with the plight of the Indian women. While they did not consider women's suffering trivial, they were more concerned that Indian domestic violence would be an obstacle to their goal of attaining Europeanized progress and modernization. Yet their proclaimed concern did mean that, at least in theory, court officials had to commit themselves to eradicating domestic violence.

The lawyers' impassioned arguments in this case were simultaneously deceptive and enlightening. The circumstances and outcome of the case were unusual. Though López was found guilty and given the two-year maximum prison term, most cases against indigenous men for domestic violence or sexual harassment went unpunished, and most were freed either for insufficient evidence or because the women's injuries were not considered serious.[50] The López case was also exceptional because Indian women rarely brought domestic violence cases to court (although they were more likely to bring charges in ecclesiastical courts). Their reluctance to do so may have been influenced by court officials' leniency in these disputes but was also because Indian peasant women had other means of addressing domestic problems. Documentary evidence suggests that abused Indian women were more likely to abandon their homes temporarily, seek the protection of other men, or even leave their husbands to live with other men, than to bring these cases to court.[51] Although Asencio López's trial was not typical, the attorneys' attitudes about domestic violence as proof of Indian barbarism, and their dispute over how to interpret and respond to such conduct, mirrored more general ideas about Indian savagery in the era.

Though Ecuadorian references to indigenous domestic violence were rare in the period, a travel account by United States official Friedrich Hassaurek in 1867 reflects deeply embedded assumptions about Indians. He wrote, "The Indian is strongly attached to his wife, and very jealous, although he treats her cruelly; but the woman does not wish to be treated otherwise. If her husband should cease to beat her, she would be convinced that he ceased to love her."[52] One must be careful using accounts by foreign visitors as historical evidence, as their authors were apt to view both indigenous peoples and whites in Latin America as "backward" on many levels. Hassaurek (like James Orton, who saw a need to beat Indian servants) interacted mainly with high society in Ecuador, and his opinions about indigenous peoples were based largely on those connections. His portrait of Indian marriages echoed the prejudice of wealthy Ecuadorians, and his statements on indigenous domestic violence suggest that Laso and Rivadeneira drew on deeply embedded racial stereotypes when they formed their arguments in the López case.

The López case also mirrored broader ideas about aberrant Indian behavior in its references to the link between alcohol and indigenous violence. A typical defense strategy in cases where Indian men were accused of violent crimes was to cite intoxication as a mitigating factor. As one lawyer proclaimed in another (superior court) case: "Our Indians surrender to intoxication and ignore the consequences; . . . *thus one can logically deduce that a cerebral congestion develops.*"[53] Indian men were allegedly prone to alcoholism, which made them violent. Pedro Fermín Cevallos, just after identifying Indians as timid and humble, continued by declaring, "When they are drunk it is another thing altogether, and they become talkative and valiant, and they would resign themselves to dying rather than ceding to something they did not want." Indeed, when discussing indigenous dances connected with the celebration of Corpus Christi in Quito, Cevallos described a level of drunkenness so extreme that "if it is not a palpable profanation of that which is most sacred, we do not know how to qualify it."[54] Drinking transformed the timid, humble, cowardly Indian into a bold and even vulgar character.[55] This idea was not new, but how those in power manipulated it changed in the republican period.

Drunkenness also helped to explain Indians' violent behavior in rebellions. After the Daquilema rebellion in Chimborazo Province in 1871, members of the central government blamed intoxication for the brutality of the event.[56] García Moreno's 1873 message to the congress described the revolt as "produced by drunkenness and vengeance and marked with various acts of ferocious savagery."[57] Minister of the Interior Francisco Javier León concurred: "The rebels, stimulated by intoxication, committed repulsive excesses, killing and cruelly defiling the cadavers, burning and robbing not only in the civil parish [of origin], but also in those of Punín, Cajabamba, and Sicalpa."[58] Drinking, it seems, unleashed a savagery that lay just under the surface of the "socialized" and "docile" Indians of the highlands.

Even "El Demonio Alcohol," while it lacked a direct reference to racial distinctions, indirectly suggested that Indians were more prone to the dangers of drunkenness and barbaraic behavior than other members of society. Moderate drinking did not undermine morals or steer a man away from his patriarchal obligations. Only the heavy drinker, the habitual drinker, lost all rationality and moral compass.[59] Moreover, some men were more vulnerable to heavy drinking than others: "If alcohol can . . . enslave the spirit of one who is devoted to good sentiments, there is even greater reason that it will produce this enslavement when such sentiments are weak, *by nature or by lack of education*, or when they are altogether absent due to an inborn moral monstrosity in which the dark passions are naturally greatly active."[60] This passage is highly suggestive, since it alludes to characteristics frequently assigned to Indians: coarseness, ignorance, habitual intoxication, and irresponsibility. Thus Indian men were again defined as aberrant and as undeserving patriarchs.

Stereotypes of Indian men as either childlike or brutal served to alleviate the contradictions underlying Indian-state relations at a time when Indians' legal equality to whites and mestizos was rendered virtually meaningless by ongoing racial oppression and political restrictions. This is evidence of what Uday Mehta refers to as the methods by which "universalistic doctrines sustained a status quo of unmistakable political exclusion."[61] Although Ecuadorian state officials did not directly declare that Indian men should be excluded from nation making, they saw them as hindrances to their goals. Identifying Indian men as childlike and subservient restored the paternalism of the colonial and early republican eras, though without the official structures or benefits that Indians had enjoyed under the old tribute system. Calling Indian men irresponsible patriarchs in their own homes questioned their trustworthiness in other ways, particularly in political matters. Therefore, whether Indian men were identified as helpless children or aberrant patriarchs, these exaggerated discussions of their supposedly inherent qualities helped to justify Indians' continuing (and even intensifying) marginalization in the nation, and they reinforced the idea that "better kinds of men" should run the country. State officials had to make these claims carefully in the post-tribute era to avoid implications of inequality among Ecuador's ethnic groups. The more tentative tone of "El Demonio Alcohol" reflects the desire to deny racial difference. The description, however, was far from neutral; references to an individual's supposed character could easily be interpreted in terms of class and race, especially by the privileged men who read the official newspaper of the central government.[62] Not only was the position of Indian men paradoxical, caught as they were between minority and adult status, but also white-mestizo elites took a hypocritical stance regarding paternalism and Indians. On the one hand, Indian men were seen as aberrant because they beat their dependents; on the other hand, they had to be whipped to be forced to work.

Indian men and women did not passively accept state-sanctioned stereotypes; they used them to their own advantage whenever possible. While it did not benefit Indian men to call attention to their reputation as irresponsible husbands and fathers, they emphasized their presumably childlike need for protection. An Indian man faced with criminal charges might allude to his membership in the *raza infeliz* (miserable race) as a means of gaining the court's sympathy and reminding state officials that despite laws, Indians were far from equal to whites and mestizos in Ecuador. (These patterns appear in the criminal court records for the province of Chimborazo.)[63] Even allegations of habitual drunkenness could be used to seek leniency in sentencing, while Indian women exploited their supposed vulnerability both as members of the miserable race and as women.

Because of its role in state formation and in Indian-state relations in particular, patriarchy must be examined (as Joseph and Nugent have indicated for hegemony, culture, and consciousness) "in historical motion."[64] Patriarchy, like state formation, is a changing phenomenon, a set of multilayered and contradictory processes that differ along class and race lines as well as over time.[65] In late nineteenth-century Ecuador, state-sanctioned patriarchal ideals not only constrained women's activities, but also relegated Indian men to a category of people that had to be forced to relinquish their backward and barbaric ways. In essence the state had to "shove civilization downward" to Indian populations.[66] Used to conceal racial inequalities in the late nineteenth century in Ecuador, gender offers contemporary scholars a tool with which to investigate the depth of racism in the process of state formation.

5

Liberalism, *Indigenismo*, and Social Mobilization in Late Nineteenth-Century Ecuador

MICHIEL BAUD

The Indian *levantamiento* (uprising) of 1994 provides an excellent point of departure for analyzing the origins of present-day indigenous movements in Ecuador.[1] Beginning in the 1950s, social movements and NGOs created a breeding ground for the emergence of organizations composed of indigenous peoples, directed by their own leaders. Indian intellectuals appropriated social and political discourses from the national and international arena and used them as the groundwork for a movement that no longer spoke for the Indians, but spoke through the voice of the indigenous population itself. We still have to see how profound this transformation will be, but an analysis of the ways social and political discourses of the ruling elites are appropriated and transformed is very pertinent. Those who study the relationship between indigenous communities and the nascent nation-state in Latin America call attention to the continuous struggle since the nineteenth century over the meaning and reality of the state's discursive practices. While the state resorted to disciplinary and centralizing measures, it could not prevent subaltern populations from taking the law into their own hands and giving it new meanings and content.[2]

Indians and the State

The relationship between state projects imposed "from above" and various forms of state formation "from below" is a central theme of modern

Andean history.[3] On the one hand, the state is seen to be fragmented and contradictory; on the other, the indigenous peasant population makes a relentless effort to influence that same state and to create more favorable conditions at the local level. The triangular relationship linking the central state, regional elites, and subaltern (indigenous) populations is particularly visible in the indigenous heartlands of the Andes and Mesoamerica. Here, the relationship between indigenous peasants and their leaders, regional "blanco-mestizo" elites, and an increasingly active state acquired all kinds of different appearances. David Nugent demonstrates the paradoxical and often contradictory results of these relationships in northern Peru.[4] For Ecuador, Andrés Guerrero and Kim Clark have done the same.[5] These contradictions are manifested both on the practical and the ideological levels, showing the complex results of implementing ideologies of progress in the late nineteenth and early twentieth centuries in Latin America and the social responses they provoked.

To address these issues in southern Ecuador, let us examine the relationship between rural society and the state in the period after the Liberal Revolution of 1895. This liberal state was informed by a strong pro Indian rhetoric that may be considered an early example of political *indigenismo*, which became so important in twentieth-century Latin America. There is some dispute as to the effectiveness of this movement among liberals, who lived in a world far apart from the daily misery and oppression of the indigenous population. However, one must look into the concrete consequences of the pro-Indian, *indigenista* rhetoric that was a result of the modernizing project of the liberal governments after 1895 and assess the influence of these ideas on popular modes of political mobilization in the countryside. Focusing on the social significance of political measures and juridical institutions may reveal to what extent peasant communities have used indigenista rhetoric to defend their way of life, to improve their living conditions, or to influence how they were incorporated into the newly created national states.[6] We also might learn to what extent this use differed from earlier attempts to find niches of autonomy within the colonial state. This analysis focuses on Cuenca, capital of the southern highland province of Azuay, where a small but powerful landed elite coexisted with a semiautonomous indigenous peasant population. It was also the region where elite opposition to Eloy Alfaro's political project was particularly vehement, giving a distinct edge to the liberal reforms of the period.[7] Notwithstanding these regional characteristics, the complex consequences of the liberal state project for the indigenous population in the rural areas can be seen throughout the country.

The 1895 Liberal Revolution in Ecuador

The year 1895 was a turbulent one for the young Ecuadorian state. Stimulated by similar movements in neighboring Colombia and Peru, the population of the coastal regions rebelled against the conservative regime of Luis Cordero in the first months of the year.[8] The rebellion took place in the name of Eloy Alfaro, living in exile in Central America, and quickly spread from the coast to the interior provinces. In June, Alfaro was declared president of the country, but it took three more months and a bloody civil war before he could effectively assume power. The first years of his government were very unstable, with repeated invasions from Colombia, civil warfare, and conservative countercoups. One of the more dangerous threats to the Alfaro regime was a conservative revolution in the southern capital of Cuenca in July 1896, which was suppressed at the cost of many lives.

During the first years of his troubled government, Alfaro tried to steer a moderate course between the conservative and radical wings of his movement. He tried to appease his conservative opponents and the church by avoiding ideological confrontation and by focusing on improving the country's infrastructure. Improving the means of communication and transportation had already been on the agenda of previous governments and symbolized a shared project by conservatives and liberals alike. Under Alfaro's relentless direction, construction of the Ferrocarril Transandino between Quito and Guayaquil now seriously began. This railroad project was meant to favor the entrepreneurial interests in Guayaquil, but in the process it became a personal obsession of Alfaro, who pushed the project through against all odds.[9] The project clearly reflected the deeply felt desire for modernity among the business elites of Ecuador.[10] The merchants, cocoa planters, and bankers of the Guayaquil region were important supporters of the Alfaro regime, and they tried to use the regime to improve their business prospects and to modernize the country.

However, the movement also had a more radical side. It must not be forgotten that the Alfarista movement was in part a real popular movement. The nucleus of Alfaro's army originated in the poor coastal population, which offered undeserved loyalty to its leader. In later years, the poor indigenous or mestizo population of the highlands also rallied behind the banner of "*Alfaro o muerte.*"[11] Unquestionably, the indigenous population of the southern provinces massively supported the liberal movement and were crucial to the victory of Eloy Alfaro over the Conservatives.[12] Led by a few radical politicians and intellectuals, Indians constituted a formidable force in the liberal movement that launched a number of radical measures that challenged the roots of the country's social structure.

An important target for this radical liberalism was the church.[13] The changing of the guard in 1895 meant the beginning of the end of the church's dominant position in social and political affairs. Initially Alfaro tried to steer a middle course. The new constitution of 1897, for instance, confirmed Roman Catholicism as the state religion. However, the continuing opposition of the church to his government led to a new wave of anticlericalism beginning in 1899 and gathering force under the government of Leonidas Plaza, who took power in 1901. A whole series of anticlerical measures was proclaimed in the first years of the twentieth century, often justified by the church's exploitation of the Indians.[14] This rhetoric became clear in 1902:

> The government is aware of the numerous abuses committed by the priests in the villages and parishes under their ecclesiastic jurisdiction. They force the poor Indians to support the religious cult with their personal possessions. They demand their presence at services and other religious practices, charging them with tithes and first fruits *[primicias]*, even though these levies have been abolished, and they punish them with fines that are always illegal and often cruel and degrading.[15]

This radical anticlerical rhetoric was rooted in the daily reality of the priests' domination of local society, and many documents and petitions from the era attest to the many attempts to limit the abuses of the clergy to which Indians were subject. However, it is doubtful whether anticlericalism was very strong among the masses. Although the church was part of the traditional system of domination in the countryside and priests could be very exacting, anticlericalism was above all a concern of the urban middle classes.

Much more important to the rural population were measures to end, or at least restrict, the abuses and taxation to which Indians were subjected. They were burdened with a number of taxes, of which the *contribución territorial* and the *diezmo* were the most significant. They were also expected to provide labor services to the government, especially constructing and maintaining roads. These demands were widely abused, and many Indians had to work as personal servants of public employees and priests.

The greatest abuse, however, was the lack of freedom of the indigenous population. A large proportion of the highland Indians lived on large haciendas in various systems of unfreedom and bondage, usually called *concertaje* (debt peonage)—although other names were used, including *huasipungo*. Most were in one way or another dependent on a landlord, for whom they had to work a certain number of days as bonded labor. In exchange, laborers lived on the hacienda and were supported by their *patrón*, who was expected to provide them with enough money and food (*socorros*) to supplement their subsistence production. Hacienda laborers could not leave if they had not paid their debts, and indebted Indians were almost always considered the property of the haciendas. When a hacienda was sold, its inventory mentioned the number of Indians assigned (*adscritos*) to it. In the labor-scarce economy of the Sierra, the "possession" of labor was of vital importance, and what little legislation governed the system of concertaje was not meant to protect the Indian laborers but to regulate the concertaje contracts and to diminish competition among haciendas.[16]

The conciertaje system was open to widely varying interpretations. Radical liberals of the period such as Abelardo Moncayo depicted it as the most cruel and inhuman form of slavery; others such as Pedro F. Cevallos saw it as proof of the Indians' backwardness and of the need for a paternalistic government that could "lead" the Indians to civilization and modernity. Others note that the *concierto* system protected the indigenous peasants against a predatory state.[17] Guerrero considers the system an expression of patron-client relations which, within a fundamentally unequal society, were the arena for extensive negotiations.[18] In any case, this bondage set the Ecuadorian Indians apart from those in regions where the indigenous population continued to live in semi-independent communities in the nineteenth century.[19]

Under Alfaro, the liberal government, which proclaimed the defense of the Indian population as a principal objective, could not leave the system of concertaje untouched. On August 18, 1895, the recently installed president abolished the contribución territorial and some of the labor services (the so-called *trabajo subsidiario*). The announced objectives of this decree read, "That the miserable situation of the Indian race must be improved by the public powers" and "that the liberal government has the duty to protect the descendants of the first inhabitants of the Ecuadorian territory."[20] Such rhetoric gained the new president the nickname "el indio Alfaro"! In the remaining six years of its first term, the government of Eloy Alfaro issued a number of laws and decrees meant to improve the situation of the indigenous population, the logical conclusion of liberal thinking which during the last half of the nineteenth century had increasingly questioned the social and legal bases of Ecuadorian rural society.

Liberalism and Indigenismo

For Charles A. Hale, Latin American liberalism in the nineteenth century embraced the ideal of a rural bourgeois society, which symbolized the liberal hope for social harmony and economic progress on the basis of small property holders. Although this ideal was unattainable in societies made up of latifundia owners and dependent peasants, it led to attempts to liberalize social and economic relations in Latin American society.[21] Around the turn of the century, this general economic project gave way to an increasingly polarized situation in which conservatives and radicalized liberals took squarely opposed positions. While conservatives were growing increasingly pessimistic about the potential for modernization in the racially mixed and socially divided Latin American societies, some liberals expressed radical ideas that envisioned a break with traditional patterns. Although both groups were convinced that Latin American society had to be modernized, radical liberalism distinguished itself by incorporating indigenista ideas that aimed at elevating and liberating the Indians.[22]

A similar current of radical indigenista liberalism can also be seen in Ecuador's earlier liberal governments under Antonio Borrero (1875–1876) and Ignacio de Veintimilla (1876–1883), when the quest for economic modernization took precedence over a coherent critique of the country's social relations. Liberal rhetoric in this period was very elitist and abstract, scarcely related to the daily reality lived by the majority of the Ecuadorian population.[23] Still, it led to the first laws which, albeit rather halfheartedly, tried to curb the most extreme forms of exploitation of the peasantry. For example, in March 1881, a new police code was issued in Quito that tried to regulate contracts between hacendados and their workers and to end the situation whereby peons were forever bound to the hacienda.[24] Similar laws were implemented in other places, an attempt by which the central government tried to improve conditions at the local level. The intention was not to protect the hacienda laborers but to confirm the status quo. Guerrero writes, "What looked like a daring innovation on the part of the State became in concrete circumstances a ratification, a simple vindication of the hacienda authorities."[25] The legislation also reflected the competition for labor between the Ecuadorian state and the hacendado class. The ambitious plans for national infrastructure development depended on the availability of labor. Rural Indians were by law obliged to build and maintain roads. Only when tied to a hacienda could they avoid these services, so the Ecuadorian state had a vested interest in "freeing" the Indian laborers. Kim Clark observes, "The 'freeing' of indigenous peasant labor . . . did not occur through a violent transformation of this sector into a proletariat or semiproletariat but rather through a series of legal regulations that gradually undermined the power of highland landowners as well as of the church."[26]

With the success of the revolutionary movement around Eloy Alfaro in 1895, Ecuadorian liberalism entered a more radical phase. Although some liberals were disillusioned with its moderate anticlericalism and evasiveness on social issues, a national convention drew up a new constitution (the eleventh since independence) in 1896–1897 that laid the foundation for more radical legislation in the future. Regarding the indigenous rural population, the tone was already set by the decree of August 18, 1895. The persistence of this indigenista rhetoric becomes clear in a circular of June 22, 1898, to the provincial governors, signed by the minister of interior and police, Abelardo Moncayo, one of Alfaro's closest and most radical collaborators. This document condemned and prohibited the illegal use of Indian labor. State and church authorities were no longer allowed to use Indian laborers "against their will and without paying them the salary due or without remuneration legally agreed upon." Moncayo admonished, "It is necessary to punish therefore the mayors who recruit laborers in the name of the government or with public works as an excuse." He concluded,

> The governors, *jefes políticos*, parish leaders, and superintendents of police are ordered to put an end . . . to so many horrible customs that clearly demonstrate the unacceptable repression and the contempt to which the Indian race is subject; such as the destruction of their houses, the taking of pledges to force them to work for private persons, taking them along tied to a rope, forcing them to work in places and climates different from those to which they had committed themselves, holding them captive in prison for months only at the whim of the landowners and without presenting them to the law, forcing wives and children to work instead of their husband or father (or pay a fine) and always without pay, demanding forcibly the sale of their goods for fixed prices, etc. These are all crimes that break the guarantees formulated in the constitution and violate the most basic principles of justice, and which we can view with so much indifference only because we are accustomed to them.[27]

Apart from illuminating the practices of Ecuadorian authorities, this circular demonstrates the ideological turn the government had made. It connected the

Bolivarian plea for citizenship for all inhabitants of the independent Latin American nations, Indians included, with an acknowledgment that the Indian population needed extra protection from exploitation. The central tenet of the new political project was that the Indians were also Ecuadorians, who "due to their wretched condition" deserved "preferential attention from the public authorities."[28]

The most important measure of the first Alfaro government was the *reglamentación del concertaje* of April 12, 1899. The second and third considerations read, "That the constitution obliges the public powers to protect the Indian race in order to improve its social situation" and that it "prohibits slavery *(esclavitud)* in the territory of the republic." This law intended to put an end to the "verdadera esclavitud" to which the abuse of the concierto system by some landowners had led.[29] The popular implementation of these efforts became clear in a letter from the governor of the province of Cañar to his jefes políticos in which he repeated the importance of the April 12 decree emphasizing "the protection that liberalism owes to the Indian race."[30] Liberalism had become synonymous with the abolition of concertaje and protection of the indigenous population.

The most extreme advocate of this form of radical liberalism was certainly Abelardo Moncayo. The vehemence of his ideas and the eloquence of his liberal indigenista rhetoric is clear in his 1895 essay, "El concertaje de indios."[31] Calling it a "barbarous custom," he describes the concertaje system as "the absolute negation of liberty, the alienation of the will and the intelligence, consequently it means the death of the personality itself; that is concertaje. . . . It is the legal condemnation to 'embrutecimiento' of an entire people."[32] In a characteristic paragraph, he describes the Indians' social condition as "the condensation of all possible evil and misery, living debasement, ignorance in its most unambiguous expression, utmost servility; this is the Indian. Here you have the master work of Christianity, of the eternal conservative domination."[33] For Moncayo, the abolition of concertaje was the most important favor the liberal governments could do the Indians, comparable to the abolition of slavery for the black population.[34] It is remarkable that a man with such a radical vision of society could become a leading politician and even minister of interior and police in Ecuador.[35]

Moncayo was certainly the most vehement of the liberal politicians, but his ideas became common sense among a considerable group of intellectuals. Like the indigenista rhetoric heard in other Andean countries, the views of these urban intellectuals were loaded with paternalism. Luis Martínez, for instance, defending the Indians in another treatise on concertaje, wrote:

> Forgive me . . . I speak in the name of justice and I speak in the name of a race, a race that deserves a different fate, because the Indian is not the stupid human being who cannot become civilized, he is not the idiot imagined by some people. In this soul there also exists gratitude, there is happiness, there exists love for the family; and in these eyes, in this endless ocean which is the gaze of the Indian, exist surprising moments of lightning of pride and dignity. It is a race that still can be what it was before the white men enslaved it in name of a religion that prohibits slavery.[36]

Much has been said about the ignorance and idealization of indigenista intellectuals and politicians regarding the daily reality in which the Indian population lived.[37] Even the category of "Indian" is hardly unequivocal, and politicians and intellectuals constructed their own image of the Indian. Their ideas were certainly also a discursive instrument in the political debates within the elite and the new needs of the Ecuadorian export economy, but this is not to say that these viewpoints and political activities were inconsequential. However unrealistic, these ideas opened up new possibilities for political action and aroused expectations that were enough to generate a degree of ferment and mobilization among the indigenous population that far exceeded the initial intentions of liberal policy.[38] If much of the liberal and indigenista rhetoric was uninformed and far from reality, it offered discursive instruments by which indigenous peasants could formulate their grievances and organize their social and political struggle.

Liberal Indigenismo and Social Change

In her influential *Peasant and Nation*, Florencia Mallon shifts her attention away from the efforts of political elites to build a central state and to unify their recently created nations, and focuses instead on the regional and local reality of these efforts and the translation and adaptation of state ideologies by the popular classes. In her view, nation building in nineteenth- and twentieth-century Latin America is the result of a continuous dialectic of different discourses on the nation. "Popular nationalism" was partly founded on the ideas of politicians and intellectuals, but at the same time was adapted to, and complemented by, existing popular perceptions and discursive practices. Mallon writes, "Only by uncovering the elements of alternative nationalism and popular political practice buried within the remaining 'official stories'—at the community, regional, and national levels—can we begin to understand the complex and conflictive processes through which rural folk, and their urban allies and antagonists, perceived and dealt with the painful political, cultural, and social questions surrounding the construction of a nation."[39] Ordinary people, sometimes helped by regional politicians or intellectuals, tried to manipulate the rhetoric of state policies and sometimes appropriated elements of the political discourse to further their own ends.

These strategies indicate the significance of liberal and indigenista projects in late nineteenth-century Ecuador. The rhetoric of the Alfaro government influenced the terms in which the indigenous peoples of the Sierra articulated the political struggle and tried to improve their position, as contemporary documents make clear. As soon as a particular law was passed, the courts were filled with complaints by Indians about abuses committed by landlords, priests, or public employees. Local scribes, the so-called *tinterillos*, translated these complaints in petitions to the regional courts or the governor. For example, on September 5, 1899, two Indians from the province of Azuay in southern Ecuador sent a letter to President Eloy Alfaro (or it was written for them, because they probably did not know how to write) asking for state protection against the powerful hacendado Benigno Ambrosi, who lived in Cuenca. They demanded the enforcement of the executive decree on the *libertad de servidumbre* proclaimed five months earlier: "It has become public knowledge how the enormous and increased debts of the *peones* who have been slaves for 60 or 70 years have come about. Some because they borrowed miserable amounts of money when they were employed; others because their forebears died in slavery and they were forced to inherit this debt and continue the sad condition of their ancestors, without receiving a centavo." They complained that in spite of the decree they were held in debt peonage by this patron and asked the president to free them: "And since our condition as miserable Indians has made us lose all hope of freeing ourselves, we appeal to the protection of Your Highness, Señor President, begging you to execute once again a deed of the most strict justice." He was their only hope, "because in Cuenca we have not encountered anyone to defend us, nor an attorney who wants to meddle with the business of Mr. Ambrosi, because of his wealth and influence."[40]

This letter is revealing about Indian-state relations in Ecuador in the late nineteenth and early twentieth centuries. The personal appeal to the president to protect his poor subjects is not unlike petitions of medieval European peasants addressed to their kings. Second, it shows the potential conflicts within the elite, indicating that the state is not monolithic, but contains different groups with different interests. Finally, the letter points to the problems in the interpretation of the era's liberal reforms and the relationship between indigenista ideology and sociopolitical processes at the rural level.

This quest for legal justice was evident in the case of the first law of 1881 providing libertad de servidumbre, also called *liquidación de cuentas.* Many

Indians leapt at the opportunity to file complaints against their masters. The provincial archive of Azuay in Cuenca contains numerous court cases attesting to the legal activity of the Indian population. I quote from one case as an example. The Indian Estanislao Guaman, living in the parish of Pucará, filed a complaint against his patron, Manuel T. Monroy, in April 1881, only one month after the proclamation of the new police code. Guaman stated:

> About 27 years ago Mr. Ygnacio Solano sold his hacienda in Yngapirca, to which I belonged as a day laborer and to which I owed a debt of thirty pesos, to Mr. Manuel Toledo Monroy. After a year went by Mr. Monroy told me I owed him another thirty pesos because my animals had, according to him, caused damage to his seed beds. Since that time I have lived on the haciendas of Yngapirca, Pue?? [illegible] and Pucallay, without receiving any salary whatsoever and working without interruption, even during the holidays. The worst is that my master has started to like a good-quality colored cow with calves which he took from me, offering to replace it with another, which he has not yet done. Since it is not in my interest to continue working for Mr. Monroy, to whom I have no commitments whatsoever, even apart from the forced sale of the cow, I beg you to declare that I am a free man and to compel Mr. Monroy to return the mentioned cow with calves, and all its other offspring, and also to pay a yearly salary of thirty pesos for the mentioned period, with the deduction of my legitimate debt.[41]

Guaman had evidently fled the hacienda before filing the complaint, perhaps indicating that it was difficult for bonded Indians to petition for their freedom while they were still living on a hacienda. But even though Guaman had fled, he needed to obtain his legal freedom because otherwise he would continue to be liable to persecution. Note also that Guaman was not an archetypical poor, defenseless Indian. He possessed at least a few cows and a small house, and his whole case suggests that he was the patriarchal leader of an extended kinship network who knew how to make himself heard and defend his rights. This impression is confirmed by his selection of José Peralta, a promising young lawyer in Cuenca who later became one of the country's leading liberal intellectuals, to defend him.[42]

The arguments of this early court case are clearly factual and juridical, without too much ideological condemnation of the concertaje system in general. The claimant's lawyer uses the word "esclavitud" only once to express his indignation at the conduct of the accused Manuel Monroy. In this period, the system of bonded labor was not itself the object of condemnation, only its abuses. Monroy was accused not because he possessed bonded laborers, but because he abused them, notably by not paying the required salary and stealing his peon's cattle. In other words, he was accused of being a "bad" master.[43] In the same vein, Indians starting a court case in this period did everything to demonstrate that they were good, law-abiding citizens. They implicitly argued that they were entitled to their freedom because the patrons they sued had mocked (*burlado*) the law. On the other hand, the accused patrons protested that they had fulfilled all their obligations. As one patron defended himself: "Antonio Yunga has received the necessary food, always when he worked on my property or under my orders."[44] None of the contending parties trespassed the boundaries set by the system of concertaje.

In the legal contention between Indians and white-mestizo landholders, discussions about the content of "Indianness" played a role. Ecuador did not have the elaborate legislation on the special obligations and rights of Indians that existed in other Andean countries, especially Peru and Bolivia, yet stereotyped images of the indigenous population strongly influenced public discussion in Ecuador. Even liberal defenders of the Indians held a whole string of stereotypes as to their moral and economic capacities. Guerrero writes: "To the extent that the 'Indian' was reduced, through colonialism and concertaje, to the position of 'raza embrutecida' [Moncayo's term], lacking 'civilization' and, therefore, unable to participate in commercial relations, [he was] reduced to an animal-like state. 'The Indian is an irrational species. It is impossible to expect social resistance on his part, even less exigencies or an economically rational attitude.'"[45] At the same time, the indigenous population tried to take advantage of these stereotypes by reversing their meaning. Court cases make clear that part of the plea for libertad de servidumbre was based on the implicit argument that the Indians, not speaking any Spanish, were fooled into contracts that they could not understand. The image of the poor, ignorant, and defenseless Indians ("los indios infelices") was confirmed by the selfsame Indians to influence the legal process and to make their abuses and exploitation look even more repugnant. Such a situation could be seen in the case of a woman who had been sold to a hacienda by her father. In rejecting this behavior, she stated, "Only the disgrace and misery that characterize some individuals of the Indian race have made it possible that my wretched father in a unprecedented act has given me away against my will."[46]

On their part, the accused landholders tried to decrease the effect of this rhetorical device by stressing the laziness, frequent drunkenness, and irresponsibility of the laborers who dared to ask for their freedom. A landlord said of a man who had worked more than 17 years for him: "That the claimant has missed work because of the fact that he is almost always drunk. That also the claimant used to leave the compound only to return after many days after having amused himself in whatever diversion he encountered. That the claimant sold on many occasions all the tools that were to be found on his land."[47] Even an Indian's understanding of Spanish became a matter of dispute. This landlord, who claimed that he had given Antonio Yunga everything he was entitled to, emphasized in his defense that Yunga "not only perfectly understands what is said in Spanish, but also speaks the language."[48]

After the victory of the Liberals and the passage of new laws, discursive practice changed almost imperceptibly. This was the result not only of the new ideological wind that was blowing, but also of the participation of thousands of Indians in the Alfarista forces who had risked their lives in the expectation that their living conditions would be improved. As happened elsewhere, by participating in the political struggle, the indigenous population became a political actor in its own right.[49] This led to a more militant legal attitude. The law of 1899 that facilitated the libertad de servidumbre for bonded laborers gave them the instrument they needed and led to countless applications. The chaotic archive of the Corte de Justicia in Cuenca contains innumerable court cases filed between May and September 1899 by Indians who wanted their freedom. Some came to the provincial capital because they were afraid to go to the local courts. As one stated, "I do not trust the judges in the place I live, because they maintain intimate relations with my master."[50] Between the lines, one detects a new self-consciousness among the Indian claimants. They knew that they could legitimately claim their freedom; at least theoretically, the government was on their side. The fact that they could refer to national laws may have made a great difference. A number of Indians in Jadán who complained about the abuses of a local landowner simply wrote the governor, "We appeal to you in name of the Indians of our parish to beg you to place us *under the protection of the law.*"[51] Indians in Gualaceo, protesting the forced labor services imposed by the local authorities, wrote in the same vein, "Every one of us counts on the guarantees of the law so that we are not obliged to do forced labor."[52]

Frequently referring to the new constitution and the abolition of a number of traditional obligations, Indians did all they could to take advantage of the new legislation. They sued landowners, public employees, and members of the clergy for breaking the new liberal rules and holding on to the old ways in their attitude toward their Indian laborers. A number of Indians from the parish of San Sebastian wrote to the provincial governor of Azuay in 1898:

> Placing our confidence in the constitutional dispositions that oblige the public powers to provide special protection for the individuals of our destitute race; that proclaim that no one can require services not defined in the law; that, ultimately, it is unacceptable in the republic that some individuals live in worse conditions than others, we believed the deeply rooted abuses of which we as a social class have been the victim to have disappeared, until the teniente político of our parish demanded from us the service of parish guards *(rondas)*. This is a much hated service that requires unpaid services which are asked only of the Indians, in this way creating a social inequality against which both justice and the fundamental law of the republic are opposed.[53]

Given their continuing ambiguous position, these petitioners added that in any case they could not perform the required service because they were bound laborers, peones conciertos, on the hacienda of a local landowner.

The Radicalization of the Indian Population

In the early twentieth century, the political and socioeconomic context of the Indian struggle became more polarized and extreme. Possibly the Liberal Revolution had failed to fulfill the expectations it had raised, especially by the vehement rhetoric of liberal politicians. In its first years, the liberal government had thrived on its political radicalism and legal energy, but then its own radicalism started to turn against it. The Ecuadorian landowning elite had certainly received blows—for some of its members possibly mortal—but it was firmly established and was capable of evading or sabotaging many aspects of the liberal legislation. Especially in the parts of the Sierra where the haciendas were the dominant social force, the Indians experienced little improvement. One has only to read Guerrero's analysis of twentieth-century life on some northern haciendas to understand that the landowners' social hegemony had hardly been affected by the liberal reforms.[54]

Also in regions where much of the population lived in more or less independent peasant communities, such as in the southern province of Azuay, Indian discontent abounded. The regional elite in Cuenca was firmly conservative and succeeded in maintaining considerable power. The anticlerical radicalism expressed by the Plaza government after 1901 did not make things much better. Most of the indigenous population was Catholic, and although they might resent clerical abuses, they had little sympathy for an abstract and generalized anticlericalism, while continuing to suffer from inequality and exactions of the government. The state's ambitious infrastructural projects caused a highly unpopular demand for indigenous labor. Although it could no longer be forced, the rural population continued to owe labor services to the government, which amounted to the same thing.

In addition, the southern provinces were hit by economic distress. The region around Cuenca had become dependent on the export of hats and manufactured textiles and was thus vulnerable to the fluctuations of the world market.[55] The region experienced a number of crises in this period. Its agricultural production no longer sufficed to feed the region's population. A famine in 1893–1894 was followed by periodic scarcity of food and subsequent inflation in the first decades of the twentieth century.[56] This was especially clear in 1910 when the boundary dispute with Peru reduced the provision of food. Although the government took measures against some merchants who manipulated the market, artificially raising prices, the population was hard hit—even more so, because only three years before a similar situation had depleted food resources.[57]

This combination of economic crisis and the exhaustion of the liberal model led to a radicalization among the rural population. Apart from the continuing quest for libertad de servidumbre, this new militancy showed itself in a growing aggression against state representatives, especially in rural areas. Liberal legislation had undermined the authority of local officials such as the tenientes políticos, who found it more difficult every day to find labor for the construction of roads. Second, there was a moderate "ethnic revival" owing to liberal measures to improve the image of the indigenous population in the Sierra. Although the self-denomination of "indios infelices" reappeared in Indian petitions time and again as a holy incantation to soften the hearts of government officials, the beginning of the twentieth century saw a new indigenous self-consciousness.

The liberal laws made the Indian struggle less desperate and gave it more perspective than it had ever had. It was no longer possible to ignore Indian demands for improvements in their position and their rejection of a society that considered them second-class citizens. In the southern provinces this became clear in the 1920s when the Indians collectively revolted and put an end to the self-evident arrogance of the regional elite.[58] These were not "Indian uprisings," born out of primitivism and social and economic backwardness, as local politicians charged. It was the response to failed liberal reforms, the sabotage of the regional elite, and the incompetence of the state. We can understand the growing militancy of this rural population only when we take into account its perception and eventual appropriation of the liberal indigenista rhetoric.

This chapter has examined how liberal indigenista rhetoric in post-1895 Ecuador changed the content and the discourse of the social and political mobilization of Ecuador's Indians, indicating some interesting directions for future research. One might be the interaction of different ideologies about society and the nation at various levels of society and how discursive symbols are manipulated and appropriated. This has been well established for elite ideologies, but it may be just as important for popular ideologies. The consistency in the indigenous population's attitudes might suggest that its legal activity and social mobilization were manipulated from above. Although in the Ecuadorian context it is difficult to find traces of an indigenous political project dating back to prerepublican or even pre-Spanish discourses, as Platt suggests was the case in nineteenth-century Bolivia,[59] nonetheless the indigenous claimants selected those elements in liberal legislation that coincided with their interests and perceptions of society. A comparison of the varying historical experiences in the Andean regions might explain the different outcomes of the complex interaction between local indigenous perceptions and the ideas and policies of nineteenth-century liberalism.

We need to know more about the persons at the local level who took care of the ideological "brokerage." Who "translated" national politics for a local audience and "translated" the local ideologies at the regional and national level? What was the social and political position of local public officials, such as the teniente político or alcalde, and the indigenous authorities generally assembled in the so-called *cabildo pequeño?*[60] In Bolivia, Rasnake suggests, their position changed over time between defending the community's interests and facilitating the intervention of the state in rural society.[61] For Ecuador, what was the relation of these authorities with the state on the one hand, and local landowners and *gamonales* on the other?

The discursive struggle between the state and the Indian population also raises the question of the position of the so-called tinterillos, who recorded the grievances of the Quichua-speaking, illiterate population. They transformed local parlance into texts that were acceptable for legal or political purposes and were frequently vilified both by politicians and landowners because they supposedly stirred up the credulous Indian peasants.[62] The tinterillos might more appropriately be called a local intelligentsia, popular intellectuals who were able to formulate more or less coherent ideas about society.[63] Since their texts are the basis of historical analysis, we need to know more about their social origins and their relations with Indian petitioners.

A second interesting theme for future research is how elements from elite ideologies found their way into popular discourse and acquired a different meaning in the process. Just as they had used Spanish colonial ideology, the Indians used arguments and symbols from the liberal analysis of society to improve their position. Which elements were worth appropriating, and how were they adapted to a different ideological context? An example is the repetition of the metaphor of "esclavitud" in Ecuador. First used in official documents, it became an important discursive device, used time and again to put pressure on state officials and judges. Similarly, the recurring self-derogatory terms such as *infelices* or *desgraciados* can be seen in all parts of the Andean region and clearly have colonial origins. The use and meaning of these terms should be analyzed in a diachronic and comparative perspective.

Research into these questions may bring us a step closer toward understanding the troubled relationship between state and rural society in nineteenth-century Latin America. It was not a dualistic contest between two separate social and political systems. However, to understand state-society relations in twentieth-century Latin America it is necessary to study the continuing interaction between various social and political spheres.[64] Mallon points to the importance of nineteenth-century nationalist projects for twentieth-century society, concluding that, in contrast to its counterparts in Peru, the Mexican elite succeeded in bringing about an "inclusive" national project.[65] The Mexican state emerged as hegemonic because it incorporated a part of the popular agenda. However, the Ecuadorian case suggests that this analysis is too simple. The relationship between state and society has two sides. It is not only the inclusion by the state of popular projects and ideologies that counts; it is just as important to look into how the indigenous rural population incorporated and appropriated elements of the state ideology. The two sides of the relationship were closely linked. When these efforts succeeded, they committed the population to the state. But they could succeed only when the state incorporated popular demands into its policies. This complex interrelationship was essential for the development of the Latin American nation-state.

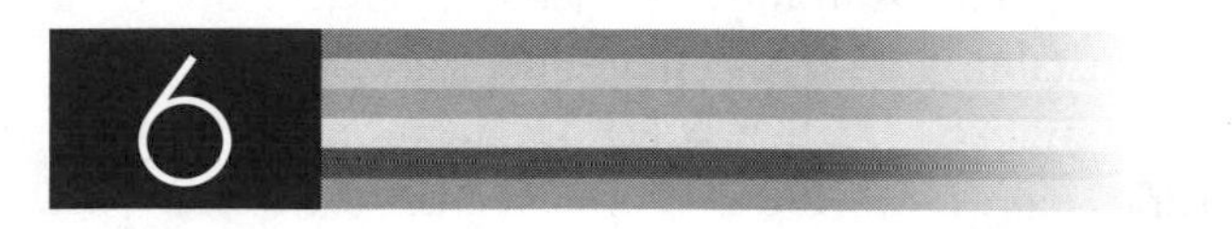

Shifting Paternalisms in Indian-State Relations, 1895–1950

A. KIM CLARK

Relations between Indians and the state in highland Ecuador exhibit a multiplicity of sites of domination in what we often homogenize as "the state." When Indians offered deference to certain state officials, it was often as part of an explicit rejection of other officials from whom they withdrew such deference. Thus, attitudes of deference were not inherent to Indians or a simple product of domination, but were part of a set of political strategies that could sometimes be quite effective.

According to E. P. Thompson's analysis of paternalism and deference, plebs defer to the gentry only when the latter fulfill their paternalistic obligations.[1] Deference quickly breaks down if the gentry proves itself undeserving, which suggests that paternalism is not accepted passively, but rather is part of a complex set of negotiations and pressures. A linked concept is that of the field of force, which Thompson represents through the suggestive image of a magnetic field in which the gentry and the plebs are at opposite poles but are held together by mutual constraint. William Roseberry points out that although this metaphor is bipolar, symmetrical, and static, "The image draws our attention to a wider field of tension and force, [and] to the importance of placing elements of 'the dominant' or 'the popular' within that field."[2]

The liberal period in Ecuador (1895–1925) was an era of relative political stability before the economic and political crises of the 1930s and 1940s. Between the Liberal Revolution in 1895 and 1925, all Ecuadorian presidents were Liberals (although Liberals seldom succeeded in dominating both congress and the executive). In 1925, disaffected military officers and members of the middle class overthrew the Liberals in the Revolución Juliana, setting off a period of extreme political instability, with fifteen presidents in the 1930s alone. This was matched by economic crisis, when Ecuadorian exports were paralyzed during the worldwide Depression (foreshadowed during the First World War). The crisis began to ease in the late 1940s, with the expansion of banana production on the coast, fueling another export boom in the 1950s. The 1930s and 1940s were characterized by rapid changes in actual governments. Indigenous peasants were able to take advantage of often brief windows of opportunity offered by changing state officials who were more or less sympathetic to their problems, when new national ideologies addressed the need to incorporate Indians through education and new local political structures.

The documentary evidence used for discussing relations between Indians and the state in the two periods is drawn from different sources.[3] I will first discuss labor issues, particularly those concerning railway construction and municipal public works, relating to community Indians in the cantón of Alausí, in the central highland province of Chimborazo. As the first highland cantón on the railway route from Guayaquil to Quito, this region was central to liberal projects to encourage labor migrations to coastal plantations. Indeed, liberal efforts to loosen Indians' ties to the highlands were effective here, resulting in early migrations of indigenous laborers to the coast. (In other highland areas, mestizo laborers were more likely to migrate during this period, while indigenous workers did not migrate until later.) Labor and land issues in the north-central highlands are most revealing about state-Indian relations in the 1930s and 1940s, when haciendas in this zone were important sites of peasant mobilizations. Relations between peasants and haciendas are particularly important for our purposes, since significantly more Indians were associated with haciendas in Ecuador than in Peru and Bolivia, where Indians were more likely to live in autonomous communities.

Labor Issues and the Liberal State

After the 1895 Liberal Revolution, state discourse regarding Indians tended to focus on labor questions for two reasons. First, a central feature of Indian-state relations in the second half of the nineteenth century was that after the revocation of Indian tribute in 1857 (and the protections this involved), Indian labor was forcibly recruited for the road-building projects of conservative President García Moreno.[4] Liberal administrators at the turn of the century were prone to regard their own stance as far better than those of previous conservative administrations regarding the treatment of Indians, as well as many other issues.[5] Second, the Liberal Revolution represented the rise to political power of the coastal elite, who suffered serious shortages of labor on their cacao plantations. (This did not prevent the expansion of these plantations, but did increase their labor costs in comparison with those of highland landowners.) Therefore a loosening of labor ties in the more populous highlands, where liberals suggested that the forces of tradition—large landowners, local political authorities and church officials—artificially monopolized indigenous labor, was central to liberal projects for national export-led development.[6]

Because Indians were seen as the victims of previous conservative administrations and of traditional highland power holders, liberals presented themselves as the protectors of indigenous rights, particularly with regard to labor issues, in the new state idea they were constructing. Indeed, it was proposed that Indians greatly needed the paternalistic protection of enlightened liberal authorities, since they were too timid and ignorant (after centuries of oppression) to defend their own rights. The liberal state's campaign to undermine highland control over labor took the form of a series of provisions that gradually undermined these power holders. This was undertaken instead of making a direct assault on Indian communities to mobilize their labor for coastal production, partly because of the continuing weight of more conservative highland elites in the congress.

To understand how liberal discourse was appropriated through indigenous action at the local level, one must recognize that local representatives of the central state often had very different interests and projects from more distant ones, differences that subordinate groups could use to their own advantage. Higher-ranking central state authorities—particularly the president and his appointees, such as cabinet ministers and provincial governors—were not merely closely aligned with the Liberal administration's projects, but were in fact the designers and administrators of these projects. At the local level, there was a political administrator (*jefe político*) in each cantón appointed by the central administration, who might be aligned with local power holders or the central government, depending on his political affiliation and whether or not he was of local origin. In turn, his subordinates, the political lieutenants (*tenientes políticos*) in each parish, may have been named by the central state but were much more immersed in local affairs as local merchants, small or medium landowners, or artisans. All were appointed by the central state (which did not necessarily guarantee their loyalty to its principles, particularly at the most local level), while at the cantonal level there were also locally elected municipal councils who responded more directly to local power relations, pressures, and projects.

An example of how Indians could maneuver between various state officials, using deference toward one to subtly threaten another, is a letter from the indigenous authority (*regidor*) of Linge community to the political lieutenant of Sibambe parish in Chimborazo Province, regarding the elimination in 1898 of a territorial tax on Indians to support the church. The executive decree declared tithes (*diezmos*), first fruits (*primicias*), and similar contributions to be voluntary and determined that the state would no longer intervene to ensure their payment. Such legal changes did not deal directly with labor issues but did undermine the power of local officials involved in the collection of these taxes (who paid a fixed amount to their superiors, rather than turning over what they collected and receiving a salary) and eliminated one of the mechanisms by which Indians became indebted and tied to their localities. As the regidor wrote,

> Regarding your order that the people of my community should pay the collector of the territorial tax, under threat of arrest by the constable, I say to you: Happily, I was in Chimbo yesterday, and I met some gentlemen who were reading a large sign with embossed print, and who said to me, "Regidor, you are in luck, along with all those of your class. Here is a decree from the president of the republic exonerating you from the territorial tax and warning all the authorities to treat you well." With this news, I returned home full of joy and advised the community, and together we gave thanks to God and the Señor President who have freed us from the continual thefts that we have suffered year after year, when we have been forced to pay any amount the collector specifies, even using the constable to help steal from us. I suggest you look around for this decree, no doubt you have it tucked away somewhere in your office; and if in spite of everything the constable is sent here, now we have someone to whom we can complain, and the thieves will suffer their punishment.[7]

While this letter reflects the tone used in many indigenous documents, it is unusual in that many more indigenous petitions were generated by labor problems than by taxes. Indeed, liberal rhetoric regarding Indians itself emphasized labor issues. Liberal officials were charged with freeing highland Indians from abusive labor recruitment and with helping them learn how to participate in national life. As the minister of justice formulated the problem in 1897,

> It is shocking to see the lamentable situation of the republic's most unfortunate group—the Indians. Their complete ignorance and the

> lack of cultivation of their intelligence does not allow them to manage their commitments with discernment, resulting in their perpetual slavery, the endless accumulation of their labor obligations.
>
> Thus it is necessary that the officials of the liberal government make an effort to rescue this neglected race from its prostration and barbarity and show themselves to be always solicitous in assuring that [the Indians] are considered and treated as beings gifted with the same rationality as civilized men.
>
> If we have labored to push forward the progress of our patria, let us make effective republican equality, such that all Ecuadorians obtain equal protection and justice from the political and judicial authorities.[8]

Now, while the liberal state might have liked to intervene directly in labor relations on highland haciendas, loosening ties and encouraging workers to move to the coast, it was not powerful enough to do so, given the influence of highland landowners, specifically their weight in congress, until at least the 1920s. A primary theme of liberal rhetoric about how Indians were abused at the local level was the recruitment of Indian labor for local public works.[9] Here the varied projects of state officials at different levels opened up possibilities for resistance to Indian laborers.

At the beginning of the liberal period, the labor recruitment system for public works functioned as follows: the locally elected municipal council would ask the political administrator of the cantón to instruct his subordinates, the political lieutenants in each parroquia, to send a certain number of day workers drawn from among the area's "free Indians" (not debt peons on haciendas) to labor sites under a system called *auxilio*. While laborers were sometimes willing to work when paid promptly, they had to be forced when they were not paid or during peak periods of the agricultural cycle; indeed, local authorities themselves frequently referred to such laborers as forced. The most common abuses, all against the law, were the nonpayment of workers, forcible recruitment, and using such peons for private rather than public projects. While this system was ostensibly used for construction of local public works, it was often used to provide agricultural enterprises with labor during peak periods, because often local landowners and local officials were one and the same. Even when the labor recruited was used for public works, these were projects approved by the municipal council that was dominated by medium landowners of the zone who benefited from the construction of paths and irrigation works, as well as urban improvements. Thus, even without directly addressing the control ("monopoly," according to liberals) of highland landowners over indigenous labor, controlling the labor recruitment practices for local public works nonetheless became an important way in which the central state undermined local landowners' power.

During the liberal period, the government's responsibility to protect Indians was institutionalized in Articles 138 of the 1897 constitution and Articles 26 and 128 of the 1906 constitution. During this era, indigenous claims were often ultimately based on these and other constitutional rights; but most important, when Indians made claims to supralocal political authorities based on these laws, the state's response (as represented by the president and his appointees) came in the form of executive decrees or specific orders to local officials reiterating indigenous rights. When specific orders were sent down, a whole web of rights was reinforced; this process was initiated through indigenous action. Laws and orders from supralocal authorities were continually undermined by racism and local vested interests, but this in turn would set off new indigenous complaints to higher authorities and new orders to local ones, including in some cases fines or dismissal of local officials.

Following is a characteristic complaint from Indians about such abuses presented to the provincial governor:

> Pablo Pedro, Felix and Juan Anasicha, Francisco and Gregorio Chacasaguay, Lorenzo Tenesaca, Gregorio Yupa Cruz Barqay, and Manuel Veintimilla respectfully expound to you the following: we are Indians of the parroquia of Tixán, belonging to the cantón Alausí, in which, infringing the principles of our constitution [and] the decisive guidelines of the Ley de Régimen Administrativo Interior, the authorities of our parroquia trample our individual rights and make us martyrs in forced labor under the name of "auxilio." If we do not present ourselves to undertake said work, they send commissions to our homes in the dead of night and they carry us away against our will, to the Señor political lieutenant, under whose order they present us in his office. And for what? To distribute us to various persons, among those favored by his authority, each of whom has his tasks to be done: they send us to Alausí with the pretext that we work in public works, carried out by those who have received contracts for these works, and that is, only if we are lucky. On the contrary, they send us to work in their fields or houses. But that is not all; if we are not encountered personally, they carry away our livestock until we present ourselves for work, and if they find no possessions, they threaten us with fines. As you are the first authority of our province, we appeal to your protection so that, out of consideration for our miserable race *[raza infeliz]*,

> you free us from this yoke and you exempt us from said labor of auxilio, for which we implore justice.[10]

The provincial governor wrote to the political administrator regarding these repeated complaints: "I have been informed that in your jurisdiction many abuses are committed against the miserable Indians, under the pretext of public works, and as these, according to our constitution, should enjoy the guarantees granted to all citizens, I urge you to convey the necessary orders to prevent such abuses, and to insinuate, instead, to the authorities under your supervision, that they favor as much as possible the improvement of this oppressed and helpless race."[11]

These are not just isolated examples of indigenous and state discourse. Rather, they formed a web of ongoing communications that eventually led to the virtual dismantling of the forced labor regime for public works construction in the Alausí region and its replacement by a system of contract labor. An important step in this process occurred when, after repeated indigenous complaints, the minister of government ordered that all local officials publicly announce that it was illegal to force Indians to work. As he stated,

> I have knowledge that the authorities of the Alausí cantón and, especially, the political lieutenants, under the pretext of needing peons of auxilio, compel the miserable Indians of that territorial section, by way of threats, fines, and other coercive means, to carry out personal services, without any remuneration, for their benefit and that of their relatives.
>
> Such an illegal and undignified proceeding has caused surprise and true indignation to the ministry under my responsibility. The government, not only in order to comply with decisive legal dispositions, but also due to the unlimited respect for human dignity which is the norm of all its actions, has pledged to improve the deplorable situation of the indigenous race, always victim of the most unspeakable abuses.
>
> The Indians are also Ecuadorians and, as such, and precisely due to their wretched condition, they deserve preferential attention from the public authorities, for whom it is appropriate to offer very efficient protection, since their ignorance and natural timidity, acquired in long years of servitude, do not permit them to oppose the arbitrariness of certain officials.
>
> Such acts, which are true crimes, punishable by law, cannot continue. And as a result I urge you, Señor Governor, to warn the author-

> ities under your supervision and especially those of the above-mentioned cantón, that they comply with the dispositions of the constitution of the republic in Articles 26 and 128, whose infraction will lead not only to immediate dismissal but to the corresponding criminal charges.
>
> To ensure that the government's intentions are realized in this regard, you will order that in each parroquia, on market day, the political lieutenant publicly declare that the Indians are not required to offer those illegal services and that, if any employee demands them, those thus affected can present the relevant denunciation to superior authorities, so that the offender receives the sanction imposed by law.[12]

It became very difficult to obtain day laborers in the following months. A political lieutenant explained to the cantonal authorities, "All of the indigenous people are aware of the order of the minister . . . which was read publicly. As a result, it is impossible for me to compel people to do forced labor, since now I know that they have their defenders and I could face criminal charges if I don't ensure that the minister's orders are strictly followed."[13] As the minister later clarified, "Of course, the political lieutenants can contract whatever number of peons the municipal council of Alausí judges necessary to carry out its public works; what this ministry wishes to avoid is the abuse committed when the Indians are obliged to undertake forced labor without remuneration."[14] Finally, in 1921 (following an indigenous uprising in another part of Chimborazo Province, provoked by different issues), there was an order from the minister in charge to suspend all recruitment of Indians for municipal public works, and the political administrator refused to participate in this system by ordering the political lieutenants to send peons.[15] Again, he suggested that the municipal inspector of public works should seek to contract people voluntarily, which of course meant offering better working conditions and higher pay.

During the liberal period, Indians repeatedly appropriated the discourse of the central state by forcefully and cogently arguing that they were timid and ignorant, thus deserving of protection, particularly in relation to labor issues. They presented themselves in this way particularly to the highest officials, while they subtly threatened more local authorities and even managed to have some local officials fined or dismissed. Thus highland Indians were able to use these legal provisions to limit abusive treatment by local powers. The central state thus strengthened its legitimacy among subordinate groups, often at the expense of its own officials at the local level. Subordinate groups drew on existing laws and government rhetoric in petitioning the central state, and their rights were reinforced or strengthened at the local level through the specific orders or decrees that formed the central state's response. By 1917 there began to be labor shortages for local projects in this zone. Indians were traveling to the coast to undertake seasonal labor on plantations, indicating that liberal efforts to weaken the ties that bound indigenous laborers to the highlands had met some success.

Indigenous Strategies in an Era of Instability

In Ecuador's Andean highlands, the 1930s and 1940s saw new forms of conflict on haciendas and new forms of organization among peasants. This was an era of profound economic crisis, a transitional period between the two principal agro-export booms based on cacao and bananas. The crisis in cacao exports began during the First World War, then deepened with the spread of crop diseases in 1920, a sharp decline in the price of cacao on the world market in 1923, then the Great Depression. The United Fruit Company bought some of the former cacao plantations in the 1930s, but banana production was not actively encouraged until the government of Galo Plaza in 1948, stimulating another economic boom in the 1950s. Yet while Ecuador experienced profound economic and political instability in these decades, their impact differed among various regions and classes, leading to economic diversification.[16] The working classes were spurred to undertake new forms of action. In addition, the national political panorama became more complex, with the founding of the Socialist and Communist parties and the emergence of urban populism. In accord with these processes, new workers' legislation was passed in the second quarter of the twentieth century, particularly during the governments associated with the Revolución Juliana (1925–1931) and the government of General Alberto Enríquez (1937–1938), who invited members of the Socialist Party to collaborate in designing a new labor code.

The following analysis draws on a series of agrarian conflicts on the haciendas of Asistencia Pública (social welfare estates) in the north-central highlands, where some of the worst clashes occurred in the 1930s and 1940s. These properties were expropriated from religious orders in 1904 with the passage of the Ley de Cultos. In 1908, under the Ley de Beneficencia, their ownership passed to the newly established Junta Central de Asistencia Pública (JCAP, Social Welfare Board), with the monies collected from their rentals going toward urban public welfare institutions. The region's large landowners rented these public properties for eight years at a time, paying a set annual rent rather than a proportion of profits. Hence, it was clearly in the interest of *arrendatarios* (leaseholders) to make as much money as possible from a property during the rental period. They did not invest in modernizing these properties because they did not own them, nor in developing good relations with peasants, which required mutual concessions from both parties, built up over time.[17] In this context, the arrendatarios tended to respond to the economic crisis by increasing demands on peasants and having them absorb arrendatario losses as much as possible.

New actors entered into labor negotiations and the resolution of agrarian conflicts during the 1930s, along with local political authorities and the members of the Junta Central de Asistencia Pública. Most important, with the passage of the 1938 labor code, labor inspectors could be called in to investigate working conditions on haciendas. After 1929, there were also "functional representatives" in the senate, representing the interests of particular social groups rather than territories. The senator for Indians was not strictly speaking a representative, but rather a defender, revealingly called the "functional senator for the tutelage and defense of the indigenous class." In addition to functional senators such as the Communist leader Ricardo Paredes, in the early 1930s the important *indigenista* intellectual Pío Jaramillo Alvarado was a member of the Consejo de Estado. These legislators often passed on indigenous complaints to the upper reaches of government and requested explanations from the JCAP about agrarian conflicts on government estates.

The evolution of peasant strategies in one conflict indicates how claims were made. In the hacienda Tolóntag in Píntag parroquia east of Quito, a peasant uprising erupted in late August 1934 when the leaseholder, José Ignacio Izurieta, increased his demands on the resident peasants, *huasipungueros*, each of whom received a subsistence plot, *huasipungo,* and a nominal wage in exchange for labor on hacienda lands. In this conflict, the peasants were able to enlist the help of President José María Velasco Ibarra, who intervened directly. The peasants rejected all efforts at resolution that did not involve the president and met with both Velasco Ibarra and Izurieta in the presidential offices, much to the arrendatario's chagrin. He was particularly incensed that at one meeting, in his words, Velasco Ibarra undermined his authority by stating in front of the peasants that "he was quite willing to go beyond the existing laws to do whatever was necessary to remedy the abuses, the injustice, and the audacity with which hacendados treat Indians." Velasco Ibarra also told them "that they were free, that debt peonage no longer existed, that no one could compel them to do anything, that they should demand a wage and a high one, that the women did not have to work, even if they were paid; in sum, all discipline was destroyed and I am at the mercy of the Indians who have been provoked to a thorough insolence by the Sr. President."[18] Tolóntag's proximity to Quito implied both ready access to a market for the crops and dairy products produced in the hacienda (which the hacienda laborers took advantage of as they progressively appropriated the hacienda's resources) and relatively easy access to political authorities in the capital. Thus in December 1934, Izurieta argued that "the hacienda Tolóntag is abandoned and its workers hang around the government offices in pursuit of what they like to call justice."[19]

The peasants in Tolóntag were fairly successful during Velasco's brief first period of rule in strategically using relations with the newly elected president to undermine both Izurieta and the Junta Central de Asistencia Pública. Velasco Ibarra took power on September 1, 1934, was overthrown on August 20, 1935, then, as a central figure in early Ecuadorian populism, became Ecuador's president four more times. Indeed, Tolóntag seems to have been a test case for extending a paternalistic, personalistic (and primarily urban) populism into the countryside. The peasants certainly played on this paternalism. They refused to agree to any solution that did not involve government officials outside the JCAP, including legislators, ministerial officials, and not least, the president. Indeed, Izurieta's lawyer asked the junta in late 1934 whom the lease holder should obey in these matters, "the honorable junta, the entity with whom he signed his contract; or the señor president of the republic who currently intervenes directly in negotiations" with the workers.[20] In this struggle, the peasants identified the hacienda as belonging directly to Velasco Ibarra, rather than to a depersonalized government institution, which justified their insistence that he continue to participate in any negotiations. The report by police lieutenant Humberto Vizuete, who had been sent to deliver the new Reglamento de Trabajo[21] to Tolóntag in February 1935, clearly expressed both the Indians' defiance and their willingness to play up to Velasco's paternalism.[22]

The report has a rather literary tone, presenting the lieutenant's dialogue with the peasants and quoting their broken Spanish in much the same style as Jorge Icaza's award-winning social realist novel *Huasipungo*, published the previous year. Among other things, the peasants refused to believe that the work regulation had been sent by Velasco. When Vizuete assured them that it had indeed been dictated by the president, the peasants responded, "If he really sent it, then we will obey. But first we have to go to Quito to make sure that what you tell us is true, *patrón*. There, speaking with Amo Velasco Ibarra, *nuestro papacito,* we'll find out if it is true that he sent you to say these things. And we'll also speak to Genaro, who is our lawyer, so that he can make the arrangements." The Indians were clearly not prepared to give in or accept the police's authority easily and wielded their deference to the president as a weapon.

Izurieta's lease was terminated in early 1936, at a great loss to him. The conflict continued as the huasipungueros occupied lands, distributing the property among themselves; in 1936, the hacienda also lost all of its livestock to the peasants. When this property was rented to two new arrendatarios in 1937, the JCAP split it into two properties to divide the indigenous movement and thus facilitate the use of the estate by the new leaseholders.[23] The junta accepted this bid for the hacienda rental only because once the junta clarified that it would not take responsibility for disciplining workers on the estate, it was the only bid that remained. This strategy was not very successful, however, and when the lease ended in 1945, the hacienda was reunified and brought under the direct administration of the junta.

In 1943, the peasants developed a new strategy for dealing with the haciendas, and their petitions take on a different tone from the claims to paternalism of the previous decade. The peasants on Tolóntag requested the use of a small area of the hacienda for community activities. As they phrased it,

> Progress through human dignity makes it urgent that we obtain an adequate place to create a plaza, a school, a community meeting place, a chapel, and a cemetery, all in accordance with the requirements of the number of families here . . . and with the norms of hygiene and supplementary needs such as sports fields, which are the most urgent and indispensable. . . . We must make our condition clear, our insistence on obtaining these particulars indicates our firm intention to progress, to become useful for ourselves and ultimately for our country *(la patria)*. These reasons . . . are highly just and imperative for the national culture and to advance the dignity of the indigenous class.[24]

Rather than using a discourse of paternalism and deference, the peasants now adopted new elements of national discourse by claiming their right to improve themselves and progress in order to better serve the nation.

As the peasants' campaign progressed, their organizational capacity also improved. By August 1943, they had organized themselves as the Comité Unión y Progreso, and their petition at this time was signed not by a mestizo in the name of the illiterate Indians, but by a number of literate indigenous leaders of this committee.[25] In addition, this time the peasants made their request not in the name of the "peons, huasipungeros, and other workers of Tolóntag" (as in the above petition), but rather in the name of the "indigenous community of the hacienda Tolóntag" and openly stated that this was a first step toward becoming an independent parroquia (the most local unit of territorial political organization).

The minister to whom this petition was addressed was Leopoldo N. Chávez, and the subsecretary of social welfare who dealt with it was Rafael Vallejo Larrea, both founding members of the Instituto Indigenista del Ecuador when it was established two months later. In describing the Indian problem and IIE's mission at the time of its inauguration, Rafael Vallejo Larrea stressed the importance of developing rural schools specifically for Indians and of disseminating knowledge of hygiene, nutrition, and related issues among the indigenous population: He concluded, "To begin to elevate the life of the Indian is a means to dignify it and make it more efficient, as part of the national community."[26] This was precisely the argument of the Comité Unión y Progreso, although they made it, significantly, just prior to the foundation of the IIE. Clearly, these ideas were in the air in 1943. While the peasants of Tolóntag may have relied less on the paternalism-deference equation that had served them so well before, they adapted their discourse to the new particular political conjuncture in which indigenistas were in charge of the ministry that oversaw their source of livelihood.

While the peasants continued to petition the JCAP and the ministry through 1943 and into 1944, they were frustrated by the lack of response. Minutes of meetings show clearly that JCAP members saw acquiescence to the peasants' request as giving them a foothold to try to form an independent community, and this was indeed the goal. However, sometime between April and August 1944, a surprising success came with their achievement of the legal status of *comuna*. This status, associated with the passage in 1937 of the Ley de Organización y Régimen de las Comunidades Indígenas y Campesinas, was technically available only to indigenous communities who possessed their own lands—that is, free communities. According to an angry member of the junta, this status had been "inadvertently approved by the minister of social welfare," after persistent peasant lobbying.[27] Indeed, this particular group of peasants, living on hacienda lands, should not have been able to register as a comuna. Becker argues that this law was aimed at bringing Indians within the purview of the state at the most local level: in several cases in Cayambe cantón north of Quito, free indigenous communities found that registering themselves as comunas in fact undermined their autonomy, since their internal governing structures came under government supervision.[28] However, since the peasants of Tolóntag were not members of a free community but hacienda laborers, achieving this status was in this case more likely a step toward increasing their autonomy vis-à-vis the hacienda and the JCAP (much to the latter's annoyance). While the status of comuna was not mentioned in an April petition, by August the peasants were proudly claiming it. It seems likely that this status was approved after the Glorious Revolution in May 1944, when Velasco Ibarra swept back into power for his second government, overthrowing Carlos Arroyo del Río.

In 1945, when the arrendatarios' leases ended, the junta decided to take over direct administration of Tolóntag. By this time the hacienda was in poor shape; in contrast, the peasants of Tolóntag were among the most prosperous in the region, according to a report written by a JCAP official.[29] Not only did they have a great deal of wealth in the form of livestock pastured on the estate, but they earned the substantial daily wage of 90 centavos, notwithstanding their usufruct of huasipungos. (On other estates in the region, wages were reduced by up to 50 percent when huasipungos were provided.) They succeeded in improving their working and living conditions by a strategic use of favorable political conjunctures and by appropriating political discourse appropriate to each one.

While in the 1940s the petitions of the Tolóntag peasants appeared to call less on paternalism than they did in the 1930s, they were not free of paternalistic-deferential overtones. The peasants explicitly identified themselves as Indians in the 1940s, drawing on both indigenista and national ideologies, and this seems to have found favor with certain state officials. Indeed, in 1945 they were described by a JCAP official as "very good and intelligent, people with whom one can work with no difficulty."[30] In contrast, farther north in Pichincha Province, the belligerent peasants of several social welfare estates in Cayambe were using a rhetoric inspired much more by class as they aggressively claimed their rights as workers in alliance with communist and socialist labor organizers.[31] Government authorities tended to see them in a less favorable light. When peasants in Cayambe established schools on the haciendas under their own initiative in 1945, both the leaseholders and the government opposed the schools. In Tolóntag, by contrast, the national government did grant the peasants 20 cuadras of land by 1945, although the junta delayed fulfillment of this promise because of disagreements about where it should be located. The peasants continued to draw on the paternalism-deference equation in a 1946 document addressed to a newly reorganized JCAP, once the hacienda was under its direct administration, requesting additional supplies and furnishings for their school. The peasants stated,

> Given the great good luck that this hacienda is directly administered by your wise management, it is only right that we are gladdened by this and manifest once again our fervent good will to work in favor of the greater exploitation of its wealth. We do not doubt that you appreciate very well that the education of the common people (*el pueblo*) will save this patria, which deserves a better future; and as our

> children now have a teacher, we urge you to provide the other necessary facilities for their education.[32]

The Tolóntag peasants made their choices within the larger regional context of peasant organizing, so that their requests were seen in comparative terms and they received a more paternalistic response from the government. But they gained far less in political experience and organizational capacity than the peasants of Cayambe, given their more localized goals.

The processes explored here raise the obvious question of why certain state officials or institutions were relatively sympathetic to some peasant claims in the 1930s and 1940s. These events responded to the broader processes leading to the foundations of modern social policy in this era: this may have been part of an official effort to subvert popular movements to avoid a more profound radicalization, an effort that was partially successful.[33] Leaders were alarmed by widespread mobilizations by peasants and workers in rural and urban areas, as well as the growing importance of populism, under the influence of Velasco Ibarra. The response of the JCAP to conflicts on its estates was also influenced by growing public perceptions that large landowners were not very efficient. Moreover, the junta recognized that its haciendas were not producing all that they could, simultaneously reducing revenues available to the junta for its urban welfare institutions (aimed precisely at soothing urban social, economic, and political tensions) and increasing food costs in the cities, which only provoked greater unrest among workers. The agrarian conflicts in the 1930s and 1940s must be understood within the broader context that generated varying degrees of support for Indians among populist leaders, leftist activists, and progressive military officers in an era of economic and political instability.

Reflections on Ecuador's State System and State Idea

What do the processes discussed here reveal about the state? Clearly, the state is not a monolithic entity, but rather encompasses various often competing projects and institutions. As Philip Abrams suggests, we need to study not "the state," but rather the state system and the state idea. The former is "a palpable nexus of practice and institutional structure centered in government and more or less extensive, unified, and dominant in any given society."[34] We must study the specific practices of various state institutions, rather than reifying the concept of a state "apparatus." A second dimension of analysis is how the state idea has changed over time. In Ecuador, there was a clear effort to present the state as a legitimate form of authority, allowing peasants to call on political authorities and government employees to live up to the state's own rhetoric about their roles.

In the liberal period, the actions of indigenous day workers were central to the very formation of the liberal state in Ecuador. Indians not only utilized law and state discourse, but in some cases even helped to generate those discursive resources when their petitions led to new government decrees. Their local struggles, in which they drew on the state idea, generated changes that became institutionalized in the state system. In the words of Gramsci, these subaltern activities led to "molecular changes which in fact progressively modif[ied] the pre-existing composition of forces, and hence bec[a]me the matrix of new changes."[35] In the 1930s and 1940s, Indian peasants actively drew on various political discourses: from the paternalism of Velasco Ibarra, and his claims to speak for the people, to the new rhetoric of indigenismo, which in Ecuador was a quasi-official project. Indians clearly manipulated the discourse of the central state—the state idea it promoted—to deal with everyday problems, increasing the legitimacy of the state. In both periods, they also took advantage of the various gaps and fissures in the Ecuadorian state system by playing off some state officials against others, further contributing to the legitimacy of the central state. This does not indicate Indians' susceptibility to false consciousness, nor does it indicate ideological consensus. Rather, it points to a hegemonic process in which political leaders were called upon, in Gramscian terms, not only to dominate, but to lead, and in so doing, they were willing to incorporate some aspects of subaltern projects into their own projects. In the process, they undermined not only other social groups, but also other state institutions or authorities. Ultimately, the fissures in the state system may have been central to the dynamic of domination, rather than being weaknesses or inadequacies of the Ecuadorian state.

State Building and Ethnic Discourse in Ecuador's 1944–1945 Asamblea Constituyente 7

MARC BECKER

On May 28, 1944, Indigenous peoples joined a coalition of workers, peasants, students, and lower-ranking military personnel in the Glorious May Revolution that overthrew the increasingly unpopular presidency of Carlos Arroyo del Río.[1] Masses of people flooded the streets to demand deep-seated reforms that would address their grievances. It was a time of euphoric optimism that seemed to signal the emergence of new social relations and the end of exclusionary state structures. Ecuador, one author observed, finally "was in the hands of its legitimate owners."[2]

This rupture in the liberal elites' domination over state structures led to an explosion of popular organizing efforts as Indians and other subalterns increasingly agitated for their concerns. Workers, women, students, peasants, and agriculturalists all held meetings during June and July to elect new leaders and put forward organizational agendas. Taking advantage of these political openings, in August Indigenous leaders formed the Federación Ecuatoriana de Indios (FEI, Ecuadorian Federation of Indians), the first successful attempt in Ecuador to establish a national organization for and by Indigenous peoples. Building on decades of Indigenous protest movements, the FEI subsequently flourished for the next several decades as it fought to improve the living and working conditions for Indigenous peoples in Ecuador.

Popular organizing efforts culminated in a Constituent Assembly that drafted a new constitution intended to codify the gains of the May 1944 revolution. Delegates did not expect the congress to stay in session for more than two months, but highly contested topics including those related to citizenship rights, suffrage, representation, and language led to lengthy debates over fundamental issues of how to conceptualize state structures and who should control them. In the glow of the aftermath of the founding of the FEI, Indians had high hopes that finally they would have a direct say in the formation of state structures. By the time the assembly promulgated Ecuador's fifteenth constitution seven months later, the limitations to reforming social relations through constitutional means were becoming obvious. Challenges to the state idea that civil society gained on the streets were lost in the halls of power. Although Indigenous peoples wished to have a seat in the assembly that debated ideas of the state, they appeared to grow more organized as part of civil society. Whether to engage the state in the electoral realm or to organize as a social movement remained an unresolved issue that Indigenous activists would debate for years to come.

Constituent Assembly

All of the delegates in the 1944–1945 Constituent Assembly were men from Ecuador's privileged white-mestizo class. Notably absent were Indians, peasants, and other marginalized sectors of society who had played important roles in the success of the Glorious May Revolution that led to this assembly. Almost all Indians in the 1940s were illiterate, and despite liberal ideals of equality, every constitution since the founding of Ecuador had made literacy a prerequisite for citizenship. The persistence of exclusionary models of state formation prevented Indians, who in the 1940s comprised about half of the population, from enjoying the benefits of citizenship, including direct access to the national congress. This ensured a continuation of a liberal model of state structures that limited participation to an educated white, urban, dominant class. By necessity, Indians had to rely on others to represent their interests to the government. With the writing of a new constitution, Indians hoped for the elimination of these restrictions that excluded them from direct participation in political discourse.

The 1944–1945 Constituent Assembly represents a significant point in the evolution of perceptions of state structures in Ecuador. The process of writing a constitution not only revealed persistent regional tensions between the coastal and highland regions as well as political tensions between conservatives, liberals, and leftists, but also exposed tensions over whether state structures should serve only the interests of wealthy elites or also include the impoverished rural masses. Indians appealed to central state structures to defend themselves from those who exploited them at the local level. As divergent and contradictory interests emerged during assembly debates, it momentarily appeared that Indians and their supporters might achieve significant conceptual shifts in the construction of Ecuadorian society. Ultimately, however, attempts to alter state structures through constitutional means ended in failure. These events reflected the limitations of employing state structures as a medium for creating ethnic spaces that would permit the development of political rights for Ecuador's Indigenous peoples.

The Role of Indians within State Structures

The first item of discussion for the Constituent Assembly that gathered in Quito on August 10, 1944 (the anniversary of independence from Spain), was to define the meanings of the Ecuadorian state, nation, sovereignty, and democracy. Generally the delegates agreed that the state was defined by its territory and people, but the meaning of Ecuadorian nationalism was much more contentious. Many searched for a sense of a unified national identity in a shared history, language, religion, territory, culture, and race. Manuel María Borrero, a liberal delegate from Cañar, pointed to the "racial duality" that divided whites and Indians as a barrier to the creation of a unified national identity, which he perceived as essential for the development of the Ecuadorian state.[3] Such comments reveal the limited knowledge of Indigenous communities and ethnic diversity that characterized discussions in the Constituent Assembly. Not only did delegates collapse the extreme diversity of more than ten different Indigenous groups into one homogenous category of "Indian" and then proceed to equate that with the Kichwa (Quichua) people living in the highlands, they largely ignored the sizable Afro-Ecuadorian population, perhaps 5–10 percent of the total. Furthermore, this search for a unified national identity submerged profound regional divisions between the coast, the northern and southern highlands, and eastern Amazonia, reflecting the continuation of classic nineteenth-century liberal ideologies that presented a homogenized construction of Ecuadorian realities. Without understanding or appreciating Ecuador's diversity, the assembly found it difficult to legislate on behalf of subaltern groups, especially given their competing concerns and interests.

If there were any discordant voices in the assembly that challenged this exclusionary model and embraced the concerns of the Indigenous peoples, they came from the Left. A small but growing literate middle class sympathetic to leftist causes helped to gives leftists a significant presence in the assembly (Socialists held 31 of the 98 seats, and Communists retained another 9 seats).

Socialists intended to use this opportunity "to write a revolution" because a "revolution is not only the triumph of arms, but more than anything it is changing the fundamental bases of the socioeconomic organization" of state structures.[4] Reflecting this goal, Socialist leader Manuel Agustín Aguirre, who represented highland workers' interests and served as the assembly's first vice president, began the debates with a critique of Ecuador's history as one of the dominant class repeatedly and constantly using state structures to exploit people and resources. "To speak of a democratic state," Aguirre argued, "we must first destroy *latifundismo* and incorporate the Indigenous masses into civilization. As long as feudalism persists, constitutions will not be democratic." He believed the duty of the congress was to accomplish what Eloy Alfaro's 1895 Liberal Revolution failed to do: destroy the existing semifeudal state structures.[5] The presence of leftists sympathetic to subaltern concerns in the halls of power created fractures in elite constructions of the purpose and exercise of state functions.

Conservative elites fought to retain their position of privilege, which necessitated the exclusion of the rural Indigenous masses from political discourse. From the beginning, signs emerged that the Left's desire not to alienate their conservative colleagues would ultimately mean failure to incorporate Indigenous peoples fully into the body politic. To calm reports in the newspaper *El Día* that the assembly was going to pass laws breaking up large estates, Socialist delegate David Altamirano from Chimborazo noted that there was no cause for alarm because they would not promulgate any agrarian reform laws. Delegate Pedro Saad, representative for coastal workers, claimed that the Communists did not want "to make a revolution of the extreme Left, as people are saying on the street."[6]

One exception was Communist leader Ricardo Paredes, who repeatedly pressed for expanding citizenship rights to allow Indigenous peoples a direct voice in designing state structures. Paredes had not been popularly elected, but rather the FEI had named him as a special representative of the "Indigenous race." On August 10, as the Constituent Assembly was engaged in its opening formalities in the legislative palace, Indigenous leaders and their supporters gathered a few blocks away in the Teatro Sucre to put the finishing touches on Ecuador's first national Indigenous organization, the FEI. In its final meeting, the FEI announced that they had selected Paredes as the functional representative for the Indigenous race to defend their interests in the Constituent Assembly.[7]

Although not himself an Indian, for two decades Paredes had been deeply involved in organizing Indigenous communities. Because of his long involvement and deep commitment, he was highly regarded in Indigenous circles and entrusted with presenting Indigenous demands to the national assembly. Paredes strove to meet these expectations as he actively lobbied for Indigenous concerns. For example, he used his position to launch an investigation into abuses on the Tiocajas and Tigua haciendas in the central highland provinces of Chimborazo and Cotopaxi and to defend Indigenous demands on the San Vicente hacienda in Otavalo. Socialist delegate Emilio Uzcátegui, representative for highland primary schools, greeted Paredes's contributions with the observation that this was "the first time that an authorized voice of a true and authentic representative of the Indigenous race has been raised in the Ecuadorian Congress."[8] It was the closest subalterns ever had come to contributing to discussions concerning the construction of state power.

Paredes was the last delegate to join the Constituent Assembly. If his late arrival almost seemed an afterthought, reflecting the marginalization of Indigenous concerns from elite constructions of state structures, he was determined not to be a minor player in the deliberations. In a lengthy speech during the discussions on concepts of state formation early in the constitutional debates, Paredes noted that extreme regional and cultural differences as well as the lack of infrastructure that further isolated areas in which Indians lived prevented the formation of a unified national identity. At most, the delegates should talk of a national identity *in formation*. Breaking from the concept of a unified Indigenous population that focused only on the highland region, he addressed the unique needs of various Indigenous groups spread throughout the Ecuadorian territory, particularly the Cayapas (Chachi) in the coastal province of Esmeraldas and forest Indians in the eastern Amazon basin. Not only more acculturated highland Indians but also isolated Indians in the Amazon, he argued, must be incorporated into the body politic. Different groups would have different concerns, and hence there was no singular, unified solution to the so-called Indigenous problem. Foreshadowing arguments that Indigenous leaders would make decades later, Paredes maintained that it was a mistake to see Indians as racial or ethnic groups because their history, language, territory, and cultural institutions made them nationalities. He repeatedly urged his fellow leftists not to see Indigenous poverty as a simple issue of class oppression, but rather a complicated issue that took into account their varying cultures and national characteristics.[9]

"The Indigenous problem is one of the most arduous issues that the country faces," Paredes noted, with "almost half of the Ecuadorian population living in a truly subhuman condition for the last five centuries." Despite their good intentions, liberals had not been able to solve Indigenous problems. Paredes blamed this on the failure of state structures to address Indigenous concerns. Only through a Ministry of Indigenous Affairs dedicated exclusively to Indigenous issues would sufficient resources be allotted to find true solutions to these problems. The few efforts that had been undertaken were focused almost entirely on the highlands, but the government's shortcomings became even more obvious when one considered those living in the eastern Amazonian basin. "We Ecuadorians must consider Indians as Ecuadorians," he argued, "but we have done nothing to benefit Amazonian Indians." The purpose of a government ministry would be to study these problems and develop concrete solutions favoring all Indigenous peoples. "The creation of a Ministry of Indigenous Affairs would be the May Revolution's greatest achievement," Paredes urged. "If the May Revolution manages truly to incorporate Indians into the Ecuadorian population, giving them all the benefits of civilization, it would be the achievement of its highest aspirations and the most beautiful of its conquests."[10] From Paredes's perspective, state structures should be utilized to expand Indigenous rights.

Years later, the formation of a ministry under Abdalá Bucaram's populist government (1996–1997) proved to be highly contentious and divided the Indigenous movement. Dissidents denounced the "ghettoization" of Indigenous concerns into only one ministry when in reality their interests should be addressed throughout government structures. Paredes recognized this problem. "The Indigenous problem is not a simple thing," he later said. "Indians belong to many social categories." In addition to being rural agricultural workers, they were also workers, street sweepers, peons, and bricklayers in the city.[11] Even with these limitations, this ministry would at least give exposure to Indigenous issues that previously had lain outside of the purview of state structures. It would be a step in the right direction.

Suffrage

Despite their exclusion from power, the role of subalterns in the conception of Ecuadorian citizenship was a common topic of debate in the Constituent Assembly, particularly as exhibited in its most public and political manifestation—the right to vote. Since independence, constitutions always had been highly exclusionary. Age, gender, wealth, and "cultural status," which generally meant the ability to read and write, limited citizenship rights. In 1945, state structures continued to be "bifurcated" with the retention of distinctions between citizens and Indians (defined as those unable to read or write). Whereas in the early republic period Indigenous peoples resisted the loss of legal recognition of their separate cultural identity represented by citizenship, by the twentieth century they increasingly desired political representation. Without citizenship, Indians could not be elected to political office or have a direct say in constructing state structures. The right to vote seemed the most visible and overt way to change the political balance of power, which led activists to defend the rights of their allies and to disenfranchise those who might side with their opponents. Highly contentious debates on the extension of suffrage indicated just how deep an impact elites feared that it could have on the nature of state structures.

By 1944, restrictions on voting based on gender and overt economic factors had been removed, but most delegates wanted to retain the age and "cultural" restrictions. Few argued for giving minors the right to vote, and apparently most delegates still believed Indians were the equivalent of minors (that is, "*niños con barbas*"). Critical observers noted that denying the vote to illiterate Indians was a throwback to debates within the Catholic Church after the European conquest as to whether the Indians could be considered human beings.[12] The desirability or even possibility of universal suffrage caused deep disagreements within the assembly. Manuel Elicio Flor, a conservative representative from Pichincha and second vice president of the congress, maintained that "pure universal suffrage does not exist" because money, ideas, class relations, and religion influenced elections.[13] Although this was a remarkable admission from someone who profited from systems of domination, it was difficult to use this logic as a basis to exclude those who did not benefit from privilege.

The debates for suffrage rights for Indigenous peoples provide interesting comparisons with the decision to grant women the right to vote. In the public mind women much like Indians, were associated with tradition and religion, and debates over extending voting rights to them followed similar lines. Rather than opening up the body politic, granting citizenship was a way to "civilize" marginalized populations. Hence, giving women the vote in 1929 was not based on a progressive impulse designed to advance women's rights, but was rather a conservative reaction intended to preempt a nascent feminist movement, to prevent women from entering the political arena, and to create a bulwark against what was perceived as a growing socialist threat in society.[14] What appeared to be a political opening for women was, in fact, an elite attempt to tighten their own grip on society. Curiously, conservatives did not embrace the same philosophy for Indians. Rather, the rhetoric of legal equality cloaked the reality of a racist attitude that viewed Indians as inherently inferior. Remnants of nineteenth-century patriarchal politics were still very evident in debates in the Constituent Assembly.

Debates over suffrage also engendered deep disagreements within the political Left, the Indians' best friends in the halls of power. Many leftists feared that if the Indians were not given a proper ideological formation, they would become susceptible to the influence of wealthy landholders who would sway their votes. This, of course, would hinder the electoral prospects of the Left in its attempt to position itself as the defender of lower-class interests. For example, Communist leader Pedro Saad advocated granting illiterate people the vote in local municipal elections to give them both more power and valuable lessons in citizenship, but he "would not dare give the vote to illiterates for higher-level political elections."[15] On the other hand, Ricardo Paredes insisted that not only more acculturated highland Indians but also isolated Indians in the eastern Amazonian rain forest must be included as part of the body politic.[16]

What emerges from these debates is that leftists were not immune to the common liberal assimilationist attitudes of the dominant culture, and in fact elements of leftist thought emerged out of that ideological formation. As a result, the 1945 constitution failed to extend citizenship rights or the vote to Indigenous peoples, even as it continued to claim that the Ecuadorian government was "republican, elected, responsible." Granting formal rights to new groups of people can be highly disruptive to existing fragile alliances, so perhaps it is not surprising that it would be 35 more years before this dream would be realized. By then, expanded access to education opened up more possibilities for electoral participation. In the 1940s, however, elites who benefited from the status quo still firmly controlled political power and saw little need to extend the franchise to subalterns who might use it to challenge their privileged position. Denied suffrage rights, Indigenous peoples could not take a seat in the National Assembly to debate the concepts and applications of state power. Rather, they were forced to work outside state structures as a social movement and to rely on sympathetic allies to represent their interests in the congress.

Functional Representation

Given the tension between a desire for universal suffrage and a fear of unchecked influences on the political system, delegates extended a system of functional deputies to guarantee congressional representation for "minority" interests, even though Indians comprised about half of the country's population in 1944 and could hardly be properly termed a minority group. Since the 1929 constitution, special interest groups—university professors, schoolteachers, students, agriculturalists, industrialists, the press, merchants, workers, peasants, and the military—had been guaranteed representation in congress. These various national bodies selected fifteen "functional" senators to represent their interests, and the Council of State selected a senator "for the guidance and defense of the Indian race."[17] Whereas others had the right to select their own representatives, Indigenous peoples, by far the single largest group of those named in the law, could not because elites found them mentally and politically incapable of exercising this right. Rather than supporting Indigenous struggles, politicians who filled this post were often antagonistic toward the very people they were to guide and defend. FEI's selection of Paredes in 1944 as their functional representative was the first and only time that Indians had direct control over this position.

Delegates in the 1944–1945 Constituent Assembly decided to retain this system of functional representation, but there was strenuous debate about how to divide up these positions. Landowners demanded two delegates but resisted granting agricultural workers an equal level of representation. Granting Indigenous peoples functional representation, writes Edison Egas Egas, "scandalized the bourgeoisie who viewed Indians only as instruments of labor and not beings with rights."[18] Conservatives argued that giving Indians representation would lead to a bloated congressional body that would make it difficult to accomplish legislative tasks; moreover, they would be an antagonistic presence in the respectable body. This, however, did not prevent conservatives from arguing that since "agriculture was the principal source of wealth" in the country, the landowners' representation should be raised from two to six delegates, which would give conservatives relatively more strength in the assembly.[19] These disagreements over exactly what interests the functional senators should represent hit at the heart of assembly debates over the purpose of state structures and whether they should be used to advance the interests of marginalized groups or maintain the status quo. These contradictory interests could not be easily reconciled.

Paredes not only advocated citizenship rights for Indigenous peoples, he also provided the strongest voice for their direct representation in the national assembly. "There are class problems and there are nationality problems," Paredes argued. Indians faced certain unique characteristics including racial discrimination and feudal-style relations on haciendas from which white and mestizo agricultural workers were largely exempt. Given their economic and social oppression, "the Indigenous problem is the deepest and most terrible problem facing the country." In Paredes's mind, these factors justified giving Indians their own representation in the assembly. He looked forward to the day when people like him would not have to represent Indigenous interests, when they would be allowed to represent themselves.[20]

Paredes succeeded in making only minor revisions to the law that granted Indians functional representation, including removing the paternalistic language of charging the representative with "guiding and defending the Indian race." Even though agricultural workers numbered more than half of the population, the assembly named only one representative for Indigenous organizations in the highlands, and two for peasant syndicates on the coast. Indians in the Amazon received no delegates. Unlike the 1929 electoral law that gave the Council of State the right to select the functional representative for the Indigenous race, the 1945 electoral law stipulated that the president of the cantonal electoral tribunal would assemble the leaders of legally recognized Indigenous communities (*comunas*) and similar associations that had operated for at least a year. These meetings would select delegates who would then elect a deputy to the congress. Yet because the comuna structure often functioned to undermine popular organizing strategies, many of the more politicized Indigenous communities rejected it. Furthermore, notable Indigenous leaders, including Dolores Cacuango and Tránsito Amaguaña, were excluded from serving in the National Assembly because of literacy restrictions on citizenship. As a result, the true representation of Indigenous concerns was limited. The FEI fought without success to claim the right, as they had done with Paredes in the 1944–1945 assembly, to name this representative.[21]

As a tool for Indigenous peoples to influence state structures, functional representation was at best a mixed bag. The high point obviously was in the 1944–1945 assembly when, taking advantage of political openings after the May Revolution, the FEI named Paredes to this position. Paredes presented the strongest, clearest, and most articulate defense of Indigenous concerns ever heard in the Ecuadorian congress, but this was no substitute for Indians representing their own interests. Because no Indians were present, they could not influence state structures directly, and as before they would continue to defend their ethnic interests as outsiders. Elites continued to control state structures to their own benefit.

Language

The role of language in the formation of state structures and national identity was also hotly debated in the Constituent Assembly. Delegates fought over the purpose of language and its practical and symbolic values, and whether Spanish should be an "official" or "national" language. Paredes, in his role as functional representative, noted that whereas everyone in the assembly agreed that Spanish was Ecuador's official language, the role and purpose of Kichwa and other Indigenous languages engendered much more contentious debate. Several delegates observed that Kichwa was not the only Indigenous language in Ecuador, that others such as Jibaro (Shuar), Zaparo (Zápara), and Cayapa (Chachi) were also important. Others questioned why this article should even be included in the constitution. "Language is a natural sociological phenomenon," remarked Gustavo Buendía, Socialist Vanguard delegate from Pichincha, "and it cannot be regulated." Having the congress declare a language official made it no more so than declaring Tulcán "tierra caliente" made it possible to grow sugarcane there.[22]

Much of this discussion about language reflected the dominance of liberal assimilationist assumptions that governed elite discourse over Indigenous rights and dictated the construction of state structures in Ecuador. Since the beginnings of European colonization, fluency in Spanish had been used as a mark of civilization. Indigenous languages were disparaged as inferior and a mark of backwardness. Daniel León Borja, Conservative delegate from Chimborazo, argued that encouraging the study of Kichwa would only result in the "deepening of existing ethnic and cultural conditions." Indian children should be taught Spanish in the schools to help civilize them, and having only one official language would also strengthen Ecuadorian national identity. Facility with European languages was also equated with intelligence. Liberal delegate Eduardo Vásconez Cuvi argued that had the Spanish taught their language to the Indians, they would have already been assimilated into white society.[23] The racist underpinnings of many such assumptions indicates how far Indians and their supporters would have to go before dominant society would recognize the value of their cultures. It also reflects the orientation of state structures to European rather than Indigenous standards.

Interestingly, dominant classes normally antagonistic toward Indigenous peoples articulated a range of ideas and opinions toward the use of languages, reflecting the contradictory attitudes of those who controlled state structures. For example, Conservative delegate Gonazalo Cordero Crespo from Azuay argued that Kichwa could be used as a tool of acculturation and assimilation. Conservative delegate Rafael Terán Coronel, one of the few delegates who spoke Kichwa, pointed out that the Inkas spoke Quechua and they were an advanced civilization.[24] While Terán Coronel maintained that language itself was not a sign of a level of intelligence, the historical value placed on a language and culture did not necessarily extend to the present. Similarly, in Cuzco in neighboring Peru, Marisol de la Cadena discovered that elites could promote Quechua as a valuable part of the great Inka culture while at the same time denigrating its use in the twentieth century.[25]

Some of the strongest reactions against Indigenous rights, including the use of language, came from delegates representing hacendados and landholding interests. Carlos Zambrano, from a powerful and influential landholding family in Chimborazo, stated that Kichwa could hardly be considered an official language. He decried the efforts of José Carlos Mariátegui's journal

Amauta in Peru to cultivate the use of Quechua as a useless and snobbish undertaking that resulted in a fiasco. Reflecting common liberal assimilationist attitudes, he maintained that the Kichwa language should be used only as a vehicle to educate and incorporate Indians into the national culture. It did not matter, he concluded, that Quechua was an ancient language. What concerned him was human progress, which could be achieved only by incorporating the Indian into Western civilization.[26]

It was not only Conservatives who desired to suppress Indigenous languages. Leftists were perhaps even more adamant on this point because of their desire to bring material progress to marginalized communities, and in their minds holding on to Indigenous cultures and languages would hinder progress and economic development. For example, Communist Pedro Saad noted that the goal of adopting Spanish as an official language should be to assimilate Indians into the national culture, not to destroy their culture.[27] With language being an important carrier of culture, however, removing a language would inevitably mean removing part of the culture.

Once again, Ricardo Paredes, the functional representative of the Indigenous peoples, provided the most strenuous defense for recognizing the value of Indigenous cultures and languages. He adamantly maintained that Indians' languages were an immensely important part of their civilization and should be encouraged rather than suppressed. "A constitution should express the reality of a country," he maintained. "The reality is that in this country about half of the people speak a language other than Spanish." Logically, these people should be allowed to use their own languages. He did not discourage the obligatory instruction of Spanish in the schools. Indeed, he considered it critical because speaking more languages meant a higher degree of culture and more economic opportunities. Encouraging the use of Kichwa was not an "anti-Ecuadorian" position, but rather a patriotic stance that would "contribute to the grandeur of the country."[28] Languages are not mutually exclusive, and Indians often recognized the benefits of multilingualism.

Unlike other Indigenous demands such as agrarian reform or increases in the minimum wage, the addition of another "official" language would not require any material concessions on the part of the elite. That it led to such contentious debates reveals the depth of ideological battles that underlay this issue. The struggle over the process of state formation extended beyond the economic realm and touched issues of racism, cultural superiority, and debates over who should be included in the body politic. Indigenous peoples and their allies sought to exploit such symbolic issues to gain a role in conceptualizing the state.

After long and heated debates, the Constituent Assembly finally yielded to some of Paredes's arguments. "The Indians have their own native civilization," Socialist Emilio Uzcátegui conceded, and the Communist Party was right not to remove them from their own civilization but to encourage their natural development, which would benefit the entire country. In the end, Paredes and his supporters carried the day; for the first time, the Ecuadorian constitution recognized the value of Indigenous languages. The fifth article of the new constitution stated, "Spanish is the Republic's official language. Kichwa and other aboriginal languages are recognized as elements of the national culture."[29] It was a small and largely symbolic victory, but it also revealed the growing strength of Indians and the Communist Party's important role in facilitating the advancement of their agenda. It is also a concrete example of Indians successfully exploiting centralized state structures to their benefit over the opposition of local elites. Concessions on these less formal issues of state formation also meant that Indians were gaining an opening that could eventually lead to more formal concessions, including a seat at the table where these issues were discussed. Indigenous pressure through their allies in the assembly increasingly forced more and more elites to acknowledge that state structures would have to be modified to take their concerns under consideration.

Aftermath

In overthrowing Arroyo del Río, according to Agustín Cueva, all Ecuadorians, "the red with the conservative, the priest with the soldier, the woman and the man, the student and worker" could momentarily unite to make the Glorious May Revolution.[30] But it became impossible to solidify these diverse forces into a common front after the ouster of the president. Many of the apparent gains of the May 1944 "revolution" were limited and failed to result in any profound or long-lasting changes, either in the state system or state idea. Although Indians had played a significant role in this political transformation, after the victory they were soon forgotten, marginalized, and excluded from participation in government affairs. The change in government failed to grant Indians citizenship or create a conceptual shift that would address the underlying structural problems of exclusionary state structures.

A definitive break that ended the possibility of using constitutional structures to gain more space for Indigenous peoples came on March 30, 1946, when President José María Velasco Ibarra dissolved the Constituent Assembly (which was supposed to remain in power until August 1946), declared himself dictator, abrogated the progressive 1945 constitution (in effect just over a year), and reinstated the 1906 constitution. In August, Velasco Ibarra convened another constitutional assembly with the task of writing a new magna carta more to his liking. Leftists refused to participate, choosing instead to adhere to the 1945 constitution. As a result, Conservatives held the upper hand in writing a document that governed the country for the next twenty years. Critics denounced it for rolling back the democratic advances embodied in the previous constitution.[31] This new document provided a legal basis for the continuation of the latifundio as the primary mode of agricultural production, directly undercutting Indigenous demands for land. Delegates struck the limited functional representation that Indians had enjoyed in the 1929 and 1945 constitutions, although Conservatives retained their own elite representatives for landholding and commercial interests.[32] The constitution also failed to acknowledge the importance of ethnicity, removing the reference to Kichwa and other Indigenous languages. This was part of a determined effort on the part of Conservative elites to exclude from government those deemed unworthy of participating in political discourse. The advance of an Indigenous rights agenda was retarded, and activists would have to await a more opportune moment to press their concerns.

Without question, the FEI saw the process of state formation as engendered by the 1944 Glorious May Revolution as a positive development and fully embraced its potential to work to their advantage. The disappointment Indians felt was not due to a failure to take power in Ecuador. In fact, over half a century later, Miguel Lluco, the national coordinator of the Indigenous Pachakutik political movement, observed that simply electing Víctor Hugo Cárdenas as vice president of Bolivia in 1993 or Alejandro Toledo as president of Peru in 2001 did not solve those countries' problems. Indeed, their neoliberal policies led to deeper economic crisis. Merely placing Indians in positions of power would not automatically mean an end to long-standing problems. Rather, the structure of the country had to be changed to build a new society.[33] Similarly in 1944, Indians were at the vanguard of redefining state structures so that they would be more inclusionary and responsive to the broader needs of *el pueblo*.

In retrospect, many participants in the events of 1944 noted the conservative outcome. Military leader Coronel Sergio Enrique Jirón called the revolution "stillborn." Others called it a "revolution betrayed." Minister of Education Alfredo Vera, a Communist, noted that Velasco Ibarra was never committed to a revolution that would open up political space for subalterns, but wanted to restore democracy only to preserve the oligarchy. Socialist leader Manuel Agustín Aguirre noted that his first meeting with Velasco Ibarra left him totally disillusioned, not only because of the leader's cold and distant personality but also because of his conservative and opportunistic political stances.[34]

Velasco Ibarra's second period in office, much like his other four terms as chief executive, resulted in deeper entrenchment of the exclusionary features of Ecuadorian politics and a denial of a voice to Indigenous peoples and popular movements in building the state.

Although Indians (as well as women, workers, and others who participated in the coalition that overthrew Arroyo del Río in 1944) had their own organizations and were able to articulate their own demands, until they gained full citizenship rights they could not directly use formal political channels to press for legal and structural changes such as raising minimum salaries and enacting agrarian reform. They faced what O'Donnell calls "low-intensity citizenship," owing to a notable gap between the liberal principle of equality and political exclusion.[35] This was a form of a polyarchic democracy in which a small group of competing elites manipulated decision making to maintain control of the system.[36] A situation of partial democracy continued to exclude the majority of people from the full exercise of their citizenship rights.

In the meantime, Indigenous peoples were left to make their presence felt through other means, including their newly formed FEI. Were electoral mechanisms and constitutional assemblies appropriate avenues for advancing Indigenous struggles? Paredes's limited success as a functional representative for the Indigenous peoples and the reversal of gains made in the 1944–1945 Constituent Assembly highlight the limitations of electoral strategies for contesting state structures. Over the next several decades, FEI would gain concessions, including agrarian reform legislation, mobilized as part of civil society. Endless debates over the most appropriate and effective methods of engaging and altering state structures would continue to follow Indigenous organizing efforts for years to come.

Indigenous Communities, Landlords, and the State

Land and Labor in Highland Ecuador, 1950–1975

WILLIAM F. WATERS

The relationship between indigenous peoples and the Ecuadorian state has evolved and grown, as shown by the extraordinary development of provincial, regional, and national indigenous organizations. The impact of this process can be gauged by the astonishing sequence of mobilizations in the 1990s and enhanced political sophistication of indigenous groups and their allies, especially with respect to demands for land, political participation, and ethnic identity.[1] However, as the indigenous leader Luis Macas suggests, today's indigenous movement in Ecuador grew out of processes that date back centuries.[2] It was preceded by the emergence of the community as an actor and protagonist vis-à-vis the country's dominant political and economic elites and the state, which has itself evolved in important ways. Moreover, agrarian reform is best understood as an extended process of transformation in the use and distribution of land and in rural labor arrangements, which between 1950 and 1975 gave rise to Ecuador's indigenous community in its present form. That is, agrarian reform was less a legislative corpus than a prolonged but dramatic social, political, and economic process of profound transformation and struggle, of which the agrarian reform laws of 1964 and 1973 were only a part.

According to some analysts, the chief protagonists in this transformation were certain fragments of the landowning elite. This view focuses attention on the *iniciativa terrateniente* (landlords' initiative) whereby economically and politically powerful landowners abolished servile forms of labor and distributed small proportions of more marginal land to indigenous households without being obliged to do so by law. They capitalized and modernized their haciendas to respond to increasing domestic demand for more specialized products, particularly dairy goods. In this view, the state's role was to promote economic development by providing legislative and regulatory mechanisms to be implemented by a technocratic apparatus. A process of orderly, directed change allowed the Ecuadorian economy to become more modern and productive while maintaining the domination of urban and rural elites. Among the chief proponents of the iniciativa terrateniente perspective were the Argentinean sociologist Oswaldo Barksy and his colleagues in the Center for Planning and Social Studies (CEPLAES); Carmen Deere makes a similar case for Cajamarca in northern Peru.[3] Another interpretation holds that indigenous and peasant movements were the driving force of agrarian transformation and that the landowners' response was more reactive than proactive. In this view, capitalist relations of production were being inserted into the Ecuadorian social formation, and demands for land and salaries augured the end of the traditional, noncapitalist relations of production. Among the proponents of this view were the Ecuadorian researchers Andrés Guerrero and Fernando Velasco.[4] These contemporary analyses were witness to and in many ways framed the original debate about the role of the indigenous community in the transformation of the rural sector.

The roles of indigenous communities and landlords were both decisive as the function of the state evolved. By virtue of the success of indigenous communities in negotiating with landlords (either directly or through technocratic state agencies) for the acquisition of land, the scenario in 1975 could hardly have been more different from that of 1950. The outcome of this transformation was that a system dominated by extensive landholdings, a largely internal smallholding sector, and various forms of servile and semiservile labor was replaced by a system consisting of: more compact haciendas; external, independent indigenous communities; and a combination of peasant, wage, and semiproletarian forms of labor. Indigenous communities were able to pursue their interests in the context of emerging state institutions and policies.

This remarkable process of agrarian transformation is illustrated by the case of Cantón Salcedo, Cotopaxi Province. As elsewhere in the highlands, much of the agricultural land in the cantón had belonged to wealthy landlords in the nineteenth and early twentieth centuries, but by 1950, the roles of landed elites, the state, and indigenous communities were changing. Agrarian reform is not a mechanical or uniform process of land redistribution (and much less a forcible expropriation) pressed on unwilling owners by an implacable reformist government; rather, between 1950 and 1975 the principal actors themselves defined new roles. The haciendas and indigenous communities of Cantón Salcedo were in many ways typical of the highland region, and the processes analyzed were general throughout that region. Out of this process, an invigorated indigenous community emerged to take its place as a pivotal institution in the development of and participation in indigenous organizations.

Indigenous communities, located for the most part within large landholdings, were empowered by law but not usually in fact by the 1937 Ley de Comunas (Law of Organization and Administration of Communes). By 1975, though, they constituted organized entities with jurisdictional authority over property and membership. Their increased organizational potential was expressed within individual communities in the form of negotiations for the purchase of individual landholdings and communal land, either directly with landlords or through the intervention of a new state agency, the Instituto Ecuatoriano de Reforma Agraria y Colonización (IERAC, Ecuadorian Institute of Agrarian Reform and Colonization).

To show the impact of agrarian reform at the local level, I discuss the case of two communities we shall call Yacucuna and Santa Marta. Data were obtained from the cantón land registry office (Registro de la Propiedad), the national land tax agency (Dirección Nacional de Catastro), and field work that involved both surveys and individual interviews.

The Ecuadorian Highlands before 1950

It is widely assumed that even as late as 1950 relatively little had changed in Ecuador over the previous century.[5] It is true that the extensive highland haciendas of the nineteenth century remained essentially intact well into the twentieth and domination of landownership was closely tied to servile and semiservile labor arrangements. After the abolition of imprisonment for debt in 1918, agricultural production in the highlands was based on obligatory labor services largely provided by Indian households in exchange for access to hacienda resources, especially land.

The most important of the traditional and obligatory rural labor arrangements was the *huasipungo* system by which a *huasipunguero* and his extended family worked four to six days a week on the hacienda. In addition to agricultural and pastoral tasks, workers provided *huasicamía* (domestic labor in the hacienda residence or in the patron's urban home), *chagracama* (guarding the fields), *cracama* (harvesting), *cuentayo* (care of the flocks in *páramos,* the high

Andean meadows), and *faena* (additional tasks performed before the day's regular duties). A variety of other duties, such as road repair and construction, were demanded on an irregular basis. In return, the household received usufruct to a small parcel of usually marginal land sufficient for a small house and subsistence farming. The hacienda's productive resources, including pastures, water, and firewood, were also available, and the household received a nominal wage (in most cases, pennies per day), which was often deducted from outstanding debts or simply not paid at all.

Households within the hacienda were nominally called communities by the 1937 Ley de Comunas, which stipulated that the community could elect its representatives and enjoy jurisdictional existence. Nevertheless, the law was not widely implemented, and before 1950 the community had only limited ability to negotiate with landlords and almost none with the state, although there were notable exceptions, especially in Chimborazo Province.[6] Moreover, Indians were not passive observers of their own fate; in addition to daily, routine acts of resistance, sporadic outbreaks of rebellion and violence were far from unknown.[7]

Independent indigenous communities during this period were either wedged between haciendas or occupied land that was so poor, often because of the absence of water, that haciendas were never established there. Members of these communities also provided various services to the patron. *Arrimado* was an arrangement by which the huasipunguero's extended family lived within the hacienda and performed certain agricultural tasks for nominal wages. Under the *yanapo* system, residents of neighboring communities worked two to three days a week in exchange for access to hacienda resources (especially pastures, firewood, and water) and the right to traverse hacienda property. *Partidario* and *arrendatario* were different forms of sharecropping and land rental by which the landowner granted the use of farmland or pastures in return for a portion of the harvest or rent in cash. Free peons were wage workers from neighboring communities who were hired by the landowner for specific tasks during times of peak labor demand, particularly sowing and harvesting. The relationship between the huasipungo and neighboring communities was not static or well defined, and there could be changes in status between huasipunguero and comunero.[8] In addition, nominally free comuneros provided labor services because of accumulated debts and mandatory marketing arrangements, and even in return for access to the hacienda (such as the right to use private roads).[9]

In summary, the agrarian system before the reform was dominated by large estates within which smallholdings were granted to indigenous households, thus comprising an internal *minifundia* sector. This internal labor force was supplemented by various other arrangements, many of them quite flexible, whereby the landowner hired other workers either paid in cash or given access to hacienda resources. This system was possible because large landowners held a virtual monopoly on landownership, for two reasons. First, because the state fostered, protected, and promoted the latifundia well into the twentieth century, hacendados had virtually unlimited authority over indigenous communities located on their estates. For example, corporal punishment and imprisonment were common, and government forces, including the rural police and the army, could be called upon to restore order in the case of overt acts of resistance. While these arrangements were not equivalent to slavery, they were similar in that debt peonage could be passed to the next generation. While Indians could not be bought and sold, their services could be, and the number of huasipungueros was regularly mentioned in advertisements for the sale of haciendas. Not surprisingly, former huasipungueros sometimes refer to their previous condition as slavery. Second, the landlords' hold on indigenous communities was strengthened and legitimized not only by racism, or a "paternalistic ideology . . . based on the idea of a 'natural' inequality among whites, mestizos, and Indians,"[10] but also by the 1937 Ley de Comunas, which gave Indians approximately the same legal status as children.[11]

Changes in Ecuador's Social Formation, 1950–1975

By 1950, various forces had begun to accelerate capitalist accumulation in both the coastal region and in the highlands. Before then, the highland agrarian system was characterized by subsistence farming and an internal market involving much of the region's area and population. Beginning around 1950, economic, political, and ideological conditions began to undergo dramatic changes. These included rural-to-urban migration, the emergence of a middle class, changes in consumption and production, an enhanced role of the state, and international influences.

Socioeconomic Change

Urbanization accelerated in the 1950s, fueling the emergence of an urban middle class. Whereas the country remained predominantly rural, towns and cities grew rapidly, principally because of migration from the countryside. This stimulated demand for a variety of consumer goods, including manufactured items, imported articles, and agricultural and dairy products by an expanding urban middle class.[12] These changes were closely related to the development of the industrial sector. From 1963 to 1974, industry grew at an average annual rate of 8.2 percent, based on investments that grew annually at a rate of 13.2 percent.

According to the landlords' initiative perspective, differences among factions of the landowning class became increasingly accentuated during this period. In 1959, the conservative government of Camilo Ponce issued an emergency decree that partitioned some state-owned haciendas and introduced settlement schemes directed at uncultivated subtropical land. The purpose was to deflect indigenous and peasant demands for land, to induce highland families to migrate to lowland areas, and to settle a segment of the peasant class on individually owned plots of land. In 1960 and 1961, José María Velasco Ibarra, president for the fourth time, avoided any measures that might provoke confrontation with rural elites, but between 1960 and 1962, six agrarian reform measures were proposed by different—often diametrically opposed—groups. All called for abolishing servile labor arrangements and for redistributing some of the land then in large holdings.[13]

Since this new conception of the role of the state in addressing the distribution of land was increasingly accepted, albeit for different reasons, by early 1964 there was no longer any doubt that there would be agrarian reform legislation. Two paths were open: change could promote either modernization of the hacienda sector or redistribution of land to the indigenous and peasant population. These strategies were not mutually exclusive, but the dominant group of modernizing landowners clearly preferred the former.[14]

The Role of the State

The Ecuadorian state grew increasingly active during this period and followed two evolving principles. First, the state directly intervened in the economy by protecting nascent national industries through import substitution policies, technical assistance, developing infrastructure (roads, water systems, and health and educational facilities), and direct participation in the production and sale of goods (such as gasoline) and services (such as telephones and the generation and transmission of electricity). Second, Ecuador created an increasingly complex juridical and administrative apparatus. New ministries and other public entities, including a dozen public corporations, were born during this period. For example, the first population census was conducted in 1950; the Ecuadorian Agency for Professional Training (SECAP) was founded to provide a trained workforce for the private sector; a stock exchange was created; and the first Ley de Compañías (Law of Companies) was promulgated to further promote business interests.[15] In the rural sector, the state was to guide and administer reform, linking public and private interests in a process that pitted traditional landowners opposed to almost any change against both reformist landowners and indigenous and peasant communities. This breach in the dominant landowning class enabled a hybrid transitional military government, which actively promoted modernization and industrialization, to take power.

Thus it was a military government, the Junta Militar de Gobierno, that promulgated the first agrarian reform and colonization law, the Ley de Reforma Agraria y Colonización, on July 11, 1964.[16] This law was designed to eliminate archaic forms of labor (particularly huasipungo) and to revitalize the production process through modernization and improved technology. The state's participation was realized in the creation of the Ecuadorian Land Reform and Colonization Agency (IERAC). Efficiently operated haciendas were to be preserved, and less efficient ones were given three years to become more efficient. Estates in the highlands were limited to 800 hectares of arable land and 1,000 hectares of páramos. Exceptions even to those generous limits were made for holdings judged to be efficiently operated or that produced raw materials for domestic industry, and for tropical or subtropical grazing lands. Huasipungo, yanapo, and other traditional labor forms were abolished, and huasipungueros were to be granted or sold land in proportion to time served on the hacienda. Here again, there were exceptions; landowners with less than 100 hectares could avoid making land grants by paying off former huasipungueros in cash, and households could be settled on land other than what they had lived on and worked. Moreover, the value of land grants was established by the landowner. Finally, rights to the hacienda's resources, especially pasture, were to be maintained for five years (and could then be suspended) but only as long as the former huasipunguero continued to work there.[17]

A second agrarian reform law was passed in 1973 by another technocratic military government. This law further impeded redistribution of land and the reduction of inequality. The central point of this legislation was that land judged by IERAC to be productively and efficiently operated was protected from expropriation, and unproductive units were given two years to improve. Limits on the amount of land that could be owned were eliminated, and IERAC was weakened by being absorbed into the Ministry of Agriculture. At the same time, other state institutions devoted to increasing productivity, such as the National Institute for Agricultural Research (INIAP), were strengthened.[18]

The state took an increasingly active role in promoting efficiency and productivity throughout the country. Agroindustry became increasingly important at this time, predating by several decades the export-driven boom in cut flowers and other nontraditional crops.[19] This change was both internally and externally driven and can be measured by the increase in land devoted to pasture from 1.9 million hectares in 1970 to 4.5 million hectares by 1980. There were similarly dramatic increases in agroindustrial crops (produced on plantations owned by coastal elites) in the same period, including oil palm (a 76 percent increase), cotton (55 percent), soy (976 percent), feed corn (52 percent), peanuts (47 percent), coffee (25 percent), and cacao (16 percent). In contrast, the area devoted to food crops for the internal market declined, particularly for corn (a 72 percent decline between 1970 and 1980), barley (80 percent), and potatoes (36 percent).

Similarly, after 1972 the oil export boom was based largely on state direction and control, and production nearly tripled in six years, from 28.5 million barrels in 1972 to 78.1 million in 1979.[20] As a new oil power (albeit one of the smallest), Ecuador joined the ranks of the Organization of Petroleum Exporting Countries (OPEC) at this time. As a consequence, GNP grew by 20 percent in 1973 alone, and by an average of 6 percent annually through the rest of the 1970s. This development had enormous repercussions for indigenous communities in the upper Amazon basin. It was no coincidence that the full name of the Agrarian Reform Law was the Law of Agrarian Reform and Colonization, just as the function of IERAC, the agency most commonly associated with highland land reform, was to promote the colonization of tropical and semitropical lands. In fact, far more land was adjudicated by the settlement of those areas than redistribution of land in the highlands.[21] Among the implications was that land previously inhabited by nomadic and seminomadic Indians in Ecuador's upper Amazon basin was increasingly occupied by oil companies, small-scale farmers (*colonos*), mining interests, plantations, and even national parks and reserves. Consequently, some of the first extracommunal indigenous organizations were founded in the Amazon region.

International Factors

Finally, international forces played an important role in changing the rural sector. The Bolivian revolution of 1952 and, to a much greater extent, the Cuban revolution of 1959–1960 were harbingers of great change throughout Latin America because they revealed the deep fissures in traditional forms of social and political organization that had appeared inviolate. In contrast, the 1961 Punta del Este conference resulted in the creation of the Alliance for Progress, which stood for orderly reform that would maintain the economic, political, and ideological status quo.

The effect of these developments on indigenous communities before the formation of regional organizations is difficult to gauge. It is true that political parties adopted revolutionary events as organizational examples or calls to action and promoted those ideas at the local level. Conversely, the Alliance for Progress model formed the basis of the Point Four program (later the U.S. Agency for International Development), which in the late 1970s supported development in Ecuador's rural sector through land reform (IERAC) as well as the intervention of state agencies like the Ecuadorian Institute of Hydraulic Resources (INHERI), responsible for irrigation, and the Secretariat for Integrated Rural Development (SEDRI), initially established in a dozen of the poorest rural areas, including Cantón Salcedo.[22]

The Landlords' Initiative

Some highland landowners responded to these changes by altering their production strategies. The process was slow and unevenly distributed, and the rate of adoption of new strategies varied within regions and even within the holdings of specific families.[23] Indeed, as early as the 1920s, some landowners in the northern highlands had begun to use slightly more advanced inputs (such as simple machinery and improved varieties of cattle). A fledgling dairy industry had developed, especially in Pichincha and Cotopaxi provinces, and mechanization had been noted on haciendas south of Quito in Machachi by the late 1940s.[24]

La iniciativa terrateniente was characterized by the replacement of huasipungo, yanapo, and other servile and semiservile arrangements with wage labor. At the same time, the need for manual labor declined, as landowners bought labor-saving machinery and invested in infrastructure. Mixed agricultural production was gradually replaced by specialized dairy production, and agricultural land was converted to pasture. Genetic improvement of dairy herds, artificial insemination, and improved herd management techniques were also adopted as part of this process. At the same time, unproductive land was discarded through sales or grants to former huasipungueros, so that haciendas became more compact, capital-intensive enterprises specializing mostly in dairy production.

These changes took place unevenly, however, and by the mid-1960s, fragments emerged in the landowning class. First, the wealthiest and most favorably situated landowners owned extensive properties with diverse resources. In the late 1950s, they began to divest themselves of the most marginal and unproductive lands, along with unprofitable labor relations. They retained the most productive land, with ready access to markets, that was worked by a smaller, more specialized labor force and used more advanced mechanical and biochemical inputs. Second, landlords in the northern and central highlands, who may have favored the changes taking place but who were hindered by poor access to markets and a more modest resource base, adapted more slowly and cautiously. Finally, traditional landowners, mainly located in the southern highlands, resisted these changes and did everything in their power to maintain traditional labor arrangements and extensive, low-productivity operations which, for them, was the most profitable strategy. In addition, extensive state-owned haciendas that had been rented out were partitioned by the government in the early 1960s and distributed to neighboring communities, which had been the most successful in organizing and demanding land.[25]

In sum, these haciendas differed according to level of capitalization, agroecological zone, and access to markets. Of equal importance, as Guerrero and Velasco point out, was that pressure from indigenous communities played a critical role in this process.[26] They collectively made important economic, political, and ethnic demands, and as in the case of Cantón Salcedo, they organized to purchase land for individual holdings and communally owned pastures. In some parts of the country, the church and nongovernmental organizations, such as the Ecuadorian Center for Agricultural Services (CESA) and the Ecuadorian Populorum Progressio Fund (FEPP), were crucial allies in this process.[27]

Agrarian Transformation and Agrarian Reform in Cantón Salcedo

Cantón Salcedo is in the southeast corner of Cotopaxi Province in the central Ecuadorian highlands. The capital, San Miguel de Salcedo, is situated in an Andean valley 2,640 meters above sea level. The twin ranges (*cordilleras*) of the Andes rise on both sides to more than 4,500 meters above sea level. Because of the altitude and the potential for soil erosion, much of the land is unsuitable for agriculture. In 1974, the cantón's population was 35,399, of which over 88 percent was rural.

Agricultural census data show that in 1954 landownership in Cotopaxi Province was extremely concentrated in the hands of a few landlords. On one hand, the vast majority of the population, almost entirely indigenous, operated more than 85 percent of farm units (of less than five hectares in extension), but they covered only 16 percent of the land. (Cantonal data were not collected in 1954.) On the other hand, only 0.3 percent of all units were 1,000 hectares or more, but they covered almost 44 percent of the land. In 1974, the situation was quite different; about 78 percent of farms had less than five hectares, and they controlled 13 percent of the land. But only 0.1 percent of units were 1,000 hectares or more, and large landowners controlled less than 28 percent of the land. The major changes between 1954 and 1974 were the emergence of farms in the 20–50 and 100–500 hectare ranges and the virtual disappearance of holdings over 1,000 hectares. (Remaining large units were mostly pastureland chiefly located in the páramos.) The data for Cantón Salcedo are similar to those for Cotopaxi Province; in 1974, over 85 percent of farms were five hectares or less, but they accounted for only 16 percent of the land. On the other hand, 0.3 percent of farms of 1,000 hectares or more occupied almost 44 percent of the land, including a single property of 21,000 hectares. (This property was part of the evolution of one of the communities discussed in this chapter.)

These figures mirror changes in the smallholding sector at the national level, where the average size of units of less than five hectares declined from 1.71 to 1.54 hectares between 1954 and 1974. This change reflects an increase in the number of small farms as a product of land grants and sales, as well as the fragmentation and subdivision of smallholdings. The average smallholding in Cantón Salcedo, though, was only 1.28 hectares in 1974, suggesting that the situation of indigenous households there was particularly precarious.

Agrarian Reform in Two Communities

The community of Yacucuna is located in the eastern cordillera 15 kilometers east of the cantón's capital. Before 1964, Yacucuna and the neighboring village of Pamba were both located within a single hacienda. At present, two separate haciendas, referred to here as Yacucuna I and Yacucuna II, lie adjacent to the two communities. The village of Santa Marta is in the western cordillera some 20 kilometers west of the capital. It also borders two haciendas, referred to here as Santa Marta I and Santa Marta II. I present the voices of former huasipungueros in Yacucuna, Santa Marta, and two other indigenous communities in Cantón Salcedo, describing their experience with labor relations before 1964.

> J. I.: "We worked for S/1.70 [per day, about U.S. 25 cents] until six o'clock. In the next few years, it went to two sucres, then . . . six sucres. And later, twelve sucres [less than 50 cents]. [The work included] leveling, harvesting, plowing. From Monday to Saturday, we worked. We worked only on Sunday for ourselves. The women would help us with some jobs, like weeding, harvesting, sowing."
>
> A. R.: "Husband and wife worked for one *raya* [a mark in the

account book] for S/1.50 . . . later, six sucres. An older son or daughter [also worked]; one account. We'd earn six sucres."

A. C.: "We would go out at six in the morning to do the faena. By faena, I mean an extra cuadra [an area 80 meters by 80 meters, or 0.64 hectare]. Irrigating barley or wheat . . . from six until seven in the morning. . . . [Then] we would work in [an area] fifty [meters] long, two meters wide, obligatorily. Orders of the *mayordomo* [boss], orders of the *ayudantes* [assistants]. If we missed a day of work, they would punish us. Here, once in a while, a push; there, a push from the mayordomo on horseback. . . . *Cuentayo* [was] taking care of so many animals. . . . We did that for five months.[28] At two in the morning, we'd eat, and work until nine or ten at night. Or, sitting in the hallway [of the landowner's residence], like a dummy. Sitting in the dining room for five months, sitting around until they would eat. . . . They would give us an advance of barley, or of corn or potatoes. . . . We would get half a bag of barley for the year coming. . . . A year that cost us! We knew how to count. And, settling the accounts [with the landowner], we'd leave crying . . . we could never, never get rid of that debt. On top of that, more . . . we always had to ask for [additional loans in kind] from the hacienda. More debts to maintain the family, maintain the wife and children. Asking favors from the hacienda."

A. J.: "The work was from six o'clock in the morning, although when we got up, we had to take the oxen to the páramo at one or two o'clock, to get to the páramo. Then, we'd work until three in the afternoon. [To walk to Quito for huasicamía duty], we'd arrive in two days."

Agrarian Reform and Community Restructuring in Yacucuna

The community of Yacucuna is composed of 219 households widely dispersed around the village center, which is situated at 3,300 meters above sea level. In addition to individual farms, the community shares 21,000 hectares of páramo with the neighboring community of Pamba, which was formerly an outlying sector of Yacucuna and which now is a separate community of 90 families.

There are now two haciendas in Yacucuna, both located below the community center at about 3,150 meters above sea level. Hacienda Yacucuna I encompasses a single parcel adjacent to the community. The owner maintains large numbers of dairy cattle and sheep and also produces barley and potatoes. Hacienda Yacucuna II consists of two separate lots, the lower devoted to pasture for dairy cattle and sheep and for potato production. Adjacent to the communities of Yacucuna and Pamba, the hacienda's high pastures rise over 3,700 meters above sea level.

In the eighteenth century, Hacienda Yacucuna belonged to the Matheu and Ascásubi families, who were among the most economically and politically powerful in the highlands. José Javier de Ascásubi was part of the intellectual elite of colonial Quito, and Manuel de Matheu was a member of the Supreme Council of Quito that was the focal point of the August 10, 1809, independence movement. The hacienda was listed in a will dated 1854 as the property of Manuel Ascásubi Matheu and Rosario Ascásubi de Alcazár. Manuel Ascásubi Matheu was vice president of the republic and interim president of Ecuador from 1849 to 1850. The hacienda later passed into the hands of Gabriel García Moreno, the powerful conservative president, whose rule in many ways defined Ecuadorian politics in the 1860s and 1870s. García Moreno married into the Ascásubi family not once but twice: he married Rosa Ascásubi y Matheu in 1843, and upon her death, her 18-year-old niece.[29]

When García Moreno was assassinated in 1875, control of Hacienda Yacucuna passed to his son, and upon his death in 1933 to his two daughters. The inheritance included all buildings, equipment, animals, and land, including the extensive páramos. As noted earlier, rural laborers were not property but were tied to the land; in this case, which was by no means unique, the will also included the services of the huasipungueros. In 1954, the hacienda was inherited by Garcia Moreno's five granddaughters, each of whom received equal portions of the cultivable land and equal shares in the extensive páramos, which remained undivided.[30]

The history of Hacienda Yacucuna in the second half of the twentieth century illustrates the complex and varied process by which indigenous households achieved landownership. In 1961 one of the five sisters sold her land and her interest in the páramos to a single buyer, a new-generation large landowner. A second sister sold a 34-hectare parcel in 1962 and the rest (totaling 469 hectares), along with her interest in the páramos, in 1965 to the buyer who had purchased the first sister's portion. Two other sisters sold portions of their inheritances to a second new landowner, who ended up with a total of 154 hectares. These two sisters, along with the fifth sister, sold or granted the balance of their land to indigenous households.

Individual households achieved landownership in different ways. Between 1963 and 1977, indigenous peasants purchased a total of 973 hectares of cultivable land that had been part of the original hacienda. Of this total, 384 hectares (or 39.4 percent) were purchased in 1963 and early 1964, before agrarian reform was formally initiated. Many of the sales agreements for this land specifically ended servile labor relations and adjudicated debts. In contrast, 116 parcels were purchased in late 1964 and 1965, following the promulgation of the law.

While the 1964 agrarian reform law abolished huasipungo and other servile labor forms, it made outright expropriation of large landholdings exceedingly unlikely (and this became practically impossible under the 1973 law). But landowners could not have known that before the law was actually issued. What is more, many were influenced less by the anticipated effect of a future law than by socioeconomic forces then in play. The 1964 law required that the value of each huasipunguero's service be balanced against that of the parcel of land to be transferred to the family. Service of more than ten years was to be compensated with a land grant and an additional cash payment for "unused vacation time." In addition, the household was to receive rights to water and firewood from the hacienda for five years and, as long as the person named in the agreement was employed on the hacienda, access to pastureland. These arrangements were mediated by functionaries of the agrarian reform agency (IERAC), but there is no evidence that the latter part of the agreement was widely respected, so that in almost all cases, Indians lost their traditional access to hacienda resources.

The process by which indigenous households gained direct access to land after 1964 is illustrated by transfers implemented in Yacucuna in 1965. Of 23 parcels adjudicated by the five sisters in that year, ten involved cash payments from the landowner in proportion to time served as huasipunguero, and three families received payments for service in excess of ten years. The largest payment in these three cases was less than $36, though, and in the other cases, no cash payment was made.

All who worked the land knew that landownership in the Ecuadorian highlands had a qualitative as well as a quantitative component. Since the time of the Incas, factors related to altitude, soil quality, and access to water have played a crucial role in determining its productive capacity. Two points reveal this complex interaction of factors. First, in addition to the large area of cultivable land purchased by indigenous households, the original hacienda had included around 21,000 hectares of páramo. This enormous parcel was used as common pastureland by the community (and neighboring Pamba), but was held in trust by the state. In 1981, though, the two communities completed negotiations with the land reform agency (IERAC) and received title in that year. This land was held in common and could not be subdivided. Its use was governed by rules drawn up by the community that restricted use of pastureland to community residents.

Second, the land acquired by Yacucuna households had very productive soils and a good supply of water from the extensive communal páramos and the abundant rainfall typical of the eastern cordillera. Indigenous households received productive land because nearly the entire hacienda had good soil and moderate slopes. Thus while in general indigenous households received marginal lands, in this case they did not. On the other hand, a second generation of large- and medium-sized landowners emerged from the same process and continued to occupy substantial amounts of highly productive land that remained out of the hands of the indigenous community.

Agrarian Reform and Community Restructuring in Santa Marta

Santa Marta is very different from Yacucuna because both the original hacienda and the land acquired by the indigenous community were smaller and of poorer quality. Nevertheless, as in Yacucuna, a new generation of landowners that emerged from the agrarian reform process retained generous portions of the best land available. Overlooking the Nagsiche River valley and the parish center of Cusubamba, the community of Santa Marta lies at 3,550 meters above sea level. Unlike the people of Yacucuna and most other dispersed highland communities, Santa Marta's population is clustered in the village center and along the single dirt road leading into the community because there is very little arable land.

Santa Marta presents a vivid example of how poorly many highland communities and households fared after smallholdings were detached from the hacienda. One-room adobe houses thatched with straw hug the vertically aligned plots on the steep slope east of the road, while on the western side are the extensive, gently rolling pastures of Hacienda Santa Marta I. Depending on the time of year, one may encounter tractors or small combines making their rounds of Hacienda Santa Marta II. Dairy cattle fill the pastures of both haciendas, and in the upper reaches of Hacienda Santa Marta II, bulls are raised for Quito's annual bullfights. By contrast, peasants plow their steeply sloped household plots with oxen or by hand, and subsistence crops are manually sown, tended, and harvested.

At the turn of the twentieth century, Hacienda Santa Marta was one of several that belonged to the wealthy Freile family of Quito.[31] In 1934, it was inherited by three sisters, and in 1949 they sold it to two urban partners, along with the buildings, animals, equipment, water sources, and even the crops then in the fields. According to property records, the two buyers were to divide the land equally, as well as "the peons, animals, and other equipment." In 1965, one of the partners severed his ties with the huasipungueros through the intervention of IERAC, the agrarian reform agency. A two-hectare village center was created and 27 parcels, totaling 36.2 hectares, were transferred to 26 former huasipungueros. The parcels ranged in size from 0.3 to 1.9 hectares, averaging only 1.42 hectares. The transfer also included the right to firewood and water from hacienda lands and the use of its pastures for five years, as provided for in the 1964 law.

The original hacienda was further subdivided in 1970, when 169 hectares were purchased directly by indigenous households and in 1973, when the community purchased 1,529 hectares of páramo on condition that it remain intact for the grazing of community members' flocks. An additional 349 hectares, which represented the lower portion of the hacienda (Santa Marta II), were sold to a veterinarian from the nearby city of Ambato. The upper portion (Santa Marta I) now covers 181 hectares.

The original Hacienda Santa Marta was not only smaller than Hacienda Yacucuna, but also situated on less productive land. Land cultivated by community households lies at 3,400–3,640 meters above sea level, while the communally owned páramo rises far higher. Land belonging to the two haciendas ranges in elevation from 3,300 to more than 3,700 meters. Although the community of Santa Marta is very high in the mountains and might be expected to receive ample precipitation, its location on the inner flanks of the western cordillera means that it gets very little rain. Moreover, land purchased by indigenous households receives virtually no irrigation water. It is steeply sloped and dominated by a heavy, unproductive clay soil known locally as *cangahua*. Moreover, since Santa Marta is so high and its temperatures are generally lower than those in the eastern chain, crops are subject to frost at virtually any time of year. In contrast, the hacienda land is better than community land: the topography is more regular (and thus suitable for mechanized production), cangahua soil is less prevalent, and, most important, irrigation water is plentiful. Thus, despite the proximity of the two haciendas to the community and their parallel vertical orientation, the haciendas control not only the better lower lands, but also the most productive higher-elevation lands.

In sum, Santa Marta's households successfully organized to collectively purchase individual household parcels and communal pasture in the páramos. They also marshaled the mediation of the land reform agency (IERAC) to that end, illustrating the activist role of IERAC, whose essential function was to facilitate the creation of independent smallholders and compact, specialized haciendas on the best remaining land. The basic difference between these two communities is that one began the postreform period already pauperized because of such poor access to land. Even in that case, though, individual households emerged as independent landowners, while the community was empowered both to negotiate with large landowners and to solicit the intervention of state functionaries.

Beginning in the late 1950s, the systematic transformation of Cantón Salcedo's haciendas and the restructuring of its indigenous communities were based on the emergence of a compact, specialized hacienda sector and the transfer of modest amounts of less productive land to indigenous households settled on smallholdings in independent communities. The process, however, was not smooth or uniform. Compared to other haciendas in the Ecuadorian highlands, those of Cantón Salcedo, including those discussed here, were neither the most modern nor the most traditional, and thus are illustrative of processes under way throughout the highlands.

The process of agrarian transformation in Ecuador can be summarized in three parts. First, until about 1950, the agrarian system in Cantón Salcedo, as in much of the highlands, was characterized by vast, often isolated haciendas owned by economically, politically, and ideologically powerful families. The haciendas were worked by indigenous households situated within the hacienda and whose members were tied to the land through debts and coercion. Other indigenous peasants, residing outside the haciendas, also provided labor services and were tied to the hacienda in different ways. Until 1964, the Ley de Comunas of 1937 had relatively little effect on promoting community participation in the political process. Nevertheless, labor relations and access to land were contested in the late 1950s and early 1960s at the community level, contributing to the evolution of the indigenous movement at the regional and national levels. In some cases, exogenous organizations supported and promoted indigenous demands. At the same time, indigenous communities themselves learned how to negotiate with both landed elites and state agencies. Outcomes differed, though, in part because access to land varied in both amounts and productive capacity, as did the ability of emerging communities to negotiate for land, access to resources, and wage labor. As haciendas adopted more specialized, capital-intensive production strategies, landowners found that a smaller labor force, available as needed, was more advantageous than a permanent labor force tied to the land.

Thus, agrarian reform, understood as a prolonged political process, was fueled by demands for land from communities themselves, and by their ability to bargain collectively for land purchases. In the cases discussed here, state agencies, particularly IERAC, acted as intermediaries to promote efficiently operated haciendas, while at the same time fostering the redistribution of some land to the communities. In this sense, state formation was enabled "from below," representing a new relationship between the state idea and state functions. In addition, landownership largely reflected communities' ability to negotiate land purchases from new landowners, sometimes with state intervention. In subsequent years, indigenous communities demonstrated a greater ability to interact with state agencies that promoted a more capital-intensive and commercially oriented rural structure. For example, both communities, like others in the highlands, used their organizational capacities, sometimes with more robust leadership, to negotiate with agencies for public works (especially waterworks and electricity), irrigation, and integrated rural development projects.

The transformation in landownership was achieved at little cost to large landowners. Land sold, granted, or ceded to former huasipungueros was of limited value, since owners generally disposed of the poorest, least productive, most marginal land. Moreover land "grants" often involved cash payments based on the value of the land, which was determined by the landowner. In addition, as in Yacucuna, debts in favor of the indigenous families, based on years of essentially unpaid labor, were often written off. Thus while the landowner was legally obliged to provide continued access to the hacienda's resources, to which families had long had the right, there is no evidence that this provision was widely respected after 1965.

Second, the different kinds of land transfers through sales and grants reflect the gradual, uneven nature of the transformation. In Santa Marta, relatively little land was granted to former huasipungueros, and what was granted was very unproductive. Despite subsequent purchases, Santa Marta's residents have little access to land, so that today the community consists of poor households that are now obliged to work on local haciendas or in the towns and cities. In contrast, those in Yacucuma and the neighboring community of Pamba have better access to land because of the availability of vast páramos and relatively productive, well-watered agricultural land.

Third, a new landowning class has grown up in the region. Because of differences in historical development and agroecological conditions, the organization of production on the new, more compact haciendas varies. Nevertheless, although landownership changed in fundamental ways in the area under study, modern haciendas have generally retained land of sufficient quantity and quality to maintain their dominant position. Their economic power is linked to political and ideological domination not only in the formal sense (mainly through state intervention in the production process), but also in relations with neighboring communities.

On the one hand, the households' ability to support themselves from the land varies. Agrarian reform left the community of Yacucuna with a resource base that enabled most of its residents to produce surpluses beyond subsistence needs. On the other hand, in Santa Marta, Indians have limited access to land, for agroecological, historical, and political reasons. In such a case, it is impossible for most households to satisfy their own needs on the land. As in many other highland communities, households combine subsistence production with temporary, cyclical, or occasional wage labor. They have been incorporated into national and even international chains of goods, services, and labor in a multiplicity of ways.[32] The very meaning of rurality is thus open to new interpretations involving complex links between different sectors of society and the economy.[33] In both cases, households retain their rural roots and thus form the bedrock of indigenous organization at the regional and national levels.[34]

9

Contesting Membership

Citizenship, Pluriculturalism(s), and the Contemporary Indigenous Movement

AMALIA PALLARES

In the post 1979 period, indigenous responses to Ecuador's pluricultural politics, embodied in literacy and bilingual education programs, led to a new political discourse and to a distinct form of citizenship that is both similar to and different from previous modes of citizenship. Indians either occupied a separate legal category, or relied on informal protections once the legal distinctions between themselves and non-Indians disappeared. Indigenous peoples in today's Ecuador rely on their distinction from non-Indians as a route to empowerment; however, they also depart from earlier patterns because they openly contest exclusionary state discourses and practices and propose a new model of citizenship.

Citizenship is not merely a status, but a negotiated relationship. It is subject to change because it is acted upon collectively within social, political, and economic relations of conflict.[1] Studies of the negotiation of citizenship generally focus on three issues: membership in political communities, the rights and obligations associated with such membership, and participation in the life of the polity. In addition, there are two traditional ways of looking at models of citizenship: liberal citizenship, based on universal rights, and communitarian citizenship, based on the notion of a common good.[2] More recently, feminist theorists of race and ethnicity have developed a model of citizenship that incorporates the notion of difference.[3]

According to Will Kymlicka and Wayne Norman,

> Many groups—blacks, women, Aboriginal peoples, ethnic and religious minorities, gays and lesbians—still feel excluded from the "common culture" despite possessing the common rights of citizenship. Members of these groups feel excluded not only because of their socioeconomic status but also because of their sociocultural identity—their "difference." . . . An increasing number of theorists, whom we will call "cultural pluralists," argue that citizenship must take account of these differences. Cultural pluralists believe that the common rights of citizenship, originally defined by and for white men, cannot accommodate the special needs of minority groups.[4]

For Iris Marion Young, a model of citizenship that does not recognize difference reinforces existing inequalities and exclusions.[5] Instead of liberal citizenship, she proposes the concept of *differentiated* citizenship as a model that will account for differences and therefore can adequately address inequalities of power. Regarding indigenous communities specifically, some scholars have pointed out the incompatibility between liberalism and collective indigenous rights to self-determination. Will Kymlicka, however, argues that such rights are not necessarily incompatible with liberalism.[6] He claims that native groups should be recognized as having specific rights that are protected from state intervention. The liberal state should intervene, he argues, only when those communal rights violate the individual rights of a group member.

Young's and Kymlicka's attempts to propose a third model of citizenship are responses to contemporary events such as mass movements of population and the increased activism of indigenous peoples around the globe. Because citizenship is the product of negotiation between parties and not merely a political abstraction, a model of citizenship based on mutual recognition of the difference will rely on the outcomes of specific political struggles.

In the late nineteenth and early twentieth centuries, Ecuador made the transition from a model of citizenship in which Indians occupied a separate republic to a liberal model of universal citizenship in which indigenous difference was not formally recognized. This led to what Iris Young would call a reinforcement of subordination. Underlying this liberal model is the premise that universal citizenship is incompatible with a recognition of indigenous distinctiveness and collective rights.

In the late 1970s and late 1980s, this purported incompatibility began to be questioned in international encounters and working groups, ranging from the Declaration of Barbados, to the United Nations Working Group on Indigenous Populations, to the International Labor Organization (ILO) convention. James Anaya describes the ILO's revision in 1989 of an earlier convention that recognized the aspirations of indigenous people to "exercise control over their own institutions, ways of life and economic development, and to maintain and develop their identities, languages and religions, within the frameworks of the States in which they live."[7] For some international agencies and state representatives, it now seemed possible to integrate indigenous rights into a model of universal citizenship without altering the fundamental model. In Ecuador, the state flirted with this idea of integration in implementing a pluricultural model in the 1980s, creating an opening that was used by indigenous activists to push for something closer to a model of differentiated citizenship. While earlier indigenous struggles in the twentieth century did not threaten the model of a liberal universal citizenship, Indian activists in the 1980s and 1990s exposed the limits of this model and any policy reforms that were bound by it.

How did Ecuadorian Indians challenge and stretch existing notions of citizenship? I would argue that the emergence of this fuller and differentiated citizenship was premised on reimagining the Ecuadorian nation. Nation and citizenship as concepts and as institutions are deeply intertwined because models of nationhood profoundly shape access to resources, patterns of solidarity, and the active and meaningful participation that we call citizenship. Hence, citizenship depends on the identity and culture provided by constructions of the nation. Negotiations over citizenship participation between Indians and the state hinged on the differences between the state's version of pluriculturalism as a new model of nationhood and indigenous activists' critique of this model, which led to another perspective that envisioned Ecuador as a compendium of multiple nations. This reenvisioning of Ecuador was both an end in itself and a means to renegotiate the forms, content, and meaning of citizenship, since a differentiated citizenship could be constructed only on the premise of a plural Ecuador.

The state's model of pluriculturalism was initiated by Jaime Roldós's newly democratic regime (1979–1981) and was continued by the administrations of Osvaldo Hurtado (1981–1984) and Rodrigo Borja (1988–1992), which proposed new cultural and educational policies for indigenous communities. Indian activists responded in a number of ways, including negotiation and cooperation as well as critique and rejection. Ultimately, the differences between indigenous organizations and the state led to a profound disenchantment that contributed in great part to the initiation of uprising politics from 1990 to the present.

The dispute between Indians and the state revolved around two central elements: how Ecuadorian plurality was defined, and what was included in and excluded from public debate. The state focused on recognizing the plurality of cultures alone while maintaining a political model of universal rights, whereas indigenous activists sought to be recognized as nationalities, a category that implied recognition of Indians as citizens of a different kind, with whom the state had to establish a relationship distinct from its relations with other citizens. They were seeking what many have termed "equality in difference." The second point of tension was the debate over what constituted indigenous affairs or claims. While the state principally sought to address literacy, bilingual education, and cultural affirmation policies, indigenous activists lobbied for a broader agenda that included resolving land claims, demands for credit and rural development, and political empowerment.

Early Pluriculturalism, 1979–1984

The 1960s and 1970s witnessed the freeing of labor relations in the highlands. The 1964 and 1973 land reforms led to the end of the *huasipungo* and the proliferation of small landholdings, or *minifundios*, as former *huasipungueros* gained access to land. Several large properties were redistributed. However, as Chiriboga, Guerrero, and Sylva point out, Ecuadorian land reform was quite limited.[8] Many landowners initiated modernization by retaining the most productive lands and relinquishing the least productive ones, while others were able to retain control of their land through numerous legal maneuverings. While the 1964 and 1973 reforms did lead to some distribution, they did not provide a dramatic transformation in the structure of landownership such as occurred in Peru or Bolivia.

The 1972 military coup was followed by two military governments, one headed by Guillermo Rodríguez Lara from 1972 to 1977, the other a military triumvirate that presided between 1977 and 1979. The two regimes were quite distinct. The Rodríguez Lara regime saw itself as a nationalist revolutionary government. As such, it sought to incorporate the popular sectors and to integrate Indians, not by addressing their uniqueness but by integrating them as yet another marginal group. This integration would be obtained by redistribution as well as through an increase in productivity that would create a national market. These two goals informed the 1973 reform, which expanded land redistribution to include communities surrounding haciendas. However, elite opposition to this and other policies led to a coup against Rodríguez Lara, resulting in the triumvirate regime. The triumvirate favored productivity over redistribution and was primarily interested in protecting the rights of landowners and establishing security measures that would impede future land invasions and protests by Indians.

The decline in land reform can be traced to the late 1970s and early 1980s, when the

Institute for Land Reform and Colonization (IERAC) had its budget slashed. Additionally, colonization in the lowlands was increasing at a dramatic speed, leading to the dispossession of several lowland groups. Contemporaneously, the transition to democracy in 1979 opened up opportunities for indigenous empowerment and marked the beginning of state pluriculturalism. In 1979, the Constitutional Assembly agreed to grant the vote to illiterates, a step that enfranchised a significant proportion of the indigenous population. The transition to democratic rule began with the election of a new president, Jaime Roldós, who represented a center-left coalition that assumed power in 1979. In contrast to military regimes, Roldós had an agenda that specifically addressed Indians as having particular needs and demands that were distinct from those of other Ecuadorians. Roldós's government became known for its symbolic appeals to Indians as well as for its active pursuit of cultural policies to improve their status. Roldós was the first president ever to include a small speech in Quichua in his inaugural address, and his regime was also the first to speak openly of a multicultural state and to carry out a full-fledged literacy campaign implemented in most of the highlands.

While the Indian as such had barely appeared in the discourse of the military regimes, the new democratic government spoke of a nation that was characterized by "pluriculturalism," referring to the respect for and support of indigenous peoples and cultures as a key component of national development. Ecuadorian pluriculturalism was inspired by a regionwide neoindigenismo that called for a new conception of national societies with indigenous populations as plurilingual, pluriethnic, pluricultural, and plurinational. This new concept called for a new role for the state, as the main agent responsible for protecting the rights of Indians.

In Ecuador the pluricultural model acknowledged the right of Indians to articulate their own concerns, organize independently of peasant class-based groups, and represent themselves in direct communications with public officials. The new regime gave indigenous activists unprecedented political opportunities and institutional mechanisms through which they could channel their demands. Furthermore, the new regime organized state-sponsored dialogues between indigenous activists and state officials at a national level. The efforts of the pluricultural state included cultural research and festivities, legal policy, encounters for discussing the specific rights and problems of Indians, and efforts to strengthen indigenous organizations.[9] While several legal and cultural initiatives were set forth by this regime, the single most important type of policy involved the literacy and bilingual education projects, handled by the Ministry of Education, that aimed at massive improvements in literacy and education rates. The design and implementation of these policies provided the site where state notions of pluriculturalism and activists' notions of pluriculturalism were aired.

The Roldós regime launched a massive literacy project that had a great impact on the countryside. Between 1974 and 1982 the national literacy level was raised from 30 percent to 55 percent.[10] Literacy was seen as having important sociological and political functions, such as promoting popular participation, helping to develop thinking, critical individuals, and expanding citizenship.[11] In addition to the general literacy program, the government focused on indigenous literacy and bilingual education as specialized tasks. State documents of this period reveal a vision of national development that was attainable, if all the components were developed, particularly the previously relegated indigenous communities. The implementation of bilingual education was preceded by a number of unprecedented meetings between state officials and indigenous activists who sought a role in decision making. During these meetings, activists struggled to obtain some control over policy and pushed for a broad agenda that included material demands. These encounters were considered necessary, argues Santana, because the policy itself "did not guarantee the benefits the Indians wanted . . . they had to secure that."[12] In a number of working meetings held from 1970 to 1981 between the government and Indians, activists insisted on playing a key role in all national decision making concerning bilingual literacy, as well as demanding local control over the selection of promoters and implementation of policy.[13]

Two pivotal events at which Indian and state differences on bilingual education were aired were the meeting of the Instituto de Culturas Aborígenes y Acción Comunitaria (INCAYAC, Institute of Aboriginal Cultures and Community Action) in 1979 and the Nueva Vida Seminar in 1980. In 1979, the government had organized the National Encounter of Aboriginal Cultures, Peasant Organizations, and Neighborhood Associations in Colta, Chimborazo, with the purpose of creating INCAYAC, an institution responsible for governing the administration of literacy. To public officials' surprise, indigenous activists asked to expand the agenda, stating that any cultural policy designed to benefit peasants could not be conceived at the margins of reality and that land and rural development issues had to be incorporated into discussions of literacy.[14] Literacy policy had to be accompanied by policies that ensured socioeconomic improvement. Additionally, activists argued that INCAYAC should be completely autonomous and managed by Indians (not jointly with the state, as government officials proposed). Activists believed that this autonomous arrangement would enable them to pressure ministries and authorities for solutions to land, education, health, and housing problems. The government rejected all of these recommendations, whereupon indigenous activists withdrew their support. The INCAYAC project was soon suspended, and several smaller encounters and meetings that followed were limited to negotiating the terms whereby efforts to increase literacy would be implemented.

The indigenous activists' agenda conflicted once again with the state during the government-sponsored Nueva Vida Seminar in April 1980, where dozens of indigenous activists from all over Ecuador gathered to unify the Quichua written alphabet. Despite its obvious limitations as a government-controlled event, Nueva Vida demonstrated the state's willingness to incorporate Indians in the literacy agenda. Indigenous activists once again demanded control over policy as well as the incorporation of socioeconomic demands into the agenda. Demands included the full representation of their organizations in the National Council of Literacy, community election of local promoters, and indigenous selection of promoters. Activists also demanded the right to register Quichua names for their children in the civil registry, elimination of the state mandated use of Spanish-language names, a solution to land problems, and the expulsion of the Summer Institute of Linguistics.[15]

After extensive discussion, public officials agreed to grant activists some power over the local administration of policy. They demanded the local selection of literacy promoters, some indigenous participation in the national and provincial literacy programs, the use of Quichua in civil registry entries, and the final removal of the Summer Institute of Linguistics. Demands for the autonomy of the literacy council and indigenous control over the national program design and implementation, however, were rejected.

The INCAYAC and Nueva Vida projects are important because, first, they provided a space for Indians to negotiate as Indians, to demand that indigenous literacy and bilingual education policies should be distinguished from other educational policies. Pluriculturalism thus demanded a focus on the specific character, or distinctiveness, of indigenous culture from white-mestizo culture. The insistence that Indians should participate in the teaching and administration of bilingual education as well as in curriculum design, that Indians should be represented at all levels of decision making, and that Quichua names be recognized, all went beyond the mere expansion of participation and stressed the specific role to be played by Indians in designing and implementing indigenous policy. This meant that Indians had to be active participants, not mere recipients of state pluricultural policy. Indigenous organizations saw that making Indians visible as distinct and different political actors was the only way to attain equal citizenship. To the extent that the state acknowledged this difference, the pluricultural model could move beyond a mere recognition of diversity to the actual empowerment of indigenous actors.

Second, these meetings marked the beginning of an unofficial and tenuous pact between the state and activists that excluded demands for economic empowerment while allowing for some local ownership of literacy policies. For Indian activists, there was a tension between participating in government incorporation and continued resistance, since this pact clearly contained its own contradictions. To generate popular support and mobilization for its literacy program, the state had forcefully laid out the politically liberating and economically empowering potential of literacy, especially its ability to raise social consciousness and enable individuals to develop social alternatives, thus expanding their own citizenship. However, in the negotiations, state officials sought to divest cultural policy of any political content, dematerializing neoindigenismo, claiming that education and language policy alone were part of a specific "cultural" public sphere in which broader political and economic demands did not have a place.[16]

Bilingual and Bicultural Education and the Second Literacy Campaign, 1988–1990

The National Literacy Program declined considerably during the León Febres Cordero regime (1984–1988). Rodrigo Borja's campaign and presidency marked an important transition, since the candidate expressed a renewed commitment to indigenous affairs. Indigenous support for Borja's candidacy followed an intense campaign effort by the Izquierda Democrática (ID, Democratic Left) Party to obtain the indigenous vote. Chiriboga and Rivera found significant support for the ID in the rural highlands, in areas with a high density of indigenous population.[17] While the Febres Cordero regime (1984–1988) had marked a hiatus in rural literacy efforts, the Borja administration began a new literacy campaign and continued bilingual education.[18]

The state's cultural policy reached a peak in 1988, when national indigenous organizations were given more control over bilingual and bicultural education. In 1988, after significant pressure from the national indigenous confederation CONAIE, the Ministry of Education signed an agreement with the confederation that established the Dirección Nacional de Educación Intercultural Bilingüe (DINEIB, National Directorate of Bilingual Intercultural Education), to be administered directly by CONAIE. Housed in the Ministry of Education and Culture, DINEIB had a primarily indigenous staff and served the dual purpose of managing literacy and bilingual education projects.

The creation of DINEIB marked the peak of indigenous empowerment within the state's pluricultural agenda. The struggles over state pluriculturalism through education had led to an unprecedented protagonistic role for Indian organizations. Giving indigenous activists input into the curriculum at the national and local levels as well as their attainment of leadership positions in the national and provincial bilingual education coordinating offices were perhaps the most important gains of the educational policy enacted since redemocratization. Educational policy became the site where mestizo hegemony was broken, even if Indians continued to be excluded from decision making in general and from leadership positions in agricultural policy.

However, this transfer of power to CONAIE also laid bare the limits of indigenous power. It appeared that the politics of cultural policy had been exhausted as a site of empowerment and political growth for activists. Cultural policy had both legitimized a pluricultural agenda and met some basic indigenous demands, but it failed to go far enough for indigenous activists. This gap between the implementation of cultural policy and the absence of significant social policy and economic redistribution became the basis for a critique that would take the movement to a new stage. Additionally, the question of the distinctive qualities of indigenous culture had also come to a halt. Recognition of difference had occurred in educational policy, but indigenous claims that the state uphold customary law or recognize territorial rights on the basis of their status as Indians had been denied.

From Pluriculturalism to Plurinationalism

While state pluricultural policies had become institutionalized by the late 1980s, they had not led to an improvement in the socioeconomic status of the majority of Indians. In fact, indigenous people's standard of living decreased substantially during the 1980s.[19] By the mid-1980s the national CONAIE and the regional highland federation ECUARUNARI had begun to express public dissatisfaction with the general direction of state pluricultural policy. They raised three sets of issues. First, cultural policy had separated indigenous culture from its producers, leading to the potential manipulation and folklorization of indigenous cultures. Second, indigenous activists still lacked control of policy. Third, material demands were still excluded.

Hence, one of the movement's main goals was to lay bare the limitations of policy efforts that considered indigenous concerns as primarily educational. Activists who had called for separating the cultural and the material had, to an extent, recognized the falseness of such a dichotomy and were actively exploring ways to reconcile the two in their own pursuit of pluriculturalism. While they were initially eager to participate in the design and implementation of this cultural policy, they were ultimately unwilling to accept what they perceived as a dematerialized notion of culture and cultural policy offered by the state.

Activists' response to this problem was to promote Indians' self-identification as nationalities. Keep in mind that identifying indigenous peoples as distinct nationalities and Ecuador as a plurinational country was a strategy designed not only to achieve public recognition of the specific nature of indigenous rights, but also to counter a state view that dematerialized these rights. Rejecting the designation of "ethnic groups," indigenous peoples declared themselves nationalities and Ecuador a plurinational country, opting for a more materially informed conception of Indian identity and difference.

For indigenous activists, plurality was composed of at least three components: cultural rights, economic rights (including land), and political empowerment. They feared that while the first component was being addressed to a certain extent, the latter two were not. The bridges that had been built during the 1980s between those who mobilized around Indian identity and politics (*indianistas*), and highland activists who relied on a peasant identity and activism (*campesinistas*), were possible because of an agreement that there was no dichotomy between material and cultural demands. In this new perspective, there was a cultural dimension to all material needs and demands, and cultural issues and policy could not be kept separate from the people's material needs. Hence, the notion of a pluricultural nation, which for the state meant artistic festivals and bilingual education, conveyed a much broader set of goals for activists. Culture was understood in a broad sense, not only subsuming artistic production and language, but also encompassing a way of life, an economic rationale, a system of law, and the right to territory.

Activists did not perceive that the state was truly pluricultural, since its protection of pluriculturalism was occurring while land reform demands were set aside in the highlands, and colonization and further investment by transnational companies were being heavily promoted in the lowlands. Almost no significant land distribution had occurred since the late 1970s. Hence, despite the significant gains obtained from cultural policy, by the mid-1980s many regional organizations as well as CONAIE were claiming that culture, as defined by the state, consisted of an excessively reduced agenda.

All three issues—the manipulation of indigenous culture, the political underrepresentation of Indians, and the neglect of material demands in the state's definition of "culture"—involved taking into account indigenous cultural and historical uniqueness as a condition for participation at all levels of politics and policy. For indigenous activists, this strategy required embodying pluriculturalism—that is, struggling against the state's notion of homogeneous subject-citizens who are acted upon (and in which they would "disappear" and in fact had disappeared in the past) and insisting on the recognition of a particularity and heterogeneity that would become the basis for Indians' empowerment. This strategy evolved into the creation of plurinationalism as an alternative model of nation.

Since the early 1980s, and in response to state pluriculturalism, Indians had defined themselves as nationalities, not merely ethnic groups. Indigenous activists had argued that as nationalities with an ancestral presence and with their own cultural history, Indians were making claims that went beyond cultural and educational policy to include demands for their own territories, ways of life, laws, and forms of government. As nationalities, they were not mere cultures or ethnic minorities, but had the right to negotiate material and political demands with the state. Their rights of membership and citizenship, in this view, stemmed not only from their individual rights as citizens born in Ecuador, but from their collective rights as ancestral groups who had first occupied and governed the land. Giving them status as nationalities, they hoped, would not only differentiate them from other socially subordinate groups with claims, including blacks and most coastal peasants, but would assign them a special place at the negotiating table with state officials and nonindigenous political actors.

Additionally, by identifying themselves as nationalities, Indian activists sought to give political and economic substance to what had been considered primarily superstructural by the state. Plurinationalism also seemed to wed the material and political dimensions that the state had previously ignored to offer a critique of the nation. Plurinationalism was a strategic response to the state's neglect of the activists' political and material concerns. It was diametrically opposed to a construction of Ecuador as a mestizo, homogeneous, and unitary nation-state.

The discrepancy between state and indigenous organizations' understanding of pluriculturalism was not a mere semantic difference. It reflected a wide chasm between two understandings of culture. For the state, indigenous affairs were primarily located in policies involving cultural rights, preservation of history, folklore, and education. For activists, the differences in customs, dress, traditions, and political and social organization were signifiers of pluriculturalism, but the struggle for economic demands and political empowerment embodied it.

Indigenous activists' response to state pluriculturalism with a plurinational model was a direct result of a decade of cultural policy in which the distance between the state's use of culture and the activists' understanding of culture was shortened but not breached. While many activists had not completely worked out the details of their plurinational platform, it was clearly something distinct from the pluricultural policy pursued by the state. It had to include the substance and effects, and not only the signs, of ethnic and racial difference. The plurinational model as a response and challenge to state pluriculturalism would become more visible after the 1990 mobilization.

Uprising Politics

The transition from institutional to extrainstitutional or uprising politics occurred when indigenous activists were more integrated into the policy process than they ever had been, yet more certain that few of their demands would be met through regular channels. The massive national uprising of June 1990 symbolized the exhaustion of pluricultural politics as usual. During the mobilization, CONAIE presented a 16-point platform that included education and cultural rights but also demanded land rights and improvements in rural development and cost of living issues.

The persistent demand for land clashed with the state's policy of privileging education over land policy. The first set of negotiations (which involved CONAIE, ECUARUNARI, and CONFENIAE) were extremely difficult because Indian leaders had a long list of land conflicts that had not been resolved in years.[20] State officials and national-level activists reached an agreement to address and attempt to resolve 56 land conflicts. Other demands included in the platform were set aside for the future. The ability to address some long-standing land conflicts was considered a significant gain. While many activists later complained that other points of the platform were not addressed, the negotiation of land cases ended the belief that mere "cultural" policy would be sufficient.

Shortly after the uprising, indigenous activists went one step further. The focus on material demands was accompanied by a quest for a plurinational state model that would both incorporate indigenous activists' economic and political demands *and* recognize indigenous nationalities as collective entities that merited specific rights and concessions. In July 1990, CONAIE presented a declaration written by the Organization of Indigenous Peoples of Pastaza (OPIP) entitled "Agreement Concerning the Territorial Rights of the Indian Peoples of Pastaza." This document enumerated rights that were claimed as specifically designed for Indians as a collective and that clearly went beyond the mere extension of universal rights to Indians. It called for the concession of land rights, self-rule, political autonomy, respect for customary law, and Indian participation in decisions concerning oil exploration in Indian-inhabited lands. It also opposed military intervention in indigenous people's affairs and asked for the revision of military statutes.

Intertwining demands for socioeconomic improvement and political autonomy, the document gave priority to self-determination, autonomy, and territorial rights. While government officials had been willing to discuss economic demands, they refused to address political ones, particularly self-determination. When President Borja met with national Indian activists to discuss the proposal, he categorically rejected it and accused Indians of threatening national sovereignty by attempting to create a parallel state. He gave the Indians a long lecture on constitutional law, explaining how they were being unconstitutional and were threatening the nation's very existence.[21]

Not only was negotiation with the state impossible at this point, but also the president's statements about the proposal had a broader social effect. Other popular movements as well as sectors of the Left also warned about this movement's threat to national sovereignty. There was no political support for the OPIP proposal outside of CONAIE, and in most government and political circles there was an overarching rejection of it.

The development of an indigenous nationalist platform was met with effective state resistance expressed in coercion and cooptation, but most important, with constructions of the movement as antinational. The state's rejection of plurinationalism did not constitute a simple rhetorical move. It had very practical effects, enabling state officials to ignore crucial questions of political empowerment at the national level. In the state's view, no discussions of empowerment were possible because Indians had proven themselves incapable of respecting the nation-state. Hence, while the state promoted some forms of Indianness, it rejected others considered too radical. While the material component of plurinationalism was understood and to a certain extent accepted, the political dimension of plurinationalism was not. While activists continued to use nationalist rhetoric, they were forced to play down the plurinationalism platform and rely on other strategies.

However, in this exchange the state's own pluricultural model was transformed. Indigenous activists had appropriated state discourse in order to challenge it. The joint indigenous pressure for material demands and recognition of the political distinctiveness and autonomy of Indians eventually led the state to adopt a more flexible model of pluriculturalism that was open to the discussion of economic demands but closed to a more radical nationalist agenda that would empower Indians as collective subjects with the right to self-determination. Borja's "We will give you land, not sovereignty" reflected which "Indians" the state was willing to accept (those with certain economic demands) and which it would not (those seeking political autonomy). True to its word, after OPIP's lowland march between Puyo and Quito (supported by CONAIE) in 1992, the government guaranteed the Indians 1,115,000 hectares (16,000 square kilometers) of land to the Quichua, Shuara, Huaorani, and Zaparo nationalities but rejected the demand that Ecuador be considered a plurinational country. The land concession had its limits (it was only 55 percent of what the OPIP had demanded, and the titling that followed was incomplete and fragmented indigenous communities), but it was nonetheless significant.[22]

The impact of indigenous political discourse and practice on state pluriculturalism was evident by the late 1990s, with the proliferation of state- and NGO-funded rural development projects that addressed some of the material demands and state support for the creation of PRODEPINE, a program designed mainly by indigenous and black political activists to address the needs of Indians and blacks as nationalities. State pluriculturalism was no longer restricted to a narrow view of culture or limited to educational and literacy policy. While state officials had rejected many aspects of plurinationalism, a serious consideration of material demands and the establishment of a relationship that upheld the specific character of indigenous issues—two main tenets of plurinationalism—were given considerable weight in the pluricultural model. While the latter concession has not necessarily given Indians political power or autonomy, it legitimized the role of Indians as collective actors in the political arena. This change in state pluriculturalism was evident in the constitutional assembly of 1998. While indigenous activists had always argued for plurinationalism against pluriculturalism, in the assembly indigenous representatives fought to include the notion that Ecuador is a pluricultural country. While to this day, CONAIE and the broad umbrella of indigenous activists working with CONAIE pursue a plurinational state model as a central objective, they do so not by positing plurinationalism as the opposite of pluriculturalism (as suggested in the OPIP document), but by stretching, redefining, and expanding the state's pluricultural model. In the process, both plurinationalism and pluriculturalism have been transformed.

We have seen that in Ecuador both state pluriculturalism and indigenous plurinationalism were negotiated and contested in the process of resistance. There was a dialectical relationship between the politics of nationalism developed by movement activists and the culturalist policy promoted by the state. If the state had a narrower conception of culture in its understanding of pluriculturalism, the yielding of land, the political access, and the constitutional reform of 1998 reveal the impact of the indigenous thesis of plurinationalism in challenging state pluriculturalism and in pressuring the state to create a more material and politically informed pluricultural model—one that is more inclusive of economic and political rights of Indians as a collective.

Indigenous discourse on nationalities and plurinationalism gained strength and legitimacy as a critique of the state's corporatism and neoindigenista approach, and as a more viable alternative for social and political organization. The tensions and differences between pluriculturalism, as defined and exercised by the state, and plurinationalism, as conceived by indigenous activists, shaped Indian collective identity and forms of resistance throughout the 1990s. This analysis of state pluriculturalism and indigenous plurinationalism contributes to our understanding of how citizenship is constructed in contemporary Ecuador. In the liberal state model, the idea of a nation that is homogeneous, mestizo, sharing a common will, and upholding the individual rights of all its citizens coexists with a reality in which racially different subordinated social groups face de facto inequality and political and economic exclusion. This distance between the idealized political model and reality means that in a "liberal" state, Indians and indigenous issues are in fact rendered invisible.

In this context, indigenous activists in Ecuador and Latin America are engaged in a struggle quite opposite to the struggles of racially subordinate groups in countries where inequality and segregation were legislated, such as South Africa and the United States. While the latter groups fought to be considered equal in a legal system that differentiated them in order to exclude them, the former fight to embody themselves, to render themselves visible and different in a system in which their invisibility has led to their de facto exclusion. They seek, therefore, the "igualdad en la diferencia," or the equality in difference that is so often mentioned by contemporary national activists. This phrase represents the desire to be recognized as distinct as a necessary step to achieving equal rights with other Ecuadorians. Moreover, it reveals the political conviction of many activists that only through the politicization and public recognition of this specificity—a key component of plurinationalism—can a fuller and more equal citizenship be obtained.

This contemporary version of differentiated citizenship is both similar to and different from previous modes of distinction arrived at in the interaction between Indians in the state. On the one hand, it is connected to long traditions of indigenous communal rights and separate indigenous republics. Group rights cannot be understood as merely the outcome of contemporary movement politics; they are also the legacy of corporatism in Ecuador and Latin America. Indians in the early national period fought to maintain the tribute, as it guaranteed their special status and protection under the Republic of Indians. However, even under a liberal model of citizenship, Indians used informal mechanisms to utilize patronage relations to their material advantage, always highlighting their special status as protégés and frequently defining themselves as "miserable Indians."

There is, however, a crucial distinction between contemporary and previous practices of "differentiated citizenship." Today's struggle for "equality in difference" questions and challenges the existing citizenship model in ways that previous struggles did not. Colonial relations were based on a corporate model in which indigenous peoples were considered childlike protégés of the state and part of a separate republic. Indians used these dynamics to their advantage to both resist and ensure survival, but they did not overturn the model. Indigenous struggles in the nineteenth and early twentieth centuries used state rhetoric and practices to their advantage, emphasizing the special status of Indians to defend their land, identity, and livelihood. They neither challenged the universal liberal citizenship model nor proposed a replacement.

Contemporary indigenous activism, by contrast, has led to the formal recognition of an embodied pluriculturalism that is now ingrained in the constitution and has become the basis for a number of collective demands. Indians are not merely recipients of state policy but central participants in state formation. The most important legacies of contemporary indigenous activism are the challenge to the liberal model of citizenship and the state's formal assumption of the tensions between liberalism and difference that may pave the way toward a new model of differentiated citizenship. In pluricultural Ecuador, the articulation between the universal and the particular has become a necessary part of the state's agenda and cannot be easily cast aside.

For some scholars, liberal citizenship and differentiated citizenship are not necessarily incompatible, as a hybrid model of citizenship could be premised on universal citizenship based on individual rights *and* differential rights for indigenous people.[23] However, this coexistence is not without tensions. For example, despite the important gains of the contemporary indigenous movement, national politicians have rejected attempts to create separate indigenous circumscriptions within the Ecuadorian polity, based on the constitutional premise that Ecuador is a pluricultural country. The attachment to a liberal model of citizenship in the face of differentiated citizenship practices underscores one way in which pluriculturalism and plurinationalism are still being contested. If Ecuadorian history teaches us anything, it is that resolving these tensions will not be in the hands of political theorists, but will emerge from the persistent and ever-changing struggles between indigenous peoples and the state.

10

Sons of Indians and Indian Sons

Military Service, Familial Metaphors, and Multicultural Nationalism

BRIAN R. SELMESKI

Indians in contemporary Ecuador are involved in the continual process of state formation through obligatory military service or conscription. Military service is mandatory for all male citizens and permanent residents eighteen years of age and over, according to Article 188 of the 1998 constitution. Unlike the situation in other parts of Latin America, where young men are recruited for military service through coercive techniques known as "club and rope," many conscripts in Ecuador are eager to complete their service.[1] Ecuador's armed forces use a carrot-and-stick approach that combines a slick marketing campaign to promote conscription to the masses with mild sanctions levied on those who fail to comply. Partly as a result, the Ecuadorian military annually conscripts approximately twenty thousand young men by lottery, with little resistance.[2]

The majority of recruits come from rural areas and includes many who identify themselves as Indians *(indígenas)*, making conscription one of the state's primary vehicles to engage native peoples on at least two levels. On the one hand, young indigenous men are directly engaged as individuals in an institution that plays a central role in the state system or apparatus.[3] Simultaneously, military service creates a discursive space where the state idea, and concomitant notions of nation and citizenship, are challenged by and forced to accommodate an increasingly autonomous and contentious process of collective Indian self-identification.

The military remains understudied and poorly understood by scholars and citizens alike, despite its centrality in many Ecuadorians' lives and in the functioning of the state. Even those unfamiliar with the details of military service realize that conscripts' sacrifices are significant and their experiences are not altogether agreeable. They are locked down for one year on stark military bases. They are subjected to strict social, moral, and disciplinary codes and incur severe punishment for violations they or their peers may commit. They live in communal dormitories with a hundred or more other recruits, with no privacy and inadequate plumbing. After basic training, their work duties are often boring and occasionally hazardous. Many conscripts become injured or ill while in service, and accidental death, while uncommon, receives heavy and sensational coverage in the popular press. Yet, in spite of these conditions, almost all young men who report to the *cuarteles* or garrisons to complete their obligatory service do so eagerly and of their own free will.[4] In fact, of the nearly eight hundred conscripts I surveyed in 1999–2000, more than 31 percent indicated that they had not been selected in the draft but volunteered for service.

Ecuadorian citizens, military officers, and Andean scholars often emphasize the obligatory nature of conscription and explain its popularity with Indians in terms of the status it confers upon veterans within their communities.[5] Likewise, public discourse emphasizes the highly valued *libreta militar* or military ID card, as it provides entrée to a gamut of civil rights. Without the document, it is difficult to gain employment with the state or in private industry, and it is impossible to leave the country, acquire a driver's license, open a bank account, or qualify for a bank loan. Yet exemptions are generously granted for men who support their parents, are married, live in a "free union," have dependent children, are matriculated students, or are disabled. Moreover, those who do not wish to serve but are not granted exemptions can easily and legally purchase the document. The price is modest and within the reach of even many poor families.

Popular opinion also suggests that many young men join the Ecuadorian Army as conscripts because they cannot find other work. In fact, in Chimborazo Province in 1999–2000, over 87 percent of the nearly eight hundred conscripts I surveyed reported working prior to entering military service.[6] While wages in the civilian economy were paltry and underemployment high, recruits' pay made those figures look generous. Conscripts earned a mere $11.20 per month, and 92 percent reported earning more prior to entering the cuartel. Military officers argued that the "free" room, board, and uniforms made up for this difference, when in fact the Army discounted $4.00 from their meager $11.20 paycheck for food, laundry, and infrequently exercised movie, pool, and gym privileges. The result was that most recruits took a pay cut upon entering the cuartel. Those from distant provinces could not even afford to go home for their bimonthly weekend passes.

While the status afforded those who complete their military service and the benefits of the libreta militar are intriguing aspects of conscription's attractiveness for subalterns, they are inadequate to explain the draft's remarkable success among the highland Indians of contemporary Ecuador. Recruits are equally motivated by a peculiar mix of civic duty, desire for self-improvement, and naturalized beliefs about military service and the nation or *Patria* (often mistranslated as fatherland, but gendered by the military as feminine). Conscripts readily embrace aspects of the military's belief system that resonate with their expectations and desires, enabling the state system from below. Yet, simultaneously, they quietly reject those elements of military culture that conflict with their core beliefs, creating tensions and fissures in the seemingly unitary state idea and nation. Gramscian hegemonic theory helps to explain consent and resistance as part of a discursive process "through which power and meaning are contested, legitimated and redefined at all levels of society" through a combination of coercion and consent.[7]

Conscripts' words and actions show them to be active and savvy participants in a negotiated social process rather than hapless pawns, victims of false consciousness and/or military authority. As William Roseberry concludes, "What hegemony constructs, then, is not a shared ideology but a common material and meaningful framework for living through, talking about, and acting upon social orders characterized by domination."[8] Or as Marisol de la Cadena describes it, hegemony is "a dynamic of power struggle characterized by constant agreements and disputes, and by domination and insubordination, [that] produces a conflict-laden consensus, usually narrow, yet politically crucial."[9]

Thus, military service, while imposed by the state, is also the forum where young men, their parents, professional soldiers, and politicians craft, express, and act upon their distinct but mutually supportive discursive frameworks. Ecuadorian conscription is so successful as a means of incorporating Indians into the state physically (as recruits) and ideologically (as contemporary citizens and primordial forefathers) for three reasons: first, the Army's distinctive style of multicultural nationalism; second, the notion of personal formation; and finally, the metaphorical portrayal of the nation—and Army—as family.

Managing "the Indian Problem": The Demise of *Mestizaje* and the Rise of Multiculturalism

Multiculturalism is a relatively new organizing framework for members of the armed forces who have not always been amenable to accepting cultural and ethnic difference in uniform. Nevertheless, Indians in particular have long been a topic of fascination and preoccupation for nationalist-minded officers. Before the early 1990s, most of the Army's efforts to approach and engage indigenous peoples were shaped by an intense preoccupation with *mestizaje.*[10] According to this belief system, the military and other elites conceived of the Ecuadorian nation in ethnic terms, as a mestizo nation. Theoretically, all inhabitants could become citizens, to a greater or lesser extent, without miscegenation by shedding their "otherness" (that is, their "Indianness" or "Blackness") and becoming cultural mestizos. A retired recruiting officer commented in 1998, "In the armed forces, we only have citizens; we don't have *indios* and non-*indios.* In fact, we have no indios in racial terms; . . . once you're in the army you're a citizen." Such thinking is not unusual among officers. In 2000, one battallion commander said: "Lately you see more indígena conscripts in the cuartel . . . precisely because we have respected their culture, so the indígena respects his obligation [to serve]." The elite's discourses of mestizaje draw heavily on *blanqueamiento* or whitening. The Ecuadorian version of this racist ideology postulates that Blacks and Indians will, if properly motivated, voluntarily abandon their respective cultures in favor of white culture in order to move up the ethnic hierarchy.[11]

Ecuadorian mestizaje was therefore never an ideologically neutral blending; it was a highly directional, charged, and biased project intimately linked to nation building. These characteristics were perhaps best summarized in President General Rodríguez Lara's now infamous proclamation, "We all become white when we accept the goals of the national culture."[12] Yet indígenas were not always cooperative from the perspective of elites; as Weismantel and Eisenman point out, historically, "the fundamental problem in the Andes lies in the inability (or stubborn refusal) of the Indian to become white—or white enough."[13] This "stubborn refusal" on the part of Ecuadorian indígenas was precisely what sparked the Army's reconsideration during the 1990s of what the Patria is and should be.

In 1990, Ecuador's nascent national indigenous movement, the Confederación de Nacionalidades Indígenas del Ecuador (CONAIE, Confederation of Indigenous Nationalities of Ecuador) orchestrated its first national strike to protest the horrendous conditions of the country's Indian population, to emphasize the need for land reform, to demand cultural rights, and to seek a constitutional amendment declaring Ecuador to be "a plurinational state." The *levantamiento,* or uprising, shut down the crucial Pan-American Highway, paralyzed the country, occupied symbolically important public buildings, and announced the indigenous movement's arrival as a powerful and organized national political actor.

In the wake of the uprising, military officers at all levels became increasingly focused on the "Indian problem" and questions of national identity. These issues quickly emerged in the theses of the military's advanced educational institutes as well as in the reports of the individual branches of the armed forces. Officers gradually came to grips with a "new" reality: there were still a lot of Indians in Ecuador after years of mestizaje-inspired programs; the indígenas were becoming increasingly organized, presenting new "threats" to national integrity; and the "Indian problem" was not going away. The conclusion of these studies and debates was as obvious as it was irrefutable: the mestizaje project had failed.

Ecuador's armed forces, drawing on a long tradition of progressive thinking, gradually developed a new belief system.[14] The military's new institutional culture is based largely on a foundation of multiculturalism that recognizes the irrefutable differences between the country's numerous indigenous, racial, and regional groups. While recognizing the right of groups to self-identify and maintain their distinctness, the military stops short of valorizing differences, emphasizing the communal over the particular. As with cultural and educational policy, official military doctrine rejects wholesale the indigenous movement's claim to represent Ecuador's indigenous *nations*; officially the military insists that the state is pluriethnic but uninational.[15] To recognize native peoples as nations would be to jeopardize both the physical and imaginary integrity of the Patria. To ignore native peoples, on the other hand, could precipitate the same unthinkable consequences.

Indians, the high command concluded, must be strategically engaged and the material roots of their discontent and misery addressed in order to assure the future of the Patria. Drawing on and modifying earlier, Vietnam era–inspired counterinsurgency projects, the Army launched a vast development assistance program. Their efforts aimed to provide medical, dental, and educational services, construct basic infrastructure, and promote the development of microenterprises in indigenous communities neglected by the state.[16] On a more personal and transformational level, conscription was thought to be the primary mechanism to facilitate this contact, control the Indian population, and diffuse the threat it posed to peace and order.[17] Respecting indigenous culture was believed to be the key to attracting Indians to the cuarteles in the first place, as the commander quoted earlier remarked.

Absent from this new "strategic engagement" doctrine is any mention of transforming native people's sense of Indianness. This is not to say that the military no longer engages in the moral regulation of indigenous conscripts, but that the focus of these efforts has changed. Thus, although today the military says it is acceptable to be an Indian, the armed forces still define what a "good Indian" is. The Ecuadorian Army's new multiculturalism, then, is simultaneously paternalistic and progressive, as it recognizes Indians as part of the nation, but only if they abide by the terms set forth by the powerful. Nor has military multiculturalism fully escaped its *mestizaje-blanqueamiento* origins.

Professional soldiers persist in their belief that Indian conscripts will voluntarily forsake foolish and detrimental aspects of their indigenous upbringing for more "modern" and "productive" (usually mestizo) alternatives. They do not believe, however, that young indigenous men must be made into cultural mestizos through conscription, as earlier military leaders advocated. As long as Indians abide by the parameters of citizenship established by the military, they are considered potential contributors to national development as Indians and need not alter their sense of self-identification.

For contemporary Army officers, being a "good Indian" means one must first be a good man and a good citizen. Yet few indigenous conscripts, nor the majority of their white and mestizo peers, meet these standards. Accordingly, conscription is more focused on transforming recruits socially than militarily. With its mere five-to-eight-week basic training period, it does not try to make young men into professional soldiers.[18] Instead, basic training initiates conscripts' social conversion through a process referred to as personal formation, or learning "good customs" or habits ranging from brushing one's teeth, to valuing hard work and honesty, to understanding the importance of a job well done.

Officers, enlisted personnel, and conscripts all distinguish personal formation from intellectual formation (that is, schooling), physical formation (fitness), and military formation (combat training). While these processes are interrelated, personal formation is the bedrock of the four, the indispensable component of complete formation. The centrality of personal formation to military service and national development is, in many ways, a continuation of the "civilizing mission" initiated by the foreign military officers contracted in the early 1900s to modernize and professionalize Latin America's armed forces.[19] Then, as today, conscription was considered fundamental to the larger nation-building process, a way to convert society's outcasts into productive citizens. As one soldier neatly summed it up, this is done through the inculcation of values, specifically "honor, truth, dignity, loyalty"; and "the formation of these values makes one's sense of patriotism and nationality grow."

The military considers personal formation to be the greatest contribution of military training because it extends beyond the individual and has the potential to renovate the whole of society. As another professional soldier noted candidly, "The problem with Ecuador is that we do things in a mediocre way. We are accustomed to doing things the way we want without exerting much effort. In the cuartel we teach these recruits how to do things right—how to comply with their duty. This, in turn, contributes to the development of the Patria." The benefits of personal formation for the nation are basic to the discursive framework that stimulates, justifies, and organizes conscription. When the military fuses this formation discourse with the nation-and-Army-as-family metaphor, they generate a model in which fathers (professional soldiers) form their sons (conscripts) into good men by teaching them to respect and love their mother (the Patria) regardless of, and at times despite, their ethnic or racial characteristics.[20]

Whether or not indigenous recruits in fact change as a result of conscription is impossible to ascertain at this point in my research. What is certain is that by accepting aspects of the military's discourse, indígenas gain favorable standing in the cuartel and tap into the reservoir of public recognition and new opportunities afforded to all former conscripts. Consequently, highland Indians in contemporary Ecuador often volunteer for conscription and espouse the military's formation rhetoric in an effort to develop a closer relationship with the Patria and state without abandoning their indigenous identity. In the Army's eyes, they are becoming "modern" Indian-citizens.

Military Myths: Creating the Patria and Ecuador's "Glorious Indian Past"

The military's contemporary discourse of multicultural nationalism is built on the collective foundation provided by a taken-for-granted nationalist account of Ecuador's territorial and cultural origins. In the words of Lieutenant Colonel Hernán Altamirano, "[We are] the inheritors of a thousand heroic acts that mark the courageousness of an Indian race such as ours that has demonstrated to the world that in Ecuador there are no fainthearted men but rather soldiers and citizens of honor."[21] The armed forces use this mythical history to portray the Patria as authentic and unique and the Army as aggrieved sons of an indomitable indigenous warrior tradition that should logically incorporate contemporary Indians as citizens. To accomplish this, conscripts receive extensive instruction in history, geography, and civics early in their basic training. Recruits must learn not only to march and to shoot, but also about the Patria they are obliged to love and defend. Once these classes have planted the seeds of multiculturalism, the myths are reinforced daily through ritual, art, music, and discourse in what Goffman calls the "total institution."[22] In the process, shared bonds and motivations are generated between Indians and non-Indians, forming the building blocks of a multicultural military and national identity. The bedrock underlying this process is the Army's national origin myth.

In the traditional anthropological sense, myths are stories people tell about their origins and history in order to understand the world and their place in it.[23] Myths are usually a delicate balance of fiction and fact; too fictional and they are unbelievable, too factual and they lose their ability to capture and persuade multiple audiences. Through their consumption and retelling, myths assume the quality of unquestionable truths and are therefore rarely scrutinized. When history becomes mythologized in literate societies, tensions and questions are minimized and deflected until all that remains is a story. As the young lieutenant explained to his conscript-pupils, the class "is like a story. We all know it, we are simply remembering. . . . History is a story, OK?"

For the Ecuadorian military, this story is based largely on eighteenth-century Jesuit Juan de Velasco's *Historia del Reino de Quito* (History of the Kingdom of Quito).[24] The Army's choice of historical touchstones is not capricious or necessarily responsible for converting the historian's work into a myth. Velasco is the foundational reference for the Ecuadorian educational system and has been interpreted in countless ways.[25] Each group molds the account slightly differently—partly consciously, partly unconsciously—to serve their ends and reflect their worldview, making their tellings parallel, though not mutually exclusive, mythologized histories.

In part, the Army's use of Velasco reflects the importance of the story to the institution's efforts to promote a unitary national identity upon which they base their efforts to integrate and engage Indians. Conscripts' lessons are essentially the same as those given to senior officers at the War Academy, where the history textbook concludes that "the Kingdom of Quito is a sociological and historical reality."[26] The preoccupation can also be seen as reflecting the military's goal of completing and/or complementing the national educational process. The military continues to cling to the education-as-emancipation philosophy of the Roldós administration.

While it is doubtful that conscripts are emancipated through this instruction, the Army's concern with supplementing their educational background is well founded. Recruits are indeed poorly educated: 33 percent have had six or fewer years of primary school and another 29 percent have completed only one to three years of secondary education. Moreover, many conscripts attended substandard rural schools where the quality of education did not meet the Army's standards. Interestingly, though, there is no data to suggest that indigenous conscripts are less educated than their mestizo and white peers. Self-identified Indians in my survey were, on average, as educated as mestizos and had one more year of formal schooling than self-identified whites. Prejudices and statistics aside, the national origin myth is actively directed at both Indians and non-Indians, since its central importance is to create a unified sense of belonging and relating to the state.

The Army is eager to reintroduce all young people to the myth to ensure that they are processing the story "correctly." Where previous exposure to Velasco may have emphasized other aspects of his work, the Army's version is not surprisingly militarized, casting the Inca as fierce and competent warriors. The story explains the Inca conquest of present-day Ecuador and subsequent civil war both by tapping into analogous myths that surround the country's twentieth-century border conflict with Peru and by drawing on a series of family metaphors that subtly reinforce the conscription model. It pays minimal attention to what may have been other motivations for territorial expansion by the Inca and earlier peoples who inhabited contemporary Ecuador.

According to the Army's version of Velasco, narrated to recruits in history classes, Ecuador was first inhabited by the simple Quitus people who occupied the present-day highland province of Pichincha, site of the capital, Quito. The Caras, a more sophisticated group who migrated from Central America to Ecuador's coastal area and then to the central highlands, subsequently conquered the Quitus. The fusion of the Quitus and Caras produced the Shyri Confederation, an empire ruled by leaders known as Shyri. While essentially peaceful, the Shyris eventually set their sights on uniting with the Puruhaes from present day Chimborazo Province. The ruling Shyri leader had only one child, a daughter, whom he offered in marriage to Duchicela, chief of the Puruhaes. After uniting the groups and subsequently crafting alliances with the Cañaris (from Ecuador's present-day Azuay Province), Caranquis (from Imbabura), and Paltas (from Loja), the Shyris formed the Kingdom of Quito.

This story conveniently connects Ecuador's major colonial highland cities (Quito, Riobamba, Cuenca, Ibarra, and Loja) in a pre-Incaic alliance. Moreover, the key union between the Shyris and the Puruhaes was achieved not through conquest, but by intermarriage. The two came together as family, both figuratively and literally. This fusion occurred in the macro sense as well, with Shyris and Puruhaes intermarrying to form Quiteños (of the Kingdom of Quito, not to be confused with the Quitus, Velasco's original inhabitants of the highlands) in a formula that predates and foreshadows mestizaje, here as miscegenation, rather than cultural mixing.

The military's account of Velasco's mythical history continues by claiming that shortly after its formation, the Incas invaded the Kingdom of Quito. Unlike the formation of the Kingdom of Quito, Inca integration was not always a peaceful process. Epic tales of Quiteño resistance include stories of

Inca Tupac Yupanqui's extended clashes necessary to subdue the rebellious Cañaris and his son Huayna Capac's slaughter of thirty thousand Caranquis at Yaguarcocha (Lake of Blood) when they refused to submit to his rule.[27] The Inca invasion and conquest brought about the end of the Kingdom of Quito and marked the birth of Tawantinsuyo, the Inca Empire of Four Parts.

Previously the Inca Empire had had only three divisions, and the Ecuadorian military insists that the fourth, Chinchasuyo, was not properly formed until Inca Huayna Capac married Princess Pacha XVI of the former Kingdom of Quito. Of this union was born Atahualpa in the city of Tomebamba, present-day Cuenca, Ecuador. Atahualpa was an exceptional child whose "mother, Princess Pacha, guided his feelings along the path of justice, honor, respect and love for all his vassals."[28] Atahualpa was neither the first-born nor the only son of Huayna Capac, who had other wives and sons, including Huascar, who resided in Cuzco. Unable to decide which son should lead the empire, and anticipating a conflict with the recently arrived Spaniards, Huayna Capac divided his empire between Atahualpa, who ruled the north (the former, and once again, Kingdom of Quito), and Huascar, who ruled the south.

Huascar, unhappy with ruling only part of Tahuantinsuyo, began making political overtures to the Cañaris and eventually occupied the region with his army. Atahualpa reluctantly mobilized his army and after a prolonged struggle defeated the "Peruvian Incas" at the Battle of Quipaypan. As the lieutenant-storyteller explained to recruits, by defeating Huascar in the "first war of Peruvian Aggression," Atahualpa became the "first Ecuadorian Inca to defeat Peru." The Inca Empire was reunited under Ecuadorian Atahualpa, but was weakened by the war and vulnerable to the advances of the recently arrived Spanish conquistadors.

The recurring and important role of family merits emphasis. Victorious Atahualpa, a moral beacon for his people, is depicted as blessed with a wise, caring, and loving mother, which leaves one questioning Huascar's maternal influence. What is more, the story suggests that had the jealous brother and expansionist-minded Peruvian not meddled in the internal matters of his half-brother's Kingdom of Quito, the war could have been averted. This rereading of prehistory casts the Inca civil war as both an international family feud and a conflict over ancient territorial rights. The myth also implies that had they worked together, Atahualpa and Huascar might have repelled the Spanish invasion. Thus, conscripts are taught that harmony, cooperation, and tolerance—as well as nurturing mothers—are the keys to national success.

In the same lesson, conscripts also learn that the definitive battle between Spaniards and the Incas was fought in Tiocajas at the foot of the Tungurahua volcano. The young lieutenant instructor pontificated, "When the Quiteño

Incas were at the point of declaring victory [against the Spaniards], [volcano] Mamá Tungurahua exploded, and the Indians, thinking it was the gods' punishment—because they believed all such elevations to be gods—all fled, terrified. Rumiñahui tried in vain to calm them, but it was impossible." This story highlights the parallels between the military's historical portrayal of indígenas and their current embodiment as conscripts by depicting Inca foot soldiers as competent warriors but undisciplined and superstitious Indians nonetheless. Likewise, it demonstrates the challenges faced by a noble officer corps—once Inca, today mestizo—to command such foolish troops, reinforcing the urgency of the formation process.

The officer responsible for telling this story made the most of every opportunity to compare his pupils with his historical subjects. At one point he extemporized, "The indios [Incas] were illiterates, just like you—no, they were worse than you. And those indios were like you [in another way too], like when you are told to march and you don't know what to do, they were like that. Worse than you recruits!" The contemptible qualities of ignorance, inaction, and illiteracy help to account for the Spanish conquest of Ecuador and reinforce the need to "form" contemporary Indians, illiterates, and other deficient individuals.[29] Not all Incas were foolish in this myth, and the officer completed the story by recounting how Atahualpa's fiercely patriotic half-brother, Rumiñahui, ensured that the city of Quito was razed, treasure hidden, and temple virgins slain to prevent the conquerors from reaping the rewards of their victory.

In this telling of Velasco's history, Rumiñahui is cast as the first commanding general of the Ecuadorian Army. While he could not stop the occupation of the Patria by the Spanish, he did prevent the rape of the capital, its treasure, and the virgins of Quito's Temple of the Sun. This highly sexualized reading of the conquest creates Rumiñahui as an honorable man who fulfills his duty to protect the nascent Patria and the integrity of its women, a key concern for contemporary soldiers. Not surprisingly, today Rumiñahui ranks high in the pantheon of Ecuadorian military heroes, and the military's bank is named after him.[30]

Moreover, the contemporary Ecuadorian Army is portrayed as the descendant of the Inca Army. The modern force is symbolically built upon the demolished institution much as the Spaniards constructed Cuzco's Santo Domingo Church on the foundation of the Inca Coricancha. Just as the architectural effort was believed to motivate Indians to convert to Catholicism, the military's myth may help convince Indians to serve today. Finally, by imagining Ecuador as "not Peru" and emphasizing Peruvian aggression, the military neatly obscures Ecuador's marginal status as an *audiencia* during the colonial period, first under the rule of the Viceroyalty of Peru then later New Granada (present-day Colombia). Thus they establish a more direct lineage from the Kingdom of Quito to the Republic of Ecuador and can more clearly juxtapose the Army of Rumiñahui to the Army of Independence.

Both the Ecuadorian Patria and Army were figuratively born through the struggles for independence. The Army is cast as both a father figure, having impregnated the colonial citizens of the *Madre Patria* in the New World with their spirit of patriotism, and midwife to the Patria's birth through their military campaigns. Thus the military both conceived the Patria through the actions of individual criollo leaders and delivered the Patria by mobilizing the population-at-arms. Present-day military officers are prone to reread this process in contemporary multicultural terms. One, for example, waxes eloquent when declaring that the Ecuadorian military "is made up of mestizos, cholos, *montuvios*, and indios, and always has been."[31] The armies of independence heroes Sucre, Bolívar, and Flores are recast in this telling as multicultural forces like the present military.

While recognizing the contributions of non-criollos to the country's history, this revisionist presentation neatly erases coercive recruiting practices and indigenous participation in the royalist forces. More fundamentally, it ignores the multiple motivations for and inequalities associated with military service. As Mallon demonstrates for Peru, Indians' motivations to serve in the creation or defense of the Patria were rarely the same as those of the elite.[32] In fact, since independence, the bulk of indígena participation in the institution has resulted from wartime conscription; peacetime integration into the Ecuadorian Army began only recently. Octogenarian veterans of early recruiting efforts are quick to note there were very few Indians in their cohorts. Nor have they ever been integrated vertically. Even today, there are no Indian generals and almost no officers who have indigenous names or who openly claim to be descendants of Indians, except in the metaphorical sense.

The military's historical "story" also minimizes indigenous contributions to (as well as direct attacks on) the early republic by portraying Ecuador as a state without a nation due to conflicts between mestizos. Between 1830 and 1895, allegiance was primarily a local phenomenon where caudillos exerted tremendous control over the population. Private armies were commonplace among large landholders throughout the country, promoting internal conflict and provincial, rather than national, loyalty. President García Moreno kept the standing Army small and favored the Catholic Church as his primary governing tool. Nevertheless, as "father figure" to the national family, he perpetuated the familial metaphor. General Eloy Alfaro's Liberal Revolution sought to secularize the state, integrate the country, and create a powerful unified national Army with which to rule. With the demise of the church as the preferred instrument of governance, Alfaro added a new layer to the metaphor by portraying the military as the "high priests of the Patria."[33]

In addition to having birthed the nation through the War of Independence, in the twentieth century, the armed forces also assumed the role of arbiter of Ecuador's future and past. Governments, charged with administering the state, come and go, failing routinely. The military perceives itself as an unvarying and competent institution, the trustees of the Patria, which is their reason for being. The relationship is symbiotic: if there were no armed forces, there would be no Patria; were there no Patria, there would be no need for a military. The consequences of this model range from military interventions in the democratic process to the variety of efforts they have launched to engage the indigenous population.

By employing their particular version of Velasco's historical myth, the military has recast native peoples from "degenerate indios," as liberal discourse portrayed them, into vanquished but once formidable combatants.[34] These conclusions, in turn, become part of the myth as it mutates, becomes reified, and is retold within the cuartel.[35] More generally, the myth helps members of the armed forces reconcile Ecuador's indigenous past with its (still) Indian present. Multicultural nationalism is far more palatable when Indians are a source of pride, albeit historically. Through conscription the Army does not aim to reinstate highland Indians as warriors so much as integrate them into the state and shape them into good citizens who will love, defend, and develop the Patria. As in the tale of the prodigal son, today the once "degenerate Indians" are being welcomed back into the family.

Fathers, Mothers, and Sons: Discipline and Duty in the Patriarchal Home

A sign at the entrance of the Riobamba basic training center reads, "The Patria does not exist without the love of her sons." A senior recruiting official confirmed the prevalence of such thinking about the Army and Patria in familial terms, commenting, "When a young citizen reports for his [military] service, the unit commander becomes like his father." When the father welcomes his prodigal indigenous sons back into the national family, he conducts the reunion in his home, the cuartel. The Army's home is a well-organized, efficient, orderly, and self-sufficient unit. The cuartel is structured both materially, with "a place for everything and everything in its place," and socially. Each family member, father, son, and Mother, has a specific, prescribed role: fathers direct, sons comply, and Mother nurtures and inspires.[36] Sons are subjected to this paternalistic moral order immediately upon entering the cuartel, yet their experiences in service are often at odds with their expectations of military life and the reality of the formation process. The family metaphor is one of the keys to negotiating this tension, yet it also contains pitfalls for indígenas' participation.

Young men, indigenous or not, are often drawn to military service by infrequently examined cultural undercurrents. Like their northern urban counterparts, most conscripts were raised in a television culture.[37] The predominance of martial arts, police, and military films translated into Spanish and shown on Ecuadorian TV is staggering. Conscripts consistently named such "fight movies" as their preferred genre of entertainment. The resulting "Rambo factor," named in honor of the muscle-bound soldier extraordinaire and quasi–patron saint of conscripts, is a powerful motivating force.[38]

Once inside the cuartel, recruits are quickly disabused of this romantic daydream by the tasks they are assigned as well as the highly regimented and routinized nature of daily life. Peeling potatoes, cutting grass, and mopping floors hardly seem like appropriate chores for the descendants of Colonel Altamirano's "courageous Indian race" and Rambo wannabes. Most of conscripts' responsibilities are menial chores, and outside the cuartel many would even be considered women's duties. Yet inside the cuartel, with a dearth of actual women, sons embrace these tasks because fathers portray them as an integral part of the formation process. If performing women's work is what one's father demands in order to become well formed—the underlying goal of conscription—most recruits comply willingly.

Nevertheless, recruits are eager to project the Rambo image to those outside the cuartel, particularly women. For example, prior to Mother's Day, conscripts line up to pay a hefty portion of their paycheck to a professional soldier-cum-photographer who snaps the young men posing behind carnival-like cardboard cutouts of a soldier of Herculean proportions. The same photographer periodically visits the barracks with a rifle and maroon airborne beret in hand to momentarily capture recruits as rugged paratroopers in photos destined for sweethearts and fiancées.

Conscripts suspect that their fathers and brothers know better, but they believe that their mothers and girlfriends, many of whom have never set foot on a military base, will be receptive to portrayals of "their men" as swashbuckling commandos. By depicting themselves in Ramboesque terms, conscripts eliminate the need to explain the formation process in all its contradictory and nuanced aspects to "their women." In fight movie terms, the Karate Kid did not brag about painting and waxing in order to learn martial arts. What mattered was his ability to fight and win. Likewise, for conscripts the important part of formation is that one is well formed, not how one achieves this status.

These photos, and the letters that accompany them, also permit conscripts to become Rambo outside the cuartel in a way they never can inside. Despite the fact that they spend their days peeling potatoes, someone sees them as tough paratroopers, ready to defend the Patria at a moment's notice. Like the petty crack dealers Philippe Bourgeois describes as portraying themselves as Vietnam veterans when they were in fact disqualified, discharged, or deserters, conscripts confabulate their identity through the skillful manipulation of images, stories, and performance.[39] While somewhat deceitful, the practice makes sense for conscripts who see military service as a way to demonstrate their stability and potential as sons and husbands to their mothers and potential wives.[40]

While conscripts consider the outside world as a place to create a self-image to suit their interests, they also recognize that life inside the cuartel is far more regimented and focused on learning. On the one hand, it is like the natal home, where basic life skills are imparted by parents. On the other hand, the cuartel is similar to a single-sex boarding school with its dormitories, dining hall, male bonding, and pranks. Also present are the unavoidable lessons to be recited, memorized, and regurgitated. One indigenous conscript's father captured the scholastic nature of the cuartel when he observed that "young people learn things here. Not spelling and math, but respect and discipline," and military officers have frequently expressed this view.[41] When the poetics are stripped away from their comments, they are speaking about the values that form the core of personal formation. Couching formation in educational terms is yet another example of the frame alignment that helps make conscription so successful in contemporary Ecuador.

Like traditional schools, the cuartel is a patriarchal space where fathers make the rules. Absent is the give-and-take between indigenous and state actors negotiating a bilingual education agenda. Instead, the Army sets the criteria for the indigenous sons' reintegration into the nation-as-family. Conscripts, as sons and students, are required to obey. If they do, they can overcome their unfortunate conditions of poverty, unemployment, lack of education, and even counterproductive indigenous characteristics. Indians must therefore submit to the process of formation like other recruits to become good sons and new men. Most do, justifying their new relationship to the state in familial terms.

While the Army's goal of forming recruits is applied to all conscripts, fathers, who administer the process, are not as uniform as one might suspect. Commanders differ in how they set standards, enforce discipline, administer punishment, and interact (or not) with conscripts. While one officer may punish his entire unit for the mistake of one recruit, another may discipline only the conscripts, and yet another may choose to punish only the offender. Conscripts adapt to the circumstances with surprisingly little protest, as all commanders are seen as fathers. Just as one cannot choose one's biological father, neither can one select one's commander, or military father. Furthermore, given that conscripts have multiple fathers during their time in the cuartel, ranging from their commander to their drill sergeant, the influence of any one individual is tempered.[42] Yet commanders, like recruits, share the basic assumptions and roles of the familial metaphor, ensuring that conscripts' formation is understood consistently, though not identically, despite their sometimes radically different styles.

The family metaphor also establishes a common goal for fathers: the formation of conscripts into good sons. Sometimes military fathers, like their biological counterparts, feel they have to castigate their sons to achieve desired results "for their own good." That sons do not resent this punishment but instead consider it to be "for their own good" might suggest false consciousness. However, it would be imprudent to assume that fathers' and sons' use of the same words implies a single, consistent rationale.

For example, while officers believe that conscripts are more inclined to learn when threatened with punishment, no recruit ever voiced this conviction to me. Instead they often interpret threats or actual punishment as conveying a sense of concern on their fathers' part. While they do not always respond as their fathers would like and recognize abuse when it occurs, recruits are eager to assume the best of their fathers. Conscripts tend to believe that fathers are taking this hard-line approach to form them properly. While recruits do not enjoy punishment, they do not seem to resent it.

Admittedly, discipline is less draconian in the Ecuadorian Army than in other South American military forces. Corporal punishment, prohibited by law since 1883 but widely practiced until recently, is exceptionally rare. Most discipline in the contemporary cuartel is either physical exertion (for example, running several kilometers around the base in boots, uniform, and helmet while carrying a backpack and rifle) or repetition.[43] One basic training commander, upon observing the recruits marching out of step, exploded, "You haven't learned anything! Doing things half-assed is no good! If you don't start paying attention and executing well, we will march until 20:00 every night and on Saturday and Sunday as well!" The conscripts giggled nervously and marched on, trying to impress their father, while silently acknowledging that this was "for their own good."

Creative officers and *voluntarios* or professional soldiers have invented even more harsh ways to inflict pain and discomfort without violating military regulations. One of the cruelest is a position known as "the tripod," where recruits assume the push-up position, then raise their rumps into the air, rest their heads on the ground, and place their hands behind their backs. The strain placed on conscripts' necks, the excessive blood flow to the cranium, and the fact that they are resting much of their body weight on the scalp, firmly planted in dirt or gravel, make this position one of the few truly reviled punishments. Given the brutality of "the tripod," it is reserved for recruits and never administered to voluntarios.

Even brutal punishment can be justified as a way for well-meaning fathers to reform or manage unruly sons, not altogether unlike the situation of a century ago. The tripod position is often described as "helping conscripts think" by increasing blood flow to the brain. This makes it a fitting penalty for infractions committed out of ignorance, commonly thought to be a particularly Indian quality, as the example from history class suggests. Conscripts do not accept this justification of the tripod, revealing one of the limits to acceptable discipline (that which is "for our own good"). Consequently, recruits' acquiescence to (and loathing of) the tripod should be interpreted as a result of coercion rather than consent.

This patriarchal model of discipline, with its emphasis on hierarchy, obedience, castigation, and reform, bears little resemblance to discipline in indigenous communities. Tibán notes that Indian discipline emphasizes consensus, reconciliation, and equality, with all community members, whether directly involved in the dispute or not, having a chance to speak their minds.[44] Yet even Indian conscripts say that military discipline is "for our own good." In addition to the aforementioned tendency to correlate discipline and personal formation, the punishment indígenas share with their mestizo counterparts helps to level the playing field. As one indigenous conscript responded when asked if he felt Indians were treated differently, "No. They treat us all the same here. Badly." Punishing conscripts collectively equalizes differences in their status and opportunities to become well formed. The fact that today the Army subjects Indians and mestizos to the same harsh disciplinary codes to form them reveals how differently the institution judges indígenas' potential as citizens in the present, compared with the early republican period.

Like disciplinary codes, the behavioral and linguistic norms that govern the formation process are drawn from urban, middle-class mestizo culture. This can produce a significant disjuncture for indigenous conscripts, who face a dilemma: Should they emulate their biological fathers or their metaphorical father? The simple solution put forward by the Army is to give up any counterproductive beliefs and practices learned from one's indigenous father. Conscripts are not always willing or able to do so.

When a conscript answered a voluntario's question in the meek and quiet voice typical of a campesino or highland Indian, he was exhorted to "speak like a man!" After he failed to comply a second time, he was ordered to run fifty meters to the middle of the parade field and to answer "like a man." When he still did not adopt the loud, brash tone of "a man," he was made to do push-ups, calling out the number of repetitions he had completed. Not surprisingly, the sergeant could not hear him because he was not "speaking manly enough," so he made the conscript start over again, taunting him to "shout like a man."

The idea of shouting for no apparent reason was so foreign to this recruit that he suffered repeated humiliation in front of his peers because he could not meet the voluntario's expectations. In North American terms, the voluntario was trying to turn a mild-mannered Midwesterner into a loud, aggressive, confrontational, and perhaps even obnoxious New Yorker. Not everyone wants or is able to speak like a New Yorker, or an urban, middle-class mestizo, as this may contradict the very essence of his culture. Moreover, adopting this foreign behavioral model would require betraying one's roots. Yet this is precisely what Indian recruits must do if they wish to exploit conscription's opportunity to redefine their relationship with the state. Those who do speak and act "appropriately" are held up as role models for Indian and non-Indian recruits alike; those who do not are subjected to public humiliation. While they are welcome and encouraged to serve as Indians, native men must do so on the state's terms. This both reinforces the asymmetrical nature of the relationship and the persistence of the Army's underlying assumption that indigenous ethnicity should be subordinate to mestizo nationalist identity, though it is not portrayed as such. Diversity is welcome in the cuartel when it does not threaten the mission or national integrity, but is not itself seen as a strength.

Ironically, despite the hypermasculine expectations applied to conscripts, their preconceived gender roles are challenged in other ways. The cuartel is a home with few women where men perform what are often considered women's jobs (as operators, nurses, or food servers, for example). There are only a handful of females in the cuartel, such as commanders' secretaries and physicians in brigade hospitals. Nevertheless, women are symbolically central to ordering the roles of men. Fathers carry out formation on the behalf of the Mother. Two primary tasks for fathers are to ensure that sons respect their

Mother and to mete out discipline when they falter. This division of labor in the metaphorical family reveals thoroughly gendered parental roles.

While fathers are disciplinarians and protectors, mothers, both metaphorical and biological, are givers of life, the providers of continuity, shelter, and sustenance. In one officer's words, mothers are "half human, half divine." Without mothers, the family would not be perpetuated; there would be no new fathers to serve the Mother, nor sons to assist through conscription. Nor would conscripts arrive at the cuartel with the foundation of culture and habits that are central to the formation process. Although formation is believed to only be fully achieved through the participation of military fathers, biological mothers initiate the process by nurturing their children from infancy.[45] The centrality of true mothers to the military mission helps explain the presence of the otherwise incongruous statue of a mother breast feeding her infant child at the entrance to the Riobamba cuartel.

Despite the absence of conscripts' literal mothers from the cuartel, their Patria is omnipresent in daily praxis and discourse. These two aspects fuse during the weekly "civic moment" where the entire brigade comes together to hear inspirational speeches, sing patriotic songs, and recognize each other's achievements. The Patria's symbols—particularly the flag, national anthem, and seal or *escudo*, as well as the men and arms of the military itself—are placed center stage during these rituals. These reminders of the conscripts' metaphorical Mother are inescapable in the cuartel.

One's biological mother, like the Patria, in the words of one army officer addressing the troops during a "civic moment," is "tireless, diligent in her duty—the care of her children—in providing the first caresses of affection to her beloved child, whom she delivers to the world and society with exceptional happiness and whose first steps she tutors, whose tears she dries, wounds she heals, fears she assuages, whom she comforts in difficult times and whose aspirations she encourages." The Patria as Mother fulfills similar metaphorical roles. She assuages the pain of past territorial losses by fixing the blame and inspiring citizens to right the wrong someday, comforts by providing a sense of origin and continuity, and unites by making individuals part of a nation.

Sons also have clear duties to their Mother: they should honor, defend, and give back to the Patria by completing their military service, expressing their patriotism—it is not enough to feel civic pride, one must express it by displaying the national flag on appropriate holidays and singing the national anthem enthusiastically—and working hard in a profession that will contribute to the country's economic development. The officer cited above concluded by insisting that we should "honor our mother as she deserves, for we are testimony to her enormous sacrifice that produced what we are today. Our flower of gratitude should exude a delicate perfume to enchant our mother. While alive we should shower her with the happiness that is within the realm of each of her children, because it is so delightful to be a loving son and cause her to smile and make our mothers happy."

Pleasing conscripts' literal mothers and making them proud provides yet another important impetus to the young men's decision to serve. In countries where military service is voluntary instead of obligatory, the popular perception is that mothers naturally protest the armed forces "stealing" their sons though conscription; preliminary data from Ecuador suggests otherwise. Ninety-nine percent of surveyed conscripts reported that their mothers were not opposed to their military service. Moreover, 63 percent reported their mothers to be "proud" of their sons' conscription, and almost half described their mothers as "happy" regarding their service. Even Indian mothers I interviewed, whom one might expect to be most suspicious of the military, generally supported their sons' decisions.

While apprehensive at first, after visiting their sons on Sunday afternoons, indigenous parents also began describing the Army in fatherly terms, suggesting that the family metaphor and formation discourse resonate outside the cuartel and with different ethnic groups and generations. National conscription authorities exploit the importance of biological mothers and their sons' desire to please them. In a 2002 television commercial promoting conscription, a young man leaves home dressed in jeans and returns to his jubilant family wearing a uniform. His first interaction is with his mother, who hugs and kisses him, while a disembodied man's voice confides, "I have never seen my mother so proud as the day I reported for my military service." His father shakes the young man's hand, and siblings congratulate the conscript as well, but the focus of the interaction is the mother-son dyad. He served for her, and she is proud.

Sons' relationships with their biological and metaphorical mothers change, but do not end, when they finish their period of active service. Conscripts' time in the cuartel culminates in the *juramento a la bandera* (pledge of allegiance to the flag) ritual where sons join their fathers—represented by their commanding officers—in their duty to protect their Mother. Conscripts come forward individually and kneel before the officer who then lifts the flag, the symbol of the Mother, with his saber. The son then professes his intention to defend the Mother, "her flag, the constitution, and the laws of the republic, the integrity of the nation, and not abandon those who command you in times of war or preparation for the same" at the top of his lungs—"like a man"—for all to hear.

Never has a conscript not sworn this oath. If duty and making one's literal mother proud were not enough motivation, the rejoinder from the officer administering the oath likely alleviates any doubt. "If you so swear," they are told, "the Patria will reward you; otherwise She shall condemn you." For conscripts, to forsake this duty would be to fail both their biological mothers and their Patria. The consequences of not swearing could put the Patria's very future at risk; as the sign at the entrance to the basic training area reminds conscripts daily: She "does not exist without the love of Her sons."

Duty-bound: Indians' Roles in Defense, Development, and the State

The popular marching cadence, "Madre Mía" concludes with these words: "Pardon me, mother of mine, if my absence causes you to suffer; / Pardon me, mother of mine, if I must die for my Patria; / Your womb gave me life, you soothed me with love; / Now that I am a grown man, I am the eternal defender of you, mother, and of my Patria." The Ecuadorian military constructs the Patria as not only the metaphorical Mother, but also a virtuous woman, pacific, patient, and persistent, who has consistently been wronged. Defending her is conscripts' duty, for they are taught that the once proud and expansive Kingdom of Quito has been reduced to a fraction of its original size and grandeur by the aggressive and expansionist desires of her neighbors. While Colombia and Brazil are historically culpable, Peru is cast as the primary perpetrator.

Peruvian aggression has not only challenged the territorial integrity of Ecuador, but in the military's prose, "dismembered," "penetrated," and "violated" her. The expansionist-minded Peruvians, beginning with the conquest and continuing through the War of Cenepa, the 1995 border conflict, have "raped" the Mother repeatedly. The armed forces alone have preserved her life through war, though like Rumiñahui they have only been able to minimize the pain inflicted by invaders, not prevent it. By portraying past incursions in powerful and graphic organic and sexual terms, the military transforms national pride from an abstract and ephemeral concept into a tangible and compelling motivation in peacetime.[46]

It is the obligation of all citizens, according to the Army, to defend virtuous women, especially their literal and figurative mothers.[47] As the lyrics of the marching cadence romantically suggest, participating in national defense may result in a conscript's death. This may cause one's biological mother emotional pain, but is better than losing one's Patria or permitting her integrity as a virtuous woman to be desecrated yet again. Although conscripts, their parents, voluntarios, and officers may all have slightly different ideas of what it means to be a "good son," none disputes the obligation of sons to defend their mothers when threatened.

As sons of the Patria, former conscripts play an integral role in national defense, bound by this unwritten but transcendental filial duty; as long as the Mother is alive they are her sons and are obliged to protect her. Nor can officers and voluntarios alone assure the Patria's longevity, they insist: they are too few and are insufficiently funded, equipped, and armed. Only a unified nation can overcome these deficits, making the integration of Indians into the state through conscription a paramount concern for military planners. In practice, fathers, as the Patria's husband, bear the primary responsibility for her defense but must enlist the day-to-day help of their sons through conscription and call on former conscripts when the Mother is in danger.

Although conscripts' duty to help the father defend the Patria does not end once they complete their service, they never become the father's equal. Once sons return to civilian life, the Army continues to define and perceive them according to their former status as conscripts, the lowliest of military personnel. While conscripts rank higher in the figurative "Order of the Patria" than their peers who evaded service, they—altar boys to the officer/high priest—are not professional soldiers and will never become fathers in the military sense, even after completing their service or reaching fifty-five years of age and being permanently discharged from the reserves. Regardless of age, unless they become voluntarios, conscripts and ex-conscripts are destined to be perpetual bachelors, in military terms.[48] Yet in conscripts' eyes, it is better to be an old, unmarried son than a bastard or an orphan, unacknowledged and forsaken by the Army and the Patria. While military service is far from idyllic, Indian recruits are offered a new sort of relationship with the state. That it is framed as an all-or-nothing affair comes as no surprise or impediment to their service.

Moreover, for Ecuador's highland Indians, being recognized by the state/Army and Patria carries as many material as symbolic advantages. Indígenas often live at the periphery, in rural and marginal urban areas frequently lacking the services and authorities that operationalize the "imagined community." While many are intimately connected to the larger economy through wage labor and consumption, few have extended contact with the state educational system, police, courts, or local government. The military is the one national institution that reaches every corner of the country and routinely affects every citizen.[49]

For many indigenous communities, consequently, the Army *is* the state. Unlike other agencies, ministries, and programs that may appear and disappear with alarming regularity, the military is enduring, orderly, progressive, efficient, honest. Even more important, the armed forces' development assistance program has persuaded most indigenous organizations today that the military is beneficent and concerned with the well-being of the people.[50] The Army does not just promise to build a school, as politicians do; they build it and provide teachers. They do not hand out food to the hungry; they instruct communities how to produce it better and more cheaply, "teaching them how to fish rather than giving them the catch." Submitting to a paternalistic military model of the state and nation that includes Indians as junior partners is generally seen as a worthwhile tradeoff. Not surprisingly, regional and national indigenous organizations have been muted in their critique of both Army development projects and conscription.

Discursively, the two are not distinct processes, but interdependent. Ecuador's current national security doctrine has so fully synthesized security and development that one is rarely mentioned without the other. Pragmatically, obligatory military service is crucial to military development efforts, with conscripts providing the labor for forestry, construction, agricultural, and other military projects.[51] Since many of these projects are carried out in indigenous communities, the projects are mutually reinforcing. The net result is a favorable image whereby indígenas see a concerned Army reaching out to them and simultaneously welcoming their youth into the cuartel, where they are converted into well-formed, but still Indian, men.

Furthermore, the military and indígenas both believe that the process of personal formation that is the focus of conscription benefits indigenous communities. While former conscripts are still Indians in the Army's eyes, they are now "well formed" and better equipped to help their communities. Their work will be better than mediocre, their techniques modern, and their work ethic redoubled. Developing indigenous communities also strengthens the country as a whole and demonstrates to the Patria the love and affection that Mother deserves, making her happy.

The applicability and importance of personal formation to local, pacific concerns as well as national, military affairs makes the framework that much more malleable and persuasive. It is also crucial to the promotion of military service among youth, since during times of peace the Patria is safe and the urgency of military service eliminated. With the addition of personal and community development to the long list of other benefits of conscription, young men are provided a compelling set of mutually reinforcing incentives to serve.

The Ecuadorian military's official discourse of the state as pluriethnic but uninational is not universally accepted. Military doctrine is contested even within the highest ranks of the armed forces. Colonel Haro openly contradicts the minister of defense by characterizing the country as "multicultural, multinational, and multiethnic." Yet he shares his superior's concern that "these characteristics threaten the very survival of the state, and therefore the military seeks the strengthening of national identity."[52] These officers disagree on the precise meaning of nationality, but they concur that the Army must ensure that indígenas and other marginal populations are securely within the embrace of the Patria. Hegemony helps facilitate a better understanding of the powerful as well as explaining the sometimes contradictory and piecemeal actions and ideas of subalterns.

Nor is the Army's vision of the nation and role of Indians shared wholeheartedly by other branches of the Ecuadorian armed forces or the highly fragmented state. What makes the Army unique here is its high degree of autonomy from the other services, from the Ministry of Defense, and from other state institutions. The Ecuadorian Army, the largest of the military branches, holding a monopoly on the use of armed force, and with a messianic mission to protect the Patria, is the state's eight-hundred-pound gorilla. Legislators are loath to critique the Army, the judiciary impotent to exercise jurisdiction over it, and elected officials envious of its power and popular appeal. This gives the institution the intellectual, financial, and political independence to envision and enact policies toward Indians and promote visions of themselves, and the state in general, which would be impossible for other actors.

This does not, however, assure success. Conscription of Indians is successful in Ecuador because aspects of its multiple and interrelated frameworks—including personal formation, the nation-as-family, and the multicultural state—are shared by legislators who write conscription laws, soldiers who execute them, the young men who serve, and their mothers, fathers, and girlfriends who encourage them. In the process, Indians renegotiate their role with the state system and the Army expands its role within the panorama of state institutions, thereby questioning and transforming the state idea.

11

Same State, Different Histories, Diverse Strategies

The Ecuadorian Amazon

JULIET S. ERAZO

Even though they share the same country, indigenous groups in Ecuador's Amazon region have experienced a very different relationship to the state than have highland groups. Until the mid-twentieth century, interactions with both the colonial government and the Ecuadorian state were more intermittent in the Amazon than in the highlands. They were more directly related to boom and bust periods for the region's natural resources—particularly gold, cinchona bark, and rubber—than to changes in state administration.[1] In general, religious missions were a more visible and important local governing force than the state.

Jesuit missionaries in particular devised methods of extracting labor, gold, and pita fiber from the indigenous population, much as colonial and state agents had done, until they were banished from the Americas in 1767, and then again after their return in 1869. In the intervening years, parish priests took over their posts and were among the worst exploiters of Indians, exacting tribute and charging them exorbitant prices for ecclesiastical services.[2] In the late nineteenth century, a variety of Catholic orders and evangelical missions took over abandoned Jesuit posts and extended into new areas, pursuing varied forms of civilizing projects. On the whole, missionaries attempted to do much more than convert indigenous people to Christianity, continuing the efforts of colonial officials to settle the indigenous population into permanent villages and to convert them into European-style peasants. It is therefore difficult to determine where the civilizing projects of the various missions ended and those of the state began. During some periods, missions even received their mandate directly from the state; at other times, they acted as one of several local governing bodies, often competing for scarce indigenous labor with civil administrators.

Given the parallels between the practices of the mission and those of the state, it is counterproductive to try to isolate a "state system" and "state idea," as Philip Abrams defines them. It is more accurate to speak of a "government idea" and a "government system" in the Amazonian context, with a definition of government that would include missions in their local governing and quasi-state roles. The best evidence is that Amazonians have used similar practices in countering the domination of both missionaries and local state representatives, although groups differed in their overall approach to government by others.

Anne-Christine Taylor describes three responses by Amazonian Indians to domination by the missions and the state, used at various times and often in combination. Use of these strategies was a second way in which Indians' relations with the government system differed in the Amazon from those of highland Indians (the first being the relative importance of the missions). One strategy was to evade colonial and mission rule at all costs, even if it meant drastic changes in livelihood and way of life. The Huaorani, who are probably descended from the complex Abijira riverside society, took this approach. The Shuar and related Jivaroan groups were also able to maintain a certain level of autonomy, with less drastic changes in livelihood and culture. A second response was ethnic dissolution through flight or transculturation (the merging and converging of diverse cultures). The third was to engage to some extent with the whites, a strategy taken by members of the colonial "tribes" created in the *reducciones* (disparate groups reduced to nucleated settlements) or around Spanish settlements, such as the Canelos, Napo, and Quijos Quichua. Taylor argues that these responses were not mutually exclusive, but mutually enabling. "Tame" Indians acted as brokers between the still relatively autonomous "wild" forest populations and the dominant society, supplying manufactured goods and providing a buffer that allowed them to continue more "traditional" or separatist lifestyles. Conversely, the ongoing existence of relatively autonomous hinterland groups provided a viable alternative for "tame" Indians when exploitation became too great. The Napo Runa were linked in this way to the western Tukanoan populations and the Huaorani, while the Canelos were linked to the Záparo and the northern Jívaro.[3] Taylor goes on to argue, "It is therefore likely that, for all their empirical divergence, *auca* [wild] and *manso* [tame] cultures share a great deal of common ground and that the differences between them are rooted in contrasting forms of contextualization of cultural knowledge operating in a few restricted, culturally stressed domains of social life, rather than in the building up of entirely distinct registers of tradition."[4] Indeed, some groups, including many of the Quichua, managed to move between "tame" and "wild" status.[5]

The tripartite configuration typical of the upper Amazon region that linked whites, "tame," and "wild" Indians did not begin to disintegrate until the rubber boom, when "wild" Indians were more directly incorporated into patron-client relationships. Even then, patterns of social and linguistic behavior that began during the colonial period continued to influence interethnic relations. For example, in the early 1970s, the Shuar Federation encouraged Achuar to allow Salesian missionaries to enter their lands, and both Quichua and Shuar encouraged other nationalities to become more active in the campaigns of CONFENIAE (Confederation of Indigenous Nationalities of the Ecuadorian Amazon, the regional umbrella organization). In the late twentieth century, socioeconomic differentiation within nationalities grew as those members with access to Western-style education stood in a privileged position vis-à-vis the state and had better access to development monies and government posts. On the other hand, long-standing networks and cultural overlap likely facilitated early interethnic collaborations in the mid-twentieth century and cohesion (albeit contested) within CONFENIAE after its formation in 1980.

The history of the Shuar people is often contrasted to that of highland Quichua, given their relative success in evading domination and the early formation of an ethnicity based rights organization. By implication, their history comes to represent that of the entire Ecuadorian Oriente. However, lowland Quichua were also key players in the formation of CONFENIAE. The latter group's longer history of strategically engaging with the white population provides interesting parallels to the maneuvers used by highland Indians to resist or appeal to the state. For example, Amazonians periodically complained to the central government about both the missionaries' and local officials' exploitative practices, much as highland Indians brought complaints about local governments to the central state. This was a form of legitimizing and enabling the central state "from below." Lowland Indians also appropriated negative stereotypes of themselves to advance their own interests with mission and state authorities, much as highland Indians appropriated stereotypes of "indios infelices," using negative stereotypes to their advantage. Recognizing the deep historical roots of Indian-state relations in highland Ecuador, let us turn to a description of those roots in lowland Ecuador, focusing on the experiences of the lowland Quichua.

The Early Republic

Ecuador's independence from Spain had little effect on the Amazon region. Rather, there was a steady decline in the white and mestizo population during the early years of the republic, a trend dating back to the mid-1700s. The nonindigenous population dropped by about two-thirds between 1768 and 1850, while the indigenous population recovered some of its numbers, after devastating drops during the colonial period, and reclaimed some of its territory.[6] Some groups that had been previously settled into reducciones, including some of the Siona and Secoya, returned to a life of itinerant horticulture, hunting, and fishing.[7]

Indians with the most regular contact with state officials were subject to corruption and extraction of native tribute through various mechanisms.[8] In particular, in the *reparto* system of forced apportionment, Indians had to purchase coarse cotton cloth made in the highlands, thread, needles, and a large number of superfluous goods at least twice a year and were required to repay the debts incurred with agave fiber and gold dust. Civil officials in Archidona and elsewhere also pressed Indians into service projects for the municipality, such as building and maintaining roads.[9] Central authorities exercised administrative control by selecting powerful members from each extended patrilineal family to act as indigenous authorities known as *varas* or staff holders; varas needed to mobilize family members and friends to complete work projects or faced time in prison.[10]

It was during this period that the strategies of the lowland Quichua Indians began to resemble those of the highland Quichua. In particular, they began to turn to central government officials to mediate their relationships with local officials. For example, in 1846 the Indian authorities of Napo and Archidona brought a complaint before the minister of the interior, reporting a long list of abuses and humiliations at the hands of local *jefes políticos* (political administrators). They demanded that the government put an end to these abuses and threatened to "abandon our villages and seek safe asylum in the remotest sites of our vast and mountainous province."[11] This resistance eventually became a serious problem for local government officials, and five months after submitting the complaint, Amazonian Indians were exempted by the national congress from the "personal contribution," one of the tributes collected by the governor's office. (Highland groups held a very different view of this tribute.)[12]

Despite the Indian labor obtained through the reparto and varayuj systems, the intense political and economic control mechanisms wielded by the state in the highlands could not be extended into the Amazon during this period because the indigenous population continued to occupy areas that whites considered inaccessible. Even the Indians who lived closest to government posts and missions spent much of their time in second homes located deeper in the forest, returning only after three or four months to obtain manufactured and imported goods such as matches, machetes, and salt. The paucity of civil administrators and constant labor shortages for public works projects also limited the state's influence. Furthermore, missionaries in the Amazon were never able to consolidate their domination through the *fiesta* system and its political and religious hierarchies as they were in the Sierra.[13]

In 1869, the Jesuits returned to the region, a century after their first expulsion. The conservative president Gabriel García Moreno sought to use them to test his concept of economic development based on "moral regeneration" of the Amazon's "pagan savages."[14] The Amazon, vast regions of which still remained largely beyond the reach of the state, gave García Moreno an opportunity to increase state paternalism, even though it was in a less direct manner than in the highlands.

In the Napo and Archidona regions, the concurrence of increased trade of various products from the region and Jesuit governance led to intense conflicts between the merchants and the missionaries, who acted both as evangelizers and representatives of the state. The Jesuits sought to create a sedentary, European-style peasantry, while the traders were primarily interested in using Indian labor to extract forest products. The traders would grant *licencias* or leaves to the Indians, exempting them from obligatory service to the Jesuits so that they could pan for gold and scrape pita fiber in the forest. In choosing between the evils of the traders and of the Jesuits, the Indians typically allied themselves with the traders. When given leave to extract products in the forest, they could balance these activities with shifting horticulture and periodic hunting, fishing, and gathering expeditions. Because the Jesuits required them to remain in the mission village, they could not travel for more than a day's walk away without punishment and therefore had to compete with their village neighbors for the limited hunting, fishing, and arable land in the surrounding area.[15]

In 1876, the indigenous residents of Archidona and Tena sent a delegation to Quito to demand the expulsion of the Jesuits "because they punish greatly" and to request that the Jesuit vicar be replaced by a single civil government for the Amazon province.[16] The Indian official from Tena directly confronted the vicar, asking him to resign his office as civil governor. Once again, the Indians' efforts to exploit cleavages between local officials and the central state were rewarded, and in 1877, political control in the region returned to the civil authorities.[17]

The 1876 incident is particularly interesting because it demonstrates an understanding of a particular government system in which civil and religious authorities were separate yet functionally equivalent. While the Indians may have seen traders, missionaries, and civil authorities as sources of imported material goods, they already understood that the central state would not expel the Jesuits and leave the traders to their own devices. Rather, the Jesuits would need to be replaced by another governing authority; the idea that some form of authority would remain and would continue to extract tribute and otherwise exploit the indigenous population was not challenged in this act of resistance. The central state's authority to determine the makeup of the local government system was also apparently firmly accepted, regardless of where the Jesuits felt their legitimacy arose.

Despite the shift in governance, the Jesuits remained in the region, continuing with their evangelizing efforts and doing everything in their power to maintain a hold on the indigenous labor force that provided for their subsistence. However, the ongoing conflicts between the Jesuits and the now relatively aligned traders and civil administrators gave the Indians of Tena-Archidona and the surrounding region a way of evading responsibility for their actions when they deemed it advantageous, even though it was ironically through self-degradation. Specifically, they appropriated stereotypes of themselves as naïve children, much as highlanders appropriated images and phrases such as the "*indios infelices.*" For example, after a revolt in 1892 in which the Loreto Indians rebelled against the Jesuits, participants attempted to excuse themselves as the gullible instruments of the traders, a justification readily believed by the Jesuits.[18]

In the southern Oriente, the government system—whether exercised by Jesuits or civil authorities—held comparatively less power, as did the idea that legitimated their presence. José Jouanen writes, "Despite the self-denial and heroic efforts of the Missionaries, almost no fruit has been obtained with the Jivaroan peoples [Jívaro was a term encompassing both the Shuar and the Achuar]; given the situation in which these heathens find themselves, there was very little hope of advancing their reducción to the civilized life and their conversion to the Christian religion."[19] A native uprising in 1873 forced the abandonment of the mission at Gualaquiza, and on December 12, 1883, the church gave the missionaries in Macas permission to abandon their efforts there.[20]

Liberalism and the Early Twentieth Century

President Eloy Alfaro and his liberal supporters sought to make a clear break between church and state. This desire, the onslaught of industrial capitalism that occurred during the rubber boom, and Amazonians' resistance to the Jesuits' civilizing projects all contributed to the second expulsion of the Jesuits from the Ecuadorian Amazon in 1896.[21] Alfaro also issued various other decrees in the final years of the nineteenth century that won him the support of both Amazonian and highland Indians. The liberals exempted Indians from the territorial tax and from subsidiary work and recognized their status as Ecuadorian citizens entitled to education and judicial protection.[22] The Special Law for the Oriente of 1899 also prohibited forced repartos, the transportation of loads without prior contract and payment of appropriate wages, and the direct sale of Indian children or their exchange for products.[23] These liberal reforms offered only partial respite to most Amazonian Indians in the face of the greed and violence between 1880 and 1914 inspired by the rubber boom. A few of the more politically savvy individuals, however, were able to use the political opening to protest abuses to the authorities, and in some cases they succeeded in having fines imposed on offending merchants.[24]

In a less positive development, the Special Law for the Oriente also provided for the settlement of "vacant lands" (*terrenos baldíos*) in the Amazon region.[25] "No sooner was this law known in the missions," writes the Jesuit chronicler Jouanen, "than all the traders and miners suddenly developed a strong vocation for ranching or farming. From September to December, the governor was flooded with claims on 'vacant lands,' but the plots involved were precisely those belonging to the Indians and under cultivation by them from time immemorial."[26] The number of settlers who actually occupied the region remained relatively small during the first decades of the twentieth century, given the difficulties in reaching the area, and there were no serious conflicts over land because of colonization. The settlers took up cattle ranching or produced cash crops, the most important of which were cotton, coffee, rice, and sugarcane. During the period of international prosperity, from 1924 until the 1929 world crisis, the overall value of exports rose and hacienda owners profited.[27]

In contrast to the now illegal reparto system of the nineteenth century, under which the Indians were "given" items by the governor's office and then forced to pay them off by working on public projects, hacienda owners gained access to Indian labor through commodity-based debt peonage. Lowland Quichua were encouraged to purchase items on credit—shotguns, cooking pots, cloth, and axes—at severely inflated prices, then forced to work to pay off their debts at minimal wages. Account books were regularly doctored by hacendados to maintain deep indebtedness and thereby ensure a constant labor supply. Yet despite such exploitation, the relationships Quichua families developed with these patrons gave them a certain degree of stability and protection, and they frequently entered willingly into debt peonage, fully aware of the exploitative terms of the arrangement.[28]

For work purposes, the civil administration divided the Indian population into three groups: the "debtors," who were dependent on patrons; the "freemen," who were used to maintain roads or to perform other public services and paid low wages; and the "*salvajizados*" (those who had returned to savagery), who eluded the control of both hacendados and state authorities. In practice, families would move among these categories, since the wages earned as "freemen" were not sufficient to cover basic necessities, forcing the Indians into debt. Furthermore, to maintain access to labor, the governor's office reinstituted the varas system, whereby the civil authorities chose indigenous leaders to manage and recruit labor for public works projects. This system allowed the governor's office to obtain access to extended families for one year of service, even though indebted to a patron. If the patron refused, the authorities' usual response was to apply fines or even send in troops to locate members of the selected family.[29]

In the southern Oriente, Alfaro granted a number of mining concessions to foreign companies and passed new regulations to facilitate corporate and individual access to rubber, cinchona bark, and *tagua* (ivory nut). These market-oriented activities pushed the Shuar into smaller areas and contaminated the rivers and forests where they hunted and fished.[30] Several new missions also opened across the Oriente. In addition to their role in "civilizing" the people of the Amazon, the state saw in the missions a means of securing its border with Peru and therefore encouraged them, despite liberal desires to separate the activities of church and state. In the north of Pastaza, Dominican missions were established in Puyo in 1889, in Mera in 1907, and in Arapicos in 1929. In 1922, the Josephines established a mission that encompassed 70,000 square kilometers in the Napo region. Additionally, starting in 1914 and continuing into the 1920s, priests from the Salesian order established missions in Shuar areas with support from the Ecuadorian state. Evangelical missions from North America also spread into various regions of the Oriente. In the southern Amazon, the Gospel Missionary Union was established in Macas in 1903 and in Sucúa in 1919. In the Upper Napo region, evangelical missions were established in Tena and Shandia in 1927, and a few years later in Pano. Starting in 1950, Protestant missionaries from the Summer Institute of Linguistics established a much more permanent presence within the Huaorani, Cofán, and Secoya territories and made significant advances in settling them into relatively permanent villages by establishing bilingual schools and health clinics.[31] The presence of missionaries often opened the door to increased colonization from the highlands.

There were large differences among the various missions established during this period in the Oriente, and some changed rather dramatically over time. The Dominicans and Franciscans were satisfied with administering and accompanying the growing number of Quichua-speaking Indians, reproducing the mechanisms of control and exploitation developed in the eighteenth century. They attempted neither to impose an educational system nor to introduce new forms of production and were thus hostile toward the commercial penetration of the region when it appeared to threaten indigenous practices.

The Salesians, on the other hand, were more modern and more interventionist; their primary weapons were facilitating colonization and their boarding schools. Families of poor mestizos from the highlands followed the missionaries and settled around the missions, appropriating or purchasing Shuar lands nearby. Between the 1920s and the 1960s, an expanding network of missions attracted an increasing number of mestizo colonists into the region.[32] The schools opened in the 1940s, and by 1960, a large portion of Shuar youth were being educated. In the schools, Shuar children were socialized to be subordinate to the state but simultaneously given knowledge of and access to Ecuadorian society that gave them leverage over other Shuar.[33] Thus, the divisions separating "wild" Indians, "civilized" Indians, and the dominant society that existed before the rubber boom repeated themselves within the Shuar population.

The nonindigenous population of the two southernmost provinces of the Oriente reached 30,787 in 1950.[34] The state did not attempt to control this colonization or to develop the Amazonian provinces until 1963, when it passed the Ley de Tierras Baldías (Law of Vacant Lands).[35] Attempts in the 1964 agrarian reform legislation to placate highland peasants over the scarcity of land were primarily limited to encouraging colonization of low-density areas (particularly in the upper Amazon), not expropriating and redistributing the land of highland haciendas. This encouragement went beyond facilitating land titles to include agricultural extension programs and other social services, making resettlement in the Oriente even more attractive to potential colonists.

The Josephines in Napo Province and the evangelical missions throughout the Oriente were also interested in "modernizing" their indigenous followers by engaging them more in the national economy and by giving their youth a more Western-style, formal education.[36] Rather than promoting bilingual education like the Salesians did, they discouraged the use of Quichua and, according to local residents, severely punished Quichua students who spoke in their native language while in the mission schools.

Achuar territories remained relatively free of colonization and other pressures until the 1970s, when Salesian and Protestant missionaries developed trading and evangelizing relations with them. The missionaries persuaded some Achuar, through heavy economic inducements, to clear jungle airstrips, cluster their homes around these strips, give up much of their violent feuding, and engage in cattle ranching. The Shuar Federation also actively encouraged the Achuar to form nucleated settlements around airstrips.[37] By 1978, about two-thirds of the Achuar population north of the Pastaza River was concentrated in half a dozen nucleated settlements, while the remaining third still lived in more traditional, dispersed residential patterns.[38] The settlements typically included a landing strip, a chapel, a school, and service buildings, all of which contributed to the permanence of these settlements.[39] Both the Salesian and evangelical missions mimicked state development programs in other parts of the Oriente, providing loans for cattle and providing formal, primary education.[40]

In recent decades, the northern Amazon has been most important for the national economy because of the presence of petroleum, wood, and agricultural industries. In 1967, Texaco discovered the country's first commercial petroleum reserve and brought subsequent reserves into production in 1972. Ecuador soon became heavily dependent on oil, and revenues from crude oil exports represented approximately 50 percent of the state budget.[41] The new oil fields, mestizo settlements, logging operations, and agribusiness enterprises of the late 1960s and 1970s invaded the territories of the Cofán, Secoya, Siona, and Tetete peoples.[42] The state increasingly made land concessions for agricultural plantations, first for tea and later for African palm, as well as to groups from the highlands and coast to relieve land pressures in those regions. Finally, the creation of large national parks, ecological reserves, and forest reserves restricted indigenous access to forest resources and lands for cultivation. While many indigenous people see value in conserving some areas of habitat for the reproduction of flora and fauna, many also view the state's new land designations with suspicion, believing that reserves are in fact set aside for future concessions to nonindigenous peasants, agroindustrial firms, and petroleum companies.[43]

The First Indigenous Federations in the Amazon

The 1960s and 1970s, as we have seen, was a critical period for indigenous-state relations in Ecuador, both in the highlands and in the Amazon. Unlike Indians in the highlands, where *huasipungeros* were able to mobilize existing "communities" of families working on the same hacienda to purchase lands made available by the 1964 agrarian reform and to negotiate with state agencies for public works, Amazonians had to build new collectivities to defend their access to land in the face of the threats posed by the same legislation. Once they were able to form collective organizations, lowland Indians gained important experience negotiating with local missions. These experiences became critical precedents for the organizing work of larger indigenous federations.

Community-level action occurred first among the Shuar, whose lands were being threatened by the growing number of colonists entering the region. Under Salesian auspices, Shuar families living near Sucúa established small administrative units, called *centros*, that replicated the colonists' hamlets to some extent. The centros included a square plaza, surrounded by a school, a chapel, a first-aid clinic, the teacher's house, and a few other dwellings occupied permanently or periodically by Shuar families.[44] The centro was an attractive development to the government as well as missionaries, as the settlement of the Shuar facilitated their further integration into the national economy as well as their evangelization.[45] While most Shuar families belonging to the centro continued to live in a more scattered fashion, the presence of the town center and administrative structure was a critical first step in convincing state officials that the Shuar deserved title to the agricultural lands surrounding the central plaza. Subsequently, several of the centros came together to form the Asociación de Sucúa, which the government recognized in 1962. Less than two years later, this association came together with others that had been formed since 1962 to create the Shuar Federation.[46]

The Salesian mission aided Shuar who wanted to establish cattle herds, first by providing them with cattle from small mission herds and later by offering credit to individuals on a rotating basis.[47] Once the Shuar Federation gained organizational experience with land legalization and cattle projects, they expanded their activities, advocating for self-determination, economic self-sufficiency, bilingual education, health care, and civil rights. The federation and the mission together founded a nonprofit publishing company, Mundo Shuar (Shuar World), which published about seventy books on Amazonian cultures.[48] Starting in 1972, they also coproduced a bilingual radio program that was broadcast widely and that focused on bilingual elementary education and adult literacy.[49]

Lowland Quichua in Napo Province, like the Shuar, received some initial assistance from Catholic missionaries in their efforts to protect their lands from colonist takeover. In the 1960s, the Josephines promoted the formation of a local affiliate of the Confederación Ecuatoriana de Organizaciones Sindicales Cristianas (CEDOC, Ecuadorian Confederation of Christian Syndical Organizations), a national organization with strong ties to the Christian Democrats, particularly in Germany.[50] The Shuar Federation was held up by this confederation as an example for Quichua leaders. While those who attended courses on leadership and organization formation sponsored by the confederation recognized their value, they soon sought to form an organization that was more independent of the mission. Some were schoolteachers, and others had learned about labor organizing while working for short stints on coastal plantations. They formed Prodefensa, an organization primarily concerned with defending Quichua lands from takeover by colonists. Prodefensa existed only a few months, but several members went on to establish cooperatives and other organizations with the primary goal of obtaining legal title to their lands. Of particular importance was the Federación Provincial de Organizaciones Campesinas de Napo (FEPOCAN, Provincial Federation of Peasant Organizations of Napo) formed by leaders from seven Quichua regions in June 1969.[51] In 1973, the group changed its name to the Federación de Organizaciones Indígenas del Napo (FOIN, Federation of Indigenous Organizations of Napo), a change seen by some analysts as indicating a growing emphasis on cultural distinctiveness.[52] However, from its founding, FEPOCAN restricted its membership to Quichua community organizations and sought to protect Quichua lands from takeover by highland peasants and commercial interests.[53]

FEPOCAN's early priorities had much in common with those of the Shuar Federation, including legalizing indigenous land claims, recruiting additional communities into the organization, and defending and promoting civil and human rights for indigenous people in Napo Province.[54] As in the case of the Shuar, before the wave of colonization inspired by the 1964 agrarian reform, most Quichua did not live in nucleated settlements. However, to obtain recognition of their land claims by the state, both groups had to adjust their residential and livelihood practices to fit the state's ideal of a modern peasantry. While both organizations were formed in part to assert the rights of indigenous peoples, their activities promoted greater state involvement in members' lives. As in the highland communities, this involvement began in 1964 with the Ecuadorian Institute for Agrarian Reform and Colonization (IERAC). In a few years it included the state development bank, the Ecuadorian Institute of Social Security (particularly through the *seguro campesino* program), the Ministry of Education (as state schools supplemented or replaced existing missionary ones), and the Ministry of Agriculture and Ranching.

By 1978, FOIN's membership had expanded from a handful of base organizations in 1969 to include 43 associations, 25 *comunas* (collective landowning communities), and 6 agricultural cooperatives.[55] Bilingual education and projects specifically designed to promote the Quichua language or cultural distinctiveness were not early priorities. Rather, FOIN's development projects in the 1970s were focused largely on increasing market-oriented agricultural production, increasing access to Western health services, and providing training on how to form local organizations to serve as intermediaries between Quichua households and FOIN.[56] Like the Shuar Federation, FOIN served as an intermediary between its constituent organizations and aid programs (financed both by the state and by international sources) and provided credit for increasing agricultural production.

The Organization of Indigenous Peoples of Pastaza (OPIP), which represented Quichua, Achuar, and Schiwiar communities in Pastaza Province, was formed in 1979 and also saw land defense as its primary purpose.[57] In August 1980, OPIP joined FOIN and the Shuar Federation to form the Confederation of Indigenous Nationalities of the Ecuadorian Amazon (CONFENIAE). While these groups differed in their history of interaction with Catholic missions, the state, and the market economy, there were also areas of historical and ideological overlap, with potential collaboration on similar political projects. Use of the words "indigenous nationalities" in the name of the confederation was a last-minute change from a previous name that spoke of "indigenous organizations,"[58] indicating that Amazonian leaders were well aware of regional discourses of *neoindigenismo.* In the meetings that led to the founding of CONFENIAE, leaders discussed resisting colonization, pushing for a greater role in national politics, promoting education and literacy, revalorizing indigenous medicine and languages, and developing "relations of solidarity with like-minded organizations within and outside of the country." They also pledged to obtain funding from the state for their various projects and to "foster the spirit of unification [and] social, economic, and cultural consolidation through seminars, meetings, courses, etc."[59] Like those in the highlands, Amazonian activists pushed the Roldós regime to expand its pluricultural model to include territorial and political rights.

The organizational representatives that came together to form CONFENIAE had no intention of suppressing their ethnic distinctiveness in the hopes of strengthening organizational unity. Despite a long history of interethnic rivalries, they were able to appreciate the diversity of cultures that were present and to work toward recognizing the commonalities in the subordination shared by all lowland Indians, regardless of ethnicity. Unlike highland activists, they were not hindered by tensions between those who wanted to pursue special rights as Indians versus those who wanted to join with other poor peasants to pursue access to land and other class-based aims. An important component of the lowland understanding of rights specific to Indians was the notion of *territory,* as opposed to simply *land,* as a site of cultural reproduction and political autonomy. This notion later influenced highland activists as they reimagined their own appeals for greater access to land.[60]

Early Campaigns and Victories

While in the 1960s and 1970s indigenous Amazonians gained experience in forming large organizations and used these organizations to increase members' access to state programs, the 1980s signaled a new use for them. Specifically, Amazonian groups began to use their organizations to challenge the state and its intermediaries. Rather than simply exploiting divisions within the state or between the mission and hacendados to their advantage, as they had done in the past, indigenous people began to understand that they were powerful enough to create their own political openings.

Before confronting the state, however, indigenous organizations used their new cross-regional alliances to imagine, and later demand, better treatment from local missions. Because the Amazonian missions were crucial to governance and paving the way for the greater incorporation of indigenous peoples into the national economy, it is not surprising that these missions were the target of some of the first organized challenges by indigenous federations.[61] Two meetings occurred in the early 1980s that inspired activists to challenge the status quo. The first occurred in November 1980, when representatives from various missions and indigenous communities from the greater Amazon region met in Manaos, Brazil. The second was held December 18–20, 1981, in Puyo, when indigenous groups from the Ecuadorian Amazon met to compare their experiences with local missions and to share ideas about improving their relationships with them.

FOIN then drafted a document called "Recommendations that FOIN Will Present to the Josephine Mission" that sought additional resources from the mission and challenged its conduct of business in Napo. The group demanded more educational scholarships and jobs for indigenous people, particularly as assistant nurses in mission hospitals and as directors of mission-operated elementary schools. It also asked the mission to use its radio broadcast for bilingual educational programming similar to that developed by the Shuar Federation in conjunction with the Salesian mission. FOIN also demanded that the Josephine mission work harder to coordinate its activities with them and with the other Amazonian missions. This was partially a response to the divisions within the indigenous community arising from antagonisms between evangelical and Catholic missions.

Furthermore, FOIN directly criticized the mission's past practices in the following demand: "Fourth, that the Josephine mission refrain from meddling in the political and internal affairs of the [indigenous] organizations [which] prohibit priests from MARXIST or COMMUNIST political proselytizing, because [we] indigenous people are not interested in China, nor Russia, nor Albania. We believe in our own indigenous reality and we are reconstructing our own politics within the Ecuadorian national context." The passage is particularly interesting, given the highland organization FEI's history of ties to the Communist Party.[62] FOIN strongly asserted both its desire to have unique political beliefs and goals as "indigenous" people and to continue to engage in the national political system as full citizens.

Interestingly, in spite of these expressed desires to form an autonomous political platform, the bilingual radio programming provided by missions was still seen as beneficial by both Shuar and Quichua, even though the Salesian mission used radio programming for evangelizing, openly stating that the radio programs were intended for "Christian inspiration," designed to make listeners "start thinking in a new way."[63] Thus, unlike in the highlands, gaining greater control over bilingual education was not an early priority for lowland activists. Just when the Shuar and lowland Quichua were meeting and drafting these recommendations, inviting the missions into their homes in the form of bilingual radio programs, highland activists were actively attempting to wrest control over bilingual education programs from the state. By 1982, however, CONFENIAE delegates had identified state-supported (but not state-controlled) bilingual education as a priority, specifying that "this education should be done according to our needs, permitting the reproduction of our culture and additionally the active participation of indigenous people in the socioeconomic life of the country."[64] This change in understanding of the power of bilingual education indicates the increased communication between highland and lowland activists.

In response to the demands made by Amazonian federations, in March 1982 members of the Josephine mission met with representatives from nine missions working in the Ecuadorian Amazon, both Catholic and evangelical. They discussed the challenges they were facing from indigenous leaders and drafted a "Declaration and Commitment for the Intermissional Coordination for the Development of the Ecuadorian Amazon Region." They pledged to work more collaboratively with one another, including working with Catholic and Protestant missions. They also responded directly to some of the recommendations listed by FOIN leaders, including complaints about religious proselytizing and party politics. Finally, they promised to support indigenous organizations and to help them pursue their goals.

The successful campaign against the missions in the Amazon demonstrated to leaders how meetings at the regional, national, and international levels allowed them, with their limited organizing experience, to come together and formulate concrete steps toward improving the political and economic situation of their constituents. By comparing experiences and ideas for political strategies, leaders could better imagine alternative futures and how to achieve them. This provided an important precedent for later organizing against state programs and policies, both through CONFENIAE and together with highland groups through CONAIE. These two federations soon became increasingly bold in their demands on the state, building on the base of confidence established with the campaigns of the early 1980s.

Because the civilizing aims of Jesuit and other church representatives in the Ecuadorian Amazon overlapped substantially with those of the state during much of the last four centuries, any examination of Indians' relationships with the state must take into account their relations with the missions. Amazonians with the greatest contact with state and church representatives used similar practices to contest domination by both missionaries and local state officials, and some of these tactics mirrored those used by highland Indians. At times, Amazonians could exacerbate tensions between the various groups who attempted to dominate them and thereby create political openings for improving their quality of life. Thus, they understood the government system with its multiple entities and existing cleavages, while they simultaneously accepted the government idea, refraining from violent rebellion except on a few occasions.

Other Amazonian groups with less extended contact rejected both state and mission governance more successfully, although they stood to suffer more intensely during economic boom periods and from early mestizo colonization when they did not have the necessary political experience or relationship with the central state to contest exploitative practices. Yet their ability to resist domination in the periods between booms provided an important alternative vision to those who engaged more fully with whites, a vision and set of techniques comparatively unavailable to highland Indians. In the nineteenth century in particular, Amazonians used the very fathomable threat of escaping farther into the forest to challenge mistreatment by missionaries. Just over a century later, conversations among multiple ethnic groups in the Amazon elicited more elaborate demands on missionaries and responses that indicated increased respect for indigenous organizations. These early successes built confidence for CONFENIAE's subsequent confrontations with the state as well as with oil companies and other transnational interests.

From *Indigenismo* to Indigenous Movements in Ecuador and Mexico

SHANNAN L. MATTIACE

Although Mexico has the largest number of indigenous peoples in the Americas, Indian organizations in Mexico have not come together to form a strong national-level Indian movement. Even after the emergence of the Ejército Zapatista de Liberación Nacional (EZLN, Zapatista Army of National Liberation) on January 1, 1994, in the southern state of Chiapas, a national Indian movement has not been consolidated.[1] The Mexican case stands in marked contrast to that of Ecuador, where, during the 1990s, the Confederación de Nacionalidades Indígenas del Ecuador (CONAIE, Confederation of Indigenous Nationalities of Ecuador) successfully united highland and lowland, local and regional Indian associations into an umbrella organization that has become a significant political force on the national level. The contrast between the two cases is striking and deeply connected to the role of the Mexican and Ecuadorian states vis-à-vis the indigenous peoples living within their borders.

Throughout the twentieth century, the Mexican state penetrated indigenous, rural areas of the country and exerted a stronger presence in these areas than its Ecuadorian counterpart. Because of the relative strength of the Mexican state and its greater presence in the countryside, Mexico was more adept at coopting independent and potentially independent indigenous organizations and leaders than the Ecuadorian state. Ecuador, in contrast, has been subject to pressure from Indian organizations, especially after the 1990 uprising. At the center of Mexican *indigenismo* was a host of government policies and programs for indigenous peoples.[2] To the contrary, in Ecuador, "protection" of indigenous peoples was left largely to the local administration of hacendados, whose power in rural areas was not seriously challenged until the agrarian reforms of the 1960s and 1970s.[3] Whereas indigenismo emerged under different circumstances in the two countries—from a revolutionary context in Mexico and from a liberal context in Ecuador—the content of indigenist policies in both cases was similar. Throughout most of the twentieth century, assimilation was the goal. By the 1990s, however, assimilationism was supplanted by new policies that emphasized cultural distinctiveness and difference. This shift was the result of many factors: new trends in international development assistance and aid, changes in international law, the decline of class-based organizations, and the increasing strength of Indian mobilization that had been building from the 1970s. In both Ecuador and Mexico, these new policies emerged in a wider context of neoliberal economic reform and political democracy.

In the 1980s and 1990s, differences between indigenist policy in Ecuador and Mexico rested less on the relative strength of the state and its ability to penetrate the countryside and more on the strength of independent Indian organizations.[4] Today, Indian organizations in Mexico and Ecuador frame their demands for land, autonomy, and rights as "equality in difference." This mix of demands—for equal rights and for rights to difference—is not new. What is new, in terms of indigenous demand making, is that Indian organizations are proposing alternative models to the classic model of the nation-state, forcing states to rethink the relationship between the state and indigenous peoples. Support for these alternative nation-building models is coming from outside as well as from within: from nongovernmental organizations (NGOs) operating on the regional and international levels, from intergovernmental organizations, such as the United Nations and the Organization of American States, and from internationally based foundations.

Forging *la Patria* in Mexico

For the leaders and the party that emerged from the revolutionary period of 1910–1917, unity among Mexico's diverse regions and peoples was a central goal. Mexican leaders sought to forge *la patria* (the nation).[5] For postrevolutionary state officials, nationalism meant progress and unity. That unity would come, in part, through racial assimilation—turning Indians into mestizos, or Mexicans. Mexican leaders coming to power in the wake of the revolution placed the mestizo at the center of their image of a modern, progressive country. The Confederación Nacional Campesina (CNC, National Peasant

Confederation), created in 1938, and the Instituto Nacional Indigenista (INI, National Indigenist Institute), created in 1948, were the two most important institutions linking indigenous peoples to the state in twentieth-century Mexico. The CNC was based explicitly on Indian assimilation, while the INI was created to deal with Indians who were not likely to assimilate.[6]

The National Peasant Confederation was part of Mexico's system of state corporatism, institutionalized during the administration of President Lázaro Cárdenas (1934–1940). Workers and peasants (and, to a lesser extent, urban dwellers after 1943) were organized into hierarchical groups based on occupation and linked directly to the state through membership in the Partido Revolucionario Institucional (PRI, Institutional Revolutionary Party). Peasants, for example, were to be organized into local-level CNC branches that were tied to subnational and national organizations. Credit from government agencies was to be funneled through the CNC, and CNC affiliates were given preference over nonaffiliates in the distribution of land. This system separated workers, peasants, and urban dwellers by organizing them in distinct confederations, thus preventing the possibility of another revolution. Yet it also kept popular sectors tied to the state and gave millions of Mexican citizens access to state largesse.

The state "encouraged" peasants and workers to join the CNC by employing both the carrot and the stick. While the state offered positive incentives for peasants to join, such as credit and crop subsidies, party officials did not hesitate to use force if peasants did not respond to state overtures. This was especially true in the heavily indigenous southern state of Chiapas, where state governors were historically closely aligned with landowners, often using state power to ensure a docile, largely Indian workforce on the region's many large estates. Peasants who operated outside the CNC were subject to harsh reprisals by landowners and the state police.[7] In exchange for access to credit and land, the PRI expected political loyalty from CNC affiliates. To put it simply, the state or party was the patron that delivered the goods (such as subsidies, credit, land), and the peasants were the clients who voted for the PRI on election day. Through corporatism, the PRI shored up solid majorities in the countryside at election time and stymied the possibility of future unrest and rebellion.[8]

From the perspective of Mexican policy makers, tying peasants to the party and state through the National Peasant Confederation was an effective way to assimilate the country's indigenous population. Yet, policy makers acknowledged that not all Indians were assimilable. For those Indians, other mechanisms had to be created. The state's first concentrated effort to coordinate its activities in indigenous areas of the country was the creation in 1936 of the Autonomous Department of Indian Affairs, proposed by Cárdenas's minister of education, Moisés Sáenz. The express purpose of the department was to coordinate the development efforts of all public agencies working in indigenous areas and to adapt them to the particular requirements of each group.[9] These efforts culminated in the creation of the National Indigenist Institute (INI) in 1948. The goal pursued by Sáenz was not the incorporation of the Indian, but the integration of Mexico "through the building of a great nation linked together in a just and efficacious economic system."[10]

Of all Latin American countries in the twentieth century, the Mexican state created the most robust set of indigenist institutions. Indeed, at the First Interamerican Indigenist Conference held in Pátzcuaro, Michoacán, in 1940, Mexican delegates urged policy makers to develop national-level indigenist institutes.[11] Under President Alemán's watch (1946–1952), the National Indigenist Institute was created "as a public, decentralized organism of the federal government in charge of designing and instituting government policy toward the indigenous peoples of Mexico."[12] Undergirding the founding of this institute was the idea, dominant during the Cárdenas administration, of respectful, noncoercive integration of Mexico's Indians into the nation. INI's original mandate was to coordinate the activities of diverse government agencies and dependencies operating in indigenous areas, not to make and implement policy.[13] Because of the absence of government agencies in many areas, however, the INI gradually began to attend to indigenous needs, as it defined them, and to design and implement various educational, medical, agricultural, and general assistance programs for Indians.

From its inception, the INI occupied an uncomfortable position within the Mexican state system and bureaucratic apparatus. INI's budget was chronically small, even compared to other federal social service agencies. Yet the INI played a key role in service of the Mexican state as idea. The postrevolutionary Mexican state (indeed, the same could be said for the postindependence state) projected the idea of a mestizo society and culture with a glorious indigenous past. This state idea remained remarkably stable over time, and the INI played a crucial role in mediating the tensions between the idea of Mexico's noble indigenous past and attempts to assimilate present-day indigenous peoples into national (that is, mestizo) life while at the same time preserving those indigenous characteristics that were "culturally and socially valuable."

In Ecuador, early expressions of political indigenismo emerged after the Liberal Revolution of 1895. After the 1895 revolution, the liberal state was informed by strong pro-Indian attitudes. Radical liberals allied with Indian peasants and leaders against regional white-mestizo elites. The indigenist rhetoric of this period, steeped in paternalism, emerged from urban, liberal intellectuals who urged citizenship for all inhabitants, Indians included, yet understood that the Indian population needed extra protection from exploitation.

Both Ecuador's liberal intellectuals at the turn of the nineteenth century and Mexican revolutionary leaders after 1920 believed fervently in progress and modernization. Elites in Mexico may have disagreed about the best method of integrating Indians into the national culture, but they both saw the integration of indigenous peoples as necessary and yoked the ultimate success of the national project (and of modernization itself) to that integration. However, because the dictator ousted in the first wave of revolutionary activity in Mexico, Porfirio Díaz, had ruled as a liberal, revolutionary leaders distanced themselves from liberalism. Public discourse by official party (PRI) leaders after 1929 stressed the party's popular origins, even as its policies showed more continuity than rupture with the liberal Díaz regime. Thus in both countries, liberal ideals and deep-seated paternalism toward indigenous peoples coexisted in government discourse and policy.

In Ecuador in the late nineteenth and early twentieth centuries, landowners, not state policy makers, were largely responsible for "protecting" Indians. Drawing on the work of Andrés Guerrero, José Antonio Lucero argues that in this era "'ethnic administration' in Ecuador was effectively localized and virtually privatized, as hacendados, the church, and other local powers were essentially given charge of 'their' Indians." This system of ethnic administration was virtually untouched by legislation passed in 1937 (the Ley de Comunas) that recognized the legal standing of indigenous communities and remained in place until the agrarian reforms of the 1960s and 1970s.[14] In Mexico, by contrast, the state took over "ethnic administration" after the revolution, supplanting the figure of patron-landowner with its own version of paternalist "protection." During most of the twentieth century, the most significant difference between Mexico's and Ecuador's versions of indigenismo was not that it was strong in Mexico and weak in Ecuador, but that indigenismo in Mexico was more state-driven and policy-oriented.

The longevity and continuity of indigenist institutions in each country also help to explain differences in the relative strength of indigenismo. Indigenist institutions in twentieth-century Mexico were initially created by the PRI and remained under its control for decades.[15] This stands in marked contrast to Ecuador (and the rest of Latin America), where there was much less regime stability and periods of liberal rule alternated with periods of conservative or military rule. As we have seen, Mexico was an early leader in calling for the creation of national-level indigenist organizations and, despite the relative lack of funding vis-à-vis other federal agencies, maintained these institutions over the course of the twentieth century.[16]

As a result, the relative strength and presence of the National Indigenist Institute (INI) and the National Peasant Confederation (CNC) in the Mexican countryside made it less likely that independent Indian organizations would emerge to challenge the state. A related point is that Mexican indigenist institutions have provided employment for a multitude of non-Indian advisors who have dominated policy making on Indian affairs, thus crowding out the voices of Indian organization leaders and would-be leaders. Since its creation in 1948, the National Indigenist Institute and its affiliate organizations around the country have generated employment for thousands of social scientists (especially anthropologists) and lower-level bureaucrats, many of them trained at the National School of Anthropology and History (ENAH) in Mexico City. While it is common across Latin America for non-Indians to serve as advisors to the government on Indian affairs, Mexico is unsurpassed in the sheer number of its non-Indian advisors. Non-Indians have also served as consultants to independent Indian organizations. Yet, while they may have crowded out the independent Indian voices that have emerged outside the state system, INI officials within the system are often viewed as having "gone native."

One of the tensions within the Mexican state system, particularly since the 1970s, has been the perceived loyalty of INI employees to the general goals of the state (the PRI party until 2000). The INI is viewed as one of the more progressive federal agencies and its officials and employees as sympathetic to indigenous "causes." During the peace negotiations between the Mexican government and the EZLN on Indian rights and culture held between October 1995 and February 1996, the government invited the INI, its official voice on Indian affairs, to serve as advisors to the government's team during the first round of negotiations. Yet the INI was not invited back to the second and third round of negotiations! While no official explication was given for this decision, observers suggested that it was because INI officials publicly supported the justness of the EZLN's demands (but not its methods) during the first round of negotiations. The mistrust between INI and other state officials is perhaps greater at the subnational level, particularly in conservative states. In one notorious incident in Chiapas in 1990, the state governor, Patrocinio González Garrido, forced the INI regional director in Las Margaritas to resign. The governor accused the INI director of helping leaders of a radical local union acquire government funding to purchase a coffee-processing plant from the Mexican Institute of Coffee (INMECAFE). Two years later, the Chiapas state government jailed three INI officials for the "crime" of having supported independent peasant organizations.[17]

If the INI played a significant role in providing employment for non-Indians, it also provided training, education, and employment for thousands of indigenous Mexicans as well. While most high-level INI administrative positions were occupied by non-Indians, many Indians received training in education, bilingual education, leadership, cultural "revival," and radio production and programming that they later used to create and sustain independent organizations.[18]

Indigenous organizations in Mexico have not forcefully separated themselves from this institutional apparatus of advisors, as has occurred in Ecuador. Amalia Pallares argues that in the late 1970s a number of Indian organizations in Ecuador's highlands broke with their mestizo advisors, passing through a period of separatist development.[19] It is difficult to locate such a moment in the history of Mexico's Indian movement. During the peace negotiations between the government and EZLN delegates in Chiapas beginning in 1994, for example, hundreds of non-Indian advisors to the Zapatistas exerted considerable influence on the process.

Negotiating Autonomy, Mapping Multiculturalism

In the late 1980s, assimilationism—the dominant orientation of indigenist policy making for decades—gave way to multiculturalism.[20] Across Latin America, reforms were passed that constitutionally enshrined rights for indigenous peoples (and in some cases Afro-descendant peoples) for the first time. These reforms took place within a context of economic liberalization and electoral democracy. In the 1990s, for example, a dozen Latin American countries ratified Convention 169, the International Labor Organization's (ILO's) legislation on Indian rights and the protection of Indian workers. Among other things, the convention obliges signatory countries to consult with indigenous peoples about development projects that affect indigenous land, resources, and culture.[21]

In both Mexico and Ecuador, institutional changes regarding Indian rights have been largely symbolic. In an era of shrinking national budgets and fiscal constraint, policy makers have amended constitutions and passed legislation granting additional rights to Indian people, while they have defunded ministries and programs that have long been important to indigenous peoples, such as the Ministry of Land Reform and social service agencies. In response, Ecuador's indigenous organizations, represented by CONAIE, have engaged in a mix of institutional and extrainstitutional politics, fielding candidates for public office, and organizing nationwide protests and blockades. In contrast, the EZLN in Mexico, after a brief engagement with institutional politics in the mid-1990s, has largely withdrawn from formal politics. Indian organizations in both countries, however, have been at the forefront of struggles opposing neoliberalism and globalization.

For most of the twentieth century, official expressions of Mexican national identity were bound to the ideals of the revolution, as articulated by the PRI. Under President Carlos Salinas de Gortari (1988–1994), these ideals shifted dramatically. Architect of the North American Free Trade Agreement (NAFTA), Salinas committed future Mexican political leaders to a regime of free trade and investment. Beyond economic reforms, Salinas proposed the "modernization" of a host of other policy arenas. Laws were passed, for example, recognizing dual citizenship for Mexicans living abroad.

In an effort to preempt rising Indian activism within Mexico, as well as to raise Mexico's international profile, Salinas pushed through several constitutional initiatives focused on the relationship between Mexico's indigenous peoples and the state. In 1990, Mexico became the second country in the world to ratify ILO Convention 169. In 1992, Salinas pushed through an amendment to the constitution (Article 4) declaring Mexico to be a multicultural nation "originally based on its indigenous peoples."[22] Article 4 states that the law "will protect and promote the development of their [Indian] languages, cultures, traditions, customs, resources, and specific forms of social organization and will guarantee their members effective access to the jurisdiction of the State." The administration, however, made no serious effort to reconcile the promises of Article 4 with current reforms in agriculture that affected millions of indigenous peoples. That same year, Salinas pushed through an amendment to Article 27 that effectively ended the government's role in distributing *ejido* land.[23] The reforms to Article 27 also allowed ejido land to be used as collateral or to be bought and sold on the private market. These reforms, and the absence of implementing legislation for Article 4, greatly reduced the latter's significance, making it largely symbolic.[24]

The 1998 Ecuadorian constitution also formally recognized Ecuador's indigenous peoples and defined the Ecuadorian state as "pluricultural and multiethnic." This symbolic recognition extended to explicitly recognizing and guaranteeing the existence of indigenous forms of social organization, the official and public nature of indigenous customary law and jurisdiction over internal community affairs, the constitutional guarantee to bilingual education, and the right of indigenous communities to own property in common.[25]

In Mexico there was little substantive consultation with indigenous organizations before Salinas pushed through the amendment to Article 4.[26] In Ecuador, by contrast, the 1997 constitutional assembly occurred within the context of a strong and growing national Indian movement. Before the 1997 assembly, CONAIE, Pachakutik (the indigenous political movement established in 1996), and several other national-level organizations met to discuss the issues that would be addressed by the assembly.[27] Two principal demands were central to the indigenous agenda: establishment of Ecuador as a plurinational nation and declaration of a series of interrelated indigenous rights; and the creation of indigenous and black electoral districts (circumscriptions). The law of indigenous and black circumscriptions has yet to be created, however, and the indigenous nationalities law designed to predate the circumscription law and initially submitted to congress in 2001 was approved but vetoed by President Lucio Gutiérrez in 2003. Until these constitutional amendments and legal initiatives are made law, they will have little or no impact on policy.

In Ecuador, as in Mexico, policy makers conceive of multiculturalism as one state consisting of a plurality of cultures. In contrast, the definition supported by the national Indian movement is based on another model, or multiple models, of nation. According to Pallares, under the state's model, Ecuador consists of different cultures that coexist within the framework of universal rights. Indigenist policy making in Ecuador has focused on education and educational policy, for example, as a way of empowering indigenous peoples and improving their living conditions. For the Indian movement led by CONAIE, in contrast, Ecuador is a plurality of *nations*, and Indians are different citizens; that is, the state's relationship with indigenous citizens is different from the state's relationship with non-Indians. For Indian activists, equality in citizenship will occur only when Indians are visible as distinct and different political actors. For the movement, pluralism has at least three components: cultural rights, economic rights, and political empowerment.

Despite these differences, in the negotiations between the two parties after the 1990 uprising, both sides modified their positions on multiculturalism. Under pressure from CONAIE, the state has moved from an exclusive focus on education to a discussion of socioeconomic rights. CONAIE, for its part, continues to hold up plurinationalism as its model for state-indigenous relations but does not make it the sine qua non for negotiating with state officials.

Indian organizations in Mexico, on the other hand, have not placed plurinationalism at the center of their demands. The EZLN and its advisors, for example, did not raise the issue in the peace negotiations between October 1995 and February 1996, but they did insist that the state envision a new relationship with its indigenous peoples. It would be protected not by an exclusive commitment to universal rights, but by a combination of universal and differential rights. For example, indigenous law was protected on a community level as long as individual human rights were also respected.[28] After months of discussion and deliberation, an accord on Indian culture and rights was signed in February 1996 that included umbrella legislation to protect Indian autonomy.[29] Indigenous communities and municipalities would have the right to practice their own law, to use their own mechanisms for electing local officials, and to control resources on their land, among other provisions. Negotiating such provisions to protect their autonomy was a notable success for the EZLN and for indigenous organizations in Mexico, given the government's refusal to acknowledge Indians' right to political autonomy on any level before 1994. Several months after the accord was signed, however, President Zedillo deemed parts of it unconstitutional, and the EZLN rejected the bill that was ultimately sent to Congress in the spring of 2001 under Fox's watch.[30]

Given the overwhelming and widespread support for the San Andrés Accords on Indian Culture and Rights among indigenous organizations, the EZLN appeared poised to consolidate its position as the leading indigenous organization in Mexico.[31] After the signing of the accords in early 1996 and as peace negotiations continued, there was considerable hope that the EZLN would make a peaceful transition from an armed movement to a civil organization and solidify its leadership of a national movement. However, after a significantly watered-down version of a bill on Indian rights and culture was passed by both houses of congress in 2001, the EZLN withdrew to the territories under its control and ceased to engage in formal politics. The EZLN has focused instead on strengthening *de facto* autonomy within its own communities and regions.

The EZLN has had a tense relationship with the political party most likely to support its demands, the left-of-center Partido de la Revolución Democrática (PRD, Party of the Democratic Revolution).[32] While national-level indigenous organizations in Mexico do exist, such as the Congreso Nacional Indígena (CNI, National Indian Congress) and the Asamblea Nacional Indígena por la Autonomía (ANIPA, National Indian Assembly in Support of Autonomy), they do not function as coordinating, or umbrella, organizations for the Indian movement. Mexico has no single national-level indigenous organization with the scope or authority of CONAIE in Ecuador, which has combined extrainstitutional activism with institutional participation and involvement in national politics.

Despite their significant differences in relative strength and level of involvement in formal institutional politics, Indian organizations in Ecuador and Mexico are at the forefront of protests against neoliberalism. CONAIE, for example, has consistently opposed the Free Trade Area of the Americas (FTAA), an economic and investment pact first proposed in 1994 by 34 Latin and North American heads of state that would extend NAFTA throughout the Americas. In a 2002 interview, CONAIE leader Luis Macas articulated his opposition:

> The Free Trade Area of the Americas is not an equitable model of integration; in such an agreement the Andean region would enter as an inferior partner. National industry cannot compete with the large transnational, U.S.-based companies that would take over the market. For example, agricultural production in the region cannot compete with subsidized North American production. Under such an agreement, an increasing number of rural industries and producers would go out of business; thus, fewer jobs would be available, resulting in increased unemployment. The United States is not willing to eliminate agricultural subsidies, nor is it willing to liberalize the barriers on international goods entering its markets. As it is now proposed, the FTAA is an economic structure of annexation that would swallow up Ecuador, the Andean region, and all of Latin America. For this reason, it is necessary to work together to create common policies in opposition to this agreement and in defense of regional integration based on sovereignty and democracy.[33]

Mexican indigenous organizations are also at the forefront of the antineoliberal, antiglobalization movement. Recently, those efforts have focused on opposition to a massive development project proposed by the Fox administration called Plan Puebla-Panamá (PPP) that would stretch from Puebla, Mexico (approximately a two-hour drive east of Mexico City) to Panamá, Central America.[34] Through a combination of public and private investment, transportation links would be built to unite the region, including highways, electricity and gas lines, airports, and seaports. These links would, in Fox's words, "rescue the south-southeast region of the country from its backwardness."[35] After he was sworn in as president on December 1, 2000, Fox assembled a team of public officials to coordinate the project, and in the spring of 2001 the Official General Coordinating Committee of Plan Puebla-Panamá was officially created.[36]

The National Indian Congress (CNI) has publicly opposed this plan, claiming that it is an attempt to "massively privatize our territories, divide up the communal property of our peoples, and appropriate—by large international consortia—our natural riches and our ancestral wisdom."[37] The CNI has been active in organizing resistance to the PPP through information-gathering forums, creating a network of opposition groups throughout the region, and spearheading public marches and protests, often in concert with the EZLN. In August 2003, the EZLN launched a counterplan, Plan La Realidad–Tijuana, which would set up a network of basic commerce between and among local and regional communities. This plan calls for respect of local autonomy efforts throughout the country. For both CONAIE and ELZN, then, organizational demands include both collective and individual rights.

Continuities and Differences in Indigenous Demand Making

A key theme that emerges in this volume is the historically dynamic relationship that has existed between state officials (operating at different levels of government) and indigenous peoples. As we have seen, nineteenth-century state officials vacillated between dealing with indigenous peoples as corporate groups and as individual citizens. As Derek Williams notes, "Midcentury liberal reformism in Ecuador was weak by Latin American standards and left an ambiguous balance between individual and corporate rights." Aleezé Sattar also characterizes the postindependence Ecuadorian state as bifurcated between colonial and republican approaches to dealing with Indians as subjects and as citizens. This point is linked to her larger claim that there has been continuity, not rupture, between colonial and postcolonial periods. Indians, in turn, alternately framed their demands in corporate or individual terms, depending on the administration in office and the shifting relations between national and local state officials.[38] While corporatist political structures have been largely dismantled across Latin America, one legacy of corporatism is the persistent demand for group rights. As we have seen, in Mexico, the chief corporatist identity in the countryside was that of peasant. Calling for autonomy, Indian activists continue to make demands for land and communal rights to land and its resources, even in the current period dominated by the emphasis on privatization and individual land titles.

A striking difference between Indian-state relations in the mid-nineteenth century and today is the presence of a new actor: the international community. The United Nations and its affiliate organizations, such as the International Labor Organization, have taken a lead both in laying out standards for protecting individual rights and codifying group rights for indigenous peoples.[39] The support of international intergovernment organizations like the UN, as well as nongovernmental organizations such as Cultural Survival, has been crucial in buttressing indigenous peoples' demands for both individual and group rights.

If nineteenth-century relations were defined principally as the state acting and Indian people responding to state directives in creative and adept ways, indigenous peoples today are increasingly shaping the terms of the debate. Empowered through pan-Indian organizations and the support of transnational networks, indigenous peoples throughout the Americas are defending and asserting their identity within the framework of a renegotiated, more inclusive citizenship.[40] Today in Mexico, Ecuador, and across Latin America, indigenous peoples are demanding multiple types of citizenship. They demand citizenship on the basis of individual rights with guarantees of equal rights and representation at the national level *and* differential rights that recognize corporate indigenous authority structures in indigenous communities and regions.[41] Proponents of Indian autonomy insist that autonomy does not mean that the state can abrogate its responsibility to its citizens. Guillermo de la Peña explains this seeming contradiction by arguing that indigenous peoples in Mexico demand "ethnic citizenship": access to both citizenship rights and preferential rights based on ethnic identity.[42] Similarly, in his work on the 1990 Indian uprising in Ecuador, León Zamosc argues that the uprising was not a reaction against modernity, as has been charged, but a response to the hypocritical modernity advanced by the current regime. Zamosc claims that the rhetoric about universal citizenship put forth by liberal Ecuadorian statesmen was not matched by democratic institutions that allowed for popular participation. Indians, he argues, are demanding a more inclusive citizenship than the Ecuadorian state has offered in practice.[43] This volume provides needed historical context for understanding the dynamic interaction of the multiple types of citizenship demands that are being made in Ecuador, and across the Americas, today.

13

Barricades and Articulations

Comparing Ecuadorian and Bolivian Indigenous Politics

All the nation's centuries are marked by uprisings or rebellions; it is as if Bolivia were nothing but that which had been built between the walls of defensive barricades erected against a territory populated by the Indian masses (la indiada).

RENÉ ZAVALETA

JOSÉ ANTONIO LUCERO

Ecuador's history gives it an important place in the study of indigenous politics. The Confederation of Indigenous Nationalities of Ecuador (CONAIE) in particular has received special attention for the remarkable accomplishment of achieving a national and panethnic confederation that includes indigenous organizations from Ecuador's coastal, Andean, and Amazonian regions. In a remarkably short time, indigenous people have gone from political invisibility to becoming among the most important political actors, and biggest obstacles to neoliberal presidents, in the country.[1]

Of course, the "peculiarity" of Ecuador, to borrow E. P. Thompson's term, can only be appreciated in comparison to indigenous politics elsewhere. While indigenous movements have emerged in striking ways throughout the region, from Chiapas to Chile, in most Latin American countries José Carlos Mariátegui's old lament remains largely accurate: "The Indians lack national linkages. Their protests have always been regional."[2] Even in Bolivia, where, unlike Ecuador, indigenous people make up a majority of the national population and where indigenous people have engaged in perhaps more impressive (and even revolutionary) mobilization, the contemporary indigenous movement has been characterized more by regional fragmentation than national unity. Ecuador's seeming indigenous coherence stands in contrast to Bolivia's plurality. Both nations have seen remarkable changes in indigenous politics since 2000. The unity of Ecuador was dealt a serious blow due to an ill-fated alliance with the former army colonel (and now former president) Lucio

Gutiérrez, while the fragmented Bolivian movement environment produced the historic presidential campaign and victory of Evo Morales, the country's first indigenous president.

Comparing indigenous politics in Ecuador and Bolivia, home to arguably the strongest movements in the continent, reveals contrasting cases of the politics of articulation as theorized by Stuart Hall, James Clifford, Tanya Li, and others.[3] The double meaning of articulation provides a language for exploring both the discursive expressions and political "cobbling together" of political identities that occur during overlapping colonial, corporatist, and neoliberal moments. The ways in which indigenous projects have been expressed and cobbled together in Ecuador (in a more unified, though still divided movement) and Bolivia (in a more regionally differentiated constellation) reveal important lessons about political opportunities, the imagining of indigenous collectivities, and the political economies of neoliberal multiculturalism.[4]

An examination of indigenous articulation also converges with a dynamic conception of the state. Both states and movements are constellations of practices and ideas that interact with broader social forces. Indigenous politics in Bolivia and Ecuador differ widely in sequence, style, and structure. First, the national convergence of Amazonian and Andean currents is enabled in Ecuador and frustrated in Bolivia by the regional nature and sequence of independent (not class-based) indigenous organizing.[5] In Ecuador, "early" Amazonian organizations (in the 1960s) emerged in some cases before, but often at the same time, as their counterparts in the Andes, while in Bolivia highland activism came years before the "late" emergence of strong lowland indigenous actors in the 1980s and 1990s.

Second, Ecuadorian indigenous forms seem more "modern" and less tied to the kind of strong pre-Columbian, colonial, and corporatist historical legacies that shape indigenous contention in Bolivia. If indigenous communities are imagined and invented in both countries (as they are), it seems that the imaginings in Ecuador have been more strategic and less constrained than in Bolivia; however, this too may be changing with the indigenous-*cocalero* socialism of the Morales government. Finally, the transition from state corporatism and dictatorship to market neoliberalism and democracy in both countries provide a last set of key differences. In the 1990s, aggressive neoliberal policies and clientelistic party politics in Bolivia fragmented indigenous politics, while in Ecuador indigenous people were able to block neoliberal projects and make important gains within the state. Recent developments in Ecuador, however, suggest that indigenous politics are far from immune to cooptation or fragmentation. At the same time, recent developments in

Bolivia, especially the electoral victory of Evo Morales, indicate the possibilities of convergences of what Nancy Postero calls "post-multiculturalism."[6] In both countries, indigenous movements advance a broad political message captured in a phrase that has become commonplace in Ecuadorian indigenous protests: "Nothing only for Indians."[7]

Articulating Regions: Amazonian and Andean Contention

Regional dynamics have always been an important part of politics in Latin America. "Regions" are hardly stable, natural, or homogenous units, but rather the products of geography, politics, and culture. In Ecuador, coast, highlands, and Amazonian lowlands are the commonsense regional reference points of politics. In Bolivia, a country that lost its coast to Chile in the late nineteenth century, the highlands of the altiplano, the inter-Andean valleys of Cochabamba, and the lowlands of Santa Cruz are the main regional poles of economic and political life. Exploring the different regional opportunity structures in each county is important, as regions both enable and constrain indigenous mobilization. This is not surprising, given the long history of uneven state formation. As Dandler and Torrico explain with regard to Bolivia, "Local and regional 'states' . . . undermined every centralizing and pro-indigenous effort by the national 'state.'"[8]

For indigenous politics in both countries, highland and lowland indigenous politics share similar styles of contention, though the timing and relative parity of regional indigenous actors has differed. Indigenous politics has evolved in some strikingly similar ways across the Andean republics. The development of highland contention was shaped by a greater and more direct contact with the national state and with traditions of class-based organizing.[9] In the twentieth century, corporatist models, based somewhat on the experience of the Mexican Partido Revolucionario Insititucional (PRI), provided a model for many Latin American states to incorporate rural people not as Indians, but in Albó's phrase, "rebaptized as peasants."[10] Resistance to state incorporation from the left opposed state schemes, but shared state labels. "Peasant" or campesino identities and organizational forms left their mark in the highland federations that were often linked to larger worker federations or leftist parties. The experience of state corporatism in the mid-twentieth century, though stronger in Bolivia than in Ecuador, encouraged rural highland populations in both countries to think in terms of the language of class struggle to organize in unionlike organizational structures. If hegemony, as William Roseberry's reading of Gramsci suggests,[11] provides a language of contention, then the hegemony of class-based discourses and models during the 1960s and 1970s can explain much of the similarity between the tactics and rhetoric of ECUARUNARI (and the Federación Nacional de Organizaciones Campesinas [FENOC, National Federation of Peasant Organizations]) in Ecuador and the Confederación Sindical Única de Trabajadores Campesinos de Bolivia (CSUTCB, Unified Confederation of Rural Laborers of Bolivia) in the 1980s. They can even shed light on the identity crises that afflicted highland movements in both countries. The great debate among highland organizations was over how to harmonize class and ethnic identities, how to "see with both eyes," as the Katarista leader and later Bolivia's vice president, Víctor Hugo Cárdenas, put it. Over time both external political events, like the fall of the Berlin Wall and the crisis of the international Left, and internal ones, like the influence of more radical *indianista* writers like Fausto Reinaga, pushed class identities into the background, though not out of the picture.

If, in both countries, the highlands were home to class-based organizing, the lowlands were more hospitable to "ethnic" alternatives in the second half of the twentieth century. Throughout the central Andean republics, "the areas where the ethnic federation has proliferated are precisely those areas which were peripheral to or outside of the integrative horizons which have swept the Andean region over the past several millennia."[12] What Smith calls the "myth of vast Amazonian emptiness" had many negative consequences for lowland populations, yet the relatively weak presence of the national state gave indigenous people greater room to craft political identities and organizations that were distinct from the dominant traditions of the state and the Left.[13] The Amazon has been the crucible in which the contemporary vocabulary of indigenous "nationalities" and "peoples" was forged in both Ecuador and Bolivia.

Thus, it is no surprise that the first indigenous ethnic federations in the Americas emerged in the 1960s in the Amazonian regions. The first was the Shuar Federation, organized in Ecuador in 1964. Amazonian organizing in Ecuador continued through the 1970s and culminated with the 1980 establishment of the Confederación de Nacionalidades Indígenas de la Amazonia Ecuatoriana (CONFENIAE, Confederation of Indigenous Nationalities of the Ecuadorian Amazon). While regional Amazonian organizations emerged later in Bolivia, in the 1980s and 1990s, the Confederación de Pueblos Indígenas de Bolivia (CIDOB, Confederation of Indigenous Peoples of Eastern Bolivia) quickly acquired a surprising political presence, since it represented only 2 percent of the national indigenous population.

Despite the striking similarity of regional styles in both Ecuador and Bolivia, the national configurations of indigenous protest are quite different. In the Ecuadorian case—something unique in Latin America—the largest highland and lowland indigenous confederations (ECUARUNARI and CONFENIAE, respectively) have since 1986 been part of the same national confederation. The emergence of the national indigenous confederation, CONAIE, is essentially the convergence of two parallel organizational struggles. In Bolivia, such a convergence has not occurred and indigenous movements remain "limited in scope and fragmented in structure."[14]

This difference in indigenous political geographies is affected by the geography of dominant power (see table 13.1). Indigenous politics in Ecuador offers a mirror image to dominant elite arrangements. While political and economic elites are clustered around coastal Guayaquil and highland Quito, the Amazon for much of the nation's history was a faraway site of war (with Peru) or a promised land of resource explorations (for oil). The relative neglect of the Ecuadorian lowlands by the state allowed indigenous actors greater freedom in consolidating regional organizations that could confront the threats of outside

TABLE 13.1. REGIONAL CLEAVAGES AND PATTERNS OF INDIGENOUS REPRESENTATION IN ECUADOR AND BOLIVIA

	ECUADOR	BOLIVIA
Largest Indigenous Groups	Highlands: Quichua (85–90% of total Indian population	Highlands: Quechua, Aymara (98% of total Indian population)
	Lowlands: Shuar, Quichua (10 smaller groups)	Lowlands: Guaraní, Quechua, Aymara (35 other groups)
Non-Indian Elite Regional Cleavages	Coast (Guayaquil)/ Highland (Quito)	Eastern Lowlands (Santa Cruz)/Highlands (La Paz)
Indian Regional Cleavages	Lowlands/Highlands Coastal groups (weak)	Lowlands/Valleys/ Highlands
Timing of Indigenous Political Organizing	Lowlands (1960s)	Highlands (1970s)
	Highlands (1970s)	Lowlands (1980s)
	National (1980s)	Valleys (1980s)
Patterns of Indigenous Representation	Relative Unity (Pan-Regional CONAIE)*	Fragmentation along Regional and Ideological Lines (Lowlands: CIDOB; Valleys: Cocaleros; Highlands: CSUTCB, CONAMAQ)

*There are other "national" organizations, though less powerful than CONAIE.

forces like highland colonizers and multinational oil companies. In Bolivia, lowland groups had less room to maneuver, largely because of the central place of the lowlands in the distribution of power in the country.

The regional structures of opportunity—in terms of the existence of regional elite opposition—were more favorable in Ecuador than in Bolivia. In Ecuador, strong indigenous organizations emerged early in an Amazonian region that was relatively marginal to national elites who were concentrated in other regions.[15] Modern indigenous organizations emerged later in the highlands, especially after agrarian reform weakened landed elites that had controlled prior systems of ethnic administration. In Bolivia, in contrast, the lowland CIDOB became a strong force only in the 1990s, long after the Aymara and Quechua highland groups had become prominent in the 1970s. Why? Part of the reason lies in location: CIDOB emerged in the very center of the economically strong and politically conservative region of Santa Cruz. Lowland indigenous groups, explains Kevin Healy, were literally "surrounded by powerful white and mestizo cattle ranchers, large commercial farmers, agrobusinesses, and timber enterprises whose holdings had been bolstered by government and international aid."[16] The presence of powerful regional elites created an obstacle to indigenous political participation in lowland Bolivia that did not exist in lowland Ecuador.

In Bolivia, the relatively late entrance of lowland groups has important implications for the possibilities of a unifying national movement. Unlike the situation in Ecuador, where lowland and highland indigenous elites were in contact for decades (the Shuar Federation had an office in Quito in the 1970s), a critical mass of Bolivian lowland indigenous elites did not emerge until the late 1980s. And by 1985, the successive blows of economic crisis and neoliberal economic reform had cut the legs from under the highland Bolivian Left, most notably in the mining sector but also in the CSUTCB. This crisis in the highlands enabled the rise of powerful movements in the valley (around the cocaleros) and in the lowlands (confederated in CIDOB), but made a national confederation less likely.

Imagining Indian and State Models

The regionalized rhythms of Ecuadorian and Bolivian state formation help us understand the importance of elite conceptual and institutional structures in constructing supralocal political actors. As with all counter-hegemonic discourses, Amazonian and Andean indigenous movements contain traces of the very elite efforts that map and order indigenous domination.[17] Efforts to "jump scales" and to bridge different sets of regional counterhegemonic discourses, also involve some reproduction of dominant models of politics, but so do they provide opportunities for radical new imaginings. Indigenous social movements are themselves "imagined communities," in Benedict Anderson's phrase; they require political creativity and communicative networks to articulate different peoples, histories, and ideas. Creating indigenous actors (or any social actor, for that matter) does not mean uncovering "authentic" essences, but rather the more pragmatic process of political invention.

When comparing social movements or any other kind of imagined political community, it is important to recall Anderson's insight that such collectivities "are distinguished not by their genuineness/falseness but by the style in which they are imagined."[18] Indigenous movements in Ecuador and Bolivia are all genuine expressions of historical and political realities, yet they have been imagined and articulated in different ways.[19] To summarize, indigenous political projects in Ecuador are a more radical departure from state and indigenous histories than Bolivian efforts, which often look to pre-Columbian or state models for organizational inspiration. In Ecuador, the novel language of "nationalities" (a term curiously out of place in the Americas) has played a crucial role in indigenous politics. In Bolivia, highland movements have borrowed both from the corporatist vocabulary of the 1952 revolutionary state and the ancient Andean geographies of ayllus to cobble together political movements. As the Aymara intellectual Carlos Mamani observes, "In Ecuador, they [indigenous leaders] tend to be linguists and lawyers, in Bolivia we are historians."[20]

In Ecuador and Bolivia, forms of organization have included class-based, religious, and "ethnic" models of organizing. These models are critical in the formation of collective identities. Note first that not all models are equally "available" to different groups; second, some models work better than others in mobilizing support and claiming legitimacy.

Since colonial and republican governments had fragmented any remaining pre-Columbian federations, it is hardly surprising that indigenous leaders in both countries turn to "Western" models. The pioneering Shuar, under the influence of Salesian missionaries, writes Janet Hendricks, "have been forced to adopt a Western form of political organization . . . to ensure their very survival."[21] The Aymara nationalism of Reinaga, which sought a state for the Aymara nation, found its first organizational expression in a party (the Partido Indio de Bolivia) and then infused a union movement through Katarismo, both Western vehicles.[22] In both Ecuador and Bolivia, sociologist José

Sánchez-Parga argues that "the state provided the forms of organization."[23] While this may overstate the case, it does recognize the role of the state in providing an important referent for indigenous organizing. However, this process of political mimesis was different in each case.

Ecuador: Ethnic Administration, Weak Corporatism, and the Nationality Consensus

In the early republican period, both highland and lowland regions in Ecuador were examples of the kind of semiprivate-semipublic system that Andrés Guerrero calls "ethnic administration": the state turned to landowners, the national church, and foreign missionaries to "civilize" indigenous people.[24] This system of ethnic administration was slowly and unevenly replaced by a relatively weak form of state corporatism in which state legislation created new legal spaces (*comunas* in the highlands, *centros* in the lowlands) that would incorporate indigenous people in official state geographies. In the 1960s and 1970s, agrarian reform provided the spark that ignited organizing in both regions. In the highlands, the social basis of ethnic administration (the hacienda) was permanently undermined and in the lowlands the state-sponsored colonization programs created a threat to lowland peoples who responded with new indigenous organization against the racially and regionally different "invaders."

In neither region did the organizational repertoires invoke a return to any kind of pre-Columbian utopia. While many indigenous traditions were (and are) practiced and celebrated in the highlands, centuries of hacienda agriculture and contact with mestizo populations enabled indigenous people to organize in line with "Western" categories (for example, peasants) and national administrative units (communities, provinces). In the lowlands, indigenous groups were more dispersed and isolated, and in the words of one Shuar leader, were "unconquered" and sought to defend their present territories, not return to a previous state.[25]

Luis Maldonado, former CONAIE leader and minister of social welfare, noted in an interview, "It is curious that Ecuador cannot claim a strong level of ethnohistory, those kinds of utopias almost don't exist here." In the next breath, Maldonado highlights the singular achievement of the Ecuadorian indigenous movement: "It has a national indigenous presence. This is a fundamental difference [from other countries]. . . . The indigenous people in Ecuador have a greater capacity to define themselves, unlike other countries, we are independent of unions and political parties that have politicized and fragmented [other movements]. Nationalities are a product of our political will."[26] In Maldonado's description, a "weak ethnohistory," a strong national presence, and political independence all fit together. Ecuador, he suggests, has not fallen into the trap of millenarian movements or the machinations of contemporary politics; greater space exists for the "political will" and creativity of indigenous elites.

While Maldonado also acknowledges the influence of leftist currents and indianista ideas, especially from Bolivia, he emphasizes the most Ecuadorian of indigenous forms: "nationality." While local and regional organizations certainly do have a trade union look to them (many organizations are called "federations" or "unions" of "peasants and Indians"), relatively late industrialization in Ecuador has meant a relatively weak labor movement.[27] Additionally, Ecuador implemented a thin form of corporatism, especially when compared to the Bolivian state that emerged from the revolution of 1952. In the absence of strong class-based political traditions in the countryside, Ecuadorian rural people have turned to more "ethnic" labels to frame their struggles. However, it is somewhat remarkable that the general category that puts a discursive roof over Amazonian and Andean heads is that of nationality. In the last two decades, indigenous activists in Ecuador have taken a term from the lexicon of Marxist and European thought and "Indianized" it.

The term *nationality* entered the vocabulary of *both* highland and lowland leaders, even if it seemed to fit better with the more autonomous and more diverse Amazonian groups. Though the term was present in debates as early as the 1930s, it did not become widely shared until after Ecuadorian social scientists reintroduced the term as an analytic tool in the 1970s, applying it first to the highlands, and subsequently to all parts of "indigenous reality."[28] Ampam Karakras, the influential Shuar leader and author of *Las nacionalidades indígenas y el estado en el Ecuador*, had spent many years in highland Quito, both as a student at the Central University and as the Shuar Federation's representative. When lowland and highland federations joined in 1986, it became not a federation of organizations but of nationalities. After convincing several political leaders and especially the armed forces that the use of *nationalities* did not imply any separatist or irredentist desires on the part of indigenous people, it became the political term of choice to encompass the diverse indigenous groups of the country. Though nationalities as such did not exist in an organizational sense—the movement remained one of local, provincial, and regional federations—they still represented important units of representation. But if we regard nationalities as subjects of representation, as Foucault understands it, the movement did not reflect what was "really there" but helped produce a political subject and project that had not existed before.

Compare for example, a reference to the nationality concept in the media in 1990 with the place of nationality in a 1998 executive decree: From *El Comercio,* June 9, 1990: "And you, politicians, historians, where do the so-called indigenous nationalities come from? Where do they come from? Did they, perchance, spend 500 years stuck in the magician's bottle, in the marvelous lamp of Aladdin? Show us!" From Executive Decree 386, December 11, 1998: "It is the duty of the national government to promote the harmonization of the secondary laws and institutional structure of the state with the existing political constitution guaranteeing the exercise of the collective rights of the nationalities and pueblos. . . . Exercising the powers provided by the current constitution, [the president of the republic] decrees . . . the creation of the Council for the Development of the Nationalities and Pueblos of Ecuador." From "Aladdin's lamp," nationalities found their way, via a constituent assembly of 1997, into the very language of the Ecuadorian state. Ecuadorian nationalities had the full attention of the president and a place within the executive branch of government in a ministry-level agency, the Consejo de Desarrollo de las Nacionalidades y Pueblos del Ecuador (CODENPE, Council for the Development of Nationalities and Peoples of Ecuador).

The power of nationality is not restricted to the upper echelons of executive power. Currently, a process is under way to transform many of the provincial and regional organizations into bodies that represent a specific nationality or its subsidiary pueblos. With this move from laborlike federations to indigenous nationalities, one notes not only a discursive and organizational shift, but also a generational one. At one CONAIE assembly I attended in 1999, a rugged and respected older Shuar leader questioned all the noise that was being made about nationalities: "Why do we have to change the way we talk, why can't we continue to defend our organization and pueblos as we always have?" A younger lowland Quichua man who has become increasingly influential in political debates responded, "We have to change our discourse in accord with the constitution, as nationalities not as organizations."[29] In other words, the organizations (ECUARUNARI, CONFENIAE, CONAIE) had through their marches and protests and negotiations forced a legal recognition of the "nationalities." Now, perhaps ironically, indigenous people must update themselves to catch up with this recognition.

Despite the political importance of the idea, not all indigenous actors in Ecuador accept this political project of recognizing indigenous nationalities. The two largest rivals to CONAIE, the class-based FENOCIN (Federation of Peasant, Indigenous, and Black Organizations) and evangelical Christian FEINE (Council of Indigenous Evangelical Peoples), argue that indigenous peoples have organized in a variety of ways that include unions and churches, and that the state should not favor one unit over another. In 2002, these organizations took the question to the Supreme Constitutional Tribunal to protest the way in which the planning agency, CODENPE, had favored the idea of nationality over others. In something of a blow to CONAIE, the tribunal ruled that it was unconstitutional to structure the agency in terms of nationalities to the exclusion of other forms of indigenous organization. Nevertheless, even given alternative indigenous challenges to the "nationalities" of CONAIE, the relative novelty of Ecuadorian indigenous politics is striking: native peoples creatively borrow and invent identities that "Indianize" the near past of union movements and Protestant evangelism rather than invoking any kind of pre-Columbian *longue durée.*

Bolivia: Ethnic Conflict, Strong Corporatism, and the Nationality Debacle

Indian-state relations have been much more violent in Bolivia than in Ecuador since the colonial period. Especially in the highlands, a "long memory" of resistance—Tupak Katari's 1781 siege of La Paz, Zarate Willka's menacing armies of 1899, the Jesús de Machaqa uprising of 1921, to name only a few critical events—is constantly referenced by contemporary scholars and activists.[30] Significantly, all the uprisings just mentioned are Aymara uprisings and inform an Aymara nationalism that propelled the pen of Fausto Reinaga in the 1960s as he dreamt of an "Indian revolution" and "Indian socialism."

Moreover, Aymara nationalism is hardly a thing of the past. In conversations with "Juan," a well-known Aymara intellectual and NGO professional, I heard references to Bolivia as an Aymara country that neither the Incas nor the Spaniards could defeat.[31] Juan labeled Bolivian Quechuas as "really" Aymaras who had lost their "true" identity and learned a new language. He also emphasized the need to learn from other struggles like that of the Palestinians (during my research, no one in Ecuador ever mentioned the PLO). Less anecdotally, the 1998 election of Felipe Quispe (popularly know as "the Mallku")[32] to the leadership of the CSUTCB suggested a return of the Reinaga-style *indianismo* that many thought was in the past. Quispe was in prison for five years for his activities with a guerrilla group known as the EGTK, the Tupak Katari Guerrilla Army. While in prison he wrote several books, all on Indian resistance.[33] One of Quispe's books takes its epigraph from Reinaga: "What I would like to emphasize is this: to know what is Indian one must be Indian. Because he who is just 'culturally' Indian can only 'reveal' (*revelar*) the Indian. But whoever is Indian of heart and flesh, cosmos and race, not only 'reveals' the Indian but rebels as Indian (*rebela al indio*)." During an interview in the cramped offices of the CSUTCB in La Paz, I spoke to Quispe about this epigraph and his thoughts about working with non-Indian (*q'ara*) sectors. After offering coca leaves (which were often chewed at indigenous organization events in Bolivia), he responded:

> Look, in that book, which was going to be much bigger, but we ran out of funds . . . I argue that we will liberate ourselves. We have experience with white-mestizo people: in 1971, the arrival of Che Guevara more or less, 1967, '66, that era, '70, '71, we have been militants in the political parties of the left, of the communist, of the liberation army, the EGTK was a product of this. Then they used us like cargo animals. "The Indian had to sleep on the ground, we sleep in the hammocks." . . . Even in the EGTK. They ate with us in the marginal zones of the city, but when we got out of jail, they returned to their lives. They only were pursuing fame. [Because of] those experiences, not only those, with the parties as well, we have said in other words, a q'ara is just a q'ara (*el q'ara es q'ara no más*).[34]

Many have doubted that such thinking would help the CSUTCB recover from the crisis dealt by the neoliberal reforms of 1985. Almost twenty years ago, during the 1988 assembly when the fundamentalism of the Red Ayllus (with whom Quispe was associated) were presented, many observers equated them with "racist" rantings, even comparing them with Nazism.[35]

While such harsh accusations did not greet the Mallku when he returned to the CSUTCB, opinions were very much divided on what Felipe "Mallku" Quispe would bring. On the optimistic side, Albó initially compared the Mallku's trajectory with that of Nelson Mandela. Ivan Arías was much more skeptical and almost dismissive of the Mallku's ability to lead, comparing him not to a statesmen but to a character from a second-rate martial arts movie, full of aggression and violence but hardly realistic.[36]

The Mallku has shown that he must be taken more seriously than that. In 2000–2001 he led the CSUCTB in protests (with other social organizations) that paralyzed the country for almost two months and announced the creation of a new political party called Pachakutik. Comparisons with Mandela are gone, and, as Bret Gustafson notes, accusations of "fascism without boots" are back.[37] More recently, Quispe has called for the refoundation of Qollasuyo, the pre-Spanish name for the part of the Inca Empire that became Bolivia. He also attracted great attention in 2004 when he called for Aymaras in Peru, some of whom had just lynched a mayor in the highland town of

Ilave, to join Aymaras in Bolivia to create a new Aymara nation. Quispe, who was in the interesting position of being a member of congress and a radical protest leader, finally resigned his congressional seat to pursue his style of indigenous politics in the streets. The multiculturalism promised by a series of reforms in the mid-1990s (Laws of Popular Participation, Bilingual Education, and Land Reform) has not been able to rid Bolivia's nervous upper classes of Zavaleta's barricades.

Related to this conflictual history is a complicated history of indigenous community. Unlike Ecuadorian leaders who have self-consciously refashioned the concept of nationality and even Protestantism to accommodate their contemporary political needs, Bolivia continues to experience what Rivera called unresolved "diachronic contradictions," as models from various national periods compete with each other.[38] Bolivia's strong tradition of state corporatism heavily influenced the structuring of the highland movement yet did not eliminate the competing models of the pre-Columbian ayllus. Highland indigenous leaders have given three contrasting responses to the question expressed by Esteban Ticona as "ayllu versus sindicato."

First, CSUTCB leaders and some social scientists note that the local "union" is often, despite the name, itself a communal form of government that acts very much in accordance with the logic of the ayllus. This is not true everywhere, they will say, but the apparent dichotomy between union and ayllu is often a false one.[39] Second, they emphasize the conflictual nature of the highlands and insist that unions are the "occidental opposition" that must be phased out if decolonization is ever to occur. This is the position that has been behind the current movement to "reconstitute" the ayllus represented by the Consejo Nacional de Ayllus y Markas del Qollasuyo (CONAMAQ, Confederation of Ayllus and Markas of Qollasuyo).[40] Finally, some suggest an instrumental logic. When agrarian reform legislation required rural folks to register as peasant unions, they did so. Now that the Law of Popular Participation allows for titling of "original communities," and international funders pledge to help in recuperating "original" forms, the countryside is responding in kind.[41]

The indígenas of the Bolivian lowlands are quite another story, a story that is more "Ecuadorian." As an assemblage of "ethnic federations," the lowland peoples have been, since their historic march to La Paz in 1990, much more in line with the "transnational" indigenous movements that identify with postleftist and proenvironmental agendas. Additionally, like its lowland Ecuadorian counterpart, CIDOB is much more prone to negotiate than the highland Aymaras. While CIDOB seeks to repeat the success of the lowland Ecuador organization CONFENIAE in negotiating with the state and transnational companies, it shows no interest in replicating CONFENIAE's alliance with the main highland confederation. When such an alliance has been attempted, it has either failed to materialize or exacerbated tensions.

There was an ill-fated effort between 1988 and 1992 to bring lowland and highland organizations together in an Assembly of Nationalities. The project of the assembly was full of mixed motives from the beginning, and adding to the problems were the motives that many nonindigenous sectors and political parties brought to the table. The very name of the proposed assembly went from emphasizing indigenous sovereignty (the Assembly of Nationalities) to a more intercultural framing that emphasized not only indigenous but also leftist and popular (nonethnic) identities (the Assembly of the First Nations and the People). Aymara sociologist Felix Patzi argues that leftist organizers assumed the role of speaking for "popular sectors" and reproduced the problems of 1952, when ethnicity was subsumed under class. "In this way, the spaces of discussion organized by NGOs become the spaces of legitimation for the very actions of NGOs and the thinking of the predominant white and mestizo caste. They were the principal expositors of the theme of the indigenous nationalities, relegating to a secondary status the indigenous actor himself."[42]

Unlike what happened in Ecuador, the idea of "nationalities" did not bring different regions together, but was used by various sectors to reconstitute a "popular" (more class-based) political and electoral proposal. Moreover, in contrast to Ecuadorian efforts to keep "nationality building" away from the pressures of political parties, the Bolivian Assembly of Nationalities could not escape the patrimonial dynamics of the political system. Still, the failure of the assembly did not necessarily make lowland-highland unity impossible.

In 1996, as land reform legislation was pending once again, another attempt was made to unite highland and lowland organizations in another march. The government successfully employed a regional strategy of divide and conquer. Negotiating separately with lowland groups, who had previously been left out of agrarian reform and had much to gain from new legislation, the government stalled the march. While the CSUTCB continued its protest, CIDOB declared victory and returned to the lowlands. Accusations of betrayal and *gobiernismo* continue to contaminate inter-regional efforts at cooperation. The confederations have held joint protests, but when they do, they present a fragile united front.

Given these difficulties, rather than merge with the CSUTCB, CIDOB and many international funders entertain hopes that CONAMAQ, the highland ayllu confederation, will become "the Bolivian ECUARUNARI [CONAIE's highland affiliate]," in the words of IBIS field director Hans Hoffmeyer.[43] In fact, CIDOB and CONAMAQ already share the same office and profess to have rather close ties.[44] Recent events, however, show that this potential unification will take some time. The burden is especially on the recently created ayllu federation, CONAMAQ, to mature politically. During the protests of 2000, which began over the privatization of water in Cochabamba and spread to a more general protest against neoliberalism led by Quispe's CSUTCB, the Apu Mallkus (maximum leaders) of CONAMAQ appeared in the national press endorsing the president and former dictator Hugo Banzer and proclaiming their support. This was a costly mistake, for as the protest proved to be widely popular, the Banzer government was forced to negotiate. CONAMAQ's international funders were forced to reconsider their support as well.[45]

In sum, the organizational repertoire in Bolivia has structured a situation very different from the one in Ecuador. Compared to Ecuador, historical models were not only more available and viable in Bolivia, but also seemed inescapable. In the highlands, the weight of different historical periods was expressed in the pervasive networks of union structure (the mirror image of the defunct corporatist state) and in the revival of an "ayllu" movement that promised to be a more authentic alternative. It is remarkable that Ecuadorians are more successful in refashioning "foreign" forms (nationality) while their highland Bolivian counterparts are, for various reasons, selecting among different and older "national" models.

In Bolivia's lowlands, as in Ecuador, a mix of regional and ethnic federations, aided by NGOs, became the preferred organizational models, given the historical weakness of union organizing in the tropical lowlands. However, unlike the situation in Ecuador, the lowland federations keep their distance from the main highland organization, unable to find ideological or organizational common ground. Even when indigenous people have a common enemy in the neoliberal ruling elites, the political economic terrain of democracy that is both multicultural and neoliberal presents contrasting opportunities for contestation and coordination in each country.

Neoliberal Articulations: Politics, Economics, and Official Multiculturalism

The 1980s were a crucial period in the Andes and in Latin America. By most economic indicators, Latin America was in the midst of its worst period since the Great Depression, prompting economists to refer to this period as the "lost decade." Interestingly, this decade also saw the consolidation of major indigenous organizations throughout the continent. As CONAIE president Luis Macas remarked, "They say this is the lost decade (*una década perdida*) for Latin America, we say that it is a decade in which Ecuadorian Indians have won (*una década ganada*)." Deborah Yashar and others recognize that the relationship between the "losing" and "winning" decades can be understood in terms of the opportunities and threats that came with economic crisis and reform. Economic crisis crippled the structures of state corporatism that had mediated state-rural relations for many years and gave indigenous people the political space to reconstitute themselves politically. Simultaneously, the withdrawal of the state in the form of disappearing rural subsidies and credit threatened the precarious livelihoods of indigenous communities and sparked protest.[46] New political opportunities and economic threats were the catalysts for a new wave of indigenous mobilization. These broad strokes are helpful for understanding the regionwide "return of the Indian," but a closer look suggests that neoliberal political economies take different forms and enable different kinds of responses in Ecuador and Bolivia.

Political Parties and Opportunities: Ecuadorian Evasions, Bolivian Conflicts

Throughout the Americas, neoliberal economic reform dealt a blow to agrarian state programs and corporatist state-society structures. Weakly institutionalized party systems, often with little presence in rural sectors, did a poor job of mediating rural discontent. Political parties were more important in the webs of patrimonial politics than they were in aggregating interests or reflecting popular anger. The party systems of Bolivia and Ecuador are among the weakest and most inchoate in Latin America. Political parties are not deeply rooted in society.[47] Moreover, the late arrival of universal suffrage meant that indigenous people could not participate in electoral life until late in the twentieth century. Universal suffrage came to Bolivia after the revolution of 1952, while in Ecuador it did not arrive until the democratic transition of 1979. The almost 30-year difference between suffrage laws in the two nations may partly explain why indigenous people have responded differently to changing political structures: Bolivian indigenous people have participated more actively in party politics than their Ecuadorian counterparts. In Bolivia, indigenous people formed political parties as early as 1969 (Reinaga's radical Bolivia Indian Party) and they often splintered into several parties (including MRTK, MITKA, MITKA-1, MITKA U, MAS-IPSP) that always trailed far behind the traditional parties of the left or right.[48]

Additionally, since 1985, when the traditional Left was severely wounded by privatization of mines and repression of the urban workers' movement, political parties that had previously been unconcerned with indigenous issues took a renewed and aggressive interest in indigenous organizing. Large and small parties began to work actively within organizations like the highland CSUTCB in hopes of cultivating clientelistic ties or placing the party faithful in high confederation positions. Internal election with the CSUTCB became fair game for various political parties. This pattern was not limited to the CSUTCB. Parties have sought to extend links to organizations in the Cochabamba valleys and the lowlands. As indigenous peoples, until recently, needed to affiliate with parties to participate in local or national elections, organizations often ask to "borrow" a traditional party's name. Parties were often happy to lend their legal status to indigenous candidates but expect political support in return.

Clientelism, and not interest aggregation, remains the hallmark of Bolivian party politics. Indigenous organizations are now seeking ways to break with party reliance and construct their own political instruments, but this too creates conflicts as regional indigenous leaders create multiple instruments. For example, the cocaleros were split by the divisions between Evo Morales (head of the MAS-IPSP and now president) and Alejo Veliz (head of the ASP). Meanwhile, Felipe Quispe established his own party, the Indigenous Movement Pachakutik (MIP). These parties have done better in the last few years, especially the MAS, which not only took Morales to the presidency in 2005 but also became the leading force in municipal and congressional elections. The success of the MAS was enabled by the decline of traditional parties, but this does not mean that indigenous organizations have ironed out all their differences. Leaders of CONAMAQ, for instance, have suggested that the Morales government is "occidental" and "leftist" and not truly an indigenous one.[49] Felipe Quispe, though no longer the head of the CSUTCB, has also been vocal in his criticisms of Morales.[50] This moment of success may highlight the fragmentation of Bolivian indigenous representation more than its institutionalization.

In Ecuador, the main indigenous organization, until 1996, consciously avoided work with parties and even boycotted national elections "as a way of rejecting traditional elections, political mismanagement, and demagogic political parties."[51] CONAIE even passed a resolution declaring that its leaders would not run for public office.[52] Parties were thus kept out of indigenous movement organizing and not allowed to participate in CONAIE congresses and assemblies. CONAIE aggressively sought to preserve its independence not only from political parties of left and right, but also from popular organizations traditionally allied with leftist political parties. One Socialist congressman complained, "CONAIE is living a policy of isolation from popular politics, even divorcing itself from the [main labor] Federation of United Workers, a kind of self-sufficiency that will cost it dearly in the struggle of the *pueblos*."[53] However, given the existing clientelistic party system and Bolivia's experiences with parties (which was actively studied in Ecuador), Ecuadorian indigenous organizations probably did well to look for space outside of formal politics.

Moreover, when CONAIE decided to depart from this strategy of so-called isolation and join other sectors in creating the Movimiento Unidad Plurinacional Pachakutik (MUPP, Pachakutik Plurinational United Movement), it did so from a position of relative strength, not as a junior partner. After leading a decade's worth of popular mobilizations, CONAIE had become a leading political actor that could negotiate with parties, social movement organizations, and the state without risking easy cooptation. Additionally, CONAIE decided to take advantage of 1994 electoral reforms that allowed Pachakutik to remain an independent electoral movement, and not a formal political party. Therefore, it was better able to signal its continuing opposition to "traditional politics" and maintain its dissenting character in civil society.

Electoral laws were not the only rules of the game that influenced Indians' political behavior. In the mid-1990s, Bolivia's sweeping decentralization law, especially the Law of Popular Participation (LPP), drastically changed the political landscape. Bolivia's President Gonzalo Sánchez de Lozada made many enemies when this law transferred state funds from regional development "corporations" to local municipalities. The legislation also recognized the legal right of indigenous people to participate in local governance. Local electoral contests became newly meaningful, as municipalities, for the first time in republican history, actually had significant resources to administer. Ecuador, by contrast, has made more tentative steps toward decentralization, perhaps because Ecuadorian regional elites do not want to lose out to localities like their Bolivian counterparts.

The incentives for working with parties, then, were different in the two countries. In more centralized Ecuador, national social movement activity was seen as more important than playing the game of national party politics. Moreover, changes in electoral laws in the 1990s allowed Indians to run as independent candidates, keeping their distance from traditional parties. In the 1990s, a decentralized political system in Bolivia, combined with stricter constraints on electoral participation (only formally recognized parties could run candidates), pushed indigenous candidates toward traditional parties. These laws did not determine the overall pattern of representation in each country but did reinforce dominant trends: centralized autonomy of indigenous protest in Ecuador, and more fragmented indigenous politics in Bolivia.

Contesting (Multicultural) Neoliberalism

For many reasons, neoliberal economic reform in Bolivia was more aggressive and sustained than similar efforts in Ecuador. As Conaghan and Malloy demonstrate, the severity of the crisis in Bolivia, where hyperinflation passed an annual rate of twenty thousand, the cohesion of technocratic policy teams, and distance from business sectors enabled a neoliberal policy approach that is comparable only with that of Chile in the region. Meanwhile, Ecuador's early neoliberal efforts were more marked by incoherence and its later ones blocked by effective indigenous opposition.[54] The turn of the millennium has meant a reversal of roles as indigenous resistance in Bolivia is undergoing a renaissance, while Ecuadorian organizations are in the midst of an internal crisis.

Bolivia: 1985–2005

In 1985, Víctor Paz Estenssoro, one of the architects of the Bolivian corporatist state, was elected president for the fourth and last time. At the age of 78, Paz Estenssoro oversaw the dismantling of the very state he had helped build.[55] The now infamous Supreme Decree 21060, part of his New Economic Policy (NEP), introduced a series of stabilization and free-market reforms that succeeded in ending the hyperinflation that the outgoing leftist party had unleashed. However, recovery came with painful side effects. Massive layoffs in the public sector (euphemistically dubbed "relocations") caused open unemployment to soar. The restructuring of the state mining company, COMIBOL, sent twenty-three thousand miners (out of thirty thousand!) to find work elsewhere, dealing a devastating blow to the Bolivian labor movement.[56]

As Bolivian neoliberal policies were implemented on a dramatic scale, the Left was in crisis. Indigenous Katarista political parties, named after the Aymara rebel Tupak Katari, found themselves in the midst of calamity. In the 1985 elections, the MRTK and MRTKL won 0.9 percent and 1.8 percent of the vote, respectively. In 1989, new parties took control of the CSUTCB, none of which was connected with indigenous Katarismo. Beginning in 1985, the labor network ceased to mediate relations between ethnic elites and indigenous populations.[57]

After the crisis in highland organizing, the altiplano began to show more signs of stress reflecting the enduring tensions between union and ayllu traditions. After 1985, a CSUTCB leader told me, the old labor model that had worked in a state capitalist system "simply no longer functioned."[58] It is in this context that a "national" Confederation of Ayllus and Markas (CONAMAQ) began. Meanwhile, in the inter-Andean valleys and tropics of Cochabamba, many "dislocated" mineworkers added to the growing ranks of the coca growers. With their union traditions and with a new cause, the cocaleros remain affiliated to the CSUTCB but enjoy a great deal of independence. They have shown an impressive ability to mobilize protests against eradication plans and have made important electoral inroads (as the 2005 electoral victory of cocalero leader Evo Morales dramatically illustrates). In the 1990s, though, rivalries within the cocaleros and the CSUTCB often limited the political impact of these groups.

As the highland labor-linked groups were in crisis, the center of indigenous protest moved to Bolivia's eastern lowlands. The lowland CIDOB saw the possibility of going from a purely regional confederation to one with national aspirations. Of all the "indigenous" organizations, CIDOB had the most success in dealing with various governments and attracting international support, largely because of the neoliberal attack on labor organizing in the highlands and the internal crisis of the CSUTCB. It is also a product of the official multiculturalism that accompanied the neoliberal policies of Sánchez de Lozada. In the mid-1990s, sweeping decentralization, education, and agrarian legislation accompanied privatization in what Sánchez de Lozada called the Plan for All (Plan de todos). This plan gave new recognition to indigenous people who could now hold political power in local municipalities, develop curricula in their own languages, and obtain land titles recognizing their territories. Sánchez de Lozada's choice of vice president, the Aymara leader Víctor Hugo Cárdenas, provided an additional connection between neoliberal and multicultural state making. The articulation of an official multicultural and neoliberal Bolivia opened opportunities for indigenous actors like CIDOB (and initially the ayllu federation CONAMAQ) that accepted the new laws and did not challenge the government's new economic agenda. The new regime of the "pluri-multi" disadvantaged the more radical element of indigenous actors like Morales and Quispe, whose anti-imperial and antineoliberal stance made them unlikely partners for the government. Víctor Hugo Cárdenas flatly announced that the only national organization that had the capacity to carry out development programs was CIDOB.[59] The effect of these official multicultural policies, as many have noted, is to divide indigenous actors into pragmatic and radical categories, and thus coopt and divide movements in ways that neutralize threats to the state while increasing its legitimacy in international eyes.[60]

Since 2000, however, a series of "wars"—first over the privatization of water in Cochabamba, then over taxes, and finally over the export of natural gas—have changed the dynamic in Bolivia. The cycle of protests began with the ill-considered privatization plan that resulted in some cases in a 400 percent increase in the cost of water to local communities. This set off a wave of protests in the valley by the cocaleros led by Evo Morales, and in the altiplano led by the radical indianista leader of the CSUTCB, Felipe Quispe. The waves of protest continued as Sánchez de Lozada returned to the presidency in 2002 and pursued widely unpopular tax hikes and a plan to export gas through the historic national enemy, Chile. Popular discontent reached the point where hundreds of thousands of protesters took to the streets and demanded Sánchez de Lozada's resignation. Violence from the state only made matters worse, and the president was forced to step down and flee the country in October 2003. Sánchez de Lozada's vice president, Carlos Mesa, moved cautiously and pragmatically but was also forced to resign in the face of growing protest. Cocalero leader Morales skillfully positioned himself for another presidential run, while Quispe escalated his rhetorical assaults by calling for an independent Aymara state.

This tension within the indigenous movement served to make Morales a more appealing candidate and contributed to his historic victory in the 2005 election. Morales became not only the first indigenous president of Bolivia but also the first presidential candidate, since electoral democracy returned to Bolivia, to win an outright majority and avoid a second-round election (in which the congress, not the voters, picks the president). His victory reflected the political space that the cocaleros, through the MAS party, had consolidated locally and regionally—thanks, in part, to the decentralization of the 1990s—as well as the political crisis of all the traditional parties that had dominated Bolivian politics.

While indigenous politics in Bolivia has not converged in one national organization or in one leader, an environment has been created in which indigenous leaders have democratically taken control of the state. Briefly put, both the "Washington consensus" economic policies and Bolivia's party system were unable to weather the "wars" over gas, taxes, and water. Morales and the MAS party were able to create a broad anti-imperialist message (in contrast to Quispe's narrower Aymara-centric one) and capitalize on the electoral gains of the 1990s. As a result, Morales has been able to ride a wave of popular support and implement such dramatic changes as the "nationalization" of the hydrocarbon sector. As these policies are not exclusively indigenous ones, Morales has articulated a broad base of support and (seemingly) put an end to Bolivia's ten-year neoliberal experience. The "multicultural neoliberalism" of the 1990s has yielded to a postmulticultural and postneoliberal moment.[61]

Ecuador, 1990–2004

Neoliberalism in Ecuador has been less extensive and intensive than in Bolivia. During the first attempts at structural adjustment in the 1980s, the relative "failures" of neoliberal policies had much to do with the policy-making limitations of President León Febres Cordero, a coastal industrialist whose close ties to business made it difficult to reconstitute state-market relations in any sustained way. In the 1990s, neoliberal policies faltered less because of government aggressiveness, which increased throughout the decade, but because of the opposition of an increasingly powerful indigenous actor, CONAIE. Beginning with the government of Rodrigo Borja in 1990, CONAIE mounted powerful national mobilizations against every president who attempted to impose neoliberal policies whose costs fell most heavily on the rural and popular sectors. Through these mobilizations and subsequent negotiations, CONAIE obtained important spaces in the national political system, gaining control of the Dirección Nacional de Educación Intercultural Bilingue (DINEIB, Directorate of Bilingual Education), the indigenous development agency (CODENPE), the Office of Indigenous Health, and a central role in the World Bank–supported Program for the Proyecto de Desarrollo para Pueblos Indígenas y Negros del Ecuador (PRODEPINE, Development of Indigenous and Afro-Ecuadorian Peoples).

Among the many conflicts of the 1990s, the last confrontation of the decade between CONAIE and the government of Harvard-trained technocrat Jamil Mahuad, former mayor of Quito, was especially significant.[62] Mahuad faced a dire economic situation: falling oil prices and the damage inflicted by the El Niño ocean current on coastal shrimp and banana industries made it impossible for exporters to repay loans that were themselves based on unsound financial decisions. Mahuad spent millions trying to rescue the banks but did not stave off a severe economic crisis, with massive capital flight, soaring deficits, and rising unemployment. The crisis triggered a radical and ultimately ill-fated response from Mahuad. Under pressure from the IMF, he froze bank accounts, halted the rescues of failing banks, announced the dollarization of the economy, privatized state industries, and eliminated subsidies on electricity, gasoline, and domestically used natural gas. Massive protests in 1998 and 1999 forced Mahuad to retreat on many of these measures; dollarization, however, was not negotiable. CONAIE, leading an ever-broader coalition of popular groups and even middle-class sectors, augmented pressure on an increasingly isolated Mahuad.

This culminated in the dramatic events of January 21, 2000, when CONAIE and sectors of the military led by Colonel Lucio Gutiérrez overthrew Mahuad and, for a few hours, held power as a "Junta of National Salvation." The military high command, under U.S. pressure, abandoned the junta and returned power to Gustavo Noboa, Mahuad's vice president. Over the following months, all those involved in the coup were granted amnesty and negotiations with the IMF were effectively stalled. Aside from dollarization, all the measures Mahuad had sought to implement were abandoned for the rest of the Noboa administration. Gutiérrez, in alliance with CONAIE again, won the presidency in 2002, seemingly opening the doors to a renewed military-indigenous alliance. However, Gutiérrez quickly disappointed his indigenous partners. He signed a letter of intent with the IMF that signaled his intention to pursue austerity measures that again would be felt most sharply in the poorest sectors. In effect, as Rafael Correa notes, "The economic policy of the [Gutiérrez] regime is hardly new; to the contrary, it is a more orthodox expression of the dominant thinking in Latin America over the past two decades."[63] The indigenous members of Gutiérrez's cabinet, Luis Macas and Nina Pacari, left the government in 2003. After less than a year in government, CONAIE returned to its opposition role.

This time, however, the constellation of forces seemed less favorable to the kind of protagonism that CONAIE had exercised in the 1990s. First, Gutiérrez was better able to divide the indigenous movement by reaching out to former CONIAE president Antonio Vargas to be minister of social welfare (who was then denounced as a traitor by CONAIE) as well as reaching out to other indigenous actors, including the national evangelical indigenous federation (FEINE) and sectors of the Amazon still loyal to fellow Amazonian Vargas. In CONAIE offices and throughout Ecuador, which I visited in the summer of 2004, I heard worries about an organizational crisis that was obvious in a noticeably small "uprising" that CONAIE convoked to protest Gutiérrez's policies. Additionally, the massive protests in 2005 that drove Gutiérrez from office were not led by CONAIE, but by other social forces that included university students and middle-class sectors.[64] As of July 2006, CONAIE was still trying to recover from the bitter experience of joint government and division. Luis Macas, the historic leader of the 1990s, was back as the president of CONAIE. His labors increased, however, when he was named the presidential candidate of the Pachakutik Party for the October 2006 elections. To say that Macas was unable to repeat the experience of Bolivian President Evo Morales is an understatement. Deciding against a coalition with the eventual winner, leftist economist Rafael Correa, Macas won just over 2 percent of the popular vote. Such a poor showing has only added to CONAIE's troubles.

At the beginning of the millennium, Bolivia and Ecuador had reached a critical juncture for indigenous politics. Bolivia's indigenous movement, especially in the highlands and valleys, has become radicalized and renovated as figures like Evo Morales and Felipe Quispe advance their struggles both in the streets and with their own parties. Ecuador's indigenous movement seems to have been weakened by a failed alliance with a government that has been able to divide CONAIE by appealing to Amazonian leaders and making alliances with other national indigenous confederations, like FEINE. The situation in both countries, however, is still very much in motion.

Things come together and things fall apart. This is at the core of the politics of articulation in social struggles. Discourses, identities, and actors are cobbled together in provisional ways that reflect the prevailing constellation of forces and political opportunities. Stuart Hall quotes Gramsci's injunction, "'Turn your face violently towards things as they exist now,'" then continues in his own words, "Not as you'd like them to be, not as you think they were ten years ago, not as they're written about in the sacred texts, but as they really are: the contradictory, stony ground of the present conjuncture."[65]

In Bolivia and Ecuador, the naturalized regions of politics (highlands and lowlands) reflect the different encounters of the state with local communities and local economies. While in both cases the highlands have been the centers of colonial and republican states, in Bolivia the relatively greater importance of the lowlands to elites hindered the emergence of strong regional actors. Thus, unlike the case in Ecuador, where two strong regional movements with long organizational histories converged in the late 1980s, in Bolivia, indigenous political activity has been fragmented and regional actors have taken turns in the national spotlight more often than they have shared it. The convergence of different regional actors in Ecuador, however, is not necessarily a permanent development. Tension has always characterized the internal conflicts of the indigenous movement, and Lucio Gutiérrez did a better job than his predecessors in exploiting them.

In both countries, ideologies and discourses have also come together in often surprising ways. The most remarked ideological articulation among indigenous civil society has been that of class and ethnic discourse. "Seeing with two eyes," as Cárdenas put it, Indians, as both rural peasants and colonized peoples, have long been able to articulate agendas that reflect their own ethnic particularities (calls for territory and bilingual education) with broader popular and leftist ones (attacks on neoliberal policies and U.S. imperialism). Given the regional articulations we have discussed, it is not surprising that CONAIE in Ecuador has been more successful in articulating both ethnic and class struggles than organizations in Bolivia, where the more radical highland laborlike CSUTCB and cocalero federation fly the flags of class and CIDOB is relatively less engaged in combating neoliberal policies.

Finally, the strategies of state agents and the tactics of social movements display the politics of articulation at work in remarkable ways. Creating official spaces in constitutions, ministries, and development agendas for indigenous people creates new terrain for state incorporation of and negotiation with indigenous people. This official multiculturalism, like other strategies of dominant power, carries the danger of what Gramsci called *trasformismo*, where reforms soften the harder edges of resistance, all to maintain a status quo where the most vital distributive issues of power and wealth remain largely untouched. Whether these spaces become their own kinds of iron cages for indigenous movements is unclear; indigenous actors can use these spaces to push and pull at different parts of the policy-making machinery. The electoral success of indigenous parties in both Bolivia and Ecuador can perhaps be characterized as an indigenous concession to dominant ("occidental") forms of governing, yet with their linkages to local communities and organizations these parties also challenge party systems that hardly served the democratic purpose of electoral representation. Ironically, Indians may have been the only actors capable of democratizing deeply clientelistic systems.

Of course, indigenous organizations have varied their tactics, often preferring contestation to negotiation, with different results. While in the 1990s Ecuadorian organizations made impressive tactical maneuvers to avoid cooptation by party or state, they entered the new millennium with a coup, a junta that lasted hours, a failed government alliance that lasted months, and now find themselves in the midst of crisis. In contrast, radical Bolivian indigenous actors (especially in the highlands) had a difficult time challenging the official multiculturalism and aggressive neoliberalism of the state in the 1990s, but have emerged with unexpected power since 2000. This may be the beginning of indigenous rearticulation which, as Charles Hale argues, may represent "a crucial facet of resistance" if it "builds bridges between authorized and condemned ways of being Indian."[66] It is too early to tell whether such bridges will be built in either country, or what kinds of structures the state will construct in these times of crisis. We can say with certainty only that the foundations of contemporary Bolivian and Ecuadorian states will rest on both the ruins of the "defensive barricades" of old forms of exclusion and the "stony, contradictory ground" of multicultural articulations.

14

In the Shadows of Success

Indigenous Politics in Peru and Ecuador

JOSÉ ANTONIO LUCERO AND
MARÍA ELENA GARCÍA

Indigenous movements in Ecuador and Peru represent different poles and even types of cases. If Ecuador is the paradigmatic successful case of powerful and unified indigenous mobilization, Peru represents a puzzling negative case of absence. In the regional and indeed global trend of growing Indian mobilization, the indigenous movement in Peru has been widely described as "marginal,"[1] "largely non-existent,"[2] and "a profound failure."[3] Unlike the powerful Confederation of Indigenous Nationalities of Ecuador (CONAIE), scholars point out that Peru, the heart of the Inca Empire and a country where roughly 40 percent of the population is indigenous, has no representative national indigenous organization.[4]

Instead of trying to explain the absence of indigenous mobilization in Peru, let us examine the assumptions and ideas that underwrite both Ecuadorian "success" and Peruvian "failure." Our aim here is not to show that Peruvian indigenous actors are equally as politically active or consequential as their Ecuadorian counterparts; rather it is to rethink this comparison.[5] While observers often use a teleological approach in which some movements are "ahead" or "behind," it is important to find alternative ways of evaluating indigenous collective action and contention to explore new analytical and political possibilities. In rethinking success, we are concerned not only with particular evaluations of "Peru" or "Ecuador," but also with a more dynamic and self-reflexive conversation over what indigenous movements look like and what they do. We conclude with questions and observations that apply beyond the Andes about the power of regimes of representation over scholarly and political imaginings. Relations between the state and society must be examined both as "system" and "idea." Following Abrams, we study social movements as both palpable networks of association and relations of meaning.

Movement Success and Failure

Why is the indigenous movement so much stronger in Ecuador than in Peru? What has made CONAIE such a powerful political actor? In comparing the indigenous movement in Ecuador to those in Bolivia and Peru, Xavier Albó notes that "Ecuador's ethnic movement shows a higher level of coherence, mobilizing all its ethnic groups in the Andes and Amazonian lowlands."[6] While tensions exist throughout the Central Andes in the rural identifications of class (campesino), or ethnicity *(indígena)*, in Ecuador "this polarity was found in each Andean community, with some people belonging to a 'class' organization and others belonging to an ethnic group (with the latter finally winning out)."[7] CONAIE, as the premier ethnic organization, has eclipsed all other organizations and for over a decade has been able to mobilize nationally, forcing frequent government retreats on neoliberal policies, and on two occasions (1997 and 2000) forcing unpopular presidents into exile.

In contrast, indigenous political actors in Peru, according to Albó and many others, are characterized by weakness. While pockets of politicized indigenous identity exist, Albó writes, "ethnic identity and indigenous organizations remained largely restricted to the smaller groups of the Amazonian region, [and] scarce among the more numerous highland Quechua and Aymara, whose organizations continue to emphasize their 'campesino' identity over ethnicity." Compounding this weakness, several scholars note that in Peru indigenous symbolic capital, and particularly highland Inca legacies, have been appropriated by elites, not popular sectors, in such a way that Indianness is emptied of its subversive potential. Even the election of the Andean born Alejandro Toledo has hardly been seen as an advance for "ethnically minded grassroots" but rather another elitist reformulation of the idea captured by Cecilia Méndez: "Incas yes, Indians no."[8]

How are we to explain this difference between a strong Ecuadorian movement and a weak Peruvian one? By what criteria do scholars distinguish between strong and weak movements? Briefly, we might call these criteria of *identity, scale,* and *tactics.* First, Indian identity is a prerequisite for Indian mobilization. New indigenous movements reject imposed "class" identities and reassert authentically "ethnic" self-representation. To transpose a familiar formulation, a movement must exist "in itself" before it can be "for itself." A second criterion is scale. A strong indigenous movement articulates local and regional organizations into a nationally cohesive political force. As Mariátegui noted long ago in Peru, without national linkages, indigenous people would not realize their full political potential. A third criterion is tactics. Political and social movements mobilize significant protests, marches, and blockades that resist state projects and influence changes in state policies. With the rise of indigenous political contestation, some observers have gone so far as to suggest that protest is not only an indigenous tactic but has become "the primary characteristic of Indian ethnicity."[9] If these help to define success, they also clearly provide the criteria for failure. A movement is in trouble if it cannot forge an independent Indian identity, if it remains regional and fragmented, and if it is unable to mobilize visible political protest.

There is reason however to be skeptical about this model of success and failure. This framework, like all theoretical constructs, could obscure important features of political landscapes that do not conform to expectations. To pose an important albeit familiar question: "Do we know only what we see, one may wonder, or do we only see what we know?"[10] Comparing Ecuadorian and Peruvian indigenous political contexts in terms of this idealized model of success and failure reveals the limitations of some of our theoretical imaginings. More specifically, a familiarity with Peruvian indigenous politics may reveal important and understudied aspects of Ecuadorian indigenous politics.

Identity: Real Indians, Ethnicity, Class, and Religion

As Albó observes, Ecuadorian organizations even in the highlands, where the Left has historically been an important influence, have moved toward ethnic identities and away from class. CONAIE is the maximum expression of this move, as its language of "nationalities" and "pueblos" suggests an alternative conception of Ecuador not as a nation-state but as a plurinational state. Indigenous people, rejecting the labels imposed by others, have created their own political categories and injected them into the official political and constitutional vocabulary. As a result of CONAIE's political strength, indigenous organizations control important spaces in the state, including agencies for intercultural bilingual education (DINEIB) and indigenous and Afro-Ecuadorian development (CODENPE).[11] Indigenous people are no longer simply "peasants" in Ecuador.

Peru, in the prevailing view, represents a contrasting case in which the use of leftist labels in forging rural "peasant" identities have not, or not yet, yielded to "ethnicity." Moreover, the appropriation of Inca histories and mythologies by elites and the complex nature of Peru's racial mixture and internal migration produce various interstitial identities, like *cholo*, that defy easy classificationas simply indigenous or nonindigenous.[12] Indeed, the contested nature of Peruvian racial identities (who is really "indigenous"?) is at the heart of recent debates over indigenous politics. As a self-identified Quechua intellectual commented, "We have a long way to go [in Peru]. Before we can organize as indigenous peoples, we must *be* indigenous people."[13] Unlike Ecuador, where *indígena* has become a political identity common to both highland and lowland groups, Peru's racial and regional landscapes are characterized by unstable and shifting labels including *campesino, andino, mestizo, nativo*, and *indígena*. The complexity of ethnic identifications in Peru has been read by many scholars as a lack of a consolidated indigenous identity that makes it difficult to speak of an indigenous movement.[14]

We suggest a different way of seeing these dynamics. It is important to be aware of the danger of teleological discussions in which social and cultural change moves in one direction, and thus some are more advanced while others must catch up. As Carlos Iván Degregori notes, "Perhaps it is not a matter of being behind or ahead, but rather of the distinct forms through which ethnicity is expressed in different countries."[15] Rather than being mutually exclusive, class and ethnic identities can and always do coexist.

Several scholars contend that the rise of class-based rural contention in Peru in the 1960s and 1970s was not a move against indigenous identity. Rather, "indigenous utilization of class-based rhetoric was a political option that did not represent the loss of indigenous culture, but was rather a strategy toward its empowerment."[16] At the center of peasant contention was a recognition of community that some see as the hallmark of indigenous struggles. "Indeed, one of the union demands was legal recognition of their communities of origin."[17] Union and federation membership can be seen as a pragmatic means toward achieving a specific goal: the "recuperation" of community lands. Between 1958 and 1964, powerful indigenous peasant unions recuperated thousand of hectares of land.[18]

Yet Peruvian organizations in the highlands have recently adopted more explicit indigenous ethnic political identities, following the example of the lowland ethnic federations founded in the 1960s. For example, the Confederación Nacional de Comunidades del Peru Afectadas por la Minera (CONACAMI, Confederation of Communities Affected by Mining Industries), emerged as a nationally and internationally recognized indigenous organization that led marches and protests against the government of Alejandro Toledo. CONACAMI was also highly critical of the official Commission for Amazonian, Andean, and Afro-Peruvian Peoples (CONAPA), formerly headed by Peru's first lady, Eliane Karp, as a threat to autonomous indigenous organizing.[19] CONACAMI, with the help of funders like Oxfam America, held exchanges with Ecuador's CONAIE and Bolivia's federation of altiplano *ayllus*, CONAMAQ. In 2006, CONACAMI, with these organizations and others from Colombia and Chile, cofounded the transnational Andean Coordinator of Indigenous Organizations. CONACAMI was selected as the political coordinator of this new international body.

While many see the rise of CONACAMI and similar organizations as evidence that Peruvian actors are following the example set by Ecuador and CONAIE, other indigenous voices see CONACAMI as illegitimate. Criticizing connections with "foreign influences" like Oxfam America (which has also supported CONAIE in Ecuador), some rival organizations see CONACAMI as not truly reflecting indigenous communities, but outside interests. In this critique, CONACAMI is not an "authentic" or representative indigenous organization, but something much more problematic: a nongovernmental organization (NGO). Echoing recent poststructural critiques of the disciplinary power of development actors, some indigenous intellectuals have cast NGOs as simply another extension of neoliberal governmentality that further colonizes indigenous subjects. The controversy over the transnational ties between indigenous groups and external development organizations reminds us of the insight of Arturo Escobar and others who have noted that "development operates as an arena for cultural contestation and identity construction."[20] These criticisms have not prevented CONACAMI from increasing in visibility and strength, but they do suggest that the question of who is "really" indigenous is hardly settled in Peru.

However, this question is not settled in Ecuador either. While CONAIE has certainly had the greatest representational strength, in terms of both mobilizing indigenous people and shaping how indigenous people are talked about, there are important alternatives. One of the most notable and surprising is the Consejo de Pueblos y Organizaciones Indígenas Evangélicas del Ecuador (FEINE, Council of Indigenous Evangelical Peoples), which represents an important number of Protestant Indians, especially from the central Sierra.[21] Recently, FEINE has moved from being considered a conservative or apolitical organization to being an active participant in the politics of protest. FEINE has succeeded in "Indianizing" Protestantism. As Blanca Muratorio argues, if Protestant evangelism "destroyed" some traditional activities that depended on alcohol consumption, it also reconstituted new spaces for cultural (re)production. Especially important for indigenous languages, evangelical organizations were pioneers in broadly publishing, teaching, and broadcasting radio programs in Quichua. Politically, in the post–agrarian reform period, evangelical indigenous organizations helped local communities obtain the rights enshrined in the reforms of the 1960s and 1970s, and emerged as "representative[s] of indigenous people before the state."[22]

Along with FEINE, the other main indigenous organization is the (still) class-based Confederación Nacional de Organizaciones Campesinas, Indígenas y Negras (FENOCIN, Federation of Peasant, Black, and Indigenous Organizations). FENOCIN grew out of the work of leftist political parties, and its leaders admit that indigenous concerns were not always at the center. Largely in response to the success of CONAIE, the organization changed much of its language and even its name. (Previously, as FENOC, it lacked the indigenous "I" and African "N" and spoke only of campesino causes.) The president of the federation, Pedro de la Cruz, a Quichua leader from the important northern Sierra canton of Cotacachi, relates how difficult it was to get the national confederation to acknowledge the problems of indigenous people in the highlands:

> We have had internal conflicts in the organization [FENOC]. As Indians we were going to disassociate ourselves . . . in order to maintain our independence due to the problems of [the lack of internal] democratization. The problem was that they did not understand the indigenous problem, that they did not understand the problem of development, that when we want electricity, when we want anything, even roads, it meant that we were moving to the "right," they said. This closed-minded Leftism, or whatever we might call it, did not include us. Therefore we had to fight, internally, and hard.[23]

But de la Cruz emphasizes that indigenous people can and should pursue contemporary political struggles in ways that do not simply "only include Indians." In his mind, and now as official FENOCIN policy, class-based organizing does not mean ethnic-blind organizing, but rather represents the only hope for true national-level "interculturality." Such a radical change from "closed-minded" leftism to "intercultural" leftism reflects the internal conflicts that de la Cruz identifies. It also reflects the ongoing conversation on how to bring indigenism into harmony with popular struggles that are often focused on the material issues of survival and subsistence.

The broader lesson for both Peru and Ecuador is that indigenous identities are plural, contested, and constructed in dialogue with a great number of actors. While political struggle means that some identities and discourses are privileged over others, the politics of recognition remain dynamic and full of surprises. For instance, few would have expected the former CONAIE president, Antonio Vargas, after leaving CONAIE, to run for the presidency of the country with an evangelical indigenous political party. He lost badly in 2002, but two years later when President Lucio Gutiérrez had his own falling out with CONAIE, he named Vargas to his government, along with a representative of FEINE. With evangelical and Amazonian support (Vargas is from the eastern lowlands), Ecuadorian indigenous movements have become fractured. Although Gutiérrez was forced out of office himself in 2005, CONAIE leaders continue to speak of crisis and division, while FEINE also struggled to recover after its alliance with Gutiérrez came to an end. Attention to alternative identities can help one understand how Ecuadorian unity has apparently come undone (at least for the moment). Religion is an important and understudied axis of indigenous identity. (Region is also part of the politics of identity, but we will explore it within the spatial politics of scale.)

Scale: Thinking Nationally?

Perhaps the main distinguishing feature of indigenous politics in Ecuador has been the ability to create CONAIE, a confederation of indigenous nationalities from the three main regions of the country: Costa, Sierra, and Oriente. Such a task may, as many suggest, be facilitated by Ecuador's small size and other demographic factors, but in any national setting with serious regional political cleavages like those in Ecuador, such an achievement is nevertheless remarkable. Peru is much more representative of countries with sizable Indian populations, as regional organizations, notably in the Amazon, have been more important than national organizations.[24] While the pattern of indigenous politics differs between the two countries, Peru's "fragmentation" is instructive about indigenous movements generally, and about the Ecuadorian one specifically. The Peruvian example provides two broad lessons of scale, calling attention to various forms of contention, local, national, global. It also suggests that the label of "national" organizing can obscure more than it reveals.

First, as we have noted elsewhere, indigenous people in Peru have been active on many levels—local, regional, national, and transnational.[25] This is clearly important for both empirical and conceptual reasons, since looking for "national-scale" activity has been a bias of much social movement theory that needs to be critically examined.[26] As Orin Starn argues, "The label 'grassroots movement' holds an assumption about the likelihood of growing taller and stronger." However, we should not automatically assume that this kind of community politics will always tend to move toward greater scales of political activity. As Starn notes in the case of the *rondas campesinas*, local community politics "force us to recognize that there is nothing natural at all about a movement going regional, national, or global. A collection of tribes in the Amazon in Peru, a neighborhood association in the United States, or any other movement may join together as a force for change, or they may not, depending on many factors, as occurred with the rondas. . . . The failure of the rondas to grow into strong federations offers confirmation that even mobilizations for change can proceed in many ways besides up."[27]

A focus on national social movement organizations tends to minimize the importance of local or regional actors that have an impact on national and transnational indigenous politics. As María Elena García's research shows, Quechua parents in local communities as well as indigenous intellectuals in transnational institutes are connected in important struggles over intercultural education policies.[28] Scholars have documented other ways in which local peoples have engaged in important forms of contention such as challenging transnational development agendas in struggles over water management.[29] Additionally, regional organizing, especially in the Amazon, has had a longer history in Peru than in many places in Ecuador or Bolivia. The Amuesha Congress was among the first indigenous organizations to form in the continent in the 1960s.[30] In the highlands, indigenous people founded peasant federations in the 1960s, self-defense rondas campesinas in the 1980s, and coca farmer federations in the 1990s.[31]

Second, national developments have added another layer of complexity. Much of the change on the national level clearly came with the end of the ugliest years of terror (from the state, Shining Path guerrillas, and other insurgents) as well as the end of the authoritarian presidency of Alberto Fujimori. The period between the fall of Fujimori and the election of Alejandro Toledo was crucial for indigenous advocacy. The interim administration of Valentín Paniagua (2000–2001) responded to the calls of Amazonian indigenous leaders by creating "*mesas de diálogo*" that convoked experts and Indian leaders from throughout the country to discuss the needs and demands of various indigenous communities. This "window of opportunity" for indigenous rights closed (somewhat surprisingly) with the election of Alejandro Toledo in 2001.

Despite making much of his Andean roots, including an unprecedented inaugural ceremony at Machu Picchu, Toledo gave indigenous issues less attention than his predecessor had done. Toledo's wife, Eliane Karp, played a much more visible role in elaborating a state response to indigenous demands by heading the new agency for indigenous and Afro-Peruvian affairs, CONAPA, often referred to as the Comisión Karp. CONAPA sought to channel the new international funds in a new development agenda for indigenous and Afro-Peruvian communities, to establish a space for indigenous representation with the Toledo government, and to advance the discussion over multicultural constitutional reforms. Some saw Karp's commission as an important opportunity for raising indigenous issues, while others criticized the paternalism exhibited in such practices as Karp's naming the members of the commission herself and the potential danger that the state might co-opt indigenous organizations.[32]

In addition to new changes in state policies, there were also important developments in civil society. Joining older Amazonian organizations like the Inter-Ethnic Association for the Development of the Peruvian Jungle (AIDESEP), CONACAMI, though primarily concerned with the impact of mining on highland communities, has become an important highland counterpart to lowland indigenous federations. CONACAMI, along with AIDESEP and others, are now part of a new national organization that was originally known as the Conferencia Permanente de los Pueblos Indígenas del Perú (COPPIP, Conference of the Indigenous Peoples of Peru). Could COPPIP, as a "national" organization, be perhaps yet another indicator that Peru is "catching up" with its neighbors? Again, we should resist the temptation to label it as such, and not only for the problematic evolutionary language involved, but also because COPPIP represents a complicated example of indigenous organization. As we detail elsewhere, there have actually emerged two COPPIPs, one that calls itself a Coordinator led by CONACAMI and a second that has kept the name of Conference, led by organizations opposed to CONACAMI.[33] The first COPPIP consciously looks to the model represented by CONAIE in Ecuador, while the second adopts a more "Indianist" nationalism that many label more politically radical and closer to the thinking of Bolivia's Aymara leader Felipe Quispe. Javier Lajo, a leading Indianist intellectual (of the COPPIP-Conference) made a telling statement in his answer to the question: "Where is the indigenous movement in Peru?" He replied, "It is in Ecuador and Bolivia."[34] This comment reflects the Indianist irredentist idea that someday the national lines will be redrawn to reconstitute the empire of Tawantinsuyo. We propose reading Lajo's comment metaphorically, by looking at the Ecuadorian case through "Peruvian" eyes. That is, if Peru is notorious for its fragmentation and (in Mariategui's phrase) lack of "national linkages," what might we learn if we look for fragmentation in Ecuador?

CONAIE is certainly not the only indigenous actor in Ecuador, even if many agree that it is the most important. Indeed, its very classification as a "national" organization is more often than not a provisional truth, since its "regional" affiliates, especially the highland ECUARUNARI and the lowland

CONFENIAE, behave independently of the wishes of the CONAIE leadership. Additionally, conflict between highland and lowland indigenous leaders is one of the durable tensions of national politics. At a CONAIE assembly in 1999 in Cayambe, a stronghold of ECUARUNARI, a Quichua Amazonian leader, reflecting on the ideological changes in the highlands, remarked unkindly: "You know the word for not knowing what you want? ECUARUNARI."[35] These tensions have become part of presidential politics, as President Gutiérrez, with the help of former CONAIE leader (and Gutiérrez's minister of social welfare) Antonio Vargas, has managed to separate Amazonian and Andean organizations even further. Unity is a difficult thing to maintain.

It is important to stress once again the old wisdom of Tip O'Neill: All politics is local. Municipalities have been an important source of political innovation, perhaps most notably in Cotacachi, where Mayor Auki Tituania was elected with the support of CONAIE's political arm, Pachakutik, but also has the support of CONAIE's rival, FENOCIN, which counts Cotacachi as one of its strongholds. In addition, local evangelical organizations, which technically form part of another CONAIE rival, FEINE, often work hand in hand with the bases of CONAIE and FENOCIN. The broad point is that national tensions and alliances are often articulated in local arenas. In short, in the study of indigenous politics, one must pay careful attention to multiple scales of politics, studying both "up" and "down," as change does not simply grow in one direction.

Tactics of Contention

The last criterion for distinguishing between the success and failure of social movements is tactics. What do they do? What are their "repertoires of contention"? The tactics of protest have been perhaps most important in this last wave of indigenous mobilizations. Unlike previous waves, when indigenous uprisings represented violent responses to the abuses of colonial and neocolonial rule, the contemporary *levantamientos* were peaceful and massive popular demonstrations made famous by CONAIE well before the Zapatistas made headlines in Mexico. The historic and much discussed 1990 levantamiento marked an important moment for indigenous contention. Through large-scale national mobilizations and blockades, indigenous people could close off important roadways and paralyze commercial transactions in places like Ecuador and Bolivia. Throughout the 1990s, such demonstrations became routinized ways to force executives to negotiate with civil society. In the classic interaction described by Tilly and others,[36] the contestation and negotiation between social movements and states has transformed political frameworks, as shown by new constitutions that recognize the collective rights of indigenous people and the pluricultural makeup of Andean and Amazonian republics.

In addition to taking to the streets, indigenous people have also taken to the polls. Indigenous parties have become a more common part of national political party systems throughout the region. Again, CONAIE's electoral arm, Pachakutik, represents one well-known example of indigenous electoral success. Since it was founded in 1996, Pachakutik has won between 6.5 and 10 percent of the vote in Ecuador's national elections.[37] While this may seem a modest vote share, in multiparty systems as fractured as those of the central Andean republics, this kind of electoral success can translate into important representation in legislative assemblies. This has been especially clear in Bolivia, where the Aymara *cocalero* leader and now President Evo Morales has been the most successful national indigenous politician. Even before his impressive victory in 2005, Morales narrowly lost the 2002 presidential race and led his party, the Movement toward Socialism (MAS), to win a greater share of the vote than any other party in the 2004 local elections. As other traditional parties confront a great crisis of legitimacy, MAS has become the leading party in the country.

Peru seems once again to trail behind its neighbors. While there have certainly been protests, especially during the remarkably unpopular presidency of Alejandro Toledo, they have been less regular and routine than in other Andean countries. CONACAMI has borrowed the language of levantamientos from CONAIE and has shown itself able to mobilize protests. Still, the political environment of Peru has always been much less permissive of sustained collective action than those of neighboring countries. The lingering fear and repressive legislation produced by two decades of war clearly affected the possibilities for large-scale mobilization. Peruvian cocaleros learned this lesson most clearly when their leader, Nelson Palomino, was arrested under national security legislation in 2003. He was finally released in 2006, long after it was clear that there was no evidence to support charges of subversion against him. Unlike Bolivia, where a cocalero leader became president, in Peru, Palomino remains on the margins of formal politics.[38]

In electoral politics, Peru has no political party quite like Ecuador's Pachakutik or Bolivia's MAS. Although, as Donna Lee Van Cott notes, Amazonian political parties have run candidates in local and regional races, there is no national indigenous political party.[39] Nevertheless, indigenous candidates have run in President Toledo's Peru Posible Party. In 2001, for example, for the first time, an Aymara woman was elected to the National Congress in

Peru. Paulina Arpasi, a former secretary general of the CCP, strongly emphasized her role in representing indigenous people in congress: "I think that it is not only necessary that indígenas know that they have a representative in the national congress, it is also very important that the national congress knows that it has within it a representative of the indígenas. I will change neither my indigenous dress, nor my constant defense (*reivindicación*) of the rights of the indigenous peoples of Peru."[40] Despite criticisms of Arpasi's congressional performance, the 2006 elections built on her 2001 victory and four indigenous women were elected to congress.[41] So while Peru may not have the same kind of political dynamics as its neighbors, one cannot speak of absence.

Additionally, as we noted in our discussion of scale, there are various local and regional forms of contention that may not resemble mainstream tactics of protest and political campaigns. For instance, to borrow once more from García's work on the politics of intercultural bilingual education, we find an unexpected example of Peruvian ethnic mobilization in the tensions between indigenous Peruvians and indigenous rights activists. Many parents saw bilingual education (designed by outsiders) as a way to keep their children from gaining access to Spanish and thus greater economic opportunities. Using the spaces activists developed to gain support from indigenous peoples, some Quechua parents have devised strategies to challenge the imposition of education reform in their communities. For instance, "parent schools" (*escuelas de padres*), designed by activists to explain their goals, quickly became a forum where parents could dispute activist interpretations of concepts such as citizenship and protest education reform. Another important strategy of indigenous leaders has been to promote the establishment of community-controlled schools that are *not* managed by the state, nor by NGOs. Discussion among Quechua community leaders about their own control of education implies a move toward self-determination, even if it does not come in the form of massive protests and marches. Such an example bears a resemblance to other movements like the Pan-Mayan movement in Guatemala, which has favored education and cultural production over mass demonstrations.[42]

What does this suggest, then, about how we think about the tactics of Ecuadorian social movements? Perhaps the most obvious lesson is that high-profile tactics may not always be the most successful (with success understood in a variety of ways). A particularly glaring example of this was provided on January 21, 2000, when Ecuadorian indigenous leaders, if for only a few hours, achieved what no other indigenous movement in the region had achieved: it removed an unpopular neoliberal president *and* formed part of a new government with elements from the military, a Junta of National Salvation.[43] The junta unraveled before dawn of the next day. Immediately, many inside and outside the movement questioned the wisdom of this "rebellion." Critics attacked the secretive and undemocratic character of the coup, which marked a departure from the kind of social movement tactics CONAIE had used for over a decade. On the other hand, defenders noted that CONAIE retained its political power, as demonstrated by recent elections. In 2002, Pachakutik helped Lucio Gutiérrez, a former colonel and leader of the January 21 "coup," to win the presidential election. This too was a pyrrhic victory, as the alliance with the new president would last less than a year. Additionally, Gutiérrez managed to split CONAIE in unprecedented ways, something facilitated perhaps by the lingering tension over whether January 21 marked a high or low point for Ecuadorian indigenous politics.

To put the broad lesson in Gramscian terms, Peru and Ecuador (and other places, to be sure) provide examples of wars of position (the slow going through many trenches of civil society) and wars of maneuver (the storming of government palaces). Peru and Ecuador seem to present contrasting trajectories. After decades of Shining Path guerrillas' bloody and destructive war of maneuver, indigenous people in Peru (the primary victims of Shining Path and state violence) have pursued social change in the various spaces and interstices of national, regional, and local civil society. Ecuador's CONAIE moved from a decade of the tactics of the war of position (in the streets and in the halls of government), only to resort momentarily to the maneuver of a coup, which has unleashed a set of dynamics that have fragmented and weakened CONAIE's place in national society.

Long ago, C. Wright Mills gave scholars the following advice: "The release of imagination can sometimes be achieved by deliberately inverting your sense of proportion. If something seems very minute, imagine it to be simply enormous, and ask yourself: What difference might that make?"[44] In this spirit, we might ask what would happen if we inverted the common wisdom about the strength of Ecuador's indigenous movement and the weakness of that in Peru?

Such an inversion, though hardly an "objective" portrait of what is actually occurring in these complex countries, prompts us to examine more critically what might be obscured by the shadows cast by discussions of movement "success" and "failure." Rather than see either as a particular configuration of movement activity at a certain scale, around a particular identity, and deploying a limited set of tactics, we should be open to other possibilities. These possibilities may involve some contradictions. Regional fragmentation may make for more democratic imaginings *and* it can sometimes weaken indigenous negotiating positions vis-à-vis the state, while at other times it may create opportunities for the emergence of strong political actors (like Bolivia's cocaleros). Multiple indigenous identities may avoid the traps of essentialism *and* create problems for social movement leaders seeking to forge solidarity and authenticity. Nonprotest tactics by indigenous people may exploit openings in the system *and* leave other elements of it unchallenged and even legitimized. In a word, all these means of contestation and negotiation are very much alive in Ecuador and Peru, and beyond. The current moment is one of change, one in which the Ecuadorian movement has faced several setbacks, including the poor showing of Luis Macas, president of CONAIE in the 2006 elections. Meanwhile, Peruvian movements are in a moment of rearticulation as they face the conservative reincarnation of Alan García, who won a narrow victory in 2006. Trying to atone for his disastrous populist government of the 1980s, García has championed foreign investment, especially in the mining sector, which will certainly lead to further confrontations with campesino communities, CONACAMI, and other indigenous organizations.

In short, here we are raising some questions about common representations of indigenous mobilization in the Andes, and in Peru and Ecuador specifically. While CONAIE has clearly been successful in mobilizing indigenous communities, and gaining important (national and international) support, its representation as *the* most important indigenous organization in the hemisphere, and as the model that other organizations should strive toward, has at times obscured the diversity of indigenous mobilizing in that country as well as elsewhere. At the same time, common representations of indigenous movements in Peru as "weak" or "negative" cases stand in the way of richer ethnographic explorations and understandings of the contentious politics taking place on many levels. To be clear, we do not want to diminish the achievements of CONAIE, which have been remarkable, nor ignore the limitations of other indigenous actors, which are often challenging. Our efforts here are meant to be both provocative and modest in suggesting some alternative ways to see and not see the patterns and consequences of indigenous challenges to state structures throughout the Americas.[45]

Bibliographic Essay

MARC BECKER

Ecuador, as a small country on South America's Pacific coast, often receives little attention in broader works on Latin America. For example, not a single chapter in the landmark volume, *Resistance, Rebellion, and Consciousness in the Andean Peasant World: 18th to 20th Centuries*, ed. Steve J. Stern (Madison: University of Wisconsin Press, 1987) is dedicated to Ecuador. Likewise, *The Cambridge History of the Native Peoples of the Americas*, ed. Frank Salomon and Stuart B. Schwartz (Cambridge: Cambridge University Press, 1999) devotes relatively little attention to Ecuador. In bibliographic essays on the Andes in that volume, Brooke Larson notes that Ecuador's nineteenth century is one of the least studied topics in the region, and Xavier Albó notes that "the first half of the twentieth century shows a deafening silence on the part of scholars, as if nonwhite Ecuador no longer existed."[1] In a 1985 survey of North American writings on Latin American history, David Bushnell counted only one book on Ecuador. In comparing the number of historical studies in English on Ecuador to its size, Bushnell noted that the country "would again lose half its territory, this time by reason of North American neglect rather than war or diplomacy."[2]

This scholarly lack of interest has not been the result of an absence of compelling themes in the country's history. In the early 1970s, political scientist John Martz observed that Ecuador, even though little studied among scholars of Latin American issues, "serves as a microcosm for a wide variety of problems, questions, and issues relevant to various of the other Latin American countries."[3] Slowly but surely Ecuador is beginning to take a more prominent place in the scholarly literature on Latin America. One notable attempt is *Historia de América Andina*, vol. 5, *Creación de las repúblicas y formación de la nación*, ed. Juan Maiguashca (Quito: Universidad Andina Simón Bolívar, 2003). As dissertations written over the past twenty years make their way into print in the form of articles, monographs, and books, the literature on Ecuador has become richer.

Although somewhat dated in its focus on the emergence of civilian government in the 1980s, a short and highly readable introductory study is David Corkill and David Cubitt, *Ecuador: Fragile Democracy* (London: Latin American Bureau,

1988). Broader in scope and also focusing primarily on political developments is Enrique Ayala Mora, *Resumen de historia del Ecuador* (Quito: Corporación Editora Nacional, 1993), which summarizes much of the information presented in *Nueva Historia del Ecuador,* 15 vols., ed. Enrique Ayala Mora (Quito: Corporación Editora Nacional, 1983–1995). Organized chronologically and thematically, the *Nueva Historia* brings together many advances in Ecuador's historiography. Particularly relevant to the themes of this book are Gerardo Fuentealba, "La sociedad indígena en las primeras décadas de la república: continuidades coloniales y cambios republicanos," in ibid., vol. 8, *Epoca republicana II: Perspectiva general del siglo XIX*, 45–77; Xavier Andrade and Fredy Rivera, "El movimiento campesino e indígena en el último período: fases, actores y contenidos políticos," in ibid., vol. 11, *Epoca republicana III: El Ecuador en el último período*, 257–82; and Diego Iturralde G., "Nacionalidades indígenas y estado nacional en Ecuador," in ibid., vol. 13, *Ensayos Generales II: Nación, Estado y Sistema Político*, 9–58.

An introductory survey of Ecuadorian anthropological studies is Segundo E. Moreno Yánez, *Antropología ecuatoriana: Pasado y presente* (Quito: Editorial Ediguias C. Ltda., 1992). More in-depth treatments include a study by the political scientist and Ecuador's former president, Osvaldo Hurtado, *Political Power in Ecuador* (Albuquerque: University of New Mexico Press, 1980); and by an economist, David W. Schodt, *Ecuador: An Andean Enigma* (Boulder, CO: Westview Press, 1987). A good volume, though now somewhat dated, that gives a broad overview of the ethnic diversity in Ecuador is *Cultural Transformations and Ethnicity in Modern Ecuador,* ed. Norman E. Whitten Jr. (Urbana: University of Illinois Press, 1981). Also essential is the updated edition, *Millennial Ecuador: Critical Essays on Cultural Transformations and Social Dynamics,* ed. Norman E. Whitten Jr. (Iowa City: University of Iowa Press, 2003). Complementing these works is Michael Handelsman, *Culture and Customs of Ecuador* (Westport, CT: Greenwood Press, 2000), with its focus on popular culture. An ambitious study is *Ecuador: una nación en ciernes,* ed. Rafael Quintero and Erika Silva (Quito: FLACSO–Abya-Yala, 1991), which provides much information on Ecuadorian history. These more recent works provide interesting contrasts to two classic studies that provided the basis for an earlier generation of research on Ecuador: Lilo Linke, *Ecuador: Country of Contrasts* (London: Oxford University Press, 1954); and George I. Blanksten, *Ecuador: Constitutions and Caudillos* (Berkeley: University of California Press, 1951), which argues that passive Indians were responsible for the creation of an authoritarian state in Ecuador.

Less archaeological research has been conducted in Ecuador than in Peru. An outstanding book that reconstructs the political and economic institutions of pre-Inka societies in the northern Andes is Frank Salomon, *Native Lords of Quito in the Age of the Incas: The Political Economy of North Andean Chiefdoms* (Cambridge: Cambridge University Press, 1986). Much of the most developed research on Ecuador concerns the colonial period, when it was known as the Audiencia of Quito. The earliest book in English on the subject is John Leddy Phelan, *The Kingdom of Quito in the Seventeenth Century* (Madison: University of Wisconsin Press, 1967). Galo Ramón, *La resistencia andina: Cayambe, 1500–1800* (Quito: Centro Andino de Acción Popular, 1987) examines indigenous resistance to colonial policies within hacienda settings. Karen Powers, *Andean Journeys: Migration, Ethnogenesis, and the State in Colonial Quito* (Albuquerque: University of New Mexico Press, 1995) examines indigenous migrations as a form of resistance to state structures. Kris Lane, *Quito 1599: City and Colony in Transition* (Albuquerque: University of New Mexico Press, 2002) extends this analysis in a variety of directions, including a look at maroon slave resistance on the coast and Shuar resistance to gold mining in the eastern Amazon.

Only recently has the nineteenth century begun to receive the attention it deserves. A useful starting point on this century is *Historia y región en el Ecuador 1830–1930*, ed. Juan Maiguashca (Quito: Corporación Editora Nacional, 1994); and in particular Juan Maiguashca, "El proceso de integración nacional en el Ecuador: el rol del poder central, 1830–1895," in ibid. Maiguashca's rethinking of state formation has influenced subsequent interpretations. One of the best essays on Indian-state relations in this century is Andrés Guerrero, "The Construction of a Ventriloquist's Image: Liberal Discourse and the 'Miserable Indian Race' in Late Nineteenth Century Ecuador," *Journal of Latin American Studies* 29, no. 3 (October 1997): 555–90 (originally published as "Una imagen ventrílocua: el discurso liberal de la 'desgraciada raza indígena' a fines del siglo XIX," in *Imágenes e imagineros: representaciones de los indígenas ecuatorianos, siglos XIX y XX*, ed. Blanca Muratorio [Quito: Facultad Latinoamericana de Ciencias Sociales-Sede Ecuador, 1994], 197–252). Guerrero examines how liberals represented indigenous concerns and exploited them for their own political gain. See also Andrés Guerrero, "Curagas y tenientes políticos: La ley de la costumbre y la ley del estado (Otavalo 1830–1875)," *Revista Andina* 7, no. 2 (no. 14) (December 1989): 321–66, which examines a shift from ethnic to secular authority in Otavalo in northern Ecuador.

The three chapters on Ecuador in *Los Andes en la encrucijada: indios, comunidades y estado en el siglo XIX*, ed. Heraclio Bonilla (Quito: Ediciones Libri Mundi–FLACSO, 1991) are also all useful treatments of nineteenth-century Indian-state relations. Conservative efforts to establish a Catholic state are described in Derek Williams, "Assembling the 'Empire of Morality': State Building Strategies in Catholic Ecuador, 1861–1875," *Journal of Historical Sociology* 14, no. 2 (June 2001): 149–74. The 1871 revolt in Chimborazo against taxation and labor drafts led by Fernando Daquilema is receiving an increasing amount of attention. See Hernan Ibarra, *Nos encontramos amenazados por todita la indiada: El levantamiento de Daquilema* (Quito: CEDIS, 1993). Innovative research on relations between gender and ethnicity may be found in Erin O'Connor, "Widows' Rights Questioned: Indians, the State, and Fluctuating Gender Ideas in Central Highland Ecuador, 1870–1900," *The Americas* 59, no. 1 (July 2002): 87–106; and Erin O'Connor, *Gender, Indian, Nation: The Contradictions of Making Ecuador, 1830–1925* (Tucson: University of Arizona Press, 2007). A chapter in *The Cambridge History of the Native Peoples of the Americas* has been expanded into Brooke Larson, *Trials of Nation Making: Liberalism, Race, and Ethnicity in the Andes, 1810–1910* (Cambridge: Cambridge University Press, 2004). The chapter on Ecuador provides an excellent synthetic treatment of this period.

The 1895 Liberal Revolution and its aftermath has begun to attract more attention from scholars. See Enrique Ayala Mora, *Historia de la Revolución Liberal Ecuatoriana* (Quito: Corporación Editora Nacional, 1994). A. Kim Clark, *The Redemptive Work: Railway and Nation in Ecuador, 1895–1930* (Wilmington, DE: SR Books, 1998) examines the political economy and culture of the railroad in Ecuador that, uniquely in Latin America, was designed to unify the country rather than create an export infrastructure. Mercedes Prieto, *Liberalismo y temor: imaginando los sujetos indígenas en el Ecuador postcolonial, 1895–1950* (Quito: FLACSO, 2004) presents a solid analysis of liberal attitudes toward race. Also see Nicola Foote, "Race, State and Nation in Early Twentieth Century Ecuador," *Nations and Nationalism* 12, no. 2 (April 2006): 261–78. For indigenous uprisings against government taxes in the 1920s, see Michiel Baud, "The Huelga de los Indígenas in Cuenca, Ecuador (1920–1921)," in *Indigenous Revolts in Chiapas and the Andean Highlands*, ed. Kevin Gosner and Arij Ouweneel (Amsterdam: CEDLA, 1996), 217–39; and Michiel Baud, "Campesinos indígenas contra el Estado. La huelga de los indígenas de Azuay, 1920/21," *Procesos: Revista Ecuatoriana de Historia* 4 (1993): 41–72.

Much of the research on twentieth-century Ecuador is composed of anthropological studies of indigenous groups in the eastern Amazonian basin, called the Oriente. Early twentieth-century accounts tended to sensationalize Amazonian "headhunters." See Rafael Karsten, *The Head-hunters of the Western Amazonas: The Life and Culture of the Jibaro Indians of Eastern Ecuador and Peru* (Helsinki: Societas Scientiarum Fennica, Commentationes Humanarum Litterarum, 1935); and M. W. Stirling, *Historical and Ethnographical Material on the Jivaro Indians* (Washington, DC: American Ethnological Society, 1939). The literature has developed significantly since then. See Blanca Muratorio, *The Life and Times of Grandfather Alonso: Culture and History in the Upper Amazon* (New Brunswick, NJ: Rutgers University Press, 1991); Norman J. Whitten Jr., *Sacha Runa: Ethnicity and Adaptation of Ecuadorian Jungle Quichua* (Urbana: University of Illinois Press, 1976); and Norman J. Whitten Jr., *Sicuanga Runa: The Other Side of Development in Amazonian Ecuador* (Urbana: University of Illinois Press, 1985). These books on lowland Quichua Indians have inspired a generation of anthropologists. An important historical perspective is presented in Anne-Christine Taylor, "El Oriente ecuatoriano en el siglo XIX: 'el otro litoral,'" in *Historia y región en el Ecuador 1830–1930*, ed. Juan Maiguashca (Quito: Corporación Editora Nacional, 1994), 17–67. Ethnographic work examines how indigenous peoples in the Amazon have confronted challenges from the imposition of state structures on traditional communities. Among the best recent treatments are Suzana Sawyer, *Crude Chronicles: Indigenous Politics, Multinational Oil, and Neoliberalism in Ecuador* (Durham: Duke University Press, 2004); Michael Uzendoski, *The Napo Runa of Amazonian Ecuador* (Urbana: University of Illinois Press, 2005); Steven L. Rubenstein, *Alejandro Tsakimp: A Shuar Healer in the Margins of History* (Lincoln: University of Nebraska Press, 2002); Laura M. Rival, *Trekking Through History: The Huaorani of Amazonian Ecuador* (New York: Columbia University Press, 2002); and Lawrence Ziegler-Otero, *Resistance in an Amazonian Community: Huaorani Organizing Against the Global Economy* (Oxford: Berghahn, 2004).

Unlike the Amazon, the western coast has received little scholarly attention outside of the port city of Guayaquil. Guayaquil has a long history of working-class struggles against capital, expressed most vividly in a strike that was repressed through a massacre of workers on November 15, 1922. The history of subaltern attempts to influence government policies in Guayaquil is examined in Ronn F. Pineo, *Social and Economic Reform in Ecuador: Life and Work in Guayaquil* (Gainesville: University Press of Florida, 1996). An interesting examination of the conformation of political and social power in Guayaquil is found in Patricia de la Torre, *Lo privado y local en el estado ecuatoriano: la Junta de Beneficencia de Guayaquil* (Quito: Abya Yala, 1999). Few indigenous peoples remain in the coastal region, with much of the rural population assimilated into a poor mestizo population; see José de la Cuadra, *El montuvio ecuatoriano* (Quito: Instituto de Investigaciones Económicas de la Universidad Central del Ecuador, 1937). Peasant struggles in the early twentieth century for recognition of their rights are covered in John F. Uggen, *Tenencia de la tierra y movilizaciones campesinas: zona de Milagro* (Quito: Andean Center for Latin American Studies, 1993). A compelling book is Steve Striffler, *In The Shadows of State and Capital: The United Fruit Company, Popular Struggle, and Agrarian Restructuring in Ecuador, 1900–1995* (Durham: Duke University Press, 2002), which examines how agrarian workers on the Tenguel banana hacienda engaged state structures in attempts to improve their lives.

Important works on highland indigenous cultures include Linda Smith Belote and Jim Belote, "Drain from the Bottom: Individual Ethnic Identity Change in Southern Ecuador," *Social Forces* 63, no. 1 (September 1984): 24–50, which examines the resurgence of ethnic consciousness in Saraguro. A now classic article on religion and ethnicity is Blanca Muratorio, "Protestantism and Capitalism Revisited, in the Rural Highlands of Ecuador," *Journal of Peasant Studies* 8, no. 1 (October 1980): 37–60. Good starting points for understanding indigenous relations with the broader society in the central highland provinces of Cotopaxi and Chimborazo include Mary J. Weismantel, *Food, Gender, and Poverty in the Ecuadorian Andes* (Philadelphia: University of Pennsylvania Press, 1988); and Barry J. Lyons, *Remembering the Hacienda: Religion, Authority, and Social Change in Highland Ecuador* (Austin: University of Texas Press, 2006).

The early emergence of peasant organizations in Cayambe in the northern highlands that challenged white hegemonic control over indigenous labor on haciendas is explored in Mercedes Prieto, "Haciendas estatales: un caso de ofensiva campesina: 1926–1948," in *Ecuador: cambios en el agro serraño*, ed. Miguel Murmis et al. (Quito: Facultad Latinoamericana de Ciencias Sociales [FLACSO]–Centro de Planificación y Estudios Sociales [CEPLAES], 1980), 101–30; Muriel Crespi, "Changing Power Relations: The Rise of Peasant Unions on Traditional Ecuadorian Haciendas," *Anthropological Quarterly* 44, no. 4 (October 1971): 223–40; and Marc Becker, "Una Revolución Comunista Indígena: Rural Protest Movements in Cayambe, Ecuador," *Rethinking Marxism* 10, no. 4 (Winter 1998): 34–51. Biographies of two important indigenous leaders are Raquel Rodas, *Dolores Cacuango: Gran líder del pueblo indio* (Quito: Banco Central del Ecuador, 2006); and Cecilia Miño, *Tránsito Amaguaña* (Quito: Banco Central del Ecuador, 2006).

In the highland region, the Otavalo Indians have received significant scholarly attention owing to their financial success and international renown for their weaving. As a result, they have not experienced the degree of racism faced by other groups, a fact that has also influenced the nature of their relations with state structures. John Collier Jr. and Aníbal Buitron, *The Awakening Valley* (Chicago: University of Chicago Press, 1949) presents the metaphor of the Otavalo Indians coming of age. Although most work on Otavalo has been ethnographic, Andrés Guerrero examines a historical shift from ethnic to secular authorities during the nineteenth century in "Curagas y tenientes políticos: La ley de la costumbre y la ley del estado (Otavalo 1830–1875)," *Revista Andina* 7, no. 2 (no. 14) (December 1989): 321–66. The role of Indians in the privatization of communal lands since the 1700s is examined in Elizabeth Marberry Rogers, "Ethnicity, Property, and the State: Legal Rhetoric and the Politics of Community in Otavalo, Ecuador," *Research in Economic Anthropology* 19 (1998): 69–113. Among the best recent studies on this region are Rudi Colloredo-Mansfeld, *The Native Leisure Class: Consumption and Cultural Creativity in the Andes* (Chicago: University of Chicago Press, 1999); and Lynn Meisch, *Andean Entrepreneurs: Otavalo Merchants and Musicians in the Global Arena* (Austin: University of Texas Press, 2003).

Politically, *indigenismo* has not been as strong a force in Ecuador as in Mexico and Peru, but the intellectual presence of this ideology has been felt culturally. A novel published in 1934 by Jorge Icaza, *Huasipungo* (Carbondale: Southern Illinois University Press, 1964), is one of the best examples of *indigenista* literature in Latin America. Icaza portrays Indians as incompetent fools who need the assistance of white liberals to save them from the worst abuses of the dominant culture. A more scholarly work along the same lines is Pío Jaramillo Alvarado, *El indio ecuatoriano,* 2 vols., 7th ed. (Quito: Corporación Editora Nacional, 1997 [1922]). Jaramillo's work contributed to the formation of the Instituto Indigenista Ecuatoriano in 1943, which published an occasional journal called *Atahualpa* and a variety of books, including *Cuestiones indígenas del Ecuador* (Quito: Edit. Casa de la Cultura Ecuatoriana, 1946). In the 1950s and 1960s, Alfredo Costales Samaniego and Piedad Peñaherrera de Costales published 24 monographs in a series entitled *Llacta* which summarized much of the contemporary scholarly research on Indians. Among significant works by indigenista intellectuals in the twentieth century is Gonzalo Rubio Orbe, *Los indios ecuatorianos: Evolución histórica y políticas indigenistas* (Quito: Corporación Editora Nacional, 1987).

Many of the discussions concerning indigenous-state relations have revolved around issues of agrarian reform. An early study that interprets this history from the peasants' point of view is Fernando Velasco, *Reforma agraria y movimiento campesino indígena de la sierra*, 2d ed. (Quito: Editorial El Conejo, 1983). Velasco's untimely death in 1978 ended his important contribution to this debate, but Osvaldo Barsky and Andrés Guerrero continued the discussion. The thesis that modernizing landowners initiated the agrarian reform process is presented in Osvaldo Barsky, *La reforma agraria ecuatoriana* (Quito: Corporación Editora Nacional, 1984).

Guerrero argues that peasant initiative forced these changes. See Andrés Guerrero, *Haciendas, capital y lucha de clases andina: disolución de la hacienda serrana y lucha política en los años 1960–64* (Quito: Editorial El Conejo, 1983). A similar view is found in Paola Sylva, *Gamonalismo y lucha campesino* (Quito: Ediciones Abya Yala, 1986). Galo Ramón criticized these authors for adhering too closely to a class analysis that blinded them to the ethnic dimensions in the peasant struggle to regain ownership over land which they historically had occupied. See Galo Ramón, *El regreso de los runas: la potencialidad del proyecto indio en el Ecuador contemporánea* (Quito: COMUNIDEC–Fundación Interamericana, 1993). A good summary of the debate is in Leon Zamosc, *Peasant Struggles and Agrarian Reform: The Ecuadorian Sierra and the Colombian Atlantic Coast in Comparative Perspective*, Latin American Issues Monograph 8 (Meadville, PA: Allegheny College, 1990).

Several works examine how specific images of Indians are formed and how the indigenous population fits into models of the Ecuadorian nation. Mary Crain, "The Social Construction of National Identity in Highland Ecuador," *Anthropological Quarterly* 63, no. 1 (January 1990): 43–59, critiques how national governments have exploited symbols of indigenous cultures for their own political gain. A now classic study of national ideologies in Ecuador is Ronald Stutzman, "El Mestizaje: An All-Inclusive Ideology of Exclusion," in *Cultural Transformations and Ethnicity in Modern Ecuador*, ed. Norman E. Whitten Jr. (Urbana: University of Illinois Press, 1981). Accounts of how images of Indians have articulated with nationalist ideologies at different times may be found in Blanca Muratorio, ed., *Imágenes e Imagineros: Representaciones de los Indígenas Ecuatorianos, Siglos XIX y XX* (Quito: FLACSO, 1994). In a rather different vein, Ecuadorian beauty pageants and how Indians participate in them figuratively and literally are examined in Mark Rogers, "Spectacular Bodies: Folklorization and the Politics of Identity in Ecuadorian Beauty Pageants," *Journal of Latin American Anthropology* 3, no. 2 (1998): 54–85. On the social construction of images of Indians, see A. Kim Clark, "Race, 'Culture' and Mestizaje: The Statistical Construction of the Ecuadorian Nation, 1930–1950," *Journal of Historical Sociology* 11, no. 2 (1998): 185–211; "Racial Ideologies and the Quest for National Development: Debating the Agrarian Problem in Ecuador (1930–1950)," *Journal of Latin American Studies* 30, no. 2 (1998): 373–93; and "La medida de la diferencia: Las imágenes indigenistas de los indios serranos en el Ecuador (1920s a 1940s)," in *Ecuador racista: Imágenes e identidades*, ed. Emma Cervone and Fredy Rivera (Quito: FLACSO, 1999), 111–26.

Andrés Guerrero, *La semántica de la dominación: el concertaje de indios* (Quito: Ediciones Libri Mundi, 1991) is a masterful study of mechanisms of domination on highland haciendas and indigenous resistance to those systems. A wide-ranging study of the highland hacienda economy is Jorge Trujillo, *La hacienda serrana, 1900–1930* (Quito: Instituto de Estudios Ecuatorianos–Ediciones Abya-Yala, 1986). Marc Becker, "Comunas and Indigenous Protest in Cayambe, Ecuador," *The Americas* 55, no. 4 (April 1999): 531–59, argues that politicized indigenous activists rejected a 1937 law that extended legal recognition to rural communities because it would deepen dependence on the dominant culture. Marc Becker examines how rural and urban activists joined together in a common struggle for social justice in "Indigenous Communists and Urban Intellectuals in Cayambe, Ecuador (1926–1944)," in *Popular Intellectuals and Social Movements: Framing Protest in Asia, Africa, and Latin America*, ed. Michiel Baud and Rosanne Rutten (Cambridge: Cambridge University Press, 2004), 41–64.

A variety of works analyze indigenous-state relations, most of them focusing on recent decades. These include Diego Iturralde G., "Nacionalidades indígenas y estado nacional en Ecuador," in *Nueva historia del Ecuador*, vol. 13, *Ensayos generales II: nación, estado y sistema político*, ed. Enrique Ayala Mora (Quito: Corporación Editora Nacional, 1995), 9–58; Diego Cornejo Menacho, ed., *Los indios y el estado-país; pluriculturalidad y multietnicidad en el Ecuador: contribuciones al debate* (Quito: Ediciones Abya-Yala, 1993); Enrique Ayala Mora et al., *Pueblos indios, estado y derecho* (Quito: Corporación Editora Nacional, 1993); Juan Carlos Ribadeneira, ed., *Derecho, pueblos indígenas y reforma del estado* (Quito: Ediciones Abya-Yala, 1993); and Ilena Almeida and Nidia Arrobo Rodas, eds., *En defensa del pluralismo y la igualdad: Los derechos de los pueblos indios y el estado* (Quito: Fundación Pueblo Indio del Ecuador; Ediciones Abya-Yala, 1998). A useful collection of essays is Víctor Bretón and Francisco García, eds., *Estado, etnicidad y movimientos sociales en América Latina: Ecuador en crisis,* ed. (Barcelona: Ausiàs Editorial, S.A., 2003).

A related theme is the interplay between class and ethnicity within indigenous movements. See Alicia Ibarra, *Los indígenas y el estado en el Ecuador: La práctica neoindigenista*, 2d ed. (Quito: Ediciones Abya-Yala, 1992), which examines the relationship between the state and indigenous peoples in Ecuador during the government of Jaime Roldós and Oswaldo Hurtado (1979–1984). Employing a Marxist analysis, she argues that the class content of an indigenous movement is more important than its ethnic elements. In contrast, Roberto Santana, *¿Ciudadanos en la etnicidad? Los indios en la política o la política de los indios* (Quito: Ediciones Abya-Yala, 1995) emphasizes the importance of ethnicity in these movements. Amalia Pallares, *From Peasant Struggles to Indian Resistance: The Ecuadorian Andes in the Late Twentieth Century* (Norman: University of Oklahoma Press, 2002), describes a shift from peasant to indigenous consciousness.

Much has been written about recent indigenous movements in Ecuador, thus expanding the discussion of indigenous relations with state structures. Anthropologists, political scientists, and sociologists have analyzed the significance of the 1990 uprising, related actions, and the corresponding ideological shift within indigenous politics and indigenous attitudes toward nationalism and state power. In a manner rarely seen in Latin America, indigenous actions spawned an academic "Generation of 1990," with countless books, articles, and doctoral dissertations on indigenous politics in Ecuador. Examples include José Almeida et al., *Sismo étnico en el Ecuador: varias perspectivas* (Quito: CEDIME-Ediciones Abya-Yala, 1993); Diego Cornejo Menacho, ed., *INDIOS: Una reflexión sobre el levantamiento indígena de 1990* (Quito: ILDIS, 1991); Segundo E. Moreno Yánez and José Figueroa, *El levantamiento indígena del inti raymi de 1990* (Quito: Ediciones Abya-Yala, 1992); Fernando Rosero, *Levantamiento indígena: tierra y precios* (Quito: Centro de Estudios y Difusión Social, 1990); Jorge León Trujillo, *De campesinos a ciudadanos diferentes: El levantamiento indígena* (Quito: CEDIME–Abya-Yala, 1994); Melina H. Selverston, "The Politics of Culture: Indigenous Peoples and the State in Ecuador," in *Indigenous Peoples and Democracy in Latin America*, ed. Donna Lee Van Cott (New York: St. Martin's Press in association with the Inter-American Dialogue, 1994), 131–52; Melina Selverston-Scher, *Ethnopolitics in Ecuador: Indigenous Rights and the Strengthening of Democracy* (Coral Gables, FL: North-South Center Press, 2001); Leon Zamosc, "Agrarian Protest and the Indian Movement in the Ecuadorian Highlands," *Latin American Research Review* 29, no. 3 (1994): 37–68; Xavier Albó, "El retorno del Indio," *Revista Andina* 9, no. 2 (December 1991): 299–345; and Lynn A. Meisch, "We Will Not Dance on the Tomb of Our Grandparents: 500 Years of Resistance in Ecuador," *Latin American Anthropology*

Review 4, no. 2 (Winter 1992): 55–74.

Building on this activism in the 1990s, a quickly exploding body of literature emerged on indigenous involvement in electoral politics. See Robert Andolina, "The Sovereign and Its Shadow: Constituent Assembly and Indigenous Movement in Ecuador," *Journal of Latin American Studies* 35, no. 4 (November 2003): 721–50; Jennifer Collins, "Linking Movement and Electoral Politics: Ecuador's Indigenous Movement and the Rise of Pachakutik," in *Politics in the Andes: Identity, Conflict, Reform*, ed. Jo-Marie Burt and Philip Mauceri (Pittsburgh: University of Pittsburgh Press, 2004), 38–57; and Pablo Dávalos, "'De paja de páramo sembraremos el mundo': Izquierda, utopía y movimiento indígena en Ecuador," in *La nueva izquierda en América Latina*, ed. César A. Rodríguez Garavito, Patrick S. Barrett, and Daniel Chavez (Bogotá: Grupo Editorial Norma, 2005), 359–403. An important collection of documents from indigenous participants is presented in Augusto Barrera, *Entre la utopía y el desencanto: Pachakutik en el gobierno de Gutiérrez* (Quito: Editorial Planeta del Ecuador, S.A., 2004). Pablo Ospina Peralta, ed., *En las fisuras del poder: Movimiento indígena, cambio social y gobiernos locales* (Quito: IIE; CLACSO, 2006) examines how Pachakutik has worked with local development projects in Cotopaxi and Cotacachi.

Recent indigenous challenges to state power continue to receive scholarly attention. The failed January 21, 2000 military-indigenous coup against Jamil Mahuad is examined in Catherine Walsh, "The Ecuadorian Political Irruption. Uprisings, Coups, Rebellions, and Democracy," *Nepantla: Views from South* 2, no. 1 (Spring 2001): 173–204; and the April 2001 issue of *Íconos*, a journal from the Ecuadorian branch of FLACSO, includes essays on this topic by Manuel Chiriboga, Fernando García, Jorge León, Eduardo Kingman, and others. A summary of recent literature is in Leon Zamosc, "The Indian Movement in Ecuador: from Politics of Influence to Politics of Power," in *The Struggle for Indigenous Rights in Latin America*, ed. Nancy Grey Postero and Leòn Zamosc (Brighton: Sussex Academic Press, 2004), 131–57. Zamosc examines the relationship between neoliberalism and political volatility, with an emphasis on the continued relevance of class conflict in an Indian movement that transcends ethnic rights.

Many works have emerged to analyze the impact of neoliberalism on Ecuador. See *Rural Progress, Rural Decay: Neoliberal Adjustment Policies and Local Initiatives,* ed. Liisa L. North and John D. Cameron (Bloomfield, CT: Kumarian Press, 2003), which uses Ecuador as an example of the adverse consequences of neoliberal macroeconomic policies on equitable development. On relations between neoliberalism and indigenous movements, see Fernando Guerrero Cazar and Pablo Ospina Peralta, *El poder de la comunidad: Ajuste estructural y movimiento indígena en los Andes ecuatorianos* (Buenos Aires: CLACSO, 2003); also see Luciano Martínez, "El campesino andino y la globalización a fines de siglo (una mirada sobre el caso ecuatoriano)," *European Review of Latin American and Caribbean*

Studies 77 (October 2004): 25–40; and Víctor Bretón Solo de Zaldívar, "Los paradigmas de la 'nueva' ruralidad a debate: El proyecto de desarrollo de los pueblos indígenas y negros del Ecuador," *European Review of Latin American and Caribbean Studies* 78 (April 2005): 7–30. On how these factors trigger rural-urban migration, see Carola Lentz, *Migración e identidad étnica: La transformación histórica de una comunidad indígena en la sierra ecuatoriana* (Quito: Ediciones Abya-Yala, 1997).

A growing arena of inquiry is indigenous justice, or how local communities use traditional authority structures to resolve internal debates rather the relying on external state structures. See *Derechos de los pueblos indígenas: Situación jurídica y políticas de estado*, ed. Ramón Torres Galarza (Quito: CONAIE/CEPLAES/Abya-Yala, 1995); *Justicia indígena. Aportes para un debate*, ed. Judith Salgado (Quito: Ediciones Abya-Yala; Universidad Andina Simón Bolívar, 2002); and Rudi Colloredo-Mansfeld, "'Don't Be Lazy, Don't Lie, Don't Steal': Community Justice in the Neoliberal Andes," *American Ethnologist* 29, no. 3 (August 2002): 637–62.

Any consideration of indigenous and state issues would be incomplete without the perspectives of the indigenous peoples themselves. Although there is no end to indigenous pronouncements and statements, most of these remain buried in archival collections. More accessible to a general audience is the CONAIE's institutional history: Confederación de Nacionalidades Indígenas del Ecuador, *Las nacionalidades indígenas en el Ecuador: Nuestro proceso organizativo*, 2d ed. (Quito: Ediciones Tincui–Abya-Yala, 1989). Also see local organizational histories such as Ecuarunari, *Historia de la nacionalidad y los pueblos quichuas del Ecuador* (Quito: Ecuarunari, FUDEC, ILDIS, CODENPE, 1998); and Lourdes Tibán, Raúl Llaquiche, and Eloy Alfaro, *Historia y proceso organizativo* (Latacunga, Ecuador: Movimiento Indígena y Campesino de Cotopaxi "MICC," 2003). Indigenous intellectuals have also published several essays presenting their view on indigenous-state relations. In particular, see Ampam Karakras, *Las nacionalidades indias y el estado Ecuatoriano* (Quito: Editorial TINCUI-CONAIE, 1990). A journal, *Yachaykuna*, along with a monthly bulletin *Rimay*, published by the Instituto Científico de Culturas Indígenas (ICCI) in Quito, is dedicated to such inquiries and is available on their web page (http://icci.nativeweb.org).

Notes

Chapter 1: Indigenous Peoples and State Formation in Modern Ecuador

1. "'Constitutional Coup' by Congress Ousts Gutiérrez on Wave of Popular Protests," *Latin American Weekly Report* WR-05-16 (April 26, 2005): 3.

2. Leon Zamosc, "The Indian Movement in Ecuador: from Politics of Influence to Politics of Power," in *The Struggle for Indigenous Rights in Latin America*, ed. Nancy Grey Postero and Leon Zamosc (Brighton: Sussex Academic Press, 2004), 131.

3. See "16 puntos," http://www.nativeweb.org/papers/statements/state/conaie16puntos.php.

4. See, for instance, Mary Crain, "The Social Construction of National Identity in Highland Ecuador," *Anthropological Quarterly* 63, no. 1 (1990): 49.

5. See Galo Ramón, *El regreso de los runas* (Quito: COMUNIDEC and Fundación Interamericana, 1993).

6. See Amalia Pallares, *From Peasant Struggle to Indian Resistance: The Ecuadorian Andes in the Late Twentieth Century* (Norman: University of Oklahoma Press), 53.

7. We are here influenced by the comments of David Nugent in a general session on state formation in Ecuador at the annual meeting of the Latin American Studies Association, 2000.

8. William Roseberry, "Hegemony and the Language of Contention," in *Everyday Forms of State Formation*, ed. Gilbert Joseph and Daniel Nugent (Durham: Duke University Press, 1994), 355–66.

9. On state formation from "above" and "below," see Philip Corrigan and Derek Sayer, *The Great Arch: English State Formation as Cultural Revolution* (Oxford and New York: Blackwell, 1985); and Gilbert Joseph and Daniel Nugent, eds., *Everyday Forms of State Formation* (Durham: Duke University Press, 1994).

10. David Nugent, *Modernity at the Edge of Empire: State, Individual and Nation in the Northern Peruvian Andes, 1885–1935* (Stanford: Stanford University Press, 1997).

11. Steve Striffler, *In the Shadows of State and Capital: The United Fruit Company, Popular Struggle, and Agrarian Restructuring in Ecuador, 1900–1995* (Durham: Duke University Press, 2002), 38.

12. Philip Abrams, "Notes on the Difficulty of Studying the State," *Journal of Historical Sociology* 1, no. 1 (1988): 82.

13. Thomas Blom Hansen and Finn Stepputat, eds., *States of Imagination: Ethnographic Explorations of the Postcolonial State, Politics, History, and Culture* (Durham: Duke University Press, 2001).

14. Linda Alexander Rodríguez, *The Search for Public Policy: Regional Politics and Government Finances in Ecuador, 1830–1940* (Berkeley: University of California Press, 1985), 202.

15. Ecuador, División de Estadística y Censos, *Primer censo de población del Ecuador, 1950* (Quito: Tall. Graf. de la Dirección, 1954); Junta Nacional de Planificación, *III censo de población 1974, Resultados definitivos* (Quito: Oficina de los Censos Nacionales, 1974).

16. For an overview of the ethnic landscape in Ecuador, see Lilyan Benítez and Alicia Garcés, *Culturas ecuatorianas: ayer y hoy*, 7th ed. (Quito: Ediciones Abya-Yala, 1993).

17. John V. Murra, "The Historic Tribes of Ecuador," in *Handbook of South American Indians*, vol. 2, *The Andean Civilizations*, ed. Julian H. Steward (Washington, DC: U.S. Government Printing Office, 1948), 786.

18. See Julian H. Steward and Alfred Métraux, "Tribes of the Peruvian and Ecuadorian Montana," in *Handbook of South American Indians*, vol. 3, *Tropical Forest Tribes*, ed. Julian H. Steward (Washington, DC: U.S. Government Printing Office, 1948), 535–657.

19. José Alcina Franch, "El proceso de pérdida de la identidad cultural entre los indios del Ecuador," *Cuadernos Hispanoamericanos* 143, no. 428 (February 1986): 94.

20. See James Lockhart, *Spanish Peru 1532–1560: A Colonial Society* (Madison: University of Wisconsin Press, 1968).

21. For example, see Robert Haskett, *Indigenous Rulers: An Ethnohistory of Town Government in Colonial Cuernavaca* (Albuquerque: University of New Mexico Press, 1991).

22. Karen Vieira Powers, *Andean Journeys: Migration, Ethnogenesis, and the State in Colonial Quito* (Albuquerque: University of New Mexico Press, 1995).

23. Andrés Guerrero, "The Construction of a Ventriloquist's Image: Liberal Discourse and the 'Miserable Indian Race' in Late 19th-Century Ecuador," *Journal of Latin American Studies* 29, no. 3 (October 1997): 560–61.

24. "Constitución de 1830," in Federico E. Trabucco, *Constituciones de la República del Ecuador* (Quito: Universidad Central, Editorial Universitaria, 1975), 34–35; Rafael Quintero and Erika Silva, *Ecuador: una nación en ciernes*, 3 vols., Colección Estudios 1 (Quito: FLACSO/Abya-Yala, 1991), 1:100.

25. Guillermo O'Donnell, "On the State, Democratization and Some Conceptual Problems: A Latin American View with Glances at Some Postcommunist Countries," *World Development* 21, no. 8 (1993): 1357. See also Uday S. Mehta, "Liberal Strategies of Exclusion," *Politics and Society* 18 (1990): 427–54.

26. Norman E. Whitten Jr., *Sacha Runa: Ethnicity and Adaptation of Ecuadorian Jungle Quichua* (Urbana: University of Illinois Press, 1976), 268.

27. "Decreta de 30 de octubre de 1857 (Supresión del tributo indígena)," in *Legislación indigenista del Ecuador*, Ediciones especiales del Instituto Indigenista Interamericano 17, ed. Alfredo Rubio Orbe (Mexico City: Instituto Indigenista Interamericano, 1954), 61.

28. Mark Thurner, *From Two Republics to One Divided: Contradictions of Postcolonial Nationmaking in Andean Peru* (Durham: Duke University Press, 1997).

29. "Decreta de 18 de agosto de 1895" and "Decreta de 12 abril de 1899," in Rubio Orbe, *Legislación*, 63, 65–68.

30. Xavier Albó, "Andean People in the Twentieth Century," in *The Cambridge History of the Native Peoples of the Americas*, ed. Frank Saloman and Stuart B. Schwartz (New York: Cambridge University Press, 1999), 783.

31. See A. Kim Clark, "Race, Culture and Mestizaje: The Statistical Construction of the Ecuadorian Nation, 1930–1950," *Journal of Historical Sociology* 11, no. 2 (1998): 185–211.

32. Jorge León and Joanne Rappaport, "The View from Colombia and Ecuador: Native Organizing in the Americas," *Against the Current*, November/December 1995, 32.

33. Ecuador, Dirección General de Estadística, *Ecuador en cifras, 1938 a 1942* (Quito: Impr. del Ministerio de Hacienda, 1944), 55. Activist indigenous-rights groups maintain that 40 percent of Ecuador's population is indigenous, while scholars sometimes give much lower figures. For example, see Confederación de Nacionalidades Indígenas del Ecuador (CONAIE), *Las nacionalidades indígenas en el Ecuador: Nuestro proceso organizativo*, 2d ed., 1992: 500 años de resistencia india, no. 0 (Quito: Ediciones Tincui–Abya-Yala, 1989), 283, and Leon Zamosc,

Estadística de las áreas de predominio étnico de la sierra ecuatoriana: Población rural, indicadores cantonales y organizaciones de base (Quito: Abya Yala, 1995).

34. By comparison, the next largest indigenous language in the Americas is Guaraní, with two to three million speakers in Paraguay and Brazil. Although parts of Mesoamerica (especially Guatemala) have a larger percentage of indigenous inhabitants than the Andean countries, they are divided among many more languages and hence the number of speakers of a particular language is smaller than that of Quechua.

35. Niels Fock, "Ethnicity and Alternative Identification: An Example from Cañar," in *Cultural Transformations and Ethnicity in Modern Ecuador*, ed. Norman E. Whitten Jr. (Urbana: University of Illinois Press, 1981), 417–18; see also Segundo E. Moreno Yánez, *Alzamientos indígenas en la Audiencia de Quito, 1534–1803*, 2d ed. (Quito: Ediciones Abya-Yala, 1989), 19.

36. Hernán Ibarra, *"Nos encontramos amenazados por todita la indiada": El levantamiento de Daquilema (Chimborazo 1871)*, Serie Movimiento Indígena en el Ecuador Contemporáneo 3 (Quito: Centro de Estudios y Difusión Social, 1993); Aleezé Sattar, "An Unresolved Inheritance: Postcolonial State Formation and Indigenous Communities in Chimborazo, Ecuador, 1820–1875" (PhD diss., New School University, 2001).

37. Lynn A. Meisch, *Andean Entrepreneurs: Otavalo Merchants and Musicians in the Global Arena* (Austin: University of Texas Press, 2003); Rudi Colloredo-Mansfeld, *The Native Leisure Class: Consumption and Cultural Creativity in the Andes* (Chicago: University of Chicago Press, 1999).

38. See Whitten, *Sacha Runa*; Norman E. Whitten Jr., *Sicuanga Runa: The Other Side of Development in Amazonian Ecuador* (Urbana: University of Illinois Press, 1985); Blanca Muratorio, *The Life and Times of Grandfather Alonso: Culture and History in the Upper Amazon* (New Brunswick, NJ: Rutgers University Press, 1991); and Michael Uzendoski, *The Napo Runa of Amazonian Ecuador* (Urbana: University of Illinois Press, 2005).

39. Michael J. Harner, *The Jivaro: People of the Sacred Waterfalls* (Garden City, NY: Doubleday/Natural History Press, 1972), 1.

40. Suzana Sawyer, "Fictions of Sovereignty: Of Prosthetic Petro-Capitalism, Neoliberal States, and Phantom-Like Citizens in Ecuador," *Journal of Latin American Anthropology* 6, no. 1 (2001): 156–97; Suzana Sawyer, *Crude Chronicles: Indigenous Politics, Multinational Oil, and Neoliberalism in Ecuador*, American Encounters/Global Interactions (Durham: Duke University Press, 2004).

41. David Stoll, *Fishers of Men or Founders of Empire? The Wycliffe Bible Translators in Latin America* (London: Zed Press, 1982), 278; see also James A. Yost, "Twenty Years of Contact: The Mechanisms of Change in Wao ("Auca") Culture," in *Cultural Transformations and Ethnicity in Modern Ecuador*, ed. Norman E. Whitten Jr. (Urbana: University of Illinois Press, 1981), 677–704.

42. Muratorio, *The Life and Times of Grandfather Alonso*, 42.

43. George I. Blanksten, *Ecuador: Constitutions and Caudillos*, University of California Publications in Political Science 3, no. 1 (Berkeley and Los Angeles: University of California Press, 1951), 22. A classic work on the montuvios is José de la Cuadra, *El montuvio ecuatoriano (ensayo de presentación)* (Quito: Instituto de Investigaciones Económicas de la Universidad Central del Ecuador, 1937).

44. "Ley de cultos," Decreto no. 1, *Registro Oficial* 3: 912 (October 14, 1904): 9381–83; "Ley de Beneficencia," Decreto no. 2, *Registro Oficial* 3: 789 (October 19, 1908): 4164–65.

45. See Andrés Guerrero, *La semántica de la dominación: El concertaje de indios* (Quito: Libri Mundi, 1991).

46. A. Kim Clark, "Racial Ideologies and the Quest for National Development: Debating the Agrarian Problem in Ecuador (1930–50)," *Journal of Latin American Studies* 30, no. 2 (May

1998): 373–93; Marc Becker, "Una Revolución Comunista Indígena: Rural Protest Movements in Cayambe, Ecuador," *Rethinking Marxism* 10, no. 4 (Winter 1998): 34–51.

47. Ecuador, División de Estadística y Censos, *Primer censo agropecuario nacional: resumen de los principales datos preliminares, 1954* (Quito: República del Ecuador, Banco Central del Ecuador: Ministerio de Economía, Banco Nacional de Fomento, 1955). Also see: Leon Zamosc, *Peasant Struggles and Agrarian Reform: The Ecuadorian Sierra and the Colombian Atlantic Coast in Comparative Perspective*, Latin American Issues Monograph 8 (Meadville, PA: Allegheny College, 1990); Fernando Velasco Abad, *Reforma agraria y movimiento campesino indígena de la sierra*, 2d ed. (Quito: Editorial El Conejo, 1983).

48. Jorge Trujillo, *La hacienda serrana, 1900–1930* (Quito: Abya Yala and Instituto de Estudios Ecuatorianos, 1986), 124.

49. See also Erin O'Connor, "Widows' Rights Questioned: Indians, the State, and Fluctuating Gender Ideas in Central Highland Ecuador, 1870–1900," *The Americas* 59, no. 1 (2002): 87–106.

50. Florencia Mallon, "The Promise and Dilemma of Subaltern Studies: Perspectives from Latin American History," *American Historical Review* 99, no. 5 (1994): 1491–1515.

51. Talal Asad, "Are There Histories of Peoples without Europe?" *Comparative Studies in Society and History* 29, no. 3 (1987): 605.

Chapter 2: *¿Indígena o Ciudadano?*

I would like to thank the director and staff of the Archivo Nacional de Historia in Riobamba for their assistance in 1997–1998. I also thank the Social Science Research Council, the Wenner-Gren Foundation, the New School University, and the American Association of University Women for generous grants.

1. See Gilbert Joseph and Daniel Nugent, eds., *Everyday Forms of State Formation in Mexico: Revolution and the Negotiation of Rule in Modern Mexico* (Durham: Duke University Press, 1994).

2. Jeremy Adelman, "The Problem of Persistence in Latin American History," in *Colonial Legacies: The Problem of Persistence in Latin American Histories*, ed. Jeremy Adelman (New York: Routledge, 1999), 1–13.

3. William Roseberry, "Images of the Peasant in the Consciousness of the Venezuelan Proletarian," in *Proletarians and Protest*, ed. Michael Hanagen and Charles Stepenson (Westport, CT: Greenwood Press, 1986), 149–69; Raymond Williams, "Traditions, Institutions and Formations"; and "Dominant, Residual, and Emergent," in *Marxism and Literature* (Oxford: Oxford University Press, 1977), 115–27.

4. Scholars have described Indians of the southern Andes (particularly Bolivia) as entering into a "pact" with the colonial state: in exchange for paying tribute and labor services, they received state protection of their communal lands and maintained their "ethnic" communities under their "traditional" authorities, the caciques. See Tristan Platt, *Estado Boliviano y ayllu andino: tierra y tributo en el norte de Potosí* (Lima: Instituto de Estudios Peruanos, 1982); see also Mark Thurner, *From Two Republics to One Divided: Contradictions of Postcolonial Nationmaking in Andean Peru* (Durham: Duke University Press, 1997).

5. "Registro Oficial de la República de Colombia. Decreto estableciendo la contribución personal de indígenas, 15-X-1828," cited in Martha Moscoso, "La tierra: espacio de conflicto y relación entre el Estado y la comunidad en el siglo XIX," in *Los Andes en la Encrucijada: Indios, Comunidades y Estado en el Siglo XIX*, ed. Heraclio Bonilla (Quito: Libri Mundi, 1991), 373.

6. See Linda Rodríguez, *The Search for Public Policy: Regional Politics and Government Finances in Ecuador, 1830–1940* (Berkeley: University of California Press, 1985), 73–75.

7. Different figures are provided by Mark Van Aken, "The Lingering Death of Indian Tribute," *Hispanic American Historical Review* 61 (1981): 429–59; and Rodríguez, *The Search for Public Policy*, 63.

8. Michael Hamerly, *Historia social y económica de la antigua provincia de Guayaquil 1763–1842* (Guayaquil: Archivo Histórico del Guayas, 1973).

9. Mahmood Mamdani, *Citizen and Subject: Contemporary Africa and the Legacy of Late Colonialism* (Princeton: Princeton University Press, 1996).

10. For a similar argument for Bolivia, see Tristan Platt, "The Janus State: Indian Sovereignty and Patrician Democracy in Republican Bolivia" (paper presented at the annual meeting of the Latin American Studies Association, 1999).

11. See Aleezé Sattar, "An Unresolved Inheritance: Postcolonial State Formation and Indigenous Communities in Chimborazo, Ecuador, 1820–1875" (PhD diss., New School University, 2001).

12. Michel Foucault, "Governmentality," in *The Foucault Effect*, ed. Graham Burchell, Colin Gordon, and Peter Miller (Chicago: University of Chicago Press, 1991), 87–104.

13. Benedict Anderson, *Imagined Communities: Reflections on the Origin and Spread of Nationalism* (London and New York: Verso, 1991).

14. Andrés Guerrero, "The Administration of Dominated Populations Under a Regime of Citizenship: The Case of Postcolonial Ecuador" (paper presented at the annual meeting of the Latin American Studies Association, 1999).

15. Andrés Guerrero, "Una imagén ventrílocua: El discurso Liberal de la 'desgraciada raza indígena' a fines del siglo XIX," in *Imágenes e imagineros: Representaciones de los indígenas ecuatorianos, siglos XIX y XX*, ed. Blanca Muratorio (Quito: FLACSO, 1994), 197–252.

16. "Decreto del 30 de septiembre de 1833 dado en Quito," in *Recopilación de leyes indígenas de 1830 a 1918*, vol. 3, *Historia social del Ecuador*, ed. Piedad Peñaherrera de Costales and Alfredo Costales Samaniego (Quito: Editorial Casa de la Cultura Ecuatoriana, 1964), 598.

17. "Decreto dado en Ambato, 29 de agosto de 1835," *Recopilación de leyes sociales indígenas*, 604, emphasis added.

18. Archivo Nacional de Historia, Riobamba (ANH/R): Cr: 18-VII-1836, "Sumario seguido contra Joaqin Osaeta por las tropelias cometidas contra los infelises indijenas y el faltamiento a la autoridad."

19. ANH/R: Cv: 1844, "Seguidos por el Sr. Dr. Andres Cevallo protector de indigenas, por el comun de Yaruquiez, contra el Diezmero Rafael Astudillo, por exceso de cobranza."

20. Ibid.

21. Ibid.

22. Contradictions and noncoherence are very much integral aspects of state formation and the "negotiation of rule." See Joseph and Nugent, eds., *Everyday Forms of State Formation*; and Sattar, "An Unresolved Inheritance."

23. ANH/R: Cv: 1847, "Seguidos por el Indijena Mariano Pacheco solicitando su titulo del cacique."

24. Andrés Guerrero illustrates this reinstitutionalization for the canton of Otavalo in "Curagas y tenientes políticos: La ley de la costumbre y la ley del estado," *Revista Andina* 7 (1991): 321–65.

25. ANH/R: Cv: 1847, "Seguidos por el Indijena Mariano Pacheco solicitando su titulo del cacique."

26. Ibid.

27. ANH/R: 1848, "Comunicación al Sr. Alcalde primero municipal."

28. "Circular, Ministerio del Estado en el Despacho de lo Interior. Quito, a 2 de octubre de 1846," *Recopilación de leyes sociales indígenas*, 621, emphasis added.

29. See William Roseberry, "Hegemony and the Language of Contention," in *Everyday Forms of State Formation*, ed. Joseph and Nugent, 355–66.

30. ANH/R: Cv: 1845, "Seguidos por el Sr. Carlos Zambrano contra varios indijenas de Calpi por despojo cometido en su hacienda de San Juan sobre los sitios y paramos de Churau, anecsos a la hacienda de San Juan." ANH/R: Cv: 1845, "Seguidos por el Sr. Carlos Zambrano, contra Manuel Duchi y mas socios por haberse introducidos en la hacienda de San Juan." ANH/R: Cv: 1845, "Causa Seguida por Manuel Echeverria, apoderado de Manuel Duchi i mas indíjenas, soliticando copia de las providencias dado por el Gobeirno Espanol a favor de dichos indijenas."

31. ANH/R, Cv: 1848, "Seguidos por el Comun de indigenas de Calpi solicitando que la Corte Suprema del distrito de Quito ordene al Gobernador del Chimborazo para que los Jueces Municipales administren justicio," emphasis added.

32. Ibid.

33. Ibid.

34. ANH/R: Cv: 28-XII-1858, "Ramon Bermudes, apoderado de Sr. Dr. Jose Manuel Beltran, en autos con los indijenas del anejo del Tolte, en Canton de Alausi, por despojo de las aguas de su hacienda Bugna."

35. "Articulo 2. de Ley de 23 noviembre de 1854," *Recopilación de leyes sociales indígenas*, 671–80.

36. Rodríguez, *The Search for Public Policy*.

37. Ley de 21-X-1857," *Recopilación de leyes sociales indígenas*, 697.

38. *Recopilación de leyes sociales indígenas*, 679.

39. Gerardo Fuentealba, "La sociedad indígena en las primera décadas de la república: continuidades coloniales y cambios republicanos," in *Nueva Historia del Ecuador*, vol. 8, *Epoca republicana II: Perspectiva general del sigo XIX*, ed. Enrique Ayala Mora (Quito: Grijalbo, 1989), 45–77.

40. AMR: 17-I-1858, "Comunicación del Gobernador de Chimborazo."

41. Philip Corrigan and Derek Sayer, *The Great Arch: English State Formation as Cultural Revolution* (Oxford and New York: Blackwell, 1985), 187.

42. See Joseph B. Casagrande and Arthur R. Piper, "La transformación estructural de una parroquia rural en las tierras altas del Ecuador," *América Indígena* 29, no. 4 (October 1969): 1039–64; see also Guerrero, "Curagas y tenientes políticos."

Chapter 3: Administering the Otavalan Indian and Centralizing Governance in Ecuador, 1851–1875

1. Enrique Ayala Mora, *Lucha política y el origen de los partidos en el Ecuador* (Quito: Corporación Editora Nacional, 1982 [1978]).

2. Juan Maiguashca, "El proceso de integración nacional en el Ecuador: el rol del poder central, 1830–1895," in *Historia y región en el Ecuador 1830–1930*, ed. Juan Maiguashca (Quito: Corporación Editora Nacional, 1994), 383; on the fall of the Urvinista government in the late 1850s, see Ayala Mora, *Lucha política y el origen de los partidos en el Ecuador*, 107–12.

3. Derek Williams, "Popular Liberalism and Indian Servitude: The Making and Unmaking of Ecuador's Anti-Landlord State, 1845–1868," *Hispanic American Historical Review* 83, no. 4 (2003): 697–733; see also Mark J. Van Aken, "The Lingering Death of Indian Tribute in Ecuador," *Hispanic American Historical Review* 61, no. 3 (1981): 429–59.

4. Maiguashca, "El proceso de integración nacional"; Williams, "Popular Liberalism and Indian Servitude."

5. Maiguashca, "El proceso de integración nacional."

6. Ibid.; Derek Williams, "The Making of Ecuador's *Pueblo Católico*, 1861–1875," in *Political Cultures in the Andes, 1750–1950*, ed. Nils Jacobsen and Cristóbal Aljovín de Losada (Durham: Duke University Press, 2005), 207–29.

7. Claudio Lomnitz-Adler, "Nationalism as a Practical System: Benedict Anderson's Theory of Nationalism from the Vantage Point of Spanish America," in *Deep Mexico, Silent Mexico* (Minneapolis: University of Minnesota Press, 2001), 12.

8. By "central government," I mean the legislative, judicial, and executive branches of governance based in Quito. From 1869 to 1878, the constitution concentrated governing power in the executive, granting extraordinary legislative and veto authority, and exclusive control over the appointment and removal of all public officers. The central government segments of the network of "executive" authorities: from provincial-level governors and canton-level *jefes politicos* (after 1869). I do not include parish-level *tenientes políticos* with more ambiguous central/local loyalties.

9. See William Roseberry, "Hegemony and the Language of Contention," in *Everyday Forms of State Formation: Revolution and the Negotiation of Rule in Modern Mexico*, ed. Gilbert Joseph and Daniel Nugent (Durham: Duke University Press, 1994), 355–66; Philip Corrigan and Derek Sayer, *The Great Arch: English State Formation as Cultural Revolution* (Oxford and New York: Blackwell, 1985).

10. On the "state idea" as separate from the state system, see Philip Abrams, "Notes on the Difficulty of Studying the State," *Journal of Historical Sociology* 1, no. 1 (1988); Monique Nuijten, "Between Fear and Fantasy: Governmentality and the Working of Power in Mexico," *Critique of Anthropology* 24, no. 3 (June 2004), 211.

11. Jorge Juan and Antonio de Ulloa, *A Voyage to South America, 1748* (London: J. Stockdale, 1807), 1:301–02; see also Padre Amable Herrera, *Monografía del cantón Otavalo* (Quito: Tipografía y Encuadernación Salesiana, 1909), 278. The Otavalans' physical beauty also impressed colonial-era observers; see William Bennett Stevenson, *Historical and Descriptive Narrative of Twenty Years' Residence in South America* (London: Longman, Rees, Orme, Brown and Green, 1825), 2:347–48.

12. Manuel Villavicencio, *Geografía de la República del Ecuador* (New York: Imprenta de Robert Craighead, 1858), 168; Eduardo André, "América equinoccial (Colombia—Ecuador)," in *América pintoresca: Descripción de viajes al nuevo continente por los más modernos exploradores, Carlos Wiener, Doctor Crevaux, D. Charnay, etc., etc.* (Barcelona: Montaner y Simon, Editores, 1884); Pedro Fermín Cevallos, *Geografía de la República del Ecuador* (Lima: Imprenta del Estado, 1888); Moisés Sáenz, *Sobre el indio ecuatoriano y su incorporación al medio nacional* (Mexico City: Publicaciones de la Secretaría de Educación Pública, 1933), 37–38. Stevenson, *Twenty Years' Residence*, 2:347–48; Joaquín de Avendaño, "Memoria sobre el comercio y la navegación del Ecuador," in *Imagen del Ecuador, Economía y Sociedad vistas por un viajero del siglo xix* (Quito: Corporación Editora Nacional, 1985 [1858]).

13. Villavicencio stressed their "special talents" as weavers, their ability to remain relatively free from hacienda servitude, and their "natural dispositions" toward civilization inherited from their pre-Inca, Quitu ancestors (*Geografía*, 168).

14. Maiguashca, "El proceso de integración nacional."

15. The vigor of Ecuador's pre-1895 liberal reforms fades in comparison with liberal projects elsewhere in the Andes and Mexico. See Jaime E. Rodríguez O., ed. *The Divine Charter: Constitutionalism and Liberalism in Nineteenth-Century Mexico* (Lanham, MD: Rowman and Littlefield, 2005); Tristan Platt, "Liberalism and ethnocide in the southern Andes," *History*

Workshop 17 (Spring 1984): 3–18; and Brooke Larson, *Trials of Nation Making: Liberalism, Race, and Ethnicity in the Andes, 1810–1910* (Cambridge: Cambridge University Press, 2004).

16. Van Aken, "The Lingering Death of Tribute in Ecuador."

17. Williams, "Popular Liberalism and Indian Servitude."

18. Villavicencio, *Geografía*, 167.

19. Ibid., 167–68.

20. Williams, "Popular Liberalism and Indian Servitude."

21. Maiguashca, "El proceso de integración nacional."

22. Popularly elected municipal governments were established not only in *cantones*, but also, for the first time, at the parish and provincial levels as well ("Ley de Régimen Municipal, 1861," *El Nacional*, no. 45, June 20, 1861).

23. Michel Foucault, "The Subject and Power," in *Michel Foucault: Beyond Structuralism and Hermeneutics*, 2d ed., ed. Hubert L Dreyfus, Paul Rabinow, and Michel Foucault (Chicago: University of Chicago Press, 1983), 221.

24. A. Kim Clark, *The Redemptive Work: Railway and Nation in Ecuador, 1895–1930*, Latin-American Silhouettes (Wilmington, DE: SR Books, 1998).

25. "Lei reglamentando la enagenación de terrenos baldios, October 24, 1863," *El Nacional*, no. 196, October 2, 1865.

26. President of Cantonal Council of Pichincha to Minister . . . of Interior, December 3, 1866, *El Nacional*, no. 264, January 29, 1867.

27. Governors were instructed to take into consideration family size and the quality of the lands in arriving at his decision. See, for example, Minister . . . of Interior to Governor of Leon, August 7, 1863, Archivo de la Gobernación de la Provincia de Cotopaxi, Latacunga (AGPC), Oficios del Ministerio de Gobierno, 1863.

28. Minister . . . of Interior to President of Cantonal Council of Pichincha, January 10, 1867, *El Nacional*, no. 265, February 5, 1867; President of Cantonal Council of Pichincha to Minister . . . of Interior, December 3, 1866, *El Nacional*, no. 264, January 29, 1867.

29. Governor of Loja to Minister . . . of Interior, January 13, 1866, *El Nacional*, no. 218, February 24, 1866.

30. Governor of Imbabura to Jefe Político (Otavalo), February 3, 1862, Archivo del Instituto Otavaleño de Antropología (IOA): Serie Municipal 23c: 58, f. 27; Governor of Imbabura to Jefe Político (Otavalo), January 7, 1862, IOA: Serie Municipal 23c: 58, f. 8; Governor of Imbabura to Jefe Político (Otavalo), February 8, 1862, IOA: Serie Municipal 23c: 58, f. 34.

31. Governor of Loja to Minister . . . of Interior, January 13, 1866 (and reply, January 31, 1866), *El Nacional*, no. 218, January 24, 1866.

32. The government repeatedly challenged the administration and legality of municipal holdings. See, for instance, Minister . . . of Interior to Governor of Leon, August 6, 1870, AGPC: bundle 121, Oficios del Ministerio of Estado [en el despacho del Interior], 1870.

33. Comunicación de la Jefatura Política, January 24, 1864, IOA: Serie Municipal 14: 1.

34. Minister . . . of Interior to President of Cantonal Council of Pichincha, December 28, 1866, *El Nacional*, no. 264, January 29, 1867; Minister . . . of Interior to President of Cantonal Council of Pichincha, December 19, 1866; *El Nacional*, no. 264, January 29, 1867.

35. The revenues at stake were typically petty, even for the poorest rural municipios. In the case of Indian lands, for example, unlike in much of neighboring Colombia or the Ecuadorian Oriente region, where large tracts of vacant land were central to economic development, the potential wealth from public land sales in the Sierra was limited.

36. Minister . . . of Interior to Governor of Leon, August 6, 1870, AGPC: bundle 121, Oficios del Ministerio of Estado [en el despacho del Interior] 1870.

37. Minister . . . of Interior to President of Cantonal Council of Quito, February 19, 1867, *El Nacional*, no. 273, April 2, 1867.

38. Minister . . . of Interior to President of Cantonal Council of Pichincha, January 10, 1867, *El Nacional*, no. 265, February 5, 1867.

39. Williams, "Popular Liberalism and Indian Servitude."

40. Governor of Loja to Minister . . . of Interior, January 13, 1866, *El Nacional*, no. 218, January 24, 1866.

41. Otavalo Municipal Council Session, February 1863 (entry: 16/15/?), reprinted in Juan Freile-Granizo, *Resúmenes de actas republicanas, cabildo de Otavalo, siglo XIX*, Colección Pendoneros: Serie Historia / Instituto Otavaleño de Antropología, 24 (Otavalo, Ecuador: Instituto Otavaleño de Antropología, 1980), 56. The council had originally considered raising the contribución to six reales across the board; Otavalo Municipal Council Session, January 1863, 55.

42. Otavalo Municipal Council Session, February 1863, 56.

43. Censo del Cantón de Otavalo (1885) IOA: cajas sueltas.

44. See Olivia Harris, "Ethnic Identity and Market Relations: Indians and Mestizos in the Andes," in *Ethnicity, Markets, and Migration in the Andes: At the Crossroads of History and Anthropology*, ed. Brooke Larson and Olivia Harris (Durham: Duke University Press, 1995), 351–90; see also Governor of Loja to Minister . . . of Interior, January 13, 1866, *El Nacional*, no. 218, January 24, 1866.

45. "Ecuador y la civilización cristiana," in *El Nacional*, no. 393, December 30, 1874; García Moreno, "1873 Mensaje," in Alejandro Noboa, *Recopilación de mensajes dirijidos por los Presidentes y Vicepresidentes de la República jefes supremos y gobiernos provisorios a las convenciones y congresos nacionales desde el año de 1819 hasta nuestros días* (Guayaquil: Impr. de A. Noboa, 1900–08), 3:124. On the link between territorial claims and missionary activity in the Oriente, see José Ignacio Víctor Eyzaguirre, *Los intereses católicos en América* (París: Librería de Garnier Hermanos, 1859), 49–50. On missions forming "bonds of nationality," see Pedro Moncayo, *Cuestión de límites entre el Ecuador y el Perú segun el uti possidetis de 1810 y los tratados de 1829* (Santiago de Chile: Imprenta Nacional, 1860), 13–24.

46. "La República del Ecuador y la civilización cristiana," *El Nacional*, no. 393, December 30, 1874.

47. "La República del Ecuador y la civilización cristiana," *El Nacional*, no. 393, December 30, 1874.

48. Indeed, underneath the rhetoric was a state concern about the Otavalans' poor church attendance, their practice of concubinage, and sacrilegious revelry during feast day celebrations. Friedrich Hassaurek, *Four Years Among the Ecuadorians* (Carbondale: Southern Illinois University Press, 1967); Derek Williams, "Assembling the 'Empire of Morality': State Building Strategies in Catholic Ecuador, 1861–1875," *Journal of Historical Sociology* 14, no. 2 (June 2001): 149–74.

49. Williams, "The Making of Ecuador's *Pueblo Católico*."

50. Loja's "skillful and intelligent" Indian population was also targeted for recruits. *El Nacional*, no. 116, November 29, 1871.

51. 'Informe . . . acerca de los métodos de enseñanza primaria . . . en el Ecuador' May 21, 1872, *El Nacional*, no. 179, June 12, 1872; see also *El Nacional*, no. 116, November 29, 1871.

52. On the colonial origins of northern roadway projects, see Rocío Rueda Novoa, "La ruta a la Mar del Sur: un proyecto de las elites serranas en Esmeraldas (s. XVIII)," *Procesos: Revista ecuatoriana de historia* 3, II semester (1992): 33–54.

53. Teniente Político of San Pablo a Jefe Político, January 29, 1871, IOA: Serie Municipal 32c, 52, f. 7; doc. 1542, IOA: Jefatura Política 1, caja 52, f. 9.

54. Similar recruitment strategies were used in road projects in the 1840s. See Samuel Ackerman, "*El Trabajo Subsidiario*: Compulsory Labor and Taxation in 19th-Century Ecuador," PhD diss., New York University, 1977, 120.

55. The church (and its *alcaldes*) played an important role in labor recruitment as well. See, for example, Teniente Político de San Pablo a Jefe Político (Otavalo), October 8, 1871, IOA: Serie Municipal 32c: 52, f. 54; see also Andrés Guerrero, "Curagas y tenientes políticos: la ley de la costumbre y el ley del estado (Otavalo, 1830–1875)," Revista Andina (Cusco) 7, no. 2 (no. 14) (1989), 321–66.

56. See Andrés Guerrero, *La semántica de la dominación: el concertaje de los indios* (Quito: Ediciones Libri Mundi, 1991); Piedad P. de Costales and Alfredo Costales Samaniego, "Historia Social del Ecuador. Tomo I: El concertaje de indios y manumission de esclavos," *Llacta* (Quito) 6, no. 17 (1964); Roque Espinoza, "Hacienda, Concertaje y Comunidad en el Ecuador," *Revista Cultura* (Quito) 19 (1984).

57. Teniente Político de San Pablo a Jefe Político, January 23, 1871, IOA: Serie Municipal 32c: 52, f6.

58. Governor of Imbabura a Jefe Político July 24, 1872, IOA: Serie Municipal 23b: 54, f. 96; and Governor of Imbabura a Jefe Político, July 27, 1872, IOA: Serie Municipal 23b: 54, f. 98.

59. Teniente Politico de San Pablo a Jefe Político, May 10, 1871, IOA: Serie Municipal 32c: 52, f26.

60. Doc. 1507, IOA: Jefatura Política 1a, caja 53, 1872. For similar instances in earlier periods, see Ackerman, "Trabajo Subsidiario," 193.

61. Governor of Imbabura circular a Jefe Político, October 26, 1871, IOA: Serie Municipal 8: 5 f. 27.

62. Governor of Imbabura circular a Jefe Político, October 26, 1871; [oficio no. 149, October 24, 1871 de Ministro de Hacienda], IOA: Serie Municipal 8: 5 f. 27; Circular a los Tenientes Políticos de San Pablo, San Luis and Jordan, November 25, 1872. IOA: Serie Municipal 3, 4, "Libro copiador del Jefe and Presidente del Ylustre Concejo Municipal," entry #702.

63. Teniente Político de San Luis a Jefe Político, July 15, 1873, IOA: Serie Municipal 26a: 3; and Jefe Político a los Tenientes Políticos de Jordan, San Pablo & San Luis, October 20, 1873, IOA: Serie Municipal 3: 9.

64. Parish Judge 2º a Jefe Político, November 18, 1870, IOA: Serie Municipal 39: 7. Estate administrators were obliged to bring hacienda books outside of the hacienda to local state offices. IOA: Jefatura Política 1ª, caja 44, doc. 1594. For similar interventions during the Urvina government, see, for example, Parish Judge 2º de Jordan a Jefe Político, January 20, 1857. IOA: Serie Municipal 39: 2.

65. On public intervention into the hacienda's customarily "private" sphere, see IOA: Jefatura Política 1a caja 49, doc. 1224 (1869); Jefetura Politica 1a caja 55, doc. 1379 (1870–1873); Circular de Minister of Interior a Jefe Político, April 6, 1876, IOA: Serie Municipal 8 exp 10, f. 19; and Governor of Imbabura a Jefe Político December 14, 1877, IOA: Serie Municipal 23b: 45.

66. "Circular del Jefe Político y Comandancia militar del cantón a los Srs. Administradores y mayordomos de las Hs de esta Comprención," February 29, 1872, IOA: Serie Municipal 26a: 3; and Teniente Político de San Luis a Jefe Político, July 15, 1873, IOA: Serie Municipal 26a: 3.

67. In the 1870s, García Moreno proposed fining those patrons who did not take an active interest in moralizing their peons by establishing education facilities. Moreno to Juan León Mera, May 24, 1873, in Wilfrido Loor, ed., *Cartas de Gabriel García Moreno* (Quito: La Prensa Católica, 1955), 347.

68. See Governor of Imbabura a Jefe Politico December 24, 1873 [Minister of Interior, circular no. 22, December 19, 1873], IOA: Serie Municipal 23b: 53? (hoja suelta). On market-day changes, see Rosemary Bromley and Robert J. Bromley, "The Debate on Sunday Markets in Nineteenth Century Ecuador," *Journal of Latin American Studies* 7, no. 1 (1975): 85–108.

69. Guerrero, "A Ventriloquist's Image," 569.

70. On the Andes, see Larson, *Trials of Nation Making*.

71. Guerrero, "A Ventriloquist's Image," 558.

72. Ibid., 569, 570.

73. Enrique Ayala de Mora, "El municipio en el siglo xix," *Procesos: Revista Ecuatoriana de Historia* (Quito) 1, no. 2 (1991): 69–70.

74. Williams, "Popular Liberalism and Indian Servitude."

75. Guerrero, "A Ventriloquist's Image," 562.

76. Michael Mann observes that state authority does not derive from "techniques" of power that are "peculiar to itself." Rather, the state must draw on means available "more generally in civil society," using resources found in "all social relationships." Michael Mann, "The Autonomous Power of the State: Its Origins, Mechanisms and Results," in *States in History*, ed. John A. Hall (Oxford and New York: Blackwell, 1986), 117.

77. Peter Guardino argues a similar point in *Peasants, Politics, and the Formation of Mexico's National State: Guerrero, 1800–1857* (Stanford: Stanford University Press, 1996).

78. Williams, "'Empire of Morality.'"

79. Lomnitz-Adler, "Nationalism as a Practical System."

Chapter 4: Helpless Children or Undeserving Patriarchs?

I thank the directors, archivists, and staff of the Archivo Nacional de Historia in Quito, the Archivo Nacional de Historia, Riobamba, and the Biblioteca Ecuatoriana "Aurelio Espinosa Pólit" in Cotocollao. This chapter derives from my monograph, *Gender, Indian, Nation: The Contradictions of Making Ecuador, 1830–1925* (Tucson: University of Arizona Press, forthcoming 2007), chap. 3.

1. See Philip Abrams, "Notes on the Difficulty of Studying the State (1977)," *Journal of Historical Sociology* 1, no. 1 (March 1988): esp. 72, 76–77.

2. Philip Corrigan and Derek Sayer, *The Great Arch: English State Formation as Cultural Revolution* (Oxford and New York: Blackwell, 1985), 4, 6, 12.

3. See William B. Taylor, *Drinking, Homicide, and Rebellion in Colonial Mexican Villages* (Stanford: Stanford University Press, 1979), esp. 42.

4. For parallels with England and France, see Corrigan and Sayer, *The Great Arch*, esp. 81, 126, 132–34; and Sarah Hanley, "Engendering the State: Family Formation and State Building in Early Modern France," *French Historical Studies* 16, no. 1 (Spring 1989): 4–27. See also Uday S. Mehta, "Liberal Strategies of Exclusion," *Politics and Society* 18, no. 4 (December 1990): 427–54.

5. Erin O'Connor, *Gender, Indian, Nation*, chap. 2; see also Mark Van Aken, "The Lingering Death of Tribute in Ecuador," *Hispanic American Historical Review* 6, no. 3 (1981): 429–59.

6. Abrams, "Notes on the Difficulty of Studying the State," 72.

7. See Galo Ramón Valarezo, "La visión andina sobre el estado colonial," *Ecuador Debate* (Quito) 12 (1986): 82, 88, 91; Gerardo Fuentealba, "La sociedad indígena en las primeras décadas de la república: continuidades coloniales y cambios republicanos," in *Nueva Historia del Ecuador*, vol. 8, *Epoca republicana II: Perspectiva general del siglo XIX*, ed. Enrique Ayala Mora (Quito: Corporación Editora Nacional, 1983), esp. 56, 66; Martha Moscoso, "La tierra: Espacio de conflicto y relación entre el Estado y la comunidad en el siglo XIX," in *Los Andes en la encrucijada: Indios, comunidades, y Estado en el siglo XIX*, ed. Heraclio Bonilla (Quito: FLACSO/Libri Mundi, 1991), 367–68; Manuel Chiriboga, *Jornaleros y gran propietarios en 135 años de explotación cacaotera (1790–1925)* (Quito: Consejo Provincial de Pichincha, 1980), 79, 95–111.

8. This pattern was distinct not only from the early nineteenth century, in which the trib-

ute system was blamed for ongoing racial inequalities, but it also differed from later state discourses on Indians, as when members of the central state blamed church officials and/or highland hacienda owners for the Indians' "backward" and oppressed state.

9. Andrés Guerrero, "The Construction of a Ventriloquist's Image: Liberal Discourse and the 'Miserable Indian Race' in Late 19th-Century Ecuador," *Journal of Latin American Studies* 29, no. 3 (October 1997): 558.

10. Seth Garfield, *Indigenous Struggle at the Heart of Empire: State Policy, Frontier Expansion, and the Xavante Indians, 1937–1988* (Durham: Duke University Press, 2001), 12.

11. República del Ecuador, *Diario de trabajos de la Convención*, 1861, cited in Enrique Ayala Mora, "El período garciano: panorama histórico (1860–1875)," in *Nueva Historia del Ecuador*, vol. 7, *Epoca republicana I*, ed. Enrique Ayala Mora (Quito: Corporación Editora Nacional, 1983), 217.

12. Ayala, "El período garciano," 226–30.

13. *El Nacional*, no. 52, September 7, 1861.

14. "La voz del deber de unas mujeres católicas," Biblioteca Ecuatoriana Aurelio Espinosa Pólit (BEAEP), hojas volantes, 1878. Thanks to Derek Williams for bringing this document to my attention.

15. Gustavo de Almenara, 1876, cited in Gladys Moscoso, "Las Imágenes de la Literatura," in *Y el amor no era todo . . . Mujeres, imágenes y conflictos*, ed. Martha Moscoso (Quito: Abya Yala/DGIS, 1996), 95.

16. *Código Civil de la República del Ecuador* (Quito: Imprenta de los Húerfanos de Valencia, 1860), art. 1734. See also arts. 124, 128, 130, 134, and 136 on the limitations on wives' actions in the public sphere. For reasons to deny women the vote based on their involvement in the private rather than public sphere, see 1910 congressional debates: República del Ecuador, *Anales de diputados*, 1910 (September 7). Ecuador was, in 1929, the first Latin American nation to grant women the vote.

17. Such use of patriarchy was typical to state formation. Corrigan and Sayer note how in England the limitations on women's legal rights helped to define the "political nation" by denying women any public existence; they also note that patriarchal ideologies in English political history helped to identify the "state" as a benevolent paternal figure and to justify paternalistic relations with men of the lower classes (*The Great Arch,* 22, 36–37, 132–34, 169).

18.See Martha Moscoso, "Discurso religioso y discurso Liberal: La mujer sumisa," in *Y el amor no era todo . . . mujeres, imágenes y conflictos*, ed. Martha Moscoso (Quito: Abya Yala/DGIS, 1996), esp. 24–25.

19. Ibid., 35–38.

20. *Código Civil* (1860), arts. 162–69.

21. *El Nacional*, no. 369, May 22, 1869. This decree also stipulated the punishment for incest, sedition, and rebellion, and "abominable offences" (most likely male homosexuality).

22. For examples of such decisions, see Archivo Nacional de Historia, Quito, Serie Criminales (hereafter cited as ANH/Q:Cr) under the following dates: October 21, 1871 (acquitted); November 3, 1871 (guilty); January 13, 1872 (acquitted); March 2, 1872 (acquitted); May 7, 1872 (acquitted); August 9, 1872 (acquitted); January 22, 1873 (acquitted); March 29, 1873 (guilty); November 29, 1873 (acquitted); October 20, 1873 (guilty); February 18, 1874 (acquitted); September 23, 1874 (guilty); September 30, 1874 (guilty).

23. For "rusticity" arguments, see ANH/Q: Cr: November 17, 1871; October 30, 1872; March 1873. For "good reputation" arguments, see the same document series: August 9, 1872; May 10, 1873; April 22, 1875.

24. ANH/Q: Cr: December 17, 1873, and May 10, 1873, respectively.

25. *El Nacional*, no. 413, March 15, 1870.

26. Concubinage charges may have sometimes been brought against innocent men and women by enemies or competitors to harm their reputations. Even in this case, the state gained power by mediating such interpersonal disputes.

27. *El Nacional* (Quito), no. 410, February 27, 1875. Though one scholar claimed that "El Demonio Alchohol" was written by García Moreno himself, no author was given in the newspaper. Segments of the piece appear in editions of no. 407 (February 17, 1875) and no. 413 (March 10, 1875).

28. Ibid., no. 410, February 27, 1875.

29. *El Nacional,* no. 407, February 17, 1875. See also "La Embriaguez," ibid., no. 98, October 6, 1871, stating that drinking brutalized and transformed the drinker into a beast; see also nos. 406–07, February 20 and 24, 1875.

30. Manuel M. Pólit Laso, *Escritos y discursos de Gabriel García Moreno*, vol. 2: *Escritos Oficiales* (Quito: Imprenta del Clero, 1888), 217–19.

31. *El Nacional*, no. 408, February 24, 1875. Similar arguments were made in no. 406 (February 13, 1875), and no. 409 (February 24, 1875).

32. Ibid., no. 408, February 20, 1875.

33. Ibid., no. 409, February 24, 1875. Other tragic consequences of drunkenness cited in this series of articles included suicide (no. 411, March 3, 1875) and beating one's own father, a different kind of disdain for patriarchal authority (no. 408, February 20, 1875).

34. See O'Connor, *Gender, Indian, Nation*, esp. chap. 5.

35. Juan León Mera, *Catecismo de geografía del Ecuador*, 2d ed. (Guayaquil: Imprenta de la Nación, 1884 [1874]), 33.

36. Ibid.

37. Ibid., 34.

38. Mehta, "Liberal Strategies of Exclusion," 437; on how the Brazilian state sought to create "better" Indians as a means to "legitimize [state] power and naturalize social inequalities," see Garfield, *Indigenous Struggle*, 11.

39. On how these notions of civilization and barbarism fit into the broader ideas of "progress" in nineteenth-century Latin America, see E. Bradford Burns, *The Poverty of Progress: Latin America in the Nineteenth Century* (Berkeley: University of California Press, 1980).

40. James Orton, *The Andes and the Amazon* (New York: Harper & Brothers, 1870), 111–12.

41. ANH/Q:Cr: May 3, 1871. Also see ANH/Q:Cr: September 5, 1872, in which the defense attorney questioned Indians' ability to understand the law, and asserted the fatherly role of employers. Both of these were concubinage cases.

42. Pedro Fermín Cevallos, *Resumen de la historia del Ecuador*, vol. 6 (Guayaquil: Imprenta de la Nación, 1889), 86.

43. Francisco J. León, Minister of the Interior, *El Nacional* (Quito), no. 449, September 21, 1870.

44. In Manuel María Pólit, *Escritos*, 283, emphasis added. García Moreno's reference to the interior provinces here reflects an important distinction made between Ecuadorian Indians in the nineteenth century in which highland Indians were seen as "socialized" and tropical Indians as completely "savage."

45. *Exposición del Ministro de Hacienda y Relaciones Interiores . . . a las cámaras legislativas, 1867* (Quito: Imprenta Nacional, 1867), 14–16.

46. See Blanca Muratorio, "Nación, identidad, y etnicidad: Imágenes de los indios ecuatorianos y sus imagineros a fines del siglo XIX," in *Imágenes e imagineros: Representaciones de los indígenas ecuatorianos, siglos XIX y XX*, ed. Blanca Muratorio (Quito: FLACSO, 1994), 169–73; a photo of the statue appears on 171.

47. ANH/Q:Cr: December 19,1874, ff. 3–4, emphasis added.

48. Ibid.

49. Ibid., emphasis added.

50. See criminal cases from the Archivo Nacional de la Historia, Riobamba (cited as ANH/R:Cr) November 11, 1880, February 6, 1875; civil cases from this archive are cited as ANH/R:Civ. Women, both Indian and non-Indian, were more likely to bring cases against abusive husbands to ecclesiastical courts; see Gladys Moscoso, "La violencia contra las mujeres," in *Y el amor no era todo . . . Mujeres, imágenes y conflictos*, ed. Martha Moscoso (Quito: Abya Yala/DGIS, 1996), 187–209. It is not clear from this article how indigenous women's complaints differed from those of non-Indian women, or whether there were different patterns between the countryside and the city. For cases of sexual assault, see ANH/R:Cr: January 21, 1875, ANH/Q: June 21, 1873, and ANH/R:Cr: June 19, 1872; see also Moscoso, "La violencia contra las mujeres," 196–200.

51. ANH/R:Cr: February 25, 1870; ANH/R:Cr: January 9, 1865; ANH/R:Cr: January 30, 1908; ANH/R:Cr: February 25, 1870; ANH/R:Cr: October 27, 1870; ANH/R: February 28, 1873; ANH/R:Cr: March 19, 1870, ff. 44–47. This evidence is available because marital problems often erupted into violent crimes, particularly homicide. Nevertheless, Indian women evidently escaped abusive marriages by kinship ties, flight, and new relationships. Patterns for Indians living on haciendas were somewhat different; see O'Connor, *Gender, Indian, Nation*, chap. 6. These responses to marital conflict reflect the dynamics of "contested patriarchy" discussed by Steve J. Stern, *The Secret History of Gender: Women, Men, and Power in Late Colonial Mexico* (Chapel Hill: University of North Carolina Press, 1995), chap. 4. Olivia Harris also notes that Indian peasant men in modern Bolivia tend to defend married sisters against domestic violence in "Complementarity and Conflict: An Andean View of Women and Men," in *Sex and Age as Principles of Social Differentiation*, ed. J. S. La Fontaine (London: Academic Press, 1978), 35.

52. Friedrich Hassaurek, *Four Years Among Spanish Americans* (Cincinnati: Robert Clarke & Co., 1892 [1867]), 132.

53. ANH/R:Cr: April 23, 1864, f. 69, emphasis added. Lawyers also used widespread ideas about Indian male drunkenness to defend whites and mestizos accused of violence against Indians. They claimed that the Indian plaintiffs were so drunk when the alleged crime occurred that they were confused about what truly happened; see, for example: ANH/R:Cr: August 16, 1870; ANH/R:Cr: October 31, 1870.

54. Cevallos, *Resumen*, 86, 131.

55. See Taylor, *Drinking*, esp. chap. 2.

56. On the "Daquilema" rebellion, see Hernán Ibarra, *Nos encontramos amenazados por todita la indiada: El levantamiento de Daquilema* (Quito: CEDIS, 1993); another discussion, although problematic because of unclear sources, is Alfredo Costales Samaniego, *Fernando Daquilema: Ultimo Guaminga* (Quito: *Llacta* 16, no. 11, 1963). One source about this rebellion remains: ANH/R:Cr: December 18, 1871 (transcribed in Ibarra, *Nos encontramos)*. Indian witnesses focused less on the drinking or "savagery" noted by government officials and remarked that the uprising began because rumors spread that a new sales tax had been announced; see testimony by Santiago Bueno, folios 15v–16.

57. Pólit, *Escritos*, 292.

58. Francisco Javier León, *Exposición del Ministro del Interior dirigida al Congreso Constitucional del Ecuador en 1873* (Quito: Imprenta Nacional), 4.

59. *El Nacional*, no. 407, February 17, 1875 and no. 408, February 20, 1875.

60. Ibid., no. 408, February 20, 1875.

61. Mehta, "Liberal Strategies of Exclusion," 439. This parallels Corrigan and Sayer's assertion that "formal equality can be violently oppressive" (*The Great Arch*, 187).

62. Mehta states: "Descriptions are seldom neutral. They effect moral and political sensibilities and therefore carry, even when intended innocently, a normative valiency" (ibid., 441). Also see Mehta's discussion of how British notions of liberty pertained only to mature adults and, specifically, not to backward nations.

63. See ANH/R:Cr: January 16, 1873; February 23, 1871; December 19, 1874; October 10, 1875.

64. Gilbert Joseph and Daniel Nugent, "Popular Culture and State Formation in Revolutionary Mexico," in *Everyday Forms of State Formation: Revolution and the Negotiation of Rule in Modern Mexico*, ed. Gilbert Joseph and Daniel Nugent (Durham: Duke University Press, 1994), 13.

65. See O'Connor, *Gender, Indian, Nation* and "Widows Rights Questioned: Indians, the State, and Fluctuating Gender Ideas in Central Highland Ecuador, 1870–1900," *The Americas* 59, no. 1 (July 2002): 87–106.

66. Corrigan and Sayer, *The Great Arch*, 128, refers to "shoving civilization downwards at the propertyless." On the "state's power to name," see William Roseberry, "Hegemony and the Language of Contention," in *Everyday Forms of State Formation: Revolution and Negotiation of Rule in Modern Mexico*, ed. Gilbert M. Joseph and Daniel Nugent (Durham: Duke University Press, 1994), 361.

Chapter 5: Liberalism, *Indigenismo*, and Social Mobilization in Late Nineteenth-Century Ecuador

Some of the material on which this chapter is based appeared in Michiel Baud, "Libertad de Servidumbre: Indigenista Ideology and Social Mobilization in Late Nineteenth Century Ecuador," in *Nation Building in Nineteenth Century Latin America: Dilemmas and Conflicts*, ed. Hans-Joachim König and Marianne Wiesebron (Leiden: CNWS, 1998), 233–53.

1. Andrés Guerrero, "El levantamiento indígena nacional de 1994: discurso y representación política (Ecuador)," *Boletín Americanista* 50 (2000): 123–51.

2. See, for example, *Nation States and Indians in Latin America*, ed. Greg Urban and Joel Sherzer (Austin: University of Texas Press, 1991); Gilbert M. Joseph and Daniel Nugent, eds., *Everyday Forms of State Formation. Revolution and the Negotiation of Rule in Modern Mexico* (Durham: Duke University Press, 1994); Florencia Mallon, *Peasant and Nation: The Making of Postcolonial Mexico and Peru* (Berkeley: University of California Press, 1995).

3. Brooke Larson, *Trials of Nation Making. Liberalism, Race, and Ethnicity in the Andes, 1810–1910* (Cambridge: Cambridge University Press, 2005).

4. David Nugent, *Modernity at the Edge of Empire: State, Individual, and Nation in the Northern Peruvian Andes, 1885–1935* (Stanford: Stanford University Press, 1997).

5. Andrés Guerrero, *La semántica de la dominación: el concertaje de indios* (Quito: Ed. Libri Mundi, 1991); A. Kim Clark, *The Redemptive Work: Railway and Nation in Ecuador, 1895–1930* (Wilmington, DE: Scholarly Resources, 1998).

6. For relevant parallels in the colonial period, see Steve J. Stern, "The Social Significance of Judicial Institutions in an Exploitative Society: Huamanga, Peru, 1570–1640," in *The Inca and Aztec States 1400–1800. Anthropology and History*, ed. George A. Collier, Renato I. Rosaldo, John D. Wirth (New York/London: Academic Press, 1982); 289–320.

7. See Silvia Palomeque, *Cuenca en el siglo XIX. La Articulación de una Región* (Quito: Flacso–Abya-Yala, 1990).

8. see, for instance: Osvaldo Hurtado, *Political Power in Ecuador* (Albuquerque: University of New Mexico Press, 1980) (Spanish original 1977), esp. 113–21.

9. Malcolm Deas, "Colombia, Ecuador and Venezuela, c. 1880–1930," in *Cambridge History*

of Latin America, vol. 5, *c. 1870 to 1930*, ed. Leslie Bethell (Cambridge: Cambridge University Press, 1986), 667.

10. Clark, *The Redemptive Work*, 42–50 and passim.

11. Oswaldo Albornoz Peralta in his *Ecuador: luces y sombras del liberalismo* (Quito: El Duende, 1989), 40, quotes a battle cry of the Alfarista indígenas: "Ñucanchic libertadta apamuy amu Alfaro, tucuy runacuna, guañushun pay ladupi" (Our liberty behind don Alfaro we are going to obtain, and all the runas have to die at his side).

12. See Ivan González and Paciente Vázquez, "Movilizaciones campesinas en Azuay y Cañar durante el siglo XIX," *Revista del Archivo Nacional de Historia, Sección del Azuay* (Cuenca) 3 (1981): 38–85, esp. 81–84.

13. Clark, *The Redemptive Work*, 61ff.

14. For instance: John Lynch, "The Catholic Church in Latin America, 1830–1930," in *The Cambridge History of Latin America*, vol. 4, *c. 1870 to 1930*, ed. Leslie Bethell (Cambridge: Cambridge University Press, 1986); 527–95, esp. 576–78.

15. Circular 24, in *Registro Oficial*, 1: 202, May 17, 1902, 2159.

16. See Guerrero, *La semántica de la dominación*.

17. For instance: Silvia Palomeque, "Historia económica de Cuenca y de sus relaciones regionales," in *Ensayos sobre historia regional. La región del sur*, ed. Universidad de Cuenca. Instituto de Investigaciones Sociales and Encuentro de Historia y Realidad Económica y Social del Ecuador (Cuenca: IDIS, 1982), 117–40.

18. Guerrero, *La semántica de la dominación*, 49–57.

19. See Tristán Platt in *Estado boliviano y ayllu andino: tierra y tributo en el norte de Potosí*, Historia andina 9 (Lima: Instituto de Estudios Peruanos, 1982). On the relation between these communities and the nineteenth-century Bolivian state, see Platt, "The Andean Experience of Bolivian Liberalism, 1825–1900: Roots of Rebellion in Nineteenth-Century Chayanta (Potosí)," in *Resistance, Rebellion, and Consciousness in the Andean Peasant World, 18th to 20th Centuries*, ed. Steve J. Stern (Madison: University of Wisconsin Press, 1987), 280–323.

20. Piedad Peñaherrera de Costales and Alfredo Costales Samaniego, *Historia Social del Ecuador*, vol. 3, *Recopilación de las leyes indígenas de 1830 a 1918* (Quito: Editorial Casa de la Cultura Ecuatoriana, 1964), 723. These laws were copied and distributed by the Ministry of the Interior in all provinces. See for instance the handwritten copy in Archivo Nacional de Historia, Cuenca (AHN/C) 12.556.

21. Charles A. Hale, "Political and Social Ideas in Latin America, 1870–1930," in *Cambridge History of Latin America*, vol. 4, *c. 1870–1930*, ed. Leslie Bethell (Cambridge: Cambridge University Press, 1988), 367–441; esp. 380–81.

22. See Marie-Danielle Demélas, *L'invention politique. Bolivie, Equateur, Pérou au XIXe siècle* (Paris: Editions Recherche sur les Civilisations, 1992), 343–99; see also Platt, "The Andean Experience of Bolivian Liberalism."

23. This is very clear in the writings of the distinguished Ecuadorian liberal Juan Montalvo (1832–1889). See Frank MacDonald Spindler and Nancy Cook Brooks, eds. *Selections from Juan Montalvo* (Tempe: Arizona State University, 1984), esp. "Lectures to the People," 67–89.

24. De Costales and Costales Samaniego, *Recopilación de las leyes indígenas de 1830 a 1918*, 714–15.

25. Guerrero, *La semántica de la dominación*, 64–79, quotation on p. 74.

26. Clark, *The Redemptive Work*, 79.

27. Circular no. 26, del Ministerio del Interior y Policia, June 22, 1898, in ANH/C, 10895, Gob. Ad., F.8.

28. A Kim Clark, chapter 6, this volume.

29. Published in de Costales/Samaniego, *Recopilación de las leyes indígenas*, 730–32; see also Guerrero, *La semántica de la dominación*, 79–85.

30. Quoted in Letter of Comandancia to Jefe de las Provincias del Sur, Cuenca, May 15, 1899, in AHN/C 6394.

31. Abelardo Moncayo, "El concertaje de indios," in *Pensamiento agrario ecuatoriano*, ed. Carlos Marchán Romero (Quito: Banco Central del Ecuador, 1986), 287–326; see also Guerrero, *La semántica de la dominación*, 49, 55.

32. Moncayo, "El concertaje de indios," 287–88.

33. Ibid., 288–89.

34. It is interesting that Moncayo explicitly makes this comparison between Indians and blacks, considering that he viewed the "free" black population as being in a better position than the bonded Indian laborers (ibid., 287–90). This seems to have been a recurrent theme in Ecuador where the coastal provinces housed a considerable Afro-American population. Eloy Alfaro also referred to the discrepancy between the "freedom" of the blacks and the "slavery" of the Indians. See Enrique Ayala, *Lucha política y origen de los partidos en Ecuador* (Quito: Ed. Nacional, 1982), 333.

35. It would be interesting to know more about the origins of these radical ideas which were rather unprecedented in Ecuadorian society. Andrés Guerrero discusses Moncayo's position to some extent in *La semántica de la dominación*, 49–50.

36. Luis A. Martínez, "Conferencia dada por el señor don Luis A. Martínez a la Sociedad Jurídico Literaria el 8 de diciembre de 1904," in *Pensamiento agrario ecuatoriano*, ed. Carlos Marchán Romero (Quito: Banco Central del Ecuador, 1986), 275–25, quotation on 281.

37. See José Luis Rénique, *Los sueños de la sierra. Cusco en el siglo XX* (Lima: CEPES, 1991); Platt, "The Andean Experience of Bolivian Liberalism"; Guerrero, *La semántica de la dominación*, 45–62.

38. For a similar analysis for Peru, see José Luis Rénique, *La batalla por Puno. Conflicto agrario y nación en los Andes peruanos, 1866–1995* (Lima: IEP/SUR/CEPES, 2004); see also Florencia E. Mallon, *The Defense of Community in Peru's Central Highlands. Peasant Struggle and Capitalist Transition, 1860–1940* (Princeton: Princeton University Press, 1983), 235.

39. Mallon, *Peasant and Nation*, 90.

40. Letter of Manuel Suguilanda y Santiago Cullcay to Gral. Presidente de la República Eloy Alfaro, September 5, 1899, in AHN/C 72.309.

41. Juicio de Estanislao Guaman contra Sr. Manuel T. Monroy sobre libertad de servidumbre, 1881, in AHN/C 95.722. Also: Juicio de Manuel Espiritu y Manuel Cruz Guaman and Resurrección Guaman contra Sr. Manuel T. Monroy, in AHN/C 95.721 and 95.729. Neither claimant could speak Spanish or sign his name.

42. See María Cristina Cárdenas Reyes, *Libertad y liberación en la obra de José Peralta* (Quito: Fundación Friedrich Naumann, 1989).

43. See Guerrero, *La semántica de la dominación*, 189–94.

44. These observations are based on: Juicio entre Sr. José Cabrera y Antonio Yunga sobre libertad de servidumbre, January 26, 1888, in AHN/C 95.412.

45. Guerrero, *La semántica de la dominación*, 56–57; see also the opinion of the Bolivian intellectual Pedro Vargas expressed in 1864, quoted in Tristán Platt, "Calendarios tributarios e intervención mercantil. La articulación estacional de los ayllus de Lipez con el mercado minero potosino (siglo XIX)," in *La participación indígena en los mercados surandinos. Estrategias y reproducción social, siglos XVI a XIX*, ed. Olivia Harris, Brooke Larson, and Enrique Tandeter (La Paz: CERES, 1987), 471–73. Also see Marta Irurozqui, *La armonía de las desigualdades* (Madrid: CSIC, 1994), 145–71.

46. AHN/C 101.288.

47. José Yunga contra Dr. Belisario Reyes, 1894, in AHN/C 86.543.

48. Juicio entre Sr. José Cabrera y Antonio Yunga sobre libertad de servidumbre, January 26, 1888, in AHN/C 95.412. This point was also legally significant, because the law said that when one of the parties of a contract did not understand Spanish an interpreter was necessary to make the contract valid. In this case no such interpreter had been present when Cabrera and Yunga had signed their contract.

49. On the Chaco War in Bolivia, see René Danilo Arze Aguirre, *Guerra y conflictos sociales. El caso rural boliviano durante la campaña del Chaco* (La Paz: CERES, 1987); on the war against Chile in the Peruvian highlands, see Mallon, *The Defense of Community in Peru's Central Highlands.*

50. Juicio de Manuel Llivisaca de Checa contra Dr. Francisco Molino, July 11, 1899, in Corte de Justicia, Cuenca (Juicios Civiles).

51. Cited in González and Vázquez, "Movilizaciones campesinas," 61–62, emphasis added.

52. Petition of "indígenas de la doctrina de Gualaceo" to Gobernador of Azuay, 1899, in AHN/C 10.369.

53. Carta al Gobernador de Azuay de Francisco Chumbe y Benigno Coraizaca, 1898, in AHN/C 140.660.

54. See also Amalia Pallares, *From Peasant Struggles to Indian Resistance: The Ecuadorian Andes in the Late Twentieth Century* (Norman: University of Oklahoma Press, 2002).

55. See Informe del Gobernador de Azuay al Ministerio de Instrucción Pública, June 12, 1902, in Gob., Copiador 1902, L 10.

56. See Letter Gobernador de Azuay to Ministerio de Beneficiencia, November 4, 1893, in AHN/C Gob.Adm. L 183; see also Petition of number of Indians to Gobernador de Azuay, February 15, 1894, in AHN/C, 12.324.

57. Letter to Sres. Comisarios Municipales del Canton de Cuenca, May 13, 1910, in Archivo del Gobierno de Azuay, Cuenca (Gob.), L 68. Also see Ordenanzas Municipales 1910 y 1911, in Gob. For the 1907 famine, see Carta de Jefatura Política de Paute to Gobernador de Azuay, May 6, 1907, in AHN/C 74.877.

58. Michiel Baud, "Campesinos indígenas contra el Estado. La huelga de los indígenas de Azuay, 1920/21," *Procesos. Revista ecuatoriana de historia* (Quito) 4 (1993): 41–72; see also Michiel Baud, "The *Huelga de los Indígenas* in Cuenca, Ecuador (1920–21). Comparative Perspectives," in *Indigenous Revolts in Chiapas and the Andean Highlands*, ed. Kevin Gosner and Arij Ouweneel (Amsterdam: CEDLA, 1996), 217–39.

59. Platt, "The Andean Experience of Bolivian Liberalism," 314.

60. See Silvia Palomeque, "Estado y comunidad en la región de Cuenca en el siglo XIX: Las autoridades indígenas y su relación con el Estado," in *Los andes en la encrucijada. Indios, comunidades y estado en el siglo XIX*, ed. Heraclio Bonilla (Quito: Libri Mundi/FLACSO, 1991), 391–417. Also see Martha Moscoso C., "Comunidad, autoridad indígena y poder republicano en siglo XIX," *Revista Andina* 7, no. 2 (1989): 481–99.

61. Roger Neil Rasnake, *Domination and Cultural Resistance. Authority and Power among an Andean People* (Durham: Duke University Press, 1988).

62. See Platt, "The Andean Experience of Bolivian Liberalism," 311; Rénique, *Los sueños de la sierra*, 39. Catherine LeGrand, *Frontier Expansion and Peasant Protest in Colombia, 1830–1936* (Albuquerque: University of New Mexico Press, 1986), 69–70, quotes a Colombian politician who defines them as "ignorant pettifoggers who defend unjust causes and complicate the controversies."

63. See for instance Michiel Baud and Rosanne Rutten, eds., *Popular Intellectuals and Social Movements: Framing Protest in Asia, Africa, and Latin America* (Cambridge: Cambridge University Press, 2004).

64. Michiel Baud, *Intelectuales y sus utopías. Indigenismo y la imaginación de América Latina* (Amsterdam: CEDLA, 2003).

65. Mallon, *Peasant and Nation.*

Chapter 6: Shifting Paternalisms in Indian-State Relations, 1895–1950

Research for this chapter was conducted in the Archivo de la Jefatura Política de Alausí (hereafter AJPA), the Biblioteca Aurelio Espinosa Pólit in Cotocollao, and the Archivo de Asistencia Pública in the Museo Nacional de Medicina in Quito (AAP/MNM). I thank the directors and staff of these archives for their assistance. I am also grateful to the Social Sciences and Humanities Research Council of Canada for both doctoral and postdoctoral fellowships, to the New School for Social Research for a dissertation fellowship, and to the Wenner-Gren Foundation for Anthropological Research for a postdoctoral research grant.

1. E. P. Thompson, "Eighteenth-Century English Society: Class Struggle without Class?" *Social History* 3, no. 2 (1978): 133–65. Thompson's insights can illuminate relations between the state and subaltern groups in rural Ecuador, a topic to which they have not been previously applied. Perhaps Thompson's most important point is that both dominant and subordinate groups are constrained by the contours of the social field that links them and which they all participate in constructing and maintaining.

2. William Roseberry, "Hegemony and the Language of Contention," in *Everyday Forms of State Formation: Revolution and the Negotiation of Rule in Modern Mexico*, ed. Gilbert Joseph and Daniel Nugent (Durham: Duke University Press, 1994), 357.

3. I went to the archives with different research questions, but found that the kinds of issues discussed in this paper were those that dominated the records. My research on the liberal period focused on the effects of railway construction on the economic and political incorporation of the region of Alausí, but I found that much local documentation concerned labor issues, particularly on municipal public works. My research in the Archivo de la Asistencia Pública began as a study of gendered social policy, but I discovered that land and labor issues on the haciendas predominated.

4. Brooke Larson, "Andean Highland Peasants and the Trials of Nation Making during the Nineteenth Century," in *The Cambridge History of the Native Peoples of the Americas*, vol. 3, *South America, part 2*, ed. Frank Salomon and Stuart B. Schwartz (Cambridge: Cambridge University Press, 1999), 558–703.

5. See A. Kim Clark, *The Redemptive Work: Railway and Nation in Ecuador, 1895–1930* (Wilmington, DE: Scholarly Resources, 1998), chap. 3.

6. See ibid., chap. 4.

7. Regidor of Linge to the Political Lieutenant of Sibambe, Sibambe, March 1, 1898, AJPA.

8. Reproduced in circular no. 11 from the Governor of Chimborazo to the Political Administrator of Alausí, Riobamba, February 23, 1897, AJPA.

9. See A. Kim Clark, "Indians, the State and Law: Public Works and the Struggle to Control Labor in Liberal Ecuador," *Journal of Historical Sociology* 7, no. 1 (1994): 49–72.

10. Petition from the Indians of Tixán to the Governor of Chimborazo, Riobamba, November 10, 1914, AJPA.

11. Governor of Chimborazo to the Political Administrator of Alausí, Riobamba, November 15, 1915, AJPA.

12. Minister of Government to the Governor of Chimborazo, transcribed in Governor of Chimborazo to the Political Administrator of Alausí, Riobamba, November 13, 1913, AJPA.

13. Political Lieutenant of Guasuntos to the Political Administrator of Alausí, Guasuntos, April 3, 1914, AJPA.

14. Minister of Public Works to the Governor of Chimborazo, transcribed in Governor of Chimborazo to the Political Administrator of Alausí, Riobamba, August 27, 1914, AJPA.

15. Political Administrator of Alausí to the Municipal Police Chief of Alausí, Alausí, August 25, 1921, AJPA.

16. Juan Maiguashca, "Los sectores subalternos en los años 30 y el aparecimiento del velasquismo," in *Las crisis en el Ecuador: los treinta y ochenta*, ed. Rosemary Thorp (Quito: Corporación Editora Nacional, 1991), 79–94; Carlos Marchán Romero, "La crisis de los años treinta: diferenciación social de sus efectos económicos," in *Las crisis en el Ecuador*, 31–60.

17. Andrés Guerrero, *La semántica de la dominación: El concertaje de indios* (Quito: Libri Mundi, 1991).

18. José Ignacio Izurieta to the Director of the JCAP, Quito, October 5, 1934, AAP/MNM LCR 1934-II h. 844–46.

19. José Ignacio Izurieta to the Director of the JCAP, Quito, December 13, 1934, AAP/MNM LCR 1934-II h. 852.

20. Carlos R. Cuvi to the Director of the JCAP, Quito, n.d. (late 1934), AAP/MNM LCR 1934-II h. 843.

21. This labor regulation was one of the results of an agreement signed on October 19, 1934, to end the peasant strike. In line with the paternalism of the era, the agreement was reached by Izurieta (the leaseholder), Gregorio Ormaza (the subsecretary of government and social welfare), Augusto Egas (director of the JCAP), and the two functional senators representing workers, Rosendo Naula and Antonio Páez. Notable for their absence were the peasant leaders and their lawyer.

22. "Memorandum que eleva el Señor Teniente Humberto Vizuete Ch., al Señor Ministro de Gobierno y Previsión Social, sobre la inspección hecha a la hacienda Tolóntag," Quito, February 27, 1935, AAP/MNM LCR 1935-I, h. 925–26, emphasis added.

23. The division of the hacienda was subsequently used by the peasants (in 1944) to argue that the estate had an excess of land, supporting their own petition to receive a plot to establish what was essentially a village center.

24. Peasants of Tolóntag to the Director of the JCAP, Tolóntag, February 15, 1943, APP/MNM LCR 1943-I, h. 989.

25. Transcribed in Minister of Social Welfare to the Director of the JCAP, Quito, August 23, 1943, AAP/MNM LCR 1944-I.

26. Rafael Vallejo Larrea, "Instituto Indigenista del Ecuador," *Previsión Social: Boletín del Ministerio de Previsión Social y Trabajo* 14 (1943): 8.

27. "Informe relacionado con la Cuestión Social de la Hacienda Tolóntag," Quito, May 2, 1945, AAP/MNM LCR 1945-I h. 2040–42.

28. Marc Becker, "Comunas and Indigenous Protest in Cayambe, Ecuador," *The Americas* 55, no. 4 (1999): 531–59.

29. "Informe relacionado con la Cuestión Social de la Hacienda Tolóntag," Quito, May 2, 1945, AAP/MNM LCR 1945-I h. 2040–42.

30. Session of the Junta Central de Asistencia Pública, May 8, 1945, AAP/MNM Libro de Actas 1945.

31. See Marc Becker, "Una Revolución Comunista Indígena: Rural Protest Movements in Cayambe, Ecuador," *Rethinking Marxism* 10, no. 4 (1998): 35–51; Muriel Crespi, "Changing Power Relations: The Rise of Peasant Unions on Traditional Ecuadorian Haciendas," *Anthropological Quarterly* 44, no. 4 (1971): 223–40; Mercedes Prieto, "Haciendas estatales: Un caso de ofensiva campesina, 1926–1948," in *Ecuador: Cambios en el Agro Serrano*, ed. Miguel Murmis (Quito: FLACSO and CEPLAES, 1980), 101–30.

32. Parents and Teacher of the Tolóntag School to the Members of the JCAP, Tolóntag, April 27, 1946, AAP/MNM LCR 1946-I h. 1917.

33. Simón Pachano, "La sociedad imperceptible," in *Las crisis en el Ecuador: Los treinta y ochenta*, ed. Rosemary Thorp (Quito: Corporación Editora Nacional, 1991), 235–58.

34. Philip Abrams, "Notes on the Difficulty of Studying the State," *Journal of Historical Sociology* 1, no. 1 (1988): 82.

35. Antonio Gramsci, "Notes on Italian History," in *Selections from the Prison Notebooks*, ed. and trans. Quintin Hoare and Geoffrey Nowell Smith (New York: International, 1971), 109.

Chapter 7: State Building and Ethnic Discourse in Ecuador's 1944–1945 Asamblea Constituyente

1. The use of a capital "I" in reference to Indigenous peoples in this chapter reflects a specific preference established by the all-Indigenous board of directors of the South and Meso American Indian Rights Center (SAIIC), a nongovernmental organization (NGO) based in Oakland, California, as an affirmation of their ethnic identity. The plural "peoples" indicates the broad diversity among Indigenous groups not only in Ecuador but throughout the Americas.

2. Raquel Rodas, *Nosotras que del amor hicimos . . .* (Quito: Raquel Rodas, 1992), 60; see also Sergio Enrique Girón, *La revolución de mayo* (Quito: Editorial Atahualpa, 1945); Universidad de Guayaquil, *El 28 de mayo de 1944: testimonio* ([Guayaquil]: Litografía e Impr. de la Universidad de Guayaquil, 1984); and Silvia Vega Ugalde, *La Gloriosa: de la revolución del 28 de mayo de 1944 a la contrarrevolución velasquista*, Colección Ecuador/Historia (Quito: Editorial El Conejo, 1987).

3. "La Asamblea Constituyente inició la discusión de la Carta Política," *El Comercio* (Quito), August 22, 1944, 11.

4. Manuel Agustín Aguirre, "Breves memorias sobre la Revolución del 28 de Mayo de 1944," in *El 28 de mayo de 1944: testimonio*, 230.

5. "La Asamblea Constituyente inició la discusión de la Carta Política," *El Comercio* (Quito), August 22, 1944, 1; "Actas de la Asamblea Constituyente de 1944," 1:618f. (August 21, 1944), Archivo Palacio Legislativo (hereafter APL), Quito, Ecuador.

6. "Actas de la Asamblea Constituyente de 1944," 1:804 (August 24, 1944), APL; "Descentralización administrativa y centralización política propunga la Asamblea," *El Comercio* (Quito), August 25, 1944, 3; "Actas de la Asamblea Constituyente de 1944," vol. 1:564f. (August 19, 1944), APL; "Sectores capitalistas no deben temer que la legislativa de emergencia haga la revolución," *El Comercio* (Quito), August 20, 1944, 12.

7. "El Dr. Francisco Arizaga Luque fue nombrado Presidente por 52 votos," *El Comercio* (Quito), August 11, 1944, 3.

8. "Actas de la Asamblea Nacional Constituyente de 1944," 3:510 (September 23, 1944), APL. Also see "Asamblea Constituyente aprobó reforma al presupuesto fiscal," *El Comercio* (Quito), September 24, 1944, 15; "Según la nueva Constitución, la provincia de Pichincha tendrá un Gobernador," *El Comercio* (Quito), October 7, 1944, 5. The assembly created a commission composed of Paredes, Liberal delegate Eduardo Vásconez Cuvi, and Conservative Humberto Gallegos to look into the abuses on the haciendas in Chimborazo and Cotopaxi.

9. "Actas de la Asamblea Nacional Constituyente de 1944," 1:720 (August 22, 1944), APL. Paredes returned to this point numerous times during the debates. See "Actas de la Asamblea Nacional Constituyente de 1944," 3:326 (September 21, 1944), APL; "Actas de la Asamblea Nacional Constituyente de 1944," 6:436–37 (November 21, 1944), APL. Compare to Shuar intellec-

tual Ampam Karakras, who later adamantly maintained that Indians were nationalities because of their cohesive and differentiated identities, cultures, history, languages, spiritual practices, and economies; see Ampam Karakras, "Indigenous Sovereignty: An Ecuadorian Perspective," *Cultural Survival Quarterly* 25 (Summer 2001): 60–62; Confederación de Nacionalidades Indígenas del Ecuador (CONAIE), *Las nacionalidades indígenas en el Ecuador: Nuestro proceso organizativo*, 2d ed. (Quito: Ediciones Abya-Yala, 1989). For at least a decade, Communists had referred to Indians as nationalities, something they had apparently borrowed from Soviet attempts to come to terms with a plurinational situation in their country. See, for example, Conferencia de Cabecillas Indios, "Indicaciones," *Ñucanchic Allpa* 1, no. 8 (March 17, 1936): 2–3.

10. "Actas de la Asamblea Nacional Constituyente de 1944," 3:325–30 (September 21, 1944), APL. Also see Ricardo Paredes, "Acerca de la nacionalidad y el estado ecuatoriano," in *Los comunistas en la historia nacional*, ed. Domingo Paredes (Guayaquil: Editorial Claridad, S.A., 1987), 74–80; "La Asamblea Nacional sesionará en Guayaquil el nueve de Octubre próximo," *El Comercio* (Quito), September 22, 1944, 12; Vega Ugalde, *La Gloriosa*, 117; Agustín Cueva, *The Process of Political Domination in Ecuador*, trans. Danielle Salti (New Brunswick, NJ: Transaction Books, 1982), 37; and Leonardo J. Muñoz, *Testimonio de lucha: memorias sobre la historia del socialismo en el Ecuador* (Quito: Corporación Editora Nacional, 1988), 86–88f.

11. "Actas de la Asamblea Nacional Constituyente de 1944," 6:435–38 (November 21, 1944), APL. On Bucaram's controversial Ethnic Ministry, see Raúl Vallejo, *Crónica mestiza del nuevo Pachakutik (Ecuador: del levantamiento indígena de 1990 al Ministerio Etnico de 1996)* (College Park: Latin American Studies Center, University of Maryland, College Park, 1996).

12. "El voto verbal para analfabetos," *Atahualpa* (Quito, Boletín del Instituto Indigenista del Ecuador) 1, no. 4 (January 1945): 3, reprinted from "El voto verbal para analfabetos," *América Indígena* 4, no. 4 (October 1944): 251.

13. "La Asamblea Constituyente inició la discusión de la Carta Política," *El Comercio* (Quito), August 22, 1944, 11; "Actas de la Asamblea Constituyente de 1944," 1:618f. (August 21, 1944), APL. By comparison, because of restrictions on the rights of immigrants, prisoners, children, and others, and the undue influence of money on the electoral process, universal suffrage also appears to be an unrealizable goal in the United States.

14. Francesca Miller, "The Suffrage Movement in Latin America," in *Confronting Change, Challenging Tradition: Women in Latin American History*, ed. Gertrude Matyoka Yeager (Wilmington, DE: Scholarly Resources Inc., 1994), 169.

15. "Actas de la Asamblea Constituyente de 1944," 1:868 (August 24, 1944), APL; Pedro Saad, "Acerca de la unidad nacional y los gobiernos seccionales," in *Los comunistas en la historia nacional*, ed. Domingo Paredes (Guayaquil: Editorial Claridad, S.A., 1987), 116.

16. Ricardo Paredes in "Actas de la Asamblea Constituyente de 1944," 3:329 (September 21, 1944), APL. Paredes was not present on October 24 when the assembly debated giving citizenship rights to illiterate Indians and peasants and did not influence the outcome.

17. Article 92 of 1929 Electoral Law in Tribunal Supremo Electoral (TSE), *Elecciones y democracia en el Ecuador*, 3, *Legislación electoral ecuatoriana* (Quito: Tribunal Supremo Electoral. Corporacion Editora Nacional, 1990), 187. Such functional representation, with its roots in Italian fascism, was said to be at odds with the liberal ideal of universal suffrage, but many argued that the system was necessary to overcome the country's feudal legacy. See interview with Pedro Jorge Vera in Edison Egas Egas, *28 de mayo de 1944: la gloriosa o la revolución traicionada y la constitución de 1945* (Quito: Departamento de Publicaciones de la Facultad de Filosofía, Letras y Ciencias de la Educación, 1992), 190–91. Functional representation is not an anomaly in Latin America. After their 1979 victory in Nicaragua, the Sandinistas granted a variety of special interest groups automatic representation in their governing Council of State;

see John A. Booth, *The End and the Beginning: The Nicaraguan Revolution*, 2d ed. (Boulder, CO: Westview Press, 1985), 191.

18. Egas, *28 de mayo de 1944*, 25.

19. "Actas de la Asamblea Nacional Constituyente de 1944," 6:380f. (November 21, 1944), APL; "La Asamblea en sesión matinal discutió la Constitución Política del Estado," *El Comercio* (Quito), November 22, 1944, 2; "La Asamblea continuó el estudio articulado de la Constitución Política," *El Comercio* (Quito), December 6, 1944, 9.

20. "Actas de la Asamblea Nacional Constituyente de 1944," 6:435–38 (November 21, 1944), APL.

21. Article 23 of the 1945 constitution in Federico E. Trabucco, *Constituciones de la República del Ecuador* (Quito: Universidad Central, Editorial Universitaria, 1975), 359–60; Article 161 of the 1945 electoral law, TSE, *Elecciones y democracia en el Ecuador*, 210. Pedro Saad was one of those who fought to expand these rights for Indians. See "Actas de la Asamblea Constituyente de 1944," 1:868 (August 24, 1944), APL; Marc Becker, "Comunas and Indigenous Protest in Cayambe, Ecuador," *The Americas* 55, no. 4 (April 1999): 531–59; Federación Ecuatoriana de Indios, *Estatutos de la Federación Ecuatoriana de Indios* (Guayaquil: Editorial Claridad, 1945), 10.

22. The debate is recorded in "Actas de la Asamblea Nacional Constituyente de 1944," 3:999 (October 3, 1944), APL.

23. "La Asamblea Constituyente inició la discusión de la Carta Política," *El Comercio* (Quito), August 22, 1944, 11; "Actas de la Asamblea Constituyente de 1944," 1:618f. (August 21, 1944), APL.

24. "La Asamblea Constituyente inició la discusión de la Carta Política," *El Comercio* (Quito), August 22, 1944, 11; "Actas de la Asamblea Constituyente de 1944," 1:618f. (August 21, 1944), APL.

25. Marisol de la Cadena, *Indigenous Mestizos: The Politics of Race and Culture in Cuzco, 1919–1991* (Durham: Duke University Press, 2000).

26. "Actas de la Asamblea Nacional Constituyente de 1944," 1:741 (August 22, 1944), APL; "Actas de la Asamblea Nacional Constituyente de 1944," 3:988–90 (October 3, 1944), APL.

27. "Actas de la Asamblea Nacional Constituyente de 1944," 3:1000, 1003 (October 3, 1944), APL.

28. "Actas de la Asamblea Nacional Constituyente de 1944," 3:984–85, 992–94 (October 3, 1944), APL.

29. Article 5 of the 1945 constitution in Trabucco, *Constituciones de la República del Ecuador*, 356.

30. Agustín Cueva, "El Ecuador de 1925 a 1960," in *Nueva Historia del Ecuador*, vol. 10, *Epoca republicana III: El Ecuador entre los años veinte y los sesenta*, ed. Enrique Ayala Mora (Quito: Corporación Editora Nacional, 1990), 110.

31. Guillermo Bossano, *Evolución del derecho constitucional ecuatoriano*, 2d ed. (Quito: Editorial Casa de la Cultura Ecuatoriana, 1975), 181.

32. Articles 129–41 of 1947 electoral law, TSE, *Elecciones y democracia en el Ecuador*, 229–31.

33. Miguel Lluco, "Pachakutik se alista para las elecciones del 2002," *Rikcharishun* (Ecuarunari), 29, no. 5 (December 2001), http://www.ecuarunari.org/rikcharishun/dic2001.html.

34. Sergio Enrique Jirón, "La transformación política del 28 de Mayo de 1944," in *El 28 de mayo de 1944: testimonio*, 30; José Vicente Ordeñana Trujillo, "Una revolución traicionada," in ibid., 55; Alfredo Vera, "Una insurrección triunfante que no pudo ser Revolución," in ibid., 105; Manuel Agustín Aguirre, "Breves memorias sobre la Revolución del 28 de Mayo de 1944," in ibid., 223.

35. Guillermo O'Donnell, "On the State, Democratization and Some Conceptual Prob-

lems: A Latin American View with Glances at Some Postcommunist Countries," *World Development* 21 (1993): 1361.

36. William I. Robinson, *Promoting Polyarchy: Globalization, US Intervention, and Hegemony* (Cambridge: Cambridge University Press, 1996).

Chapter 8: Indigenous Communities, Landlords, and the State

1. See, for example, Comisión por la Defensa de los Derechos Humanos, *El levantamiento indígena y la cuestión indígena* (Quito: Ediciones Abya Yala/CDDH, 1990); Janet Hendricks, "Symbolic Counterhegemony Among the Ecuadorian Shuar," in *Nation-States and Indians in Latin America*, ed. G. Urban and J. Sherzer (Austin: University of Texas Press, 1991), 53–71; Tanya Korovkin, "Indigenous Peasant Struggles and the Capitalist Modernization of Agriculture: Chimborazo, 1964–1991," *Latin American Perspectives* 24 (1997): 25–49; Kintto Lucas, *La rebelión de los indígenas* (Quito: Ediciones Abya Yala, 2000); Nina Pacari, "Taking on the Liberal Agenda," *NACLA Report on the Americas* 29 (1996): 23–32; Fernando Rosero, *Levantamiento indígena: tierra y precios*, 2d ed. (Quito: Centro de Estudios y Difusión Social, 1991); Suzana Sawyer, "The 1992 Indian Mobilization in Lowland Ecuador," *Latin American Perspectives* 24 (1997): 65–82; Melina Selverston-Scher, *Ethnopolitics in Ecuador: Indigenous Rights and the Strengthening of Democracy* (Miami: North-South Center Press, 2001).

2. Luis Macas, "Foreword," in Selverston-Scher, *Ethnopolitics in Ecuador*, xi–xix.

3. Oswaldo Barsky, *La reforma agraria ecuatoriana* (Quito: Corporación Editora Nacional/Facultad Latinoamericana de Ciencias Sociales, 1984); Carmen Diana Deere, *Household and Class Relations: Peasants and Landlords in Northern Peru* (Berkeley: University of California Press, 1990).

4. Andrés Guerrero, *La hacienda precapitalista y la clase terrateniente en América Latina y su inserción en el modo de producción capitalista: El caso ecuatoriano* (Quito: Universidad Central, 1975); see also Andrés Guerrero, *Haciendas, capital, y lucha de clases andina* (Quito: Editorial El Conejo, 1983); and Fernando Velasco, *Reforma agraria y movimiento campesino indígena de la sierra*, 2d ed. (Quito: Editorial El Conejo, 1983). Analyses of this process were by no means limited to local researchers. See, for example, Michael Redclift and David R. Preston, "Agrarian Reform and Rural Change in Ecuador," in *Environment, Society, and Rural Change in Latin America*, ed. D. Preston (New York: John Wiley, 1980).

5. See, for example, J. V. D. Saunders, "Man-Land Relations in Ecuador," *Rural Sociology* 26 (1961): 57–69.

6. Tanya Korovkin, "Indigenous Peasant Struggles and the Capitalist Modernization of Agriculture"; Luis Macas, "Foreword"; Paola Sylva, *Gamonalismo y lucha campesina* (Quito: Ediciones Abya Yala, 1986).

7. Velasco, *Reforma agraria y movimiento campesino*. See also José Almeida, "Luchas campesinas del siglo XX (primera parte)," in *Nueva historia del Ecuador*, vol. 10, *Epoca republicana III, El Ecuador entre los veinte y los sesenta*, ed. E. Ayala (Quito: Corporación Editora Nacional/Grijalbo, 1990), 163–86.

8. Guerrero, *La hacienda precapitalista y la clase terrateniente*.

9. Leslie Ann Brownrigg, "Variaciones del parentesco Cañari," in *Temas sobre la continuidad y adaptación cultural ecuatoriana*, ed. M. Naranjo, J. Pereija, and N. Whitten (Quito: Pontificia Universidad Católica del Ecuador, 1977).

10. Velasco, *Reforma agraria y movimiento campesino*, 56.

11. Oswaldo Hurtado, *Political Power in Ecuador* (Albuquerque: University of New Mexico Press, 1983).

12. Oswaldo Barsky, "Iniciativa terrateniente en la reestructuración de las relaciones so-

ciales en la sierra ecuatoriana, 1959–1964," *Revista Ciencias Sociales* 2 (1978): 74–126; Oswaldo Barsky, "Ideologías terratenientes en los procesos de modernización en la sierra ecuatoriana," in *Terratenientes y Desarrollo Capitalista en el Agro*, ed. Centro de Planificación y Estudios Sociales (Quito: CEPLAES, 1978), 91–149; Oswaldo Barsky, "Los terratenientes serranos y el debate político previo al dictado de la Ley de Reforma Agraria de 1964 en el Ecuador," in *Ecuador: Cambios en el Agro Serrano*, ed. FLACSO/CEPLAES (Quito: FLACSO/CEPLAES, 1980); Oswaldo Barsky and Gustavo Cosse, *Tecnología y cambio social: Las haciendas lecheras del Ecuador* (Quito: FLACSO, 1981).

13. Barsky, "Los terratenientes serranos y el debate político."

14. Barsky, "Iniciativa terrateniente en la reestructuración de las relaciones sociales"; Barsky, "Ideologías terratenientes en los procesos de modernización"; Barsky, "Los terratenientes serranos y el debate político."

15. Hurtado, *Political Power in Ecuador*.

16. Barsky, "Iniciativa terrateniente en la reestructuración de las relaciones sociales"; Gustavo Cosse, "Reflexiones acerca del estado, el proceso político y la política agraria en el caso ecuatoriano," in *Ecuador: Cambios en al agro serrano*, ed. FLACSO/CEPLAES (Quito: FLACSO/CEPLAES, 1980).

17. Barsky, "Los terratenientes serranos y el debate político"; Cosse, "Reflexiones acerca del estado, el proceso político y la política agraria en el caso ecuatoriano."

18. Cosse, "Reflexiones acerca del estado, el proceso político y la política agraria en el caso ecuatoriano."

19. For example, see Lori Ann Thrupp, Gilles Bergeron, and William F. Waters, *Bittersweet Harvests for Global Supermarkets: Challenges in Latin America's Agricultural Export Boom* (Washington, DC: World Resources Institute, 1995).

20. See the analysis of former president Oswaldo Hurtado, *Political Power in Ecuador*; and Judith Kimmerling, "Rights, Responsibilities, and Realities: Environmental Protection Law in Ecuador's Amazon Oil Fields," *Southwestern Journal of Law and Trade in the Americas* 2 (1995): 294–384.

21. Oswaldo Barsky, Emilio Díaz Bonilla, Carlos Furche, and Roberto Mizrahi, *Políticas agrarias, colonización y desarrollo rural en el Ecuador* (Quito: Organization of American States, Centro de Planificación y Estudios Sociales, 1982); Gustavo Cosse, "Reflexiones acerca del estado, el proceso político y la política agraria en el caso ecuatoriano"; see also Víctor Bretón, *Capitalismo, reforma agraria y organización comunal en los Andes: Una introducción al caso ecuatoriano* (Lledida, Spain: Adreca Científica, 1997).

22. Velasco, *Reforma agraria y movimiento campesino*, 1983.

23. Guerrero, *Haciendas, capital, y lucha de clases andina*.

24. Carlos Arcos and Carlos Marchán, "Apuntes para una discusión sobre los cambios en la estructura agraria serrana," *Revista Ciencias Sociales* 2 (1978): 13–64; Aníbal Buitron and Bárbara Salisbury Buitron, *Condiciones de vida y trabajo del campesino de la provincia de Pichincha* (Quito: Impresa Caja del Seguro, 1947); Alex Barril, "Modernización agropecuaria y economías campesinas," in *Tecnología agropecuaria y economías campesinas* (Quito: Fundaciones Brethren-Unida/CEPLAES, 1978), 57–78; Alex Barril, "Desarrollo tecnológico, producción agropecuaria y relaciones de producción en la sierra ecuatoriana," in *Ecuador: Cambios en al agro serrano* (Quito: FLACSO/CEPLAES, 1980), 207–48.

25. Barsky, "Iniciativa terrateniente en la reestructuración de las relaciones sociales"; Barsky, "Ideologías terratenientes en los procesos de modernización."

26. Guerrero, *Haciendas, capital y lucha de clases andina*; Velasco, *Reforma agraria y movimiento campesino indígena de la sierra*.

27. For example, see Christophe Eberhart, *El campesino de Chimborazo: Situación*.

28. Huasicamía usually referred to duties performed in landlord's residence, either in the hacienda or in Quito. A. C. refers to taking care of cattle in lower pastures near the residence, rather than in the páramo (*cuentayo*).

29. Luis Robalino, *Orígenes del Ecuador de hoy*, vol. 1, *García Moreno* (Quito: Talleres Gráficos Nacionales, 1948).

30. The size of the original hacienda can only be approximated; in the colonial and republican eras, estates were not precisely measured and exact boundaries were rarely established with any precision. According to available records, the hacienda in 1950 must have comprised about 2,267 hectares of cultivable land and approximately 21,000 hectares of páramo.

31. The size of the property was not recorded in the property registry, but it can be inferred from land records that the original hacienda comprised more than 2,000 hectares of cultivable land and thousands of hectares of pastures in the páramo.

32. For international links, see David Kyle, *Transnational Peasants* (Baltimore: Johns Hopkins University Press, 2000); William M. Loker, ed., *Globalization and the Rural Poor in Latin America* (Boulder, CO: Lynn Reinner, 1999). For temporary internal migration, see William F. Waters, "The Road of Many Returns: Rural Bases of the Informal Urban Economy in Ecuador," *Latin American Perspectives* 24 (1997): 50–64.

33. Norma Giarracca, ed., *Una nueva ruralidad en América Latina* (Buenos Aires, Argentina: Consejo Latinoamericano de Ciencias Sociales and Agencia Sueca de Desarrollo Internacional, 2001).

34. William F. Waters and Frederick H. Buttel, "Diferenciación sin descampesinización: acceso a la tierra y persistencia del campesinado andino ecuatoriano," *Estudios Rurales Latinoamericanos* 10 (1987): 355–81.

Chapter 9: Contesting Membership

1. Abigail B. Bakan and Daiva Kristina Stasiulis, *Not One of the Family: Foreign Domestic Workers in Canada* (Toronto: University of Toronto Press, 1997).

2. See Will Kymlicka and Wayne Norman, "Return of the Citizen: A Survey of Recent Work on Citizenship Theory," *Ethics* 104 (January 1994): 352–81.

3. See Iris Marion Young, "Polity and Group Difference: A Critique of the Ideal of Universal Citizenship," *Ethics* 99 (January 1989): 250–74; Carole Pateman, "Equality, Difference, Subordination: The Politics of Motherhood and Women's Citizenship," in *Beyond Equality and Difference: Citizenship, Feminist Politics, and Female Subjectivity*, ed. Gisela Bock and Susan James (London: Routledge, 1992), 17–31; see also Will Kymlicka, "Liberalism and the Politicization of Ethnicity," *Canadian Journal of Law and Jurisprudence* 4 (1991): 239–56; Will Kymlicka, *Multicultural Citizenship: A Liberal Theory of Minority Rights* (Oxford: Clarendon Press, 1995); S. James Anaya, *Indigenous Peoples in International Law*, 2d ed. (New York: Oxford University Press, 2004).

4. Kymlicka and Norman, "Return of the Citizen," 370.

5. Young, "Polity and Group Difference."

6. Kymlicka, *Multicultural Citizenship*.

7. Anaya, *Indigenous Peoples in International Law*.

8. Manuel Chiriboga V., "La reforma agraria ecuatoriana y los cambios en la distribución de la propiedad rural agrícola, 1974–1985," in *Transformaciones agrarias en el Ecuador*, ed. Pierre Gondard et al. (Quito: CEDIG, 1988), 39–57; Andrés Guerrero, *Haciendas, capital y lucha de clases andina: disolución de la hacienda serrana y lucha política en los años 1960–64*, 2d ed., Colección Ecuador Hoy 10 (Quito: Editorial El Conejo, 1984); Paola Sylva Charvet, *Gamonalismo y lucha campesina* (Quito: Ediciones Abya Yala, 1986).

9. Amalia Pallares, *From Peasant Struggles to Indian Resistance: The Ecuadorian Andes in the Late Twentieth Century* (Norman: University of Oklahoma Press, 2002).

10. José Sánchez-Parga, "Comunidad indígena y estado nacional," in *Pueblos indios, estado y derecho*, ed. Enrique Ayala Mora et al. (Quito: Corporación Editora Nacional, 1993), 61–78.

11. Oficina Nacional de Alfabetización, *La Alfabetización participatoria, como proceso sociopolítico* (Quito: Oficina Nacional de Alfabetización, 1981).

12. Roberto Santana, "La cuestión étnica y la democracia en el Ecuador," *Ecuador Debate* 12 (December 1986): 105–06.

13. Ibid.

14. "Alfabetización o proselitismo?" *Nueva* 72 (December 1980).

15. Pallares, *From Peasant Struggles to Indian Resistance.*

16. Alicia Ibarra, *Los indígenas y el estado en el Ecuador: la práctica neoindigenista*, 2d ed. (Quito: Ediciones Abya-Yala, 1992).

17. Manuel Chiriboga and Fredy Rivera, "Elecciones de Enero de 1988 y participación indígena," *Ecuador Debate* 17 (March 1989): 181–221.

18. Pallares, *From Peasant Struggles to Indian Resistance.*

19. Fernando Rosero, *Levantamiento indígena: tierra y precios*, Serie Movimiento Indígena en el Ecuador Contemporáneo 1 (Quito: Centro de Estudios y Difusión Social, 1990).

20. For a statistical study of this, and a more in-depth analysis of the land redistribution situation see Rosero, *Levantamiento indígena*. Rosero shows, additionally, that while there were many legal land transfers during the Febres Cordero and even Borja regimes, most of these were simply the giving of land titles to people who had lived on the land for many decades, not actual land redistributions.

21. Cited in "Despierta el gigante," *Vistazo* 550 (July 15, 1990).

22. See Suzana Sawyer, *Crude Chronicles: Indigenous Politics, Multinational Oil and Neoliberalism in Ecuador* (Durham: Duke University Press, 2004).

23. See Kymlicka, *Multicultural Citizenship*.

Chapter 10: Sons of Indians and Indian Sons

This work was made possible thanks to funding from the Social Science Research Council (SSRC), the Fulbright Commission of Ecuador, and Syracuse University, as well as institutional support of the Pontificia Universidad Católica del Ecuador (PUCE), the Facultad Latinoamericana de Ciencias Sociales (FLACSO), and Ministerio de Defensa Nacional del Ecuador.

1. Peter M. Beattie, *The Tribute of Blood: Army, Honor, Race, and Nation in Brazil, 1864–1945*, Latin America Otherwise (Durham: Duke University Press, 2001).

2. Although the constitution considers military service to be the obligation of all citizens and residents, the armed forces consider conscription to be "men's work" and therefore do not draft women.

3. Philip Abrams, "Notes on the Difficulty of Studying the State," *Journal of Historical Sociology* 1, no. 1 (March 1988): 58–89.

4. *Cuartel*, while literally translated as barracks, is better understood as a military base or garrison.

5. See, for example, Hans C. Buechler and Judith-Maria Buechler, *The Bolivian Aymara*, Case Studies in Cultural Anthropology (New York: Holt, Rinehart, and Winston, 1971).

6. Most of those who did not work were full-time students; many other students attended night school and worked during the day.

7. Florencia E. Mallon, *Peasant and Nation: The Making of Postcolonial Mexico and Peru* (Berkeley: University of California Press, 1995), 6.

8. William Roseberry, "Hegemony and the Language of Contention," in *Everyday Forms of State Formation: Revolution and Negotiation of Rule in Modern Mexico*, ed. Gilbert M. Joseph and Daniel Nugent (Durham: Duke University Press, 1994), 355–66.

9. Marisol de la Cadena, *Indigenous Mestizos: The Politics of Race and Culture in Cuzco, Peru, 1919–1991* (Durham: Duke University Press, 2000), 9.

10. Ronald Stutzman, "El Mestizaje: An All-Inclusive Ideology of Exclusion," in *Cultural Transformations and Ethnicity in Modern Ecuador*, ed. Norman E. Whitten Jr. (Urbana: University of Illinois, 1981), 45–94.

11. Norman E. Whitten Jr., *Sicuanga Runa: The Other Side of Development in Amazonian Ecuador* (Urbana: University of Illinois Press, 1985), 41–44.

12. Quoted in Norman E. Whitten Jr., *Sacha Runa: Ethnicity and Adaptation of Ecuadorian Jungle Quichua* (Urbana: University of Illinois Press, 1976), 268.

13. Mary Weismantel and Stephen F. Eisenman, "Race in the Andes: Global Movements and Popular Ontologies," *Bulletin of Latin American Research* 17 (May 1998): 123.

14. The Ecuadorian military has no history of committing genocide against native peoples as in Guatemala or widespread oppression of the Left as occurred in the Southern Cone. On the contrary, liberal military dictatorships have introduced many of the country's most progressive laws. Most notable are those associated with secularization of the state (such as introduction of civil marriage, divorce, and lay education) following the 1895 Liberal Revolution led by General Eloy Alfaro, the 1938 labor code enacted by General Alberto Enríquez, and the agrarian reforms carried out by successive juntas in the sixties and seventies. Nevertheless, few of these laws have been fully or vigorously enacted, and after the January 21, 2000, indigenous-military coup, relations between soldiers and Indians have been fragile. On the January 21 uprising (none of which adequately examines its cultural roots), see Vladimir Álvarez Grau, *El golpe detrás de los ponchos* (Quito: Edino, 2001); Fernando Bustamante, "Y después de la insurrección qué . . . ?" *Ecuador Debate* 49 (April 2000): 43–56; Heinz Dieterich, ed., *La Cuarta vía al Poder: el 21 de enero desde una perspectiva latinoamericana* (Quito: Abya-Yala, 2000); José Hernández, Marco Arauz, Byron Rodríguez V., and Leonel Bejarano, eds., *21 de enero: la vorágine que acabó con Mahuad* (Quito: El Comercio, 2000); Eduardo Kingman, "La ciudad como reinvención: el levantamiento indígena de enero de 2000 y la toma de Quito," *Íconos* 10 (2001): 68–77; Juan J. Paz y Miño Cepeda, *Golpe y contragolpe: la "rebelión de Quito" del 21 de enero de 2000* (Quito: Abya-Yala, 2002).

15. José Gallardo Román, "Nación ecuatoriana o plurinacionalidad?," *Revista de las Fuerzas Armadas del Ecuador* 123 (1998): 19–25.

16. Brian R. Selmeski, "Blurred Lines Between Defense, Development and Institutional Enrichment: the Ecuadorian Army's Apoyo Al Desarrollo Program" (paper presented at the Primer Encuentro de LASA Sobre Estudios Ecuatorianos, FLACSO, Quito, Ecuador, July 18–20, 2002).

17. Dirección de Movilización, *Borrador de la planificación de la Dirección de Movilización del Comando Conjunto de las Fuerzas Armadas* (internal document, 1993).

18. Conscripts are marginal soldiers in the military sense, though at the same time they are central to many of the armed forces' other efforts. Moreover, while an impressive 45 percent of conscripts surveyed indicated a desire to become voluntarios upon completion of their military service, only 26 percent of these met the educational requirement of having finished high school.

19. Brian Loveman, *For la Patria: Politics and the Armed Forces in Latin America*, Latin American Silhouettes (Wilmington, DE: SR Books, 1999); Frederick M. Nunn, *Yesterday's Soldiers: European Military Professionalism in South America, 1890–1940* (Lincoln: University of Nebraska Press, 1983).

20. Unless otherwise specified, the terms *family, father, son,* and *Mother* denote metaphorical rather than literal roles.

21. Hernán Altamirano Escobar, "La Identidad Histórica del Estado Ecuatoriano y sus Fuerzas Armadas Jamás Pueden Rescribirse," in *Tarqui: Fuerza Terrestre* 4 (1999): 18–21.

22. Erving Goffman, *Asylums: Essays on the Social Situation of Mental Patients and Other Inmates* (Garden City, NY: Anchor Books, 1961).

23. Bronislaw Malinowski, "Myth in Primitive Psychology," in *New Science Series 1* (New York: Norton, 1926), 11–94.

24. The inclusion of portions of Velasco's mythical history on the armed forces' home page is testimony to its importance in creating the institution's sense of identity. See Ministerio de Defensa Nacional, "Historia del Ecuador: El Reino de Quito" in *El Ecuador y sus Fuerzas Amadas* (http://www.fuerzasarmadasecuador.org/espanol/historia/reinoquito.htm, 2002). The central role of the military in circulating the myth is evidenced by the fact that their homepage is the first hit that Google.com generated for a search of "'de Velasco' + 'Historia del Reino de Quito.'"

25. Eileen Willingham, "Creating the Kingdom of Quito: Patria, History, Language and Utopia in Juan de Velasco's Historia del Reino de Quito (1789)" (PhD diss., University of Wisconsin, Madison, 2001).

26. Comandancia General del Ejército, *Materias Generales: Historia del Ecuador* (Quito: Academia de Guerra, 1981).

27. John V. Murra, "The Historic Tribes of Ecuador," in *Handbook of South American Indians*, vol. 2, *The Andean Civilizations*, ed. Julian H. Steward (Washington, DC: U.S. Government Printing Office, 1946), 785–821.

28. Ministerio de Defensa Nacional, "Historia del Ecuador."

29. The officer in question unfairly slighted Indians by suggesting they were illiterate; while statistics reveal a low overall level of schooling (as noted), all were literate. The officer also insulted nonindigenous recruits by comparing them to the supposedly illiterate Indians.

30. Willingham, "Creating the Kingdom of Quito," notes that in the original telling, Velasco portrayed Rumiñahui as a scoundrel and traitor, which demonstrates both the disparity between versions of the myth and the military's ability to alter earlier beliefs to serve its ends.

31. Patricio Haro Ayerve, *La influencia del poder militar en la historia del Ecuador* (Quito: Ministerio de Defensa Nacional, 1997). In Ecuador, *cholo* may mean merely a mestizo, or a lower-status mestizo, or a social mestizo of "pure Indian blood," or a person of mixed Indian and mestizo blood (Muriel Crespi, "When Indios Become Cholos: Some Consequences of the Changing Ecuadorian Hacienda," in *The New Ethnicity, Perspectives from Ethnology: 1973 Proceedings of the American Ethnological Society*, ed. John W. Bennett [St. Paul, MN: West Publishing, 1975], 148–66). *Montuvio*, on the other hand, is best understood as a rugged inhabitant of the country's rural coastal area.

32. Mallon, *Peasant and Nation.*

33. Brian Loveman, *For la Patria.*

34. Andrés Guerrero, "The Construction of a Ventriloquist's Image: Liberal Discourse and the 'Miserable Indian Race' in Late 19th-Century Ecuador," *Journal of Latin American Studies* 29 (October 1997): 555–90.

35. Gananath Obeyesekere, *The Apotheosis of Captain Cook: European Mythmaking in the Pacific* (Princeton: Princeton University Press, 1992).

36. Daughters are conspicuously absent from the cuartel both literally and metaphorically because they are being groomed to be mothers, a process carried out at home. Only recently have women been admitted to the military academy in small numbers, a change that will likely mean a revision of the family metaphor in the coming years.

37. Television ownership is extensive in Ecuador, even within poor and rural sectors of society. According to the *CIA Factbook*, there are over 5 million televisions in the country, one for every 2.7 residents.

38. Cynthia Enloe, "Beyond Rambo: Women and the Varieties of Militarized Masculinity," in *Women and the Military System*, ed. Eva Isaksson (New York: Harvester Wheatsheaf, 1988), 71–93.

39. Philippe Bourgeois, "Masculinidades lumpenizadas: Dos perspectivas etnográficas de vendedores de crack puertorriqueños y heroinomanos desamparados blancos" (paper presented at the Seminario Internacional: Masculinidades en América Latina, FLACSO, Quito, Ecuador, April, 23–24, 2002).

40. Lesley Gill, "Creating Citizens, Making Men: The Military and Masculinity in Bolivia," *Cultural Anthropology* 12 (1997): 527–50.

41. José Flores Recalde, *Conscriptos . . . ¿Para qué?* (Quito: Editorial Belén, 1983). The cuartel is like school in other senses as well. Loveman in *For la Patria* notes that conscription has historically been referred to as the "school of citizenship." Lip service is also paid to conscription's role in combating illiteracy, although judging from ethnographic and historical evidence I find this claim dubious. In practice, literacy has often been an informal prerequisite for conscription, and the time for conventional schooling for conscripts during their service is severely limited.

42. The fact that conscripts have minimal exposure to officers, who exercise broad fatherly authority by virtue of their rank, and extensive contact with enlisted voluntarios, whose mandate is more circumscribed, further compounds this situation.

43. However, conscripts consistently stated that it was more important to be capable than physically strong. Capability, in this sense, is a proxy for personal formation.

44. Lourdes Tibán, "Justicia Indígena: Procedimientos y Prácticas" (paper presented at the panel Interculturalidad y Justicia Indígena, Universidad Andina Simón Bolívar, Quito, Ecuador, July 19, 2002).

45. The Army recognizes the inability of mothers to control the influences their adolescent sons are subjected to when they leave home to work or study in the city.

46. Leslie W. Hepple, "Metaphor, Geopolitical Discourse, and the Military in South America," in *Writing Worlds: Discourse, Text, and Metaphor in the Representation of Landscape*, ed. Trevor J. Barnes and James S. Duncan (London: Routledge, 1992).

47. Loveman, *For la Patria.*

48. This characterization applies to Indian and non-Indian recruits alike and may help to explain the high percentage of conscripts who want to become voluntarios after completing their service.

49. Alberto Molina, *Las Fuerzas Armadas Ecuatorianas: paz y desarrollo* (Quito: Asociación Latinoamericana de Derechos Humanos, 1993).

50. Brian R. Selmeski, "Blurred Lines Between Defense, Development and Institutional Enrichment."

51. In this sense, national defense is analogous to a family business where fathers must employ the labor of their sons—through conscription, in this case—to reduce associated costs and ensure the enterprise's success.

52. Haro Ayerve, *La influencia del poder militar en la historia del Ecuador*, 166.

Chapter 11: Same State, Different Histories, Diverse Strategies

1. Anne-Christine Taylor, "El Oriente Ecuatoriano en el Siglo XIX: 'El Otro Litoral,'" in *Historia y región en el Ecuador: 1830–1930*, ed. Juan Maiguashca (Quito: Corporación Editora Nacional/FLACSO-Sede Ecuador/CERLAC, 1994).

2. Udo Oberem, *Los Quijos: Historia de la transculturación de un grupo indígena en el Oriente Ecuatoriano, 1538–1956* (Otavalo, Ecuador: Instituto Otavaleño de Antropología, 1980), 109–10.

3. Anne-Christine Taylor, "The Western Margins of Amazonia from the Early Sixteenth to the Early Nineteenth Century," in *The Cambridge History of the Native Peoples of the Americas*, vol. 3, *South America, part 2*, ed. Frank Salomon and Stuart B. Schwartz (Cambridge: Cambridge University Press, 1999).

4. Taylor, "The Western Margins of Amazonia from the Early Sixteenth to the Early Nineteenth Century," 237.

5. Blanca Muratorio, *The Life and Times of Grandfather Alonso: Culture and History in the Upper Amazon* (New Brunswick, NJ: Rutgers University Press, 1991), 146–47.

6. Udo Oberem, *Los Quijos*, 41; Taylor "El Oriente Ecuatoriano en el Siglo XIX," 37.

7. CONAIE, *Las Nacionalidades Indígenas en el Ecuador: Nuestro proceso organizativo* (Quito: TINCUI-CONAIE/Abya-Yala, 1989), 69.

8. By this time, it is possible to refer to this group as "the lowland Quichua," although the term encompassed peoples who came from diverse linguistic groups. While Quichua was most likely spoken as a trade language in the region even prior to the Spanish conquest, the Jesuits were fundamental in establishing Quichua as the lingua franca in the region; see Muratorio, *The Life and Times of Grandfather Alonso*, 36–38.

9. Oberem, *Los Quijos*, 113.

10. Muratorio, *The Life and Times of Grandfather Alonso*, 80–81.

11. Quoted in ibid., 75.

12. Muratorio, *The Life and Times of Grandfather Alonso*, 75.

13. Ibid., 72–76.

14. Ibid., 76.

15. Theodore MacDonald Jr. "Processes of Change in Amazonian Ecuador: Quijos Quichua Indians become Cattlemen" (PhD diss., University of Illinois, 1979), 225–27.

16. José S. J. Jouanen, *Los Jesuitas y el Oriente Ecuatoriano: 1868–1898* (Guayaquil: Editorial Arquidiocesana, 1977), 107.

17. Muratorio, *The Life and Times of Grandfather Alonso*, 83–84.

18. Lorenzo López San Vicente, *La Misión del Napo* (Quito: Imprenta de la Universidad Central, 1894), 70.

19. Jouanen, *Los Jesuitas*, 78.

20. Ibid., 78; see also Steven Rubenstein, "Colonialism, the Shuar Federation, and the Ecuadorian State," *Environment and Planning D: Society and Space* 19 (2001): 266.

21. Muratorio, *The Life and Times of Grandfather Alonso*, 77–78.

22. Alfredo Rubio Orbe, *Recopilación de la legislación indigenista del Ecuador* (Mexico City: Fondo de Cultura, 1954), 63–67.

23. César Cisneros Cisneros, *Demografía y estadística sobre el indio ecuatoriano* (Quito: Talleres Gráficos Nacionales, 1948), 61–62.

24. Muratorio, *The Life and Times of Grandfather Alonso*, 100–101.

25. *Terrenos baldíos* can mean uncultivated land, but could also include insufficiently cultivated land. Amazonian indigenous horticultural techniques were extensive rather than intensive, and their fields often seemed unkempt and underutilized to government agents from the highlands. Thus, the law had racist implications as well, suggesting that indigenous people were lazy and that only people who knew the "proper" way of cultivating should be able to claim lands. Finally, the term implies that forested land is somehow valueless (since it is "vacant") until converted to agriculture.

26. Jouanen, *Los Jesuitas*, 203; see also Muratorio, *The Life and Times of Grandfather Alonso*, 142.

27. Muratorio, *The Life and Times of Grandfather Alonso*, 142–45.

28. Theodore Macdonald Jr., *Ethnicity and Culture amidst New "Neighbors"* (Boston: Allyn and Bacon, 1999), 52.

29. Muratorio, *The Life and Times of Grandfather Alonso*, 146–47.

30. CONAIE, *Las Nacionalidades Indígenas*, 43; Rubenstein, "Colonialism, the Shuar Federation, and the Ecuadorian State," 267–68.

31. CONAIE, *Las Nacionalidades Indígenas*, 74; William Vickers, "The Modern Political Transformation of the Secoya," in *Millennial Ecuador: Critical Essays on Cultural Transformations and Social Dynamics*, ed. Norman E. Whitten Jr. (Iowa City: University of Iowa Press), 52.

32. Thomas K. Rudel, Diane Bates, and Rafael Machinguiashi, "Ecologically Noble Amerindians? Cattle Ranching and Cash Cropping among Shuar and Colonists in Ecuador," *Latin American Research Review* 37 (2002): 146.

33. Taylor, "El Oriente Ecuatoriano en el Siglo XIX," 51; CONAIE, *Las Nacionalidades Indígenas*, 42; Rubenstein, "Colonialism, the Shuar Federation, and the Ecuadorian State," 270–71.

34. Taylor, "El Oriente Ecuatoriano en el Siglo XIX," 48.

35. Ibid., 49.

36. Muratorio, *The Life and Times of Grandfather Alonso*, 163.

37. Philippe Descola, "From Scattered to Nucleated Settlement: A Process of Socioeconomic Change among the Achuar," in *Cultural Transformations and Ethnicity in Modern Ecuador*, ed. Norman E. Whitten Jr. (Urbana: University of Illinois Press, 1981), 614; Anne-Christine Taylor, "God-Wealth: The Achuar and the Missions," in *Cultural Transformations and Ethnicity in Modern Ecuador*, ed. Norman E. Whitten Jr. (Urbana: University of Illinois Press, 1981), 649–50.

38. Descola, "From Scattered to Nucleated Settlement," 636.

39. Ibid., 639.

40. Taylor, "God-Wealth: The Achuar and the Missions," 652–64.

41. Suzanna Sawyer, *Crude Chronicles: Indigenous Politics, Multinational Oil, and Neoliberalism in Ecuador* (Durham: Duke University Press, 2004), 11.

42. Vickers, "The Modern Political Transformation of the Secoya," 55.

43. CONAIE, *Las Nacionalidades Indígenas*, 40–41.

44. Salazar, "The Federación Shuar and the Colonization Frontier," in *Cultural Transformations and Ethnicity in Modern Ecuador*, ed. Norman E. Whitten Jr. (Urbana: University of Illinois Press, 1981), 589–613.

45. Rubenstein, "Colonialism, the Shuar Federation, and the Ecuadorian State," 274–75. Rubenstein writes that the centros "looked like, and were meant by the Salesians to function as, minimissions without priests" (274).

46. Ernesto Salazar, "The Federación Shuar and the Colonization Frontier," 594.

47. Rudel et al., "Ecologically Noble Amerindians?" 146.

48. Marc Becker, "Class and Ethnicity in the Canton of Cayambe: The Roots of Ecuador's Modern Indian Movement" (PhD diss., Department of History, University of Kansas, 1997), 314–15.

49. Salazar, "The Federación Shuar and the Colonization Frontier," 599.

50. Patricio Ycaza, *Historia del movimiento obrero ecuatoriano, segunda parte* (Quito: CEDIME, 1991), 224.

51. Juliet Erazo, "Constructing Autonomy: Indigenous Organizations, Governance, and Land Use in the Ecuadorian Amazon, 1964–2001" (PhD diss., University of Michigan, 2003), 62–63.

52. See, for example, Thomas Perreault, "Shifting Ground: Agrarian Change, Political Mo-

bilization, and Identity Construction among Quichua of the Alto Napo, Ecuadorian Amazon" (PhD diss., Department of Geography, University of Colorado, 2000).

53. Erazo, "Constructing Autonomy," chap. 1.

54. Perreault, "Shifting Ground," 214.

55. Ibid., 223.

56. Ibid., 218–23.

57. Suzana Sawyer, "The 1992 Indian Mobilization in Lowland Ecuador," *Latin American Perspectives* 24 (1997): 65–82.

58. Perreault, "Shifting Ground," 225. This concept dates back at least until the 1940s, when Communist leader Ricardo Paredes utilized his role in the constituent assembly to educate other delegates about the diversity of Ecuador's indigenous population.

59. CONFENIAE, "Estatuto de la Confederación de Nacionalidades Indígenas de la Amazonía Ecuatoriana–CONFENIAE" (Puyo, Ecuador, 1980).

60. Amalia Pallares, *From Peasant Struggles to Indian Resistance: The Ecuadorian Andes in the Late Twentieth Century* (Norman: University of Oklahoma Press, 2002), 169–73.

61. One Shuar Federation publication even goes as far as to say that the Salesian missionaries were government agents because of the integration policies they advocated; see Federación de Centros Shuar, *Federación de Centros Shuar: solución original a un problema actual* (Sucúa, Ecuador: La Federación, 1976), 107.

62. See Becker, "Class and Ethnicity in the Canton of Cayambe."

63. See Salazar, "The Federación Shuar and the Colonization Frontier," 604–05. Salazar notes that the federation worked for years to have the government institutionalize the radio schools as "public" schools, which would have freed them from religious interference. However, the schools remained a point of pride among Shuar activists, and their ambivalence regarding the connection to the mission did not stop the FOIN delegates from requesting a similar program from the Josephines.

64. CONAIE, *Las Nacionalidades Indígenas*, 102.

Chapter 12: From *Indigenismo* to Indigenous Movements in Ecuador and Mexico

1. On January 1, 1994, the EZLN took over and briefly occupied seven towns in eastern and central Chiapas. The EZLN rank and file were Mayan Indians, but their demands applied to all Mexicans lacking access to the most basic needs: adequate food, housing, and health care. By late 1994, the movement's demands expanded to include Indian rights, such as autonomy.

2. I define indigenism, or *indigenismo*, as state policies designed for indigenous peoples by non-Indians. Favre defines indigenismo as "a current of thought and of ideas that is organized and developed around the image of the Indian. It is presented as an interrogation of Indianness by non-Indians in function of the preoccupations and ends of the latter" (cited in Marie-Chantal Barre, *Ideologías indigenistas y movimientos indios*, 2d ed. [Mexico City: Siglo Veintiuno Editores, 1985], 30). While this definition is helpful in highlighting the crucial role of the state, it obscures the significant role played by indigenous peoples in shaping indigenista policies and politics. Here I focus principally on one dimension of state formation, that of state projects "from above."

3. See José Antonio Lucero, "Locating the 'Indian Problem': Community, Nationality, and Contradiction in Ecuadorian Indigenous Politics," *Latin American Perspectives* 30, no. 1 (128) (January 2003): 26.

4. Indeed, in the era of neoliberal economic reforms states sought to reduce their intervention in the countryside.

5. Manuel Gamio, *Forjando patria*, 2d ed. (Mexico City: Editorial Porrúa, 1960 [1916]).

6. A consensus formed among political leaders that Indians, as mestizos, would be incorporated by noncoercive means into the nation-state. However, there were various positions as to how this incorporation would take place. Moisés Sáenz, vice minister of education in the 1920s, defended the total incorporation of indigenous peoples, but later advocated cultural pluralism as a result of his experience with failed community development projects designed in Mexico City and applied to Indian communities elsewhere. See Cynthia Hewitt de Alcántara, *Anthropological Perspectives on Rural Mexico* (London: Routledge, 1984). Vicente Lombardo Toledano, a Marxist intellectual and influential labor leader from the 1920s to the 1940s, also challenged the notion of total incorporation. For him, problems in the Mexican countryside were rooted in unjust economic relations rather than in "backward" systems of belief. He believed that local cultures should be respected and preserved, promoting rapid rural economic development while defending cultural pluralism (ibid., 16). From the revolution through the administration of Lázaro Cárdenas (1934–1940), the central debate among policy makers centered on the necessity of incorporating the Indians into the national population without losing distinctive Indian traits.

7. For example, for the 1974–1987 period in Chiapas state, Araceli Burguete documented 165 political assassinations that took place primarily in rural areas where poor peasants demanding land were the target of state-sponsored violence. See Araceli Burguete, *Chiapas: Cronología de un etnocidio reciente (Represión política a los indios, 1974–1987)* (Mexico City: Academia Mexicana de Derechos Humanos A.C., n.d.), x.

8. This corporatist system dominated twentieth-century Mexican politics but was never all-powerful. Even in its heyday in the 1940s and 1950s, there was open resistance to the CNC from outside and even from competing peasant organizations such as the Central Campesina Independiente (Independent Peasant Confederation) formed in 1961 and the Unión General de Obreros y Campesinos Mexicanos (General Union of Mexican Workers and Peasants) that organized as early as 1949. See Armando Bartra, *Los herederos de Zapata: Movimientos campesinos posrevolucionarios en México, 1920–1980*, Colección Problemas de México (Mexico City: Ediciones Era, 1985). In the 1990s, several scholars of Mexico critically examined the common view that the Mexican state was a Leviathan. Jeffrey Rubin, for example, argues that Zapotec Indians in Juchitán, Oaxaca, actively resisted the national and state governments for decades and that the Mexican state is not as hegemonic as scholars have claimed (Jeffrey W. Rubin, *Decentering the Regime: Ethnicity, Radicalism, and Democracy in Juchitán, Mexico* [Durham: Duke University Press, 1997]); see also Gil Joseph and Daniel Nugent, *Everyday Forms of State Formation* (Durham: Duke University Press, 1994).

9. Hewitt, *Anthropological Perspectives*, 15.

10. Quoted in ibid., 16.

11. Ecuador's Instituto Indigenista Ecuatoriano (IIE) was created in 1943 as a direct outgrowth of the 1940 Pátzcuaro Conference. Unlike Mexico's INI, which became a hub of a host of government programs and initiatives after 1948, Ecuador's IIE was relatively insignificant and was quickly overshadowed by the Federación Ecuatoriana de Indios (FEI), founded a year later. (I am indebted to Marc Becker for this insight.)

12. The timing of INI's creation was due more to policy recommendations issued at the Pátzcuaro Conference than to President Alemán's commitment to the issue. Alfonso Caso was instrumental in its creation (Instituto Nacional Indigenista [Mexico], *INI 30 años después: Revisión crítica* [Mexico City: Instituto Nacional Indigenista. Secretaría de Desarrollo Social, 1978], vii).

13. INI coordinated or had a significant impact on the coordination of more than 3,000 first-tier indigenous organizations, working with the Ministry of Education, the Ministry of

Health, the Ministry of Agrarian Reform, the Office of the Agrarian Comptroller, the Ministry of Social Development, the Ecology Institute, the National Commission for Human Rights, and the National Institute of Anthropology and History (Julio C. Tresierra, "Mexico: Indigenous Peoples and the Nation-State," in *Indigenous Peoples and Democracy in Latin America*, ed. Donna Lee Van Cott [New York: St. Martin's; Inter-American Dialogue, 1994], 196).

14. Lucero, "Locating the 'Indian Problem,'" 26. Interestingly, Ecuadorian policy makers looked to the Mexican case as an example to avoid. Figueroa argues that the 1937 Ley de Comunas "came to serve as a compromise between the concessions that were still given to large landowners and the project of indigenistas who, worried about the experience of the Mexican revolution, saw in the agrarian conditions the ferment of social conflict" (cited in ibid., 29).

15. Mexico's ruling party for 71 years (1929–2000) underwent several name changes before it became the Institutional Revolutionary Party, or PRI, in 1946. The National Revolutionary Party (PNR) was formed in 1929, then was replaced by the Party of the Mexican Revolution (PRM) in 1938, which later became the PRI.

16. In May 2003, the National Indigenist Institute ceased to function and its duties were taken over by the National Commission for the Development of Indigenous Peoples (Comisión Nacional para el Desarrollo de los Pueblos Indígenas, or Conadepi). Xóchitl Gálvez, an Otomí indigenous woman and head of Fox's Presidential Office for the Development of Indigenous Peoples (Oficina Presidencial para el Desarrollo de los Pueblos Indígenas) became the new agency's first director (Judith Amador and Columba Vértiz, "El INI, convertido en oficina de gobierno," *Proceso* 1387 [June 1, 2003]).

17. See Shannan L. Mattiace, *To See with Two Eyes: Peasant Activism and Indian Autonomy in Chiapas, Mexico* (Albuquerque: University of New Mexico Press, 2003): 78–81.

18. Virtually every regional and national-level indigenous leader I interviewed in the Tojolabal region of eastern Chiapas in 2003 had participated, often quite extensively, in an INI-sponsored training program and generally had positive things to say about it.

19. Amalia Pallares, *From Peasant Struggles to Indian Resistance: The Ecuadorian Andes in the Late Twentieth Century* (Norman: University of Oklahoma Press, 2002).

20. Assimilationism was the dominant orientation of Mexico's indigenist policies from the INI's creation in 1948 to the late 1980s. The mid-1970s, however, saw a shift away from assimilationism and toward what officials called "participatory indigenism." In a 1978 INI document outlining indigenist plans of action, INI recommended the end of "compulsive methods that have homogenization and cultural mestizaje as their goal, as well as paternalistic methods that supplant the communities' own initiative and inhibit the development of their creative potential." State officials now defined the nation as "ethnically and culturally plural" (INI, *INI 30 años después*, xxvi). This shift toward participatory indigenism, however, did not mean that the administration of President López Portillo (1976–1983) or the new national director of the INI, Ignacio Ovalle Fernández, supported independent organization. While participatory indigenismo opened up greater opportunities for Indian participation, state officials closely monitored any independent organization. See Mattiace, *To See with Two Eyes*, 65–69. This policy shift was the result of an unusual alliance between radical and moderate reformers within the López Portillo administration.

21. ILO Convention 169 was the most progressive and far-reaching single document on indigenous rights to date, replacing the ILO Convention 107 of 1957 (Hurst Hannum, *Autonomy, Sovereignty, and Self-determination: The Accommodation of Conflicting Rights* [Philadelphia: University of Pennsylvania Press, 1990], 77). It implies the recognition of some form of self-rule, autonomy, or internal self-determination for indigenous peoples, meaning their right to possess a separate and distinct administrative structure and judicial system, as well as to retain customs, institutions, and customary laws (see Willem Assies, Gemma van der Haar, and

André Hoekema, eds., *The Challenge of Diversity: Indigenous Peoples and Reform of the State in Latin America* [Amsterdam: Thela Thesis, 2000], 3). The convention's principal limitation is that while it refers to indigenous peoples as *peoples*, it does not imply that Indians can exercise the rights accorded to *peoples* in international law.

22. Just when the Salinas administration was proposing reforms to Article 4, activists were preparing counter celebrations of Columbus's "discovery" of America. In Mexico, a grassroots campaign entitled "500 years of Indian, Black, and Popular Resistance" began in 1989 and increased in intensity until the quincentenary year of 1992 (Mattiace, *To See with Two Eyes*, 95).

23. The ejido is an inalienable form of communal property enshrined in the 1917 constitution (Article 27). Until 1992, when Article 27 was amended, rural community assemblies administered ejido land granted by the state.

24. Despite these limitations, Mexico's Indians have used the language of Article 4 and of Convention 169 to push for deeper reforms. We may be witnessing a disjunction between the idea of the state, which appears to be undergoing significant changes regarding its cultural and ethnic foundations, and the state system—the institutions responsible for making and enforcing laws.

25. Donna Lee Van Cott, *The Friendly Liquidation of the Past: The Politics of Diversity in Latin America* (Pittsburgh: University of Pittsburgh Press, 2000), 271–74.

26. See Mattiace, *To See with Two Eyes*, 94–95.

27. Robert Andolina, "The Sovereign and Its Shadow: Constituent Assembly and Indigenous Movement in Ecuador," *Journal of Latin American Studies* 35, no. 4 (November 2003): 721–50.

28. Conversations about the relationship between individual human rights and Indian law were spearheaded by indigenous women, who participated in several forums held during the negotiations on Indian rights and culture. Female indigenous and nonindigenous advisors to the EZLN were also key in bringing these debates to the fore; see Rosalva Aída Hernández Castillo, "Indigenous Law and Identity Politics in México: Indigenous Men´s and Women´s Perspective for a Multicultural Nation," *Political and Legal Anthropology Review* 25, no. 1 (2002): 90–110.

29. In addition to Indian culture and rights, other topics to be discussed were democracy and justice, social welfare and development, and women's rights. During the second topic, or "table" of discussion, in August 1996, the dialogue was suspended and has not been reinitiated.

30. The bill that was passed by both houses of congress in April 2001 was substantially altered by senators from Fox's own party. (Fox had publicly supported the legislation based on the original San Andrés Accords signed in February 1996.) The final version of the bill passed in April 2001 gives subnational states authority to negotiate autonomy.

31. After the Zapatista uprising, the National Indian Congress (CNI) emerged as the indigenous voice of the EZLN at the national level, but as the EZLN has reduced its national profile, the CNI has waned in importance and visibility.

32. In October 1995, the EZLN boycotted Chiapas state and municipal elections, souring an already tense relationship. (The PRD was expected to win many of the municipalities where EZLN support was heavy.)

33. Miguel Lluco, "El ALCA no es un modelo equitativo, Entrevista con Luis Macas," http://www.lainsignia.org/2002/octubre/econ_001.htm, September 29, 2002. The translation is mine.

34. The Mexican states included in the PPP are Campeche, Chiapas, Guerrero, Oaxaca, Puebla, Quintana Roo, Tabasco, Veracruz, and Yucatán.

35. Vicente Fox, Office of the Presidency, http://nt.presidencia.gob.mx/, accessed March 19, 2005.

36. Instituto Nacional Indigenista (Mexico), *Instituto Nacional Indigenista, 1989–1994* (Mexico City: Instituto Nacional Indigenista. Secretaría de Desarrollo Social, 1994), 27. An official announcement of the Plan Puebla-Panamá appeared in the *Diario Oficial,* June 5, 2001.

37. Congreso Nacional Indígena, "Declaración Final; Octava Asamblea Nacional," http://www.laneta.apc.org/cni/8an-decf.htm, November 18–20, 2001. U.S.-based NGOs have joined the CNI in opposing the PPP. San Francisco-based Global Exchange, for example, describes the goal of the project to "create an elaborate infrastructure of highway and railway systems connecting an extensive network of maquiladora and agroexportation industries with ports on either side of the Isthmus" (http://www.globalexchange.org). Another U.S.-based NGO with links to southern Mexico and Central America, Acerca, Action for Community and Ecology in the Rainforests of Central America, is equally blunt in its description of PPP goals: "The PPP is clear about its plan to remove rural and indigenous communities from the lands that have sustained them for thousand of years, and to place them in urban slums located adjacent to sweatshop factories" (http://www.acerca.org/plan_pueblo_panama.html).

38. In discussing the Otavalan Indians, Derek Williams argues that "Indian engagement with state discourse in Otavalo during the 1850s and early 1860s was characterized by a selective assertion of both citizenship rights and neocolonial corporate rights as indígenas." He observes different conceptions of progress and indeed of citizenship between the national and local governments, such as when the García Moreno administration sought to curb municipal power by portraying itself as the protector of the "*clase de indígenas.*"

39. Alison Brysk, *From Tribal Village to Global Village: Indian Rights and International Relations in Latin America* (Stanford: Stanford University Press, 2000).

40. Sarah A. Radcliffe and Sallie Westwood, *Remaking the Nation: Identity and Politics in Latin America* (London: Routledge, 1996).

41. Deborah J. Yashar, "Contesting Citizenship: Indigenous Movements and Democracy in Latin America," *Comparative Politics* 31, no. 3 (October 1998): 39.

42. Guillermo de la Peña, "Discourses on Ethnic Citizenship in Mexico" (Wednesday Seminar Series, Center for U.S.-Mexican Studies at the University of California, San Diego, 1996).

43. Leon Zamosc, "Agrarian Protest and the Indian Movement in the Ecuadorian Highlands," *Latin American Research Review* 29, no. 3 (1994): 37–68.

Chapter 13: Barricades and Articulations

Unless otherwise noted, all translations are my own.

1. See Robert Andolina, "Colonial Legacies and Plurinational Imaginaries: Indigenous Movement Politics in Ecuador and Bolivia" (PhD diss., University of Minnesota, 1999); Amalia Pallares, *From Peasant Struggle to Indian Resistance* (Norman: University of Oklahoma Press, 2002); Jorge Leon, *De campesinos a ciudadanos diferentes* (Quito: CEDIME/Abya Yala, 1994); León Zamosc, "Agrarian Protest and the Indian Movement in the Ecuadorian Highlands," *Latin American Research Review* 29, no. 3 (1994): 37–68; Augusto Barrera, *Acción colectiva y crisis política: El movimiento indígena ecuatoriano en la década de los noventa* (Quito: Abya Yala/Ciudad/Osal, 2001); José Antonio Lucero, "Arts of Unification: Political Representation and Indigenous Movements in Bolivia and Ecuador" (PhD diss., Princeton University, 2002).

2. José Carlos Mariátegui, *Siete Ensayos Interpretativos de la Realidad Peruana* (Madrid: Edición Minerva, 1979 [1928]), 45.

3. Stuart Hall, "On Post-Modernism and Articulation: An Interview with Stuart Hall," in *Critical Dialogues in Cultural Studies*, ed. David Morley and Kuan-Hsing Chen (New York: Routledge, 1996); James Clifford, "Taking Identity Politics Seriously: 'The Contradictory, Stony Ground . . . ,'" in *Without Guarantees: In Honour of Stuart Hall*, ed. Paul Gilroy et al. (London:

Verso, 2000); James Clifford, "Indigenous Articulations," *Contemporary Pacific* 13, no. 2 (2001); Tanya Murray Li, "Articulating Indigenous Identity in Indonesia: Resource Politics and the Tribal Slot," *Comparative Studies in Society and History* 42, no. 1 (2000): 149–79; see also Nancy Postero, "Articulations and Fragmentations: Indigenous Politics in Bolivia," in *The Struggle for Indigenous Rights in Latin America*, ed. Nancy Grey Postero and Leon Zamosc (Brighton: Sussex Academic Press, 2004), 189–216; for a similar analysis of Central America, see Charles Hale, "Does Multiculturalism Menace? Governance, Cultural Rights, and the Politics of Identity in Guatemala," *Journal of Latin American Studies* 34 (2002): 485–524.

4. See José Antonio Lucero, *Voices of Struggle, Struggles of Voices: Indigenous Representation in the Andes* (Pittsburgh: University of Pittsburgh Press, forthcoming).

5. Indigenous people have a long history of organizing in a variety of forms and often in alliance with other, nonindigenous actors like the Communist Party or the state. This kind of representation Andrés Guerrero called "ventriloquist's representation." I refer to organizations that claim an autonomous and indigenous political voice, distinct from traditional popular organizing, even if it has ties to traditional actors like trade unions or communist parties. Thus, my periodization of indigenous politics would not include the Communist-created Federation of Ecuadorian Indians (FEI) in the 1940s. Scholars disagree over the degree of "ventriloquism" that was involved in earlier efforts.

6. Nancy Grey Postero, *Now We Are Citizens: Indigenous Politics in Post Multicultural Bolivia* (Stanford: Stanford University Press, 2007).

7. Augusto Barrera, "Nada sólo para los indios: A propósito del último levantamiento indígena," *Observatoria Social de América Latina* 4 (June 2001): 85–92.

8. Jorge Dandler and Juan Torrico A., "From the National Indigenous Congress to the Ayopaya Rebellion: Bolivia, 1945–1947," in *Resistance, Rebellion, and Consciousness in the Andean World, 18th to 20th Centuries*, ed. Steve J. Stern (Madison: University of Wisconsin Press, 1987), 334–78.

9. See, for example, Xavier Albó, *Pueblos indios en la política* (La Paz: Plural/CIPCA, 2002); Richard Chase Smith, "A Search for Unity within Diversity: Peasant Unions, Ethnic Federations, and Indianist Movements in the Andean Republics," in *Native Peoples and Economic Development*, ed. Theodore MacDonald (Cambridge: Cultural Survival, 1984).

10. Xavier Albó, "From *MNRistas* to *Kataristas* to *Katari*," in *Resistance, Rebellion and Consciousness in the Andean Peasant World*, ed. Steve Stern (Madison: University of Wisconsin Press, 1987).

11. William Roseberry, *Anthropologies and Histories: Essays in Culture, History, and Political Economy* (New Brunswick, NJ: Rutgers University Press, 1989).

12. Smith, "A Search for Unity within Diversity," 17.

13. Richard Chase Smith, "The Dialectics of Domination in Peru: Native Communities and the Myth of the Vast Amazonian Emptiness," Occasional Paper 8 (Cambridge: Cultural Survival, 1982).

14. Laurence Whitehead, "Bolivia and the Viability of Democracy," *Journal of Democracy* 12, no. 2 (2001): 11.

15. This is not to say that Amazonian indigenous people in Ecuador faced no adversaries; oil and timber companies were powerful and disruptive forces. But as a classic enclave setting, these opponents were targets against which to mobilize as opposed to the more pervasive webs of local elites like those in the Bolivian lowlands. Using a Gramscian metaphor, there were more trenches in lowland Bolivia than Ecuador to block collective action.

16. Kevin Healy, *Llamas, Weaving, and Organic Chocolate* (Notre Dame: University of Notre Dame Press, 2001), 75.

17. See Roger M. Keesing, "Creating the Past: Custom and Identity in the Contemporary Pacific," *Contemporary Pacific* 1 (1989): 19–42; and Charles Hale, *Resistance and Contradiction* (Stanford: Stanford University Press, 1994).

18. Benedict Anderson, *Imagined Communities: The Origin and Spread of Nationalism* (New York: Verso, 1991).

19. See Jean Jackson, "Culture, Genuine and Spurious: The Politics of Indianness in the Vaupés, Colombia," *American Ethnologist* 22 (1995): 3–27.

20. Carlos Mamani, personal communication, La Paz, Bolivia, March 9, 1999.

21. Janet Hendricks, "Symbolic Counterhegemony among the Ecuadorian Shuar," in *Nation States and Indians in Latin America*, ed. Greg Urban and Joel Sherzer (Austin: University of Texas Press, 1991), 60.

22. Andolina, "Colonial Legacies and Plurinational Imaginaries."

23. José Sánchez Parga, interview, 1997.

24. Andrés Guerrero, "La desintegración de la adminstración étnica en el Ecuador," in *Sismo Étnico en el Ecuador*, ed. Jose Almeida et al. (Quito: CEDIME–Abya-Yala, 1993).

25. Ampam Karakras, personal communication, Quito, Ecuador, March 27, 2000.

26. Luis Maldonado, interview, 1997.

27. See Dietrich Rueschemeyer, Evelyne Huber Stephens, and John D. Stephens, *Capitalist Development and Democracy* (Chicago: University of Chicago Press, 1992).

28. See Lucero, *Voices of Struggle*. The main Ecuadorian social scientist who helped introduce the concept of nationalities is Ileana Almeida; the main indigenous architect of the term is the Shuar Ampam Karakras.

29. Field notes, CONAIE Assembly, February 2, 1999.

30. See, for example, Silvia Rivera, *Oprimidos pero no vencidos. Luchas del campesinado aymara y quechwa de Bolivia. 1900–1980* (La Paz: Hisbol-CSUTCB, 1984); and Felix Patzi Paco, *Insurgencia y sumisión: Movimientos indígeno-campesinos (1983–1998)* (La Paz: Editores Muela del Diablo, 1999).

31. I have used pseudonyms when quoting without explicit permission.

32. *Mallku* in Quechua and Aymara means condor, but it also refers to the traditional authorities of pre-Columbian ayllus.

33. Quispe indicates in *El indio en escena* (roughly, The Indian on Stage [La Paz: Pachakuti, 1999]) that the following books have been or are about to be published: *Tupak Katari vive y vuelve carajo* (Tupak Katari Lives and Returns Dammit [La Paz: Editorial Ofensiva Roja, 1990]), *Indianismo (Indianism)*, and *El pensamiento vivo de Fausto Reinaga* (The Living Thought of Fausto Reinaga).

34. Felipe Quispe, interview, 1999.

35. See Ricardo Calla, "Hallu hayllisa huti: Identificación étnica y procesos políticos en Bolivia," in *Democracia, etnicidad, y violencia política en los países andinos*, ed. Alberto Adrienzén et al. (Lima: Instituto de Estudios Peruanos, 1993).

36. See debate in Rafael Archondo, "La CSUTCB con alas de Mallku: Coloquio sobre sindicalismo agrario," *Tinkazos* 2 (1999): 72–84.

37. Bret Gustafson, "Paradoxes of Liberal Indigenism: Indigenous Movements, State Processes, and Intercultural Reform in Bolivia," in *The Politics of Ethnicity: Indigenous Peoples and Latin American States*, ed. David Maybury-Lewis (Cambridge: Harvard University Press, 2002).

38. Silvia Rivera, "Liberal Democracy and Ayllu Democracy in Bolivia: The Case of Northern Potosí," in *The Challenge of Rural Democratisation: Perspectives from Latin America and the Philippines*, ed. Jonathan Fox (London: F. Cass, 1990).

39. Felix Santos, interview, 1999; Juan de la Cruz Willka, interview, 1999; Felipe Quispe, interview, 1999; Esteban Ticona, Xavier Albó and Gonzalo Rojas, *Votos y Wiphalas* (La Paz: CIPCA, 1995).

40. See "Manifiesto de CONAMAQ" (press release, e-mail distribution, August 5, 2002); Robert Andolina, "Between Local Authenticity and Global Accountability: the Ayllu Movement in Contemporary Bolivia," in *Beyond the Lost Decade: Indigenous Movements, Democracy, and Development in Latin America*, ed. José Antonio Lucero (Princeton: Princeton University Program in Latin American Studies, 2003); and Lucero, *Voices of Struggle.*

41. Santiago Pérez, interview, 1999; Juan Morales, interview, 1999; Felix Patzi, *Insurgencia y sumisión.*

42. Patzi, *Insurgencia y sumisión*, 71.

43. Hans Hoffmeyer, interview, 1999.

44. Nicolás Montero, interview, 1999; Vicente Choquetilla, interview, 1999.

45. Igidio Naveda, personal communication, 2001.

46. Deborah Yashar, "Contesting Citizenship in Latin America: Indigenous Movements and Democracy in Latin America," *Comparative Politics* 31 (1997): 23–42.

47. Catherine Conaghan, "Politicians Against Parties: Discord and Disconnection in Ecuador's Party System," in *Building Democratic Institutions: Party Systems in Latin America*, ed. Scott Mainwaring and Timothy Scully (Stanford: Stanford University Press, 1995), 434–58; Eduardo Gamarra and James Malloy, "The Patrimonial Dynamics of Party Politics in Bolivia," in *Building Democratic Institutions,* ed. Mainwaring and Scully.

48. This situation has changed drastically in the last two years as older populist parties have declined, opening more space for indigenous parties. See Donna Lee Van Cott, "From Exclusion to Inclusion: Bolivia's 2002 Elections," *Journal of Latin American Studies* 35 (November 2003): 751–75.

49. Anonymous CONAMAQ interview, Cuzco, Peru, July 16, 2006.

50. See, for example, "Líder indígena Felipe Quispe da plazo de 90 días a Morales para ejecutar cambios ofrecidos," *Aporrea*, January 27, 2006, http://www.aporrea.org/dameverbo.php?docid=72317, accessed February 18, 2006.

51. Luis Macas, quoted in *El Hoy*, September 9, 1991.

52. Kenneth Mijeski and Scott H. Beck, "Mainstreaming the Indigenous Movements in Ecuador: The Electoral Strategy" (paper presented at the annual meeting of the Latin American Studies Association, September 24–26, 1998).

53. Enrique Ayala Mora, cited in Ninfa Patiño, *El discurso de los políticos frente al otro* (Quito: Abya-Yala, 1996), 175.

54. Catherine Conaghan and James Malloy, *Unsettling Statecraft: Democracy and Neoliberalism in the Central Andes* (Pittsburgh: University of Pittsburgh Press, 1994).

55. Víctor Paz Estenssoro died on June 7, 2001. The obituary in *The Economist* (2001): 84, recognized the magnitude of his impact on Bolivian politics: "It is given to few individuals to change the course of their country's history, let alone to do so twice."

56. Conaghan and Malloy, *Unsettling Statecraft*, 184–87.

57. Calla, "Hallu hayllisa huti," 75.

58. Ricardo Montevilla, interview, 1999.

59. Victor Hugo Cárdena, interview, 1999.

60. See, for example, Hale, "Does Multiculturalism Menace"; Gustafson, "Paradoxes of Liberal Indigenism"; and Peter Wade, *Race and Ethnicity in Latin America* (London: Pluto Press, 1997).

61. Ben Kohl, "Stablizing Neoliberalism in Bolivia: Privatization and Participation in Bo-

livia," *Political Geography* 21 (2003), 449–72; Ben Kohl, "Neoliberal Adventures in Bolivia" (paper presented at the annual meeting of the American Association of Geographers, March 14–19, 2004); Gustafson, "Paradoxes of Liberal Indigenism"; Van Cott, "From Exclusion to Inclusion"; Aaron Luoma, Gretchen Gordon, and Jim Shultz, "Oil and Gas Policy in Bolivia—Post-election Update" (La Paz: Democracy Center, April 6, 2006), http://www.democracyctr.org/bolivia/oilgas.htm, accessed on April 13, 2006; Postero, *Now We Are Citizens.*

62. See Leon Zamosc, "The Indian Movement in Ecuador: From Politics of Influence to Politics of Power," in *The Struggle for Indigenous Rights in Latin America*, ed. Nancy Grey Postero and Leon Zamosc (Brighton: Sussex Academic Press, 2004), 131–57; Andolina, "Colonial Legacies and Plurinational Imaginaries"; Pallares, *From Peasant Struggles to Indian Resistance*; and Lucero, *Voices of Struggle.*

63. Rafael Correa, "La política económica del Gobierno de Lucio Gutiérrez," *Íconos* 16 (May 2003): 6.

64. Arturo Cano, "La CONAIE, gran ausente en la lucha para deponer a Lucio Gutiérrez," *La Jornada*, April 26, 2005, http://www.jornada.unam.mx/2005/04/26/030n1mun.php, accessed April 27, 2005.

65. Stuart Hall, "Then and Now: A Re-evaluation of the New Left," in *Out of Apathy: Voices of the New Left Thirty Years On*, ed. Oxford University Socialist Group (London: Verso, 1989), 151.

66. Charles Hale, "Rethinking Indigenous Politics in the Era of the 'Indio Permitido,'" *NACLA Report in the Americas* 38 (2004): 20.

Chapter 14: In the Shadows of Success

1. Xavier Albó, "El Retorno del Indio," *Revista Andina* 9 (1991): 299–357.

2. Deborah Yashar, "Contesting Citizenship in Latin America: Indigenous Movements and Democracy in Latin America," *Comparative Politics* 31 (1998): 23–42.

3. Enrique Mayer, quoted in ibid., 24.

4. Luis Millones, "Hay un país sin indígenas entre Ecuador y Bolivia," in *Conversaciones para la conviencia*, ed. Marta Bulnes (Lima: GTZ, 2000), 79–88.

5. See María Elena García, *Making Indigenous Citizens: Identities, Education, and Multicultural Development in Peru* (Stanford: Stanford University Press, 2005); María Elena García and José Antonio Lucero, "'Un País Sin Indígenas'? Re-thinking Indigenous Politics in Peru," in *Indigenous Struggles in Latin America*, ed. Nancy Grey Postero and Leon Zamosc (Brighton: Sussex Academic Press, 2004), 158–88; María Elena García and José Antonio Lucero, "Authenticating Indians and Movements: Interrogating Indigenous Authenticity, Social Movements, and Fieldwork in Contemporary Peru," in *From Purity of Blood to Indigenous Social Movements*, ed. Laura Gotkowitz, in preparation; José Antonio Lucero, *Voice of Struggle, Struggles of Voice: Indigenous Representation in the Andes* (Pittsburgh: University of Pittsburgh Press, forthcoming); see also Shane Greene, "Getting Over the Andes: The Geo-Eco-Politics of Indigenous Movements in Peru's Twenty-First Century Inca Empire," *Journal of Latin American Studies* 38 (May 2006): 327–54.

6. Xavier Albó, "Ethnic Identity and Politics in the Central Andes: The Cases of Ecuador, Bolivia, and Peru," in *Politics in the Andes: Identity, Conflict, Reform*, ed. Jo-Marie Burt and Philip Mauceri (Pittsburgh: University of Pittsburgh Press, 2004), 32; see also García, *Making Indigenous Citizens;* and García and Lucero, "'Un País Sin Indígenas'?"

7. Albó, "Ethnic Identity and Politics," 32.

8. Ibid., 32–33; Cecilia Méndez G., *Incas sí, indios no: apuntes para el estudio del nacionalismo criollo en el Perú*, 2d ed., Documento de trabajo: Serie Historia (Instituto de Estudios Peru-

anos) 56. no. 10 (Lima: IEP, 1995); on Toledo's (in)action regarding indigenous politics, see García and Lucero, "'Un País Sin Indígenas'?"; and Greene, "Getting Over the Andes."

9. Les Field, "Who Are the Indians? Re-conceptualizing Indigenous Identity, Resistance, and the Role of Social Science in Latin America," *Latin American Research Review* 29 (1994): 239.

10. See Kenneth Waltz, *Theory of International Politics* (Reading, MA: Addison-Wesley, 1979), 8.

11. On DINEIB, see Melina Selverston-Scher, *Ethnopolitics in Ecuador* (Miami: North-South Press, 2002); on CODENPE, see José Antonio Lucero, "Locating the 'Indian Problem': The Politics of Community and Nationality in Ecuador," *Latin American Perspectives* 30 (January 2003): 23–48.

12. Carlos Iván Degregori, "Ethnicity and Democratic Governability in Latin America: Reflections from Two Central Andean Countries," in *Faultlines of Democracy in Post-Transition Latin America*, ed. Felipe Aguero and Jeffrey Stark (Miami: North-South Center Press, 1998), 203–34; Paul Gelles, "Andean Culture, Indigenous Identity, and the State in Peru," in *The Politics of Ethnicity: Indigenous Peoples and Latin American States*, ed. David Maybury-Lewis (Cambridge: Harvard University Press, 2002), 239–66; Marisol de la Cadena, *Indigenous Mestizos: The Politics of Race and Culture in Cuzco, Peru, 1919–1991* (Durham: Duke University Press, 2000); García, *Making Indigenous Citizens*; García and Lucero, "Authenticating Indians and Movements"; and Albó, "Ethnic Identity and Politics."

13. Quoted in García, *Making Indigenous Citizens*, 135.

14. The peculiarity of Peruvian racial formation is beyond the scope of this essay. However, as de la Cadena has shown (*Indigenous Mestizos;* and "Reconstructing Race: Racism, Culture and Mestizaje in Latin America," *NACLA Report on the Americas* 34 [May–June 2001]: 15–23), while all identity boundaries are fluid, the opposition between mestizo and indigenous identities is much less marked in Peru than in Mexico or Ecuador.

15. Carlos Iván Degregori, "Identidad étnica: movimientos sociales y participación política en el Perú," in *Democracia, etnicidad, y violencia política en los países andinos*, ed. Alberto Adrianzén et al. (Lima: IEP/IFEA, 1993), 128.

16. De la Cadena, "Reconstructing Race," 20.

17. María Isabel Remy, "The Indigenous Population and the Construction of Democracy in Peru," in *Indigenous Peoples and Democracy in Latin America*, ed. Donna Lee Van Cott (New York: St. Martin's Press, 1994), 114.

18. Carlos Iván Degregori, "Identidad étnica," 122.

19. CONAPA was later moved from the first lady's office and reconstituted at the ministry-level Institute for the Development of Andean, Amazonian, and Afro-Peruvian Peoples (INDEPA). Eliane Karp resigned in the face of intense criticism of maladministration of funds.

20. Arturo Escobar, *Encountering Development: The Making and Unmaking of the Third World* (Princeton: Princeton University Press, 1995), 15.

21. FEINE claims to represent close to three million indigenous people. While that number is probably exaggerated, indigenous evangelical communities have grown very numerous in the central highlands. FEINE, "FEINE: Una esperanza en el camino," *Informativo Amauta* 1 (March 2001): 1–5.

22. Blanca Muratorio, "Protestantism and Capitalism Revisited, in the Rural Highlands of Ecuador," *Journal of Peasant Studies* 8 (October 1980): 37–60; Blanca Muratorio, *Etnicidad, evangelización y protesta en el Ecuador: una perspectiva antropológica* (Quito: Centro de Investigaciones y Estudios Socio-Económicos, 1982).

23. Pedro de la Cruz, interview, 1999, quoted in José Antonio Lucero, "Arts of Unification:

Indigenous Movements and Political Representation in Bolivia and Ecuador" (PhD diss., Princeton University, 2002), 84.

24. Greene, "Getting Over the Andes."

25. García and Lucero, "'Un País Sin Indígenas'?"

26. Part of the bias stems from the genealogy of "social movement" that scholars like Charles Tilly (*Social Movements, 1768–2004* [New York: Paradigm Press, 2004]) have popularized. Tilly argues that the social movement as a form of contention emerged in reaction to the rise of national state structures. The emergence of the social movement marked a shift from local and direct (eighteenth-century) forms to national and indirect (nineteenth-century) forms.

27. Orin Starn, *Nightwatch* (Durham: Duke University Press, 1999), 256.

28. García, *Making Indigenous Citizens.*

29. Paul Gelles, "Andean Culture, Indigenous Identity, and the State in Peru."

30. Richard Chase Smith, "A Search for Unity Within Diversity: Peasant Unions, Ethnic Federations, and Indianist Movements in the Andean Republics," in *Native Peoples and Economic Development: Six Case Studies from Latin America*, ed. Theodore MacDonald (Cambridge: Cultural Survival, 1985), 5–38.

31. Orin Starn, "Villagers at Arms: War and Counterrevolution in the Central-South Andes," in *Shining and Other Paths: War and Society in Peru, 1980–1995*, ed. Steve Stern (Durham: Duke University Press, 1998), 224–57; Isaías Rojas, *The Push for Zero Coca: Democratic Transition and Counternarcotics Policy in Peru* (Washington, DC: WOLA, 2003).

32. On Karp and CONAPA, now renamed INDEPA, see García and Lucero, "'Un País Sin Indígenas'?"

33. García and Lucero, "Authenticating Indians and Movements."

34. Javier Lajo, "Commentary on 'Un País Sin Indígenas': Indigenous Invisibility in Peru" (unpublished manuscript).

35. José Antonio Lucero, "Arts of Unification," 85.

36. See, for example, Charles Tilly, *Social Movements.*

37. Leon Zamosc, "The Indian Movement in Ecuador: From Politics of Influence to Politics of Power," in *The Struggle for Indigenous Rights in Latin America*, ed. Nancy Grey Postero and Leon Zamosc (Brighton: Sussex Academic Press, 2004), 131–57.

38. Isaías Rojas, *The Push for Zero Coca.*

39. Donna Lee Van Cott, "Broadening Democracy: Latin America's Indigenous Peoples Movements," *Current History* (February 2004): 80–85.

40. Paulina Arpasi, "Entrevista," *Perfiles del Siglo XXI*, no. 101, http://www.revistaperfiles.com, December 2001.

41. Eduardo Ballón, interview, Lima, Peru, August 7, 2006. Felix Julca Guerrero, personal communication, April 28, 2007.

42. Kay Warren, "Indigenous Movements as a Challenge to the Unified Social Movement Paradigm for Guatemala," in *Cultures of Politics, Politics of Cultures: Re-visioning Latin American Social Movements*, ed. Sonia Alvarez, Evelina Dagnino, and Arturo Escobar (Boulder, CO: Westview Press, 1998), 165–95.

43. Bolivia is a different example of indigenous strength. Indigenous and popular protests in Bolivia forced President Gonzalo Sánchez de Lozada out of office in 2002. It is true that an Aymara political leader, Víctor Hugo Cárdenas, had participated in an earlier Sánchez de Lozada administration as vice president. At that time, the indigenous presence in Bolivia's executive was more the result of elite electoral consideration than social movement pressure. The 2005 victory of cocalero leader Evo Morales succeeded in translating social movement power into

electoral victory. In presidential, congressional, and local elections, Morales and his MAS Party have done much better than their Ecuadorian or Peruvian counterparts.

44. C. Wright Mills, *The Sociological Imagination* (Oxford: Oxford University Press, 1959), 215.

45. On the importance of exploring "seeing and not seeing," see Jeffrey Rubin, "Meanings and Mobilizations: A Cultural Politics Approach to Social Movements and States," *Latin American Research Review* 39 (2004): 106–42.

Bibliographic Essay

This essay does not attempt to cover all writings on Ecuador, but rather focuses on those most relevant to the themes of this book.

1. Brooke Larson, "Andean Highland Peasants and the Trials of Nation Making during the Nineteenth Century," in *The Cambridge History of the Native Peoples of the Americas,* ed. Frank Salomon and Stuart B. Schwartz (Cambridge: Cambridge University Press, 1999), 691; Xavier Albó, "Andean People in the Twentieth Century, in ibid., 867. A more recent volume also fails to include essays on Ecuador. See *Indigenous Movements, Self-Representation, and the State in Latin America,* ed. Kay B. Warren and Jean E. Jackson (Austin: University of Texas Press, 2003).

2. David Bushnell, "South America," *Hispanic American Historical Review* 65, no. 4 (November 1985): 772.

3. John D. Martz, *Ecuador: Conflicting Political Culture and the Quest for Progress* (Boston: Allyn and Bacon, 1972), vii.

Bibliography

Archives

AAP/MNM	Archivo de Asistencia Pública in the Museo Nacional de Medicina
AGPC	Archivo de la Gobernación de la Provincia de Cotopaxi, Latacunga
AHN/C	Archivo Nacional de Historia, Cuenca
AJPA	Archivo de la Jefatura Política de Alausí
ANH/Q	Archivo Nacional de Historia, Quito
ANH/R	Archivo Nacional de Historia, Riobamba
APL	Archivo Palacio Legislativo
BEAEP	Biblioteca Ecuatoriana Aurelio Espinosa Pólit
IOA	Archivo del Instituto Otavaleño de Antropología

Newspapers

Atahualpa
El Comercio
El Hoy
El Nacional
Registro Oficial

Books and Articles

Abrams, Philip. "Notes on the Difficulty of Studying the State." *Journal of Historical Sociology* 1, no. 1 (March 1988): 58–89.

Ackerman, Samuel. "*El Trabajo Subsidiario*: Compulsory Labor and Taxation in 19th-Century Ecuador." PhD diss., New York University, 1977.

Adelman, Jeremy. "The Problem of Persistence in Latin American History." In *Colonial Legacies: The Problem of Persistence in Latin American History*, edited by Jeremy Adelman, 1–13. New York: Routledge, 1999.

Adrianzén, Alberto, et al. *Democracia, etnicidad y violencia política en los países andinos.* América Problema 16. Lima: Instituto Francés de Estudios Andinos; Instituto de Estudios Peruanos, 1993.

Albó, Xavier. "Andean People in the Twentieth Century." In *The Cambridge History of the Native Peoples of the Americas*. Vol. 3, *South America, part 2*, edited by Frank Salomon and Stuart B. Schwartz, 765–871. Cambridge, England, New York: Cambridge University Press, 1999.

———. "El retorno del Indio." *Revista Andina* 9, no. 2 (December 1991): 299–345.

———. "Ethnic Identity and Politics in the Central Andes: The Cases of Bolivia, Ecuador, and Peru." In *Politics in the Andes: Identity, Conflict, Reform*, edited by Jo-Marie Burt and Philip Mauceri, 17–37. Pittsburgh: University of Pittsburgh Press, 2004.

———. "From MNRistas to Kataristas to Katari." In *Resistance, Rebellion, and Consciousness in the Andean World, 18th to 20th Centuries*, edited by Steve J. Stern, 379–419. Madison: University of Wisconsin Press, 1987.

———. *Pueblos indios en la política*. Cuadernos de investigación 55. La Paz: Plural/CIPCA, 2002.

Albornoz Peralta, Osvaldo. *Ecuador: luces y sombras del liberalismo*. Quito: El Duende, 1989.

Alcina Franch, José. "El proceso de pérdida de la identidad cultural entre los indios del Ecuador." *Cuadernos Hispanoamericanos* 143, no. 428 (February 1986): 91–108.

"Alfabetización o proselitismo?" *Nueva* 72 (December 1980).

Almeida, Ilena, and Nidia Arrobo Rodas, eds. *En defensa del pluralismo y la igualdad: Los derechos de los pueblos indios y el estado*. Colección Biblioteca Abya-Yala 58. Quito: Fundación Pueblo Indio del Ecuador; Ediciones Abya-Yala, 1998.

Almeida, José, et al. *Sismo étnico en el Ecuador: varias perspectivas*. Quito: CEDIME-Ediciones Abya-Yala, 1993.

Almeida Vinueza, José. "Luchas campesinas del siglo XX (primera parte)." In *Nueva Historia del Ecuador*. Vol. 10, *Epoca republicana III: El Ecuador entre los años veinte y los sesenta*, edited by Enrique Ayala Mora, 163–86. Quito: Corporación Editora Nacional, 1990.

Altamirano Escobar, Hernán. "La identidad histórica del Estado Ecuatoriano y sus Fuerzas Armadas jamás pueden rescribirse." *Tarqui: Fuerza Terrestre* 4, no. 4 (1999): 18–21.

Álvarez Grau, Vladimiro. *El golpe detrás de los ponchos*. Guayaquil, Ecuador: Edino, 2001.

Amador, Judith, and Columba Vértiz. "El INI, convertido en oficina de gobierno." *Proceso*, no. 1387 (June 1, 2003).

Anaya, S. James. *Indigenous Peoples in International Law*. 2d ed. New York: Oxford University Press, 2004.

Anderson, Benedict. *Imagined Communities: Reflections on the Origin and Spread of Nationalism*, Revised and extended edition. New York: Verso, 1991.

Andolina, Robert. "Between Local Authenticity and Global Accountability: The Ayllu Movement in Contemporary Bolivia." In *Beyond the Lost Decade: Indigenous movements, development, and democracy in Latin America*, edited by José Antonio Lucero. Princeton: Princeton University Press, 2003.

———. "Colonial Legacies and Plurinational Imaginaries: Indigenous Movement Politics in Ecuador and Bolivia." PhD diss., University of Minnesota, 1999.

———. "The Sovereign and Its Shadow: Constituent Assembly and Indigenous Movement in Ecuador." *Journal of Latin American Studies* 35, no. 4 (November 2003): 721–50.

Andrade, Xavier, and Fredy Rivera. "El movimiento campesino e indígena en el último período: fases, actores y contenidos políticos." In *Nueva Historia del Ecuador*. Vol. 11, *Epoca republicana III: El Ecuador en el último período*, edited by Enrique Ayala Mora, 257–82. Quito: Corporación Editora Nacional, 1991.

André, Eduardo. "América equinoccial (Colombia—Ecuador)." In *América pintoresca: Descripcion de viages al nuevo continente por los mas modernos exploradores Carlos Wiener, Doctor Crevaux, D. Charnay, etc., etc.* Barcelona: Montaner y Simon, 1884.

Archondo, Rafael. "La CSUTCB con alas de Mallku: Coloquio sobre sindicalismo agrario." *Tinkazos* 2, no. 3 (1999): 72–84.

Arcos, Carlos, and Carlos Marchán. "Apuntes para una discusión sobre los cambios en la estructura agraria serrana." *Revista Ciencias Sociales* 2, no. 5 (1978): 13–64.

Arpasi, Paulina. "Entrevista por Juan Pina." *Perfiles del Siglo XXI*, no. 101. December 2001. http://www.revistaperfiles.com.

Arze Aguirre, René Danilo. *Guerra y conflictos sociales: el caso rural boliviano durante la campaña del Chaco*. Serie Movimientos sociales. La Paz, Bolivia: Centro de Estudios de la Realidad Económica y Social, 1987.

Asad, Talal. "Are There Histories of Peoples without Europe?" *Comparative Studies in Society and History* 29, no. 3 (July 1987): 594–607.

Assies, Willem, Gemma van der Haar, and André Hoekema, eds. *The Challenge of Diversity: Indigenous Peoples and Reform of the State in Latin America*. Thela Thesis Latin America series. Amsterdam: Thela Thesis, 2000.

Avendaño, Joaquín de. *Imagen del Ecuador: economía y sociedad, vistas por un viajero del siglo XIX*, Introducción y organización documental por Leoncio López-Ocon. Colección Ecuador, testimonios de autores extranjeros, 6. Quito: Corporación Editora Nacional, 1985 [1858].

Ayala Mora, Enrique. "El municipio en el siglo xix." *Procesos: Revista Ecuatoriana de Historia* 1, no. 2 (1991): 69–86.

———. "El período garciano: panorama histórico (1860–1875)." In *Nueva Historia del Ecuador*. Vol. 7, *Epoca republicana I*, edited by Enrique Ayala Mora, 197–235. Quito: Corporación Editora Nacional, 1983.

———. *Historia de la revolución liberal ecuatoriana*. Colección Temas, vol. 5. Quito: Corporación Editora Nacional, 1994.

———. *Lucha política y origen de los partidos en Ecuador*. 4th ed. Biblioteca de Ciencias Sociales, vol. 4. Quito: Corporación Editora Nacional, 1988.

———. *Resumen de historia del Ecuador*. Biblioteca General de Cultura, vol. 1. Quito: Corporación Editora Nacional, 1993.

Ayala Mora, Enrique, ed. *Nueva Historia del Ecuador*. 15 vols. Quito: Corporación Editora Nacional, 1983–1995.

Ayala Mora, Enrique, et al. *Pueblos indios, estado y derecho*. Biblioteca de Ciencias Sociales 36. Quito: Corporación Editora Nacional, 1993.

Bakan, Abigail B., and Daiva Kristina Stasiulis. *Not One of the Family: Foreign Domestic Workers in Canada*. Toronto: University of Toronto Press, 1997.

Barre, Marie-Chantal. *Ideologías indigenistas y movimientos indios*. 2d ed. Mexico City: Siglo Veintiuno Editores, 1985.

Barrera, Augusto. *Acción colectiva y crisis política: el movimiento indígena ecuatoriano en la década de los noventa*. Quito: Centro de Investigaciones CIUDAD. OSAL. Abya-Yala, 2001.

———. *Entre la utopía y el desencanto: Pachakutik en el gobierno de Gutiérrez*. Quito: Editorial Planeta del Ecuador, S.A., 2004.

———. "Nada sólo para los indios. A propósito del último levantamiento indígena," *Observatorio Social de América Latina* 2, no. 4 (June 2001): 89–92.

Barril, Alex. "Desarrollo tecnológico, producción agropecuaria y relaciones de producción en la sierra ecuatoriana." In *Ecuador: cambios en el agro serrano*, edited by Miguel Murmis et al., 207–48. Quito: Facultad Latinoamericana de Ciencias Sociales (FLACSO)–Centro de Planificación y Estudios Sociales (CEPLAES), 1980.

———. "Modernización agropecuaria y economías campesinas." In *Tecnología agropecuaria y economías campesinas*, 57–78. Quito: Fundaciones Brethren-Unida/CEPLAES, 1978.

Barsky, Osvaldo. "Ideologías terratenientes en los procesos de modernización de la sierra ecuatoriana." In *Terratenientes y desarrollo capitalista en el agro*, edited by Miguel Murmis, José Bengoa, and Osvaldo Barsky, 91–149. Quito: Ediciones CEPLAES, 1978.

———. "Iniciativa terrateniente en la reestructuración de las relaciones sociales en la sierra ecuatoriana, 1959–1964." *Revista Ciencias Sociales* 2, no. 5 (1978): 74–126.

———. "Los terratenientes serranos y el debate político previo al dictado de la ley de reforma agraria de 1964 en el Ecuador." In *Ecuador: cambios en el agro serrano*, edited by Miguel Murmis et al., 133–205. Quito: Facultad Latinoamericana de Ciencias Sociales (FLACSO)—Centro de Planificación y Estudios Sociales (CEPLAES), 1980.

———. *La reforma agraria ecuatoriana*. 2d ed. Biblioteca de Ciencias Sociales 3. Quito: Corporación Editora Nacional, 1988.

Barsky, Osvaldo, and Gustavo Cosse. *Tecnología y cambio social: Las haciendas lecheras del Ecuador*. Quito: FLACSO, 1981.

Barsky, Osvaldo, et al. *Políticas agrarias, colonización y desarrollo rural en Ecuador: reflexiones sobre el proyecto de desarrollo rural integral Quinindé-Malimpia-Nueva Jerusalem*. Quito: Ediciones CEPLAES, 1982.

Bartra, Armando. *Los herederos de Zapata: Movimientos campesinos posrevolucionarios en México, 1920–1980*. Colección Problemas de México. Mexico City: Ediciones Era, 1985.

Baud, Michiel. "Campesinos indígenas contra el Estado. La huelga de los indígenas de Azuay, 1920/21." *Procesos: Revista Ecuatoriana de Historia* 4 (1993): 41–72.

———. "The *Huelga de los Indígenas* in Cuenca, Ecuador (1920–1921)." In *Indigenous Revolts in Chiapas and the Andean Highlands*, edited by Kevin Gosner and Arij Ouweneel, 217–39. Amsterdam: CEDLA, 1996.

———. *Intelectuales y sus utopías: Indigenismo y la imaginación de América Latina*. Amsterdam: CEDLA, 2003.

———. "*Libertad de Servidumbre*: Indigenista Ideology and Social Mobilization in Late Nineteenth Century Ecuador." In *Nation Building in Nineteenth Century Latin America: Dilemmas and Conflicts*, edited by Hans-Joachim König and Marianne Wiesebron, 233–53. Leiden: CNWS, 1998.

Baud, Michiel, and Rosanne Rutten, eds. *Popular Intellectuals and Social Movements:*

Framing Protest in Asia, Africa, and Latin America. International Review of Social History 12. Cambridge: Cambridge University Press, 2004.

Beattie, Peter M. *The Tribute of Blood: Army, Honor, Race, and Nation in Brazil, 1864–1945*. Latin America Otherwise. Durham: Duke University Press, 2001.

Becker, Marc. "Class and Ethnicity in the Canton of Cayambe: The Roots of Ecuador's Modern Indian Movement." PhD diss., University of Kansas, 1997.

———. "Comunas and Indigenous Protest in Cayambe, Ecuador." *The Americas* 55, no. 4 (April 1999): 531–59.

———. "Indigenous Communists and Urban Intellectuals in Cayambe, Ecuador (1926–1944)." *International Review of Social History*. Supplement 12, no. 49 (2004): 41–64.

———. "Una Revolución Comunista Indígena: Rural Protest Movements in Cayambe, Ecuador." *Rethinking Marxism* 10, no. 4 (Winter 1998): 34–51.

Belote, Linda Smith, and Jim Belote. "Drain from the Bottom: Individual Ethnic Identity Change in Southern Ecuador." *Social Forces* 63, no. 1 (September 1984): 24–50.

Benítez, Lilyan, and Alicia Garcés. *Culturas ecuatorianas: ayer y hoy*. 7th ed. Quito: Ediciones Abya-Yala, 1993.

Blanksten, George I. *Ecuador: Constitutions and Caudillos*. University of California Publications in Political Science 3, no. 1. Berkeley and Los Angeles: University of California Press, 1951.

Bonilla, Heraclio, ed. *Los Andes en la encrucijada: indios, comunidades y estado en el siglo XIX*. Quito: Ediciones Libri Mundi–Facultad Latinoamericana de Ciencias Sociales (FLACSO), 1991.

Booth, John A. *The End and the Beginning: The Nicaraguan Revolution*. 2d ed. Boulder, CO: Westview Press, 1985.

Bossano, Guillermo. *Evolución del derecho constitucional ecuatoriano*. 2d ed. Quito: Editorial Casa de la Cultura Ecuatoriana, 1975.

Bourgeois, Philippe. "Masculinidades lumpenizadas: dos perspectivas etnográficas de vendedores de crack puertorriqueños y heroinómanos desamparados blancos." Paper presented at the Seminario Internacional: Masculinidades en América Latina, Quito, April, 23–24, 2002.

Bretón, Víctor. *Capitalismo, reforma agraria y organización comunal en los Andes: una introducción al caso ecuatoriano*. Espai/temps 29. Lleida, Espanya: Edicions de la Universitat de Lleida, 1997.

———. "Los paradigmas de la 'nueva' ruralidad a debate: El proyecto de desarrollo de los pueblos indígenas y negros del Ecuador." *European Review of Latin American and Caribbean Studies* 78 (April 2005): 7–30.

Bretón, Víctor, and Francisco García, eds. *Estado, etnicidad y movimientos sociales en América Latina: Ecuador en crisis*. Barcelona: Ausirs Editorial, S.A., 2003.

Bromley, Rosemary D. F., and R. J. Bromley. "The Debate on Sunday Markets in Nineteenth-Century Ecuador." *Journal of Latin American Studies* 7, no. 1 (May 1975): 85–108.

Brownrigg, Leslie Ann. "Variaciones del parentesco canari." In *Temas sobre la continuidad y adaptación cultural ecuatoriana*, edited by Marcelo Fernando Naranjo, Jose L.

Pereira V., and Norman E. Whitten Jr. Quito: Ediciones de la Universidad Católica, 1984.

Brysk, Alison. *From Tribal Village to Global Village: Indian Rights and International Relations in Latin America.* Stanford: Stanford University Press, 2000.

Buechler, Hans C., and Judith-Maria Buechler. *The Bolivian Aymara.* Case Studies in Cultural Anthropology. New York: Holt, Rinehart, and Winston, 1971.

Buitron, Aníbal, and Bárbara Salisbury Buitron. *Condiciones de vida y trabajo del campesino de la provincia de Pichincha.* Quito: Instituto Nacional de Previsión, Dept. de Propaganda, 1947.

Burguete, Araceli. *Chiapas: Cronología de un etnocidio reciente (Represión política a los indios, 1974–1987).* Mexico City: Academia Mexicana de Derechos Humanos A.C., n.d.

Burns, E. Bradford. *The Poverty of Progress: Latin America in the Nineteenth Century.* Berkeley: University of California Press, 1980.

Bushnell, David. "South America." *Hispanic American Historical Review* 65, no. 4 (November 1985): 767–87.

Bustamante, Fernando. "Y después de la insurrección qué . . . ?" *Ecuador Debate* 49 (April 2000): 43–56.

Cadena, Marisol de la. *Indigenous Mestizos: The Politics of Race and Culture in Cuzco, 1919–1991.* Latin America Otherwise. Durham: Duke University Press, 2000.

———. "Reconstructing Race: Racism, Culture and Mestizaje in Latin America." *NACLA Report on the Americas* 34, no. 6 (May/June 2001): 15–23.

Calla Ortega, Ricardo. "Hallu hayllisa huti. Identificación étnica y procesos políticos en Bolivia." In *Democracia, etnicidad y violencia política en los países andinos*, edited by Alberto Adrianzén et al., 57–81. Lima: Instituto Francés de Estudios Andinos; Instituto de Estudios Peruanos, 1993.

Cano, Arturo. "La Conaie, gran ausente en la lucha para deponer a Lucio Gutiérrez." *La Jornada,* April 26, 2005. http://www.jornada.unam.mx/2005/04/26/030n1mun.php (accessed April 27, 2005).

Cárdenas Reyes, María Cristina. *Libertad y liberación en la Obra de José Peralta.* Quito: Fundación Friedrich Naumann, 1989.

Casagrande, Joseph B., and Arthur R. Piper. "La transformación estructural de una parroquia rural en las tierras altas del Ecuador." *América Indígena* 29, no. 4 (October 1969): 1039–64.

Cevallos, Pedro Fermín. *Geografía de la República del Ecuador.* Lima: Imprenta del estado, 1888.

———. *Resumen de la historia del Ecuador.* Guayaquil: Imprenta de la Nación, 1889.

Chiriboga, Manuel, and Fredy Rivera. "Elecciones de Enero de 1988 y participación indígena." *Ecuador Debate* 17 (March 1989): 181–221.

Chiriboga V., Manuel. *Jornaleros y gran propietarios en 135 años de exportación cacaotera, 1790–1925.* Quito: Consejo Provincial de Pichincha, 1980.

———. "La reforma agraria ecuatoriana y los cambios en la distribución de la propiedad rural agrícola, 1974–1985." In *Transformaciones agrarias en el Ecuador*, edited by Pierre Gondard et al., 39–57. Quito: CEDIG, 1988.

Cisneros Cisneros, César. *Demografía y estadística sobre el indio ecuatoriano.* Quito: Tall. Graf. Nacionales, 1948.

Clark, A. Kim. "Indians, the State and Law: Public Works and the Struggle to Control Labor in Liberal Ecuador." *Journal of Historical Sociology* 7, no. 1 (1994): 49–72.

———. "La medida de la diferencia: Las imágenes indigenistas de los indios serranos en el Ecuador (1920s a 1940s)." In *Ecuador racista: Imágenes e identidades*, edited by Emma Cervone and Fredy Rivera V., 11–27. Quito: FLACSO, Sede Ecuador, 1999.

———. "Race, 'Culture,' and Mestizaje: The Statistical Construction of the Ecuadorian Nation, 1930–1950." *Journal of Historical Sociology* 11, no. 2 (June 1998): 185–211.

———. "Racial Ideologies and the Quest for National Development: Debating the Agrarian Problem in Ecuador (1930–50)." *Journal of Latin American Studies* 30, no. 2 (May 1998): 373–93.

———. *The Redemptive Work: Railway and Nation in Ecuador, 1895–1930*. Latin-American Silhouettes. Wilmington, DE: SR Books, 1998.

Clifford, James. "Indigenous Articulations." *Contemporary Pacific* 13, no. 2 (2001): 468–90.

———. "Taking Identity Politics Seriously: 'The Contradictory, Stony Ground . . .'" In *Without Guarantees: In Honour of Stuart Hall*, edited by Paul Gilroy et al. London: Verso, 2000.

Collier, John, Jr., and Aníbal Buitron. *The Awakening Valley*. Chicago: University of Chicago Press, 1949.

Collins, Jennifer. "Linking Movement and Electoral Politics: Ecuador's Indigenous Movement and the rise of Pachakutik." In *Politics in the Andes: Identity, Conflict, Reform*, edited by Jo-Marie Burt and Philip Mauceri, 38–57. Pittsburgh: University of Pittsburgh Press, 2004.

Colloredo-Mansfeld, Rudi. "'Don't Be Lazy, Don't Lie, Don't Steal': Community Justice in the Neoliberal Andes." *American Ethnologist* 29, no. 3 (August 2002): 637–62.

———. *The Native Leisure Class: Consumption and Cultural Creativity in the Andes*. Chicago: University of Chicago Press, 1999.

Comandancia General del Ejército. *Materias Generales: Historia del Ecuador*. Quito: Academia de Guerra, 1981.

Comisión por la Defensa de los Derechos Humanos (CDDH). *El levantamiento indígena y la cuestión nacional*. Quito: Abya Yala–Comisión por la Defensa de los Derechos Humanos, 1990.

Conaghan, Catherine M. "Politicians against Parties: Discord and Disconnection in Ecuador's Party System." In *Building Democratic Institutions: Party Systems in Latin America*, edited by Scott Mainwaring and Timothy R. Scully, 434–58. Stanford: Stanford University Press, 1995.

Conaghan, Catherine M., and James M. Malloy. *Unsettling Statecraft: Democracy and Neoliberalism in the Central Andes*. Pitt Latin American Series. Pittsburgh: University of Pittsburgh Press, 1994.

Confederación de Nacionalidades Indígenas de la Amazonía Ecuatoriana (CONFENIAE). "Estatuto de la Confederación de Nacionalidades Indígenas de la Amazonía Ecuatoriana CONFENIAE." Puyo, Ecuador. 1980.

Confederación de Nacionalidades Indígenas del Ecuador (CONAIE). *Las nacionalidades indígenas en el Ecuador: Nuestro proceso organizativo*. 2d ed. 1992: 500 años de resistencia india, no. 0. Quito: Ediciones Tincui–Abya-Yala, 1989.

Conferencia de Cabecillas Indios. "Indicaciones." *Ñucanchic Allpa* 1, no. 8 (March 17, 1936): 2–3.

Congreso Nacional Indígena. "Declaración Final; Octava Asamblea Nacional." November 2001. http://www.laneta.apc.org/cni/8an-decf.htm.

"'Constitutional Coup' by Congress Ousts Gutiérrez on Wave of Popular Protests." *Latin American Weekly Report*. WR-05–16 (April 26, 2005): 3.

Corkill, David, and David Cubitt. *Ecuador: Fragile Democracy*. London: Latin American Bureau, 1988.

Cornejo Menacho, Diego, ed. *INDIOS: Una reflexión sobre el levantamiento indígena de 1990*. 2d ed. Quito: ILDIS, 1992.

———. *Los indios y el estado-país; pluriculturalidad y multietnicidad en el Ecuador: contribuciones al debate*. Quito: Ediciones Abya-Yala, 1993.

Correa, Rafael. "La política económica del Gobierno de Lucio Gutiérrez." *Íconos* 16 (May 2003): 6–10.

Corrigan, Philip Richard D., and Derek Sayer. *The Great Arch: English State Formation as Cultural Revolution*. Oxford and New York: Blackwell, 1985.

Cosse, Gustavo. "Reflexiones acerca del estado, el proceso político y la política agraria en el caso ecuatoriano." In *Ecuador: cambios en el agro serrano*, edited by Miguel Murmis et al., 387–436. Quito: Facultad Latinoamericana de Ciencias Sociales (FLACSO)–Centro de Planificación y Estudios Sociales (CEPLAES), 1980.

Costales, Piedad Peñaherrera de, and Alfredo Costales Samaniego. "Historia social del Ecuador, Tomo I: El concertaje de indios y manumisión de esclavos." *Llacta* 6, no. 17 (1964).

Costales Samaniego, Alfredo. *Fernando Daquilema, último guaminga*. 2d ed. *Llacta* 16. Quito: Instituto Ecuatoriano de Antropología y Geografía, 1963.

Crain, Mary. "The Social Construction of National Identity in Highland Ecuador." *Anthropological Quarterly* 63, no. 1 (January 1990): 43–59.

Crespi, Muriel. "Changing Power Relations: The Rise of Peasant Unions on Traditional Ecuadorian Haciendas." *Anthropological Quarterly* 44, no. 4 (October 1971): 223–40.

———. "When Indios Become Cholos: Some Consequences of the Changing Ecuadorian Hacienda." In *The New Ethnicity, Perspectives from Ethnology: 1973 Proceedings of the American Ethnological Society*, edited John W. Bennett, 148–66. St. Paul, MN: West Publishing Co., 1975.

Cuadra, José de la. *El montuvio ecuatoriano (ensayo de presentación)*. Quito: Instituto de Investigaciones Económicas de la Universidad Central del Ecuador, 1937.

Cueva, Agustín. "El Ecuador de 1925 a 1960." In *Nueva Historia del Ecuador*. Vol. 10, *Epoca republicana III: El Ecuador entre los años veinte y los sesenta*, edited by Enrique Ayala Mora, 86–121. Quito: Corporación Editora Nacional, 1990.

———. *The Process of Political Domination in Ecuador*. New Brunswick, NJ: Transaction Books, 1982.

Dandler, Jorge, and Juan Torrico A. "From the National Indigenous Congress to the Ayopaya Rebellion: Bolivia, 1945–1947." In *Resistance, Rebellion, and Consciousness in the Andean World, 18th to 20th Centuries*, edited by Steve J. Stern, 334–78. Madison: University of Wisconsin Press, 1987.

Dávalos, Pablo. "'De paja de páramo sembraremos el mundo': Izquierda, utopía y movimiento indígena en Ecuador." In *La nueva izquierda en América Latina*, edited by César A. Rodríguez Garavito, Patrick S. Barrett, and Daniel Chávez, 359–403. Bogotá: Grupo Editorial Norma, 2005.

De la Peña, Guillermo. "Discourses on Ethnic Citizenship in Mexico." Wednesday Seminar Series, Center for U.S.-Mexican Studies at the University of California, San Diego, 1996.

Deas, Malcolm. "Colombia, Ecuador and Venezuela, c. 1880–1930." In *The Cambridge History of Latin America*. Vol. 5, *C. 1870 to 1930*, edited by Leslie Bethell, 641–82. Cambridge: Cambridge University Press, 1986.

Deere, Carmen Diana. *Household and Class Relations: Peasants and Landlords in Northern Peru*. Berkeley: University of California Press, 1990.

Degregori, Carlos Ivan. "Ethnicity and Democratic Governability in Latin America: Reflections from Two Central Andean Countries." In *Fault Lines of Democracy in Post-Transition Latin America*, edited by Felipe Agüero and Jeffrey Stark, 203–34. Coral Gables, FL, Boulder, CO: North-South Center Press/University of Miami, 1998.

———. "Identidad étnica: movimientos sociales y participación política en el Perú." In *Democracia, etnicidad y violencia política en los países andinos*, edited by Alberto Adrianzén et al., 113–33. Lima: Instítuto Francés de Estudios Andinos; Instituto de Estudios Peruanos, 1993.

Demélas, Marie-Danielle. *L'invention politique. Bolivie, Equateur, Pérou au XIXe siècle*. Paris: Editions Recherche sur les civilisations, 1992.

Descola, Philippe. "From Scattered to Nucleated Settlement: A Process of Socioeconomic Change among the Achuar." In *Cultural Transformations and Ethnicity in Modern Ecuador*, edited by Norman E. Whitten Jr., 614–46. Urbana: University of Illinois Press, 1981.

"Despierta el gigante." *Vistazo*, no. 550 (July 15, 1990).

Dieterich, Heinz. *La cuarta vía al poder: el 21 de enero desde una perspectiva latinamericana*. Quito: Editorial Abya Yala, 2000.

Dirección de Movilización. *Borrador de la planificación de la Dirección de Movilización del Comando Conjunto de las Fuerzas Armadas*. Internal document, 1993.

Eberhart, Christophe. *El campesino de Chimborazo: Situación actual y perspectivas*. Quito: Central Ecuatoriana de Servicios Agrícolas, 1997.

Ecuador. *Código civil de la Republica del Ecuador*. Quito: Imprenta de los Húerfanos de Valencia, 1860.

Ecuador. Dirección Nacional de Estadística. *Ecuador en cifras, 1938 a 1942*. Quito: Impr. del Ministerio de Hacienda, 1944.

Ecuador. División de Estadística y Censos. *Primer censo agropecuario nacional: resumen de los principales datos preliminares, 1954*. Quito: República del Ecuador, Banco Central del Ecuador: Ministerio de Economía, Banco Nacional de Fomento, 1955.

———. *Primer censo de población del Ecuador, 1950*. Quito: Tall. Graf. de la Dirección, 1954.

Ecuarunari. *Historia de la nacionalidad y los pueblos quichuas del Ecuador*. Quito: Ecuarunari, FUDEC, ILDIS, CODENPE, 1998.

Egas Egas, Edison. *28 de mayo de 1944: la gloriosa o la revolución traicionada y la constitución de 1945*. Quito: Departamento de Publicaciones de la Facultad de Filosofía, Letras y Ciencias de la Educación, 1992.

Enloe, Cynthia. "Beyond Rambo: Women and the Varieties of Militarized Masculinity." In *Women and the Military System*, edited by Eva Isaksson, 71–93. New York: St. Martin's, 1988.

Erazo, Juliet. "Constructing Autonomy: Indigenous Organizatons, Governance, and Land Use in the Ecuadorian Amazon, 1964–2001." PhD diss., University of Michigan, 2003.

Escobar, Arturo. *Encountering Development: The Making and Unmaking of the Third World*. Princeton: Princeton University Press, 1995.

Espinosa, Roque. "Hacienda, concertaje y comunidad en el Ecuador." *Cultura* 7, no. 19 (1984): 135–209.

Exposición del Ministro de Hacienda y Relaciones Interiores . . . a las cámaras legislativas, 1867. Quito: Imprenta Nacional, 1867.

Eyzaguirre, José Ignacio Víctor. *Los intereses católicos en América*. París: Librería de Garnier Hermanos, 1859.

Federación de Centros Shuar. *Federación de Centros Shuar: solución original a un problema actual*. Sucúa, Ecuador: La Federación, 1976.

Federación Ecuatoriana de Indios. *Estatutos de la Federación Ecuatoriana de Indios*. Guayaquil: Editorial Claridad, 1945.

FEINE. "FEINE: Una esperanza en el camino." *Informativo Amauta* 1 (March 2001): 1–5.

Field, Les W. "Who are the Indians? Reconceptualizing Indigenous Identity, Resistance, and the Role of Social Science in Latin America." *Latin American Research Review* 29, no. 3 (1994): 237–48.

Flores Recalde, José. *Conscriptos . . . Para qué?* Quito: Editorial Belén, 1983.

Fock, Niels. "Ethnicity and Alternative Identification: An Example from Cañar." In *Cultural Transformations and Ethnicity in Modern Ecuador*, edited by Norman E. Whitten Jr., 402–19. Urbana: University of Illinois Press, 1981.

Foote, Nicola. "Race, State and Nation in Early Twentieth Century Ecuador." *Nations and Nationalism* 12, no. 2 (April 2006): 261–78.

Foucault, Michel. "Governmentality." In *The Foucault Effect: Studies in Governmentality: with Two Lectures by and an Interview with Michel Foucault*, edited by Graham Burchell, Colin Gordon, and Peter Miller, 87–104. Chicago: University of Chicago Press, 1991.

———. "The Subject and Power." In *Michel Foucault: Beyond Structuralism and Hermeneutics*. 2d ed, edited by Hubert L Dreyfus, Paul Rabinow, and Michel Foucault. Chicago: University of Chicago Press, 1983.

Fox, Vicente. Office of the Presidency. http://nt.presidencia.gob.mx/ (accessed March 15, 2005).

Freile-Granizo, Juan. *Resúmenes de actas republicanas, cabildo de Otavalo, siglo XIX*. Colección Pendoneros: Serie Historia/Instituto Otavaleño de Antropología 24. Otavalo: Instituto Otavaleño de Antropología, 1980.

Fuentealba, Gerardo. "La sociedad indígena en las primera décadas de la república: continuidades coloniales y cambios republicanos." In *Nueva Historia del Ecuador*. Vol. 8,

Epoca republicana II: Perspectiva general del siglo XIX, edited by Enrique Ayala Mora, 45–77. Quito: Corporación Editora Nacional, 1983.

Gallardo Román, José. "Nación ecuatoriana o plurinacionalidad?" *Revista de Las Fuerzas Armadas del Ecuador* 123 (1998): 19–25.

Gamarra, Eduardo, and James Malloy. "The Patrimonial Dynamics of Party Politics in Bolivia." In *Building Democratic Institutions: Party Systems in Latin America*, edited by Scott Mainwaring and Timothy R. Scully, 399–433. Stanford: Stanford University Press, 1995.

Gamio, Manuel. *Forjando patria*. 2d ed. Mexico City: Editorial Porrúa, 1960 [1916].

García, María Elena. *Making Indigenous Citizens: Identities, Education, and Multicultural Development in Peru*. Stanford: Stanford University Press, 2005.

García, María Elena, and José Antonio Lucero. "Authenticating Indians and Movements: Interrogating Indigenous Authenticity, Social Movements, and Fieldwork in Contemporary Peru." In *From Purity of Blood to Indigenous Social Movements*, edited by Laura Gotkowitz. In preparation.

———. "'Un País Sin Indígenas'?: Re-thinking Indigenous Politics in Peru." In *The Struggle for Indigenous Rights in Latin America*, edited by Nancy Grey Postero and Leon Zamosc, 158–88. Brighton: Sussex Academic Press, 2004.

Garfield, Seth. *Indigenous Struggle at the Heart of Brazil: State Policy, Frontier Expansion, and the Xavante Indians, 1937–1988*. Durham: Duke University Press, 2001.

Gelles, Paul. "Andean Culture, Indigenous Identity, and the State in Peru." In *The Politics of Ethnicity: Indigenous Peoples in Latin American States*, edited by David Maybury-Lewis, 239–66. Cambridge: David Rockefeller Center for Latin American Studies, Harvard University, 2002.

Giarracca, Norma, ed. *Una nueva ruralidad en América Latina?* Colección Grupos de Trabajo de CLACSO. Buenos Aires: Consejo Latinoamericano de Ciencias Sociales and Agencia Sueca de Desarrollo Internacional, 2001.

Gill, Lesley. "Creating Citizens, Making Men: The Military and Masculinity in Bolivia." *Cultural Anthropology* 12, no. 4 (1997): 527–50.

Girón, Sergio Enrique. *La revolución de mayo*. Quito: Editorial Atahualpa, 1945.

Goffman, Erving. *Asylums: Essays on the Social Situation of Mental Patients and Other Inmates*. Garden City, NY: Anchor Books, 1961.

González, Iván, and Paciente Vázquez. "Movilizaciones campesinas en Azuay y Cañar durante el siglo XIX." *Revista del Archivo Nacional de Historia, Sección del Azuay*, no. 3 (1981): 38–91.

Gramsci, Antonio. *Selections from the Prison Notebooks*. Translated and edited by Quintin Hoare and Geoffrey Nowell Smith. New York: International Publishers, 1971.

Greene, Shane. "Getting Over the Andes: The Geo-Eco-Politics of Indigenous Movements in Peru's Twenty-First-Century Inca Empire." *Journal of Latin American Studies* 38, no. 2 (May 2006): 327–54.

Guardino, Peter F. *Peasants, Politics, and the Formation of Mexico's National State: Guerrero, 1800–1857*. Stanford: Stanford University Press, 1996.

Guerrero, Andrés. "The Administration of Dominated Populations Under a Regime of Citizenship: The Case of Postcolonial Ecuador." Paper presented at the annual meeting of the Latin American Studies Association, 1999.

———. “The Construction of a Ventriloquist’s Image: Liberal Discourse and the ‘Miserable Indian Race’ in Late 19th-Century Ecuador.” *Journal of Latin American Studies* 29, no. 3 (October 1997): 555–90.

———. “Curagas y tenientes políticos: La ley de la costumbre y la ley del estado (Otavalo 1830–1875).” *Revista Andina* 7, no. 2 (no. 14) (1989): 321–66.

———. “El levantamiento nacional de 1994: discurso y representación política (Ecuador).” *Boletín Americanista* 50 (2000): 123–51.

———. “La desintegración de la administración étnica en el Ecuador.” In *Sismo étnico en el Ecuador: varias perspectivas*, edited by José Almeida et al., 91–112. Quito: CEDIME–Ediciones Abya-Yala, 1993.

———. *La hacienda precapitalista y la clase terrateniente en América Latina y su inserción en el modo de producción capitalista: el caso ecuatoriano*. Quito: Universidad Central, 1975.

———. *Haciendas, capital y lucha de clases andina: disolución de la hacienda serrana y lucha política en los años 1960–64*. 2d ed. Colección Ecuador/hoy 10. Quito: Editorial El Conejo, 1984.

———. “Una imagen ventrilocua: el discurso liberal de la ‘desgraciada raza indígena’ a fines del siglo XIX.” In *Imágenes e imagineros: representaciones de los indígenas ecuatorianos, siglos XIX y XX*, edited by Blanca Muratorio, 197–252. Quito: Facultad Latinoamericana de Ciencias Sociales-Sede Ecuador, 1994.

———. *La semántica de la dominación: el concertaje de indios*. Quito: Ediciones Libri Mundi, 1991.

Guerrero Cazar, Fernando, and Pablo Ospina Peralta. *El poder de la comunidad: Ajuste estructural y movimiento indígena en los Andes ecuatorianos*. Becas de investigación. Buenos Aires: CLACSO, 2003.

Gustafson, Bret. “Paradoxes of Liberal Indigenism: Indigenous Movements, State Processes, and Intercultural Reform in Bolivia.” In *The Politics of Ethnicity: Indigenous Peoples in Latin American States*, edited by David Maybury-Lewis, 267–306. Cambridge: David Rockefeller Center for Latin American Studies, Harvard University, 2002.

Hale, Charles A. “Political and Social Ideas in Latin America, 1870–1930.” In *The Cambridge History of Latin America*. Vol. 4, *c. 1870–1930*, edited by Leslie Bethell, 367–441. Cambridge: Cambridge University Press, 1986.

Hale, Charles R. “Does Multiculturalism Menace? Governance, Cultural Rights and the Politics of Identity in Guatemala.” *Journal of Latin American Studies* 34, no. 3 (August 2002): 485–524.

———. *Resistance and Contradiction: Miskitu Indians and the Nicaraguan State, 1894–1987*. Stanford: Stanford University Press, 1994.

———. “Rethinking Indigenous Politics in the Era of the ‘Indio Permitido.’” *NACLA Report on the Americas* 38, no. 2 (September/October 2004): 16–21.

Hall, Stuart. “Then and Now: A Re-evaluation of the New Left.” In *Out of Apathy: Voices of the New Left Thirty Years On: Papers Based on the Conference Organized by the Oxford University Socialist Discussion Group*, edited by Oxford University Socialist Discussion Group. London and New York: Verso, 1989.

———. “On Post-Modernism and Articulation: An Interview with Stuart Hall.” In *Criti-*

cal Dialogues in Cultural Studies, edited by David Morley and Kuan-Hsing Chen. New York: Routledge, 1996 [1986].

Hamerly, Michael T. *Historia social y economica de la antigua Provincia de Guayaquil, 1763–1842*. Publicaciones del Archivo Historico del Guayas: colección monografica 3. Guayaquil: Archivo Histórico del Guayas, 1973.

Handelsman, Michael. *Culture and Customs of Ecuador*. Latin America and the Caribbean. Westport, CT: Greenwood Press, 2000.

Hanley, Sarah. "Engendering the State: Family Formation and State Building in Early Modern France." *French Historical Studies* 16, no. 1 (Spring 1989): 4–27.

Hannum, Hurst. *Autonomy, Sovereignty, and Self-determination: The Accommodation of Conflicting Rights*. Philadelphia: University of Pennsylvania Press, 1990.

Hansen, Thomas Blom, and Finn Stepputat, eds. *States of Imagination: Ethnographic Explorations of the Postcolonial State*. Politics, History, and Culture. Durham: Duke University Press, 2001.

Harner, Michael J. *The Jívaro, People of the Sacred Waterfalls*. Garden City, NY: Doubleday/Natural History Press, 1972.

Haro Ayerve, Patricio. *La influencia del poder militar en la historia del Ecuador*. Quito: Ministerio de Defensa Nacional, 1997.

Harris, Olivia. "Complementarity and Conflict: An Andean View of Women and Men." In *Sex and Age as Principles of Social Differentiation*, edited by J. S. La Fontaine. London and New York: Academic Press, 1978.

———. "Ethnic Identity and Market Relations: Indians and Mestizos in the Andes." In *Ethnicity, Markets, and Migration in the Andes: At the Crossroads of History and Anthropology*, edited by Brooke Larson and Olivia Harris, 351–90. Durham: Duke University Press, 1995.

Haskett, Robert. *Indigenous Rulers. An Ethnohistory of Town Government in Colonial Cuernavaca*. Albuquerque: University of New Mexico Press, 1991.

Hassaurek, Friedrich. *Four Years among Spanish-Americans*. New York: Hurd and Houghton, 1867.

———. *Four Years Among the Ecuadorians*. Edited and with an introduction by C. Harvey Gardiner. Latin American Travel. Carbondale: Southern Illinois University Press, 1967.

Healy, Kevin. *Llamas, Weavings, and Organic Chocolate: Multicultural Grassroots Development in the Andes and Amazon of Bolivia*. Notre Dame, IN: University of Notre Dame, 2001.

Hendricks, Janet. "Symbolic Counterhegemony among the Ecuadorian Shuar." In *Nation-States and Indians in Latin America*, edited by Greg Urban and Joel Sherzer, 53–71. Austin: University of Texas Press, 1991.

Hepple, Leslie W. "Metaphor, Geopolitical Discourse, and the Military in South America." In *Writing Worlds: Discourse, Text, and Metaphor in the Representation of Landscape*, edited by Trevor J. Barnes and James S. Duncan. London and New York: Routledge, 1992.

Hernández Castillo, Rosalva Aída. "Indigenous Law and Identity Politics in Mexico: Indigenous Men´s and Women´s Perspective for a Multicultural Nation." *Political and Legal Anthropology Review* 25, no. 1 (2002): 90–110.

Hernández Díaz, José, et al., eds. *21 de enero: la vorágine que acabó con Mahuad*. Ecuador: El Comercio, 2000.

Herrera, Padre Amable. *Monografía del Cantón de Otavalo*. Quito: Tipografía y Encuadernación Salesiana, 1909.

Hewitt de Alcántara, Cynthia. *Anthropological Perspectives on Rural Mexico*. International Library of Anthropology. London: Routledge and Kegan Paul, 1984.

Hudelson, John Edwin. *La cultura quichua de transición su expansión y desarrollo en el alto amazonas*. Guayaquil, Quito: Museo Antropológico del Banco Central del Ecuador. Ediciones Abya-Yala, 1987.

Hurtado, Osvaldo. *Political Power in Ecuador*. Albuquerque: University of New Mexico Press, 1980.

Ibarra, Alicia. *Los indígenas y el estado en el Ecuador: la práctica neoindigenista*. 2d ed. Quito: Ediciones Abya-Yala, 1992.

Ibarra C., Hernán. *"Nos encontramos amenazados por todita la indiada": El levantamiento de Daquilema (Chimborazo 1871)*. Serie Movimiento Indígena en el Ecuador Contemporáneo 3. Quito: Centro de Estudios y Difusión Social (CEDIS), 1993.

Icaza, Jorge. *Huasipungo: The Villagers, a Novel*. Contemporary Latin American classics. Carbondale: Southern Illinois University Press, 1964.

Instituto Indigenista Ecuatoriano. *Cuestiones indígenas del Ecuador*. Quito: Edit. Casa de la Cultura Ecuatoriana, 1946.

Instituto Nacional Indigenista (Mexico). *INI 30 años después: revisión crítica*. Mexico City: Instituto Nacional Indigenista. Secretaría de Desarrollo Social, 1978.

———. *Instituto Nacional Indigenista, 1989–1994*. Mexico City: Instituto Nacional Indigenista. Secretaría de Desarrollo Social, 1994.

Irurozqui, Marta. *La armonía de las desigualdades: élites y conflictos de poder en Bolivia, 1880–1920*. Archivos de historia andina, 18. Madrid, España, and Cusco, Perú: Consejo Superior de Investigaciones Científicas. Centro de Estudios Regionales Andinos "Bartolomé de Las Casas," 1994.

Iturralde G., Diego. "Nacionalidades indígenas y estado nacional en Ecuador." In *Nueva historia del Ecuador*. Vol. 13, *Ensayos generales II: nación, estado y sistema político*, edited by Enrique Ayala Mora, 9–58. Quito: Corporación Editora Nacional, 1995.

Jackson, Jean. "Culture, Genuine and Spurious: The Politics of Indianness in the Vaupés, Colombia." *American Ethnologist* 22, no. 1 (1995): 3–27.

Jaramillo Alvarado, Pío. *El indio ecuatoriano: Contribución al estudio de la sociología indoamericana*. 2 vols., 6th ed. Quito: Corporación Editora Nacional, 1983 [1922].

Joseph, Gilbert M., and Daniel Nugent. "Popular Culture and State Formation in Revolutionary Mexico." In *Everyday Forms of State Formation: Revolution and Negotiation of Rule in Modern Mexico*, edited by Gilbert M. Joseph and Daniel Nugent, 3–23. Durham: Duke University Press, 1994.

Joseph, Gilbert M., and Daniel Nugent, eds. *Everyday Forms of State Formation: Revolution and Negotiation of Rule in Modern Mexico*. Durham: Duke University Press, 1994.

Jouanen, José. *Los jesuítas y el Oriente ecuatoriano, 1868–1898: monografía histórica*. Guayaquil: Editorial Arquidiocesana Justicia y Paz, 1977.

Juan, Jorge, and Antonio de Ulloa. *A Voyage to South America, 1748*. 5th ed. London: Printed for J. Stockdale etc., 1807.

Junta Nacional de Planificación. *III censo de población 1974, Resultados definitivos*. Quito: Oficina de los Censos Nacionales, 1974.

Karakras, Ampam. "Indigenous Sovereignty: An Ecuadorian Perspective." *Cultural Survival Quarterly* 25, no. 2 (Summer 2001): 60–62.

———. *Las nacionalidades indias y el estado Ecuatoriano*. Quito: Editorial TINCUI–CONAIE, 1990.

Karsten, Rafael. *The Head-hunters of the Western Amazonas: The Life and Culture of the Jibaro Indians of Eastern Ecuador and Peru*. Helsinki: Societas Scientiarum Fennica, Commentationes Humanarum Litterarum, 1935.

Keesing, Roger M. "Creating the Past: Custom and Identity in the Contemporary Pacific." *Contemporary Pacific* 1, nos. 1–2 (1989): 19–42.

Kimerling, Judith. "Rights, Responsibilities, and Realities: Environmental Protection Law in Ecuador's Amazon Oil Fields." *Southwestern Journal of Law and Trade in the Americas* 2, no. 2 (1995): 294–384.

Kingman, Eduardo. "La ciudad como reinvención: el levantamiento indígena de enero de 2000 y la toma de Quito." *Íconos* 10 (April 2001): 68–77.

Kohl, Ben. "Neoliberal Adventures in Bolivia." Paper presented at the annual meeting of the American Association of Geographers, March 14–19, 2004.

———. "Stablizing Neoliberalism in Bolivia: Privatization and Participation in Bolivia." *Political Geography* 21, no. 4 (2003): 449–72.

Korovkin, Tanya. "Indigenous Peasant Struggles and the Capitalist Modernization of Agriculture: Chimborazo, 1964–1991." *Latin American Perspectives* 24, no. 3 (94) (May 1997): 25–49.

Kyle, David. *Transnational Peasants: Migrations, Networks, and Ethnicity in Andean Ecuador*. Baltimore: Johns Hopkins University Press, 2001.

Kymlicka, Will, "Liberalism and the Politicization of Ethnicity." *Canadian Journal of Law and Jurisprudence* 4, no. 2 (1991): 239–56.

———. *Multicultural Citizenship: A Liberal Theory of Minority Rights*. Oxford and New York: Clarendon Press, 1995.

Kymlicka, Will, and Wayne Norman. "Return of the Citizen: A Survey of Recent Work on Citizenship Theory." *Ethics* 104, no. 2 (January 1994): 352–81.

Lajo, Javier. "Commentary on 'Un País Sin Indígenas': Indigenous Invisibility in Peru." Unpublished manuscript.

Lane, Kris E. *Quito 1599: City and Colony in Transition*. Diálogos. Albuquerque: University of New Mexico Press, 2002.

Larson, Brooke. "Andean Highland Peasants and the Trials of Nation Making during the Nineteenth Century." In *The Cambridge History of the Native Peoples of the Americas*. Vol. 3, *South America, part 2*, edited by Frank Salomon and Stuart B. Schwartz, 558–703. Cambridge: Cambridge University Press, 1999.

———. *Trials of Nation Making: Liberalism, Race, and Ethnicity in the Andes, 1810–1910*. Cambridge: Cambridge University Press, 2004.

Larson, Brooke, Olivia Harris, and Enrique Tandeter, eds. *Ethnicity, Markets, and Migration in the Andes: At the Crossroads of History and Anthropology*. Durham: Duke University Press, 1995.

LeGrand, Catherine. *Frontier Expansion and Peasant Protest in Colombia, 1850–1936*. Albuquerque: University of New Mexico Press, 1986.

Lentz, Carola. *Migración e identidad étnica la transformación histórica de una comunidad indígena en la sierra ecuatoriana*. Quito: Ediciones Abya-Yala, 1997.

León, Francisco Javier. *Exposición del Ministro del Interior Dirigido al Congreso Constitucional del Ecuador en 1873*. Quito: Imprenta Nacional, 1873.

León, Jorge, and Joanne Rappaport. "The View from Colombia and Ecuador: Native Organizing in the Americas." *Against the Current* 10, no. 5 (59) (November/December 1995): 27–32.

León Trujillo, Jorge. *De campesinos a ciudadanos diferentes: El levantamiento indígena*. Quito: CEDIME/Abya-Yala, 1994.

Li, Tanya Murray. "Articulating Indigenous Identity in Indonesia: Resource Politics and the Tribal Slot." *Comparative Studies in Society and History* 42, no. 1 (2000): 149–79.

"Líder indígena Felipe Quispe da plazo de 90 días a Morales para ejecutar cambios ofrecidos." *Aporrea*. January 27, 2006. http://www.aporrea.org/dameverbo.php?docid=72317 (accessed February 18, 2006).

Linke, Lilo. *Ecuador: Country of Contrasts*. 2d ed. London: Oxford University Press, 1955.

Lluco, Miguel. "El ALCA no es un modelo equitativo, Entrevista con Luis Macas." September 2002. http://www.lainsignia.org/2002/octubre/econ_001.htm.

———. "Pachakutik se alista para las elecciones del 2002." *Rikcharishun* 29, no. 5 (December 2001).

Lockhart, James. *Spanish Peru 1532–1560: A Colonial Society*. Madison: The University of Wisconsin Press, 1968.

Loker, William M. *Globalization and the Rural Poor in Latin America*. Directions in Applied Anthropology. Boulder, CO: Lynne Rienner Publishers, 1999.

Lomnitz-Adler, Claudio. *Deep Mexico, Silent Mexico: An Anthropology of Nationalism*. Public Worlds 9. Minneapolis: University of Minnesota Press, 2001.

Loor, Wilfrido, ed. *Cartas de Gabriel García Moreno*. Quito: La Prensa Catolica, 1955.

López San Vicente, Lorenzo. *La Misión del Napo*. Quito: Imprenta de la Universidad Central, 1894.

Loveman, Brian. *For la Patria: Politics and the Armed Forces in Latin America*. Latin American Silhouettes. Wilmington, DE: SR Books, 1999.

Lucas, Kintto. *La rebelión de los indios*. Quito: Ediciones Abya-Yala, 2000.

Lucero, José Antonio. "Arts of Unification: Political Representation and Indigenous Movements in Bolivia and Ecuador." PhD diss., Princeton University, 2002.

———. "Locating the 'Indian Problem': Community, Nationality, and Contradiction in Ecuadorian Indigenous Politics." *Latin American Perspectives* 30, no. 1 (128) (January 2003): 23–48.

———. *Voices of Struggle, Struggles of Voices: Indigenous Representation in the Andes*. Pittsburgh: University of Pittsburgh Press, forthcoming.

Lucero, José Antonio, ed. *Beyond the Lost Decade: Indigenous Movements, Development, and Democracy in Latin America*. PLAS cuadernos 6. Princeton: Princeton University Press, 2003.

Luoma, Aaron, Gretchen Gordon, and Jim Shultz. "Oil and Gas Policy in Bolivia—Post-election Update." La Paz: Democracy Center, April 6, 2006. http://www.democracyctr.org (accessed April 13, 2006).

Lynch, John. "The Catholic Church in Latin America, 1830–1930." In *The Cambridge History of Latin America*. Vol. 4, *c. 1870 to 1930*, edited by Leslie Bethell, 527–95. Cambridge: Cambridge University Press, 1986.

Lyons, Barry J. *Remembering the Hacienda: Religion, Authority, and Social Change in Highland Ecuador*. Austin: University of Texas Press, 2006.

Macdonald, Theodore. "Ecuador's Indian Movement: Pawn in a Short Game or Agent in State Reconfiguration?" In *The Politics of Ethnicity: Indigenous Peoples in Latin American States*, edited by David Maybury-Lewis, 169–98. Cambridge: David Rockefeller Center for Latin American Studies, Harvard University, 2002.

———. *Ethnicity and Culture amidst New "Neighbors": The Runa of Ecuador's Amazon region*. Cultural Survival Studies in Ethnicity and Change. Boston: Allyn and Bacon, 1999.

———. "Processes of Change in Amazonian Ecuador: Quijos Quichua Indians become Cattlemen." PhD diss., University of Illinois, 1979.

Maiguashca, Juan. "El proceso de integración nacional en el Ecuador: el rol del poder central, 1830–1895." In *Historia y región en el Ecuador 1830–1930*, edited by Juan Maiguashca, 355–420. Quito: Corporación Editora Nacional, 1994.

———. "Los sectores subalternos en los años 30 y el aparecimiento del velasquismo." In *Las crisis en el Ecuador: los treinta y ochenta*, edited by Rosemary Thorp, 79–94. Quito: Corporación Editora Nacional, 1991.

Maiguashca, Juan, ed. *Historia de América Andina*. Vol. 5, *Creación de las repúblicas y formacion de la nación*. Quito: Universidad Andina Simón Bolívar, 2003.

———. *Historia y región en el Ecuador 1830–1930*. Proyecto FLACSO-CERLAC: Biblioteca de ciencias sociales, 4. v. 30. Quito: Corporación Editora Nacional, 1994.

Mainwaring, Scott, and Timothy R Scully, eds. *Building Democratic Institutions: Party Systems in Latin America*. Stanford: Stanford University Press, 1995.

Malinowski, Bronislaw. "Myth in Primitive Psychology." In *New Science Series 1*, 11–94. New York: W. W. Norton and Company, Inc., 1926.

Mallon, Florencia E. *The Defense of Community in Peru's Central Highlands: Peasant Struggle and Capitalist Transition, 1860–1940*. Princeton: Princeton University Press, 1983.

———. *Peasant and Nation: The Making of Postcolonial Mexico and Peru*. Berkeley: University of California Press, 1995.

———. "The Promise and Dilemma of Subaltern Studies: Perspectives from Latin American History." *American Historical Review* 99, no. 5 (December 1994): 1491–1515.

Mamdani, Mahmood. *Citizen and Subject: Contemporary Africa and the Legacy of Late Colonialism*. Princeton: Princeton University Press, 1996.

Mann, Michael. "The Autonomous Power of the State: its Origins, Mechanisms and Results." In *States in History*, edited by John A. Hall, 109–36. Oxford and New York: Blackwell, 1986.

Marchán Romero, Carlos, ed. *Pensamiento agrario ecuatoriano*. Biblioteca Básica del Pensamiento Ecuatoriano 23. Quito: Banco Central del Ecuador; Corporación Editora Nacional, 1986.

Marchán Romero, Carlos. "La crisis de los años treinta: diferenciación social de sus efectos económicos." In *Las crisis en el Ecuador: los treinta y ochenta*, edited by Rosemary Thorp, 31–60. Quito: Corporación Editora Nacional, 1991.

Mariátegui, José Carlos. *Siete ensayos de interpretación de la realidad peruana*. Madrid: Edición Minerva, 1979 [1928].

Martínez, Luciano. "El campesino andino y la globalización a fines de siglo (una mirada sobre el caso ecuatoriano)." *European Review of Latin American and Caribbean Studies* 77 (October 2004): 25–40.

Martínez, Luis A. "Conferencia dada por el señor don Luis A. Martínez a la Sociedad Jurídico-Literaria el 8 de diciembre de 1904." In *Pensamiento agrario ecuatoriano*, edited by Carlos Marchán Romero, 275–85. Quito: Banco Central del Ecuador; Corporación Editora Nacional, 1986.

Martz, John D. *Ecuador: Conflicting Political Culture and the Quest for Progress*. Boston: Allyn and Bacon, 1972.

Mattiace, Shannan L. *To See with Two Eyes: Peasant Activism and Indian Autonomy in Chiapas, Mexico*. Albuquerque: University of New Mexico Press, 2003.

Maybury-Lewis, David, ed. *The Politics of Ethnicity: Indigenous Peoples in Latin American States*. Cambridge: David Rockefeller Center for Latin American Studies, Harvard University, 2002.

Mehta, Uday S. "Liberal Strategies of Exclusion." *Politics and Society* 18, no. 4 (December 1990): 427–54.

Meisch, Lynn A. *Andean Entrepreneurs: Otavalo Merchants and Musicians in the Global Arena*. Joe R. and Teresa Lozano Long Series in Latin American and Latino Art and Culture. Austin: University of Texas Press, 2003.

———. "We Will Not Dance on the Tomb of Our Grandparents: 500 Years of Resistance in Ecuador." *Latin American Anthropology Review* 4, no. 2 (Winter 1992): 55–74.

Méndez G., Cecilia. *Incas sí, indios no: apuntes para el estudio del nacionalismo criollo en el Perú*. 2d ed. Documento de trabajo: Serie Historia (Instituto de Estudios Peruanos) 56, no. 10. Lima: IEP, 1995.

Mera, Juan León. *Catecismo de geografía de la República del Ecuador, para uso de las escuelas de esta República*. Quito: n.p., 1875.

Mijeski, Kenneth J., and Scott H. Beck. "Mainstreaming the Indigenous Movement in Ecuador: The Electoral Strategy." Paper presented at the annual meeting of the Latin American Studies Association, Chicago, September 24–26, 1998.

Miller, Francesca. "The Suffrage Movement in Latin America." In *Confronting Change, Challenging Tradition: Women in Latin American History*, edited by Gertrude Matyoka Yeager, 157–76. Wilmington, DE: Scholarly Resources Inc, 1994.

Millones, Luis. "Hay un país sin indígenas entre Ecuador y Bolivia." In *Conversaciones para la conviencia*, edited by Marta Bulnes, 79–88. Lima: GTZ, 2000.

Mills, C. Wright. *The Sociological Imagination*. New York: Oxford University Press, 1959.

Ministerio de Defensa Nacional. "Historia del Ecuador: El Reino de Quito in El Ecuador y sus Fuerzas Amadas." 2002.

Miño, Cecilia. *Tránsito Amaguaña*. Quito: Banco Central del Ecuador, 2006.

Molina, Alberto. *Las Fuerzas Armadas Ecuatorianas: paz y desarrollo*. Quito: Asociación Latinoamericana de Derechos Humanos (ALDHU), 1993.

Moncayo, Abelardo. "El concertaje de indios." In *Pensamiento agrario ecuatoriano*, edited by Carlos Marchán Romero, 287–326. Quito: Banco Central del Ecuador; Corporación Editora Nacional, 1986.

Moncayo, Pedro. *Cuestión de límites entre el Ecuador y el Perú segun el uti possidetis de 1810 y los tratados de 1829*. Santiago de Chile: Imprenta Nacional, 1860.

Moreno Yánez, Segundo E. *Alzamientos indígenas en la Audiencia de Quito, 1534–1803*. 2d ed. Quito: Ediciones Abya-Yala, 1989.

———. *Antropología ecuatoriana: Pasado y presente*. Colección Primicias de la Cultura de Quito 1. Quito: Editorial Ediguias C. Ltda., 1992.

Moreno Yánez, Segundo E., and José Figueroa. *El levantamiento indígena del inti raymi de 1990*. Quito: Ediciones Abya-Yala, 1992.

Moscoso, Gladys. "Las Imágenes de la Literatura." In *Y el amor no era todo . . . mujeres, imágenes y conflictos*, edited by Martha Moscoso. Quito: Abya Yala/DGIS, 1996.

———. "La violencia contra las mujeres." In *Y el amor no era todo . . . mujeres, imágenes y conflictos*, edited by Martha Moscoso, 187–209. Quito: Abya Yala/DGIS, 1996.

Moscoso, Martha. "Discurso religioso y discurso Liberal: La mujer sumisa." In *Y el amor no era todo . . . mujeres, imágenes y conflictos*, edited by Martha Moscoso. Quito: Abya Yala/DGIS, 1996.

———. "La tierra: Espacio de conflicto y relación entre el Estado y la comunidad en el sigo XIX." In *Los Andes en la encrucijada: indios, comunidades y estado en el siglo XIX*, edited by Heraclio Bonilla, 367–90. Quito: Ediciones Libri Mundi–Facultad Latinoamericana de Ciencias Sociales (FLACSO), 1991.

Moscoso C., Martha. "Comunidad, autoridad indígena, y poder republicano." *Revista Andina* 7 (2), no. 14 (1989): 481–500.

Muñoz, Leonardo J. *Testimonio de lucha: memorias sobre la historia del socialismo en el Ecuador*. Colección Testimonios 1. Quito: Corporación Editora Nacional, 1988.

Muratorio, Blanca. *Etnicidad, evangelización y protesta en el Ecuador: una perspectiva antropológica*. Quito: Centro de Investigaciones y Estudios Socio-Económicos, 1982.

———. *The Life and Times of Grandfather Alonso: Culture and History in the Upper Amazon*. Hegemony and Experience: Critical Studies in Anthropology and History. New Brunswick, NJ: Rutgers University Press, 1991.

———. "Nación, identidad, y etnicidad: Imágenes de los indios ecuatorianos y sus imagineros a fines del siglo XIX." In *Imágenes e imagineros: representaciones de los indígenas ecuatorianos, siglos XIX y XX*, edited by Blanca Muratorio. Quito: Facultad Latinoamericana de Ciencias Sociales–Sede Ecuador, 1994.

———. "Protestantism and Capitalism Revisited, in the Rural Highlands of Ecuador." *Journal of Peasant Studies* 8, no. 1 (October 1980): 37–60.

Muratorio, Blanca, ed. *Imágenes e imagineros: representaciones de los indígenas ecuatorianos, siglos XIX y XX*. Quito: Facultad Latinoamericana de Ciencias Sociales-Sede Ecuador, 1994.

Murra, John V. "The Historic Tribes of Ecuador." In *Handbook of South American Indians*. Vol. 2, *The Andean Civilizations*, edited by Julian H. Steward, 785–821. Washington, DC: U.S. Government Printing Office, 1946.

Noboa, Alejandro. *Recopilación de mensajes dirijidos por los Presidentes y Vicepresidentes de la República jefes supremos y gobiernos provisorios a las convenciones y congresos na-*

cionales desde el año de 1819 hasta nuestros días. Guayaquil: Impr. de A. Noboa, 1900–08.

North, Liisa L., and John D. Cameron, eds. *Rural Progress, Rural Decay: Neoliberal Adjustment Policies and Local Initiatives*. Bloomfield, CT: Kumarian Press, 2003.

Nugent, David. *Modernity at the Edge of Empire: State, Individual, and Nation in the Northern Peruvian Andes, 1885–1935*. Stanford: Stanford University Press, 1997.

Nuijten, Monique. "Between Fear and Fantasy: Governmentality and the Working of Power in Mexico." *Critique of Anthropology* 24, no. 3 (June 2004): 209–30.

Nunn, Frederick M. *Yesterday's Soldiers: European Military Professionalism in South America, 1890–1940*. Lincoln: University of Nebraska Press, 1983.

Oberem, Udo. *Los Quijos: historia de la transculturación de un grupo indígena en el Oriente Ecuatoriano*. Colección Pendoneros. Otavalo, Ecuador: Instituto Otavaleño de Antropología, 1980.

Obeyesekere, Gananath. *The Apotheosis of Captain Cook: European Mythmaking in the Pacific*. Princeton: Princeton University Press, 1992.

O'Connor, Erin. *Gender, Indian, Nation: The Contradictions of Making Ecuador, 1830–1925*. Tucson: University of Arizona Press, 2007.

———. "Manliness and Nation Making: Indian Men and the Abolition of Tribute in Ecuador, 1830–1857." Unpublished manuscript.

———. "Widows' Rights Questioned: Indians, the State, and Fluctuating Gender Ideas in Central Highland Ecuador, 1870–1900." *The Americas* 59, no. 1 (July 2002): 87–106.

O'Donnell, Guillermo. "On the State, Democratization and Some Conceptual Problems: A Latin American View with Glances at Some Postcommunist Countries." *World Development* 21, no. 8 (1993): 1355–69.

Oficina Nacional de Alfabetización. *La Alfabetización participatoria, como proceso sociopolítico*. Quito: Oficina Nacional de Alfabetización, 1981.

Orton, James. *The Andes and the Amazon; or, Across the Continent of South America*. New York: Harper, 1870.

Ospina Peralta, Pablo, coordinador. *En las fisuras del poder: Movimiento indígena, cambio social y gobiernos locales*. Quito: IIE; CLACSO, 2006.

Pacari, Nina. "Taking on the Neoliberal Agenda." *NACLA Report on the Americas* 29, no. 5 (March/April 1996): 23–32.

Pachano, Simón. "La sociedad imperceptible." In *Las crisis en el Ecuador: los treinta y ochenta*, edited by Rosemary Thorp, 235–58. Quito: Corporación Editora Nacional, 1991.

Pallares, Amalia. *From Peasant Struggles to Indian Resistance: The Ecuadorian Andes in the Late Twentieth Century*. Norman: University of Oklahoma Press, 2002.

Palomeque, Silvia. *Cuenca en el siglo XIX: la articulación de una región*. Colección Tesis. Historia 2. Quito: Facultad Latinoamericana de Ciencias Sociales. Abya-Yala, 1990.

———. "Estado y comunidad en el siglo XIX. Las autoridaes indígenas y su relación con el Estado." In *Los Andes en la encrucijada: indios, comunidades y estado en el siglo XIX*, edited by Heraclio Bonilla, 391–417. Quito: Ediciones Libri Mundi-Facultad Latinoamericana de Ciencias Sociales (FLACSO), 1991.

———. "Historia económica de Cuenca y de sus relaciones regionales." In *Ensayos sobre historia regional: La región centro sur*, edited by Universidad de Cuenca. Instituto de

Investigaciones Sociales and Encuentro de Historia y Realidad Económica y Social del Ecuador, 117–40. Cuenca, Ecuador: Instituto de Investigaciones Sociales de la Universidad de Cuenca. Casa de la Cultura Ecuatoriana, Nucleo del Azuay, 1982.

Paredes, Ricardo. "Acerca de la nacionalidad y el estado ecuatoriano." In *Los comunistas en la historia nacional*, edited by Domingo Paredes, 59–80. Guayaquil: Editorial Claridad, S.A., 1987.

Pateman, Carole. "Equality, Difference, Subordination: The Politics of Motherhood and Women's Citizenship." In *Beyond Equality and Difference: Citizenship, Feminist Politics, and Female Subjectivity*, edited by Gisela Bock and Susan James, 17–31. London and New York: Routledge, 1992.

Patiño, Ninfa. *El discurso de los políticos frente al otro*. Quito: Ediciones Abya-Yala; Editorial Guaymuras, 1996.

Patzi Paco, Felix. *Insurgencia y sumisión: Movimientos indígeno-campesinos (1983–1998)*. La Paz: Editores Muela del Diablo, 1999.

Paz y Miño Cepeda, Juan J. *Golpe y contragolpe: La "Rebelión de Quito" del 21 de enero de 2000*. Serie *THEmas*, "Taller de Historia Económica." Quito: Ediciones Abya-Yala, 2002.

Peñaherrera de Costales, Piedad, and Alfredo Costales Samaniego. *Recopilación de las leyes indígenas de 1830 a 1918*. Vol. 3, *Historia social del Ecuador*. Llacta 18. Quito: Editorial Casa de la Cultura Ecuatoriana, 1964.

Perreault, Thomas Albert. "Shifting Ground, Agrarian Change, Political Mobilization, and Identity Construction Among Quichua of the Alto Napo, Ecuadorian Amazonia." PhD diss., University of Colorado, 2000.

Phelan, John Leddy. *The Kingdom of Quito in the Seventeenth Century: Bureaucratic Politics in the Spanish Empire*. Madison: University of Wisconsin Press, 1967.

Pineo, Ronn F. *Social and Economic Reform in Ecuador: Life and Work in Guayaquil*. Gainesville: University Press of Florida, 1996.

Platt, Tristán. "The Andean Experience of Bolivian Liberalism, 1825–1900. Roots of Rebellion in 19th-Century Chayanta (Potosí)." In *Resistance, Rebellion, and Consciousness in the Andean Peasant World, 18th to 20th Centuries*, edited by Steve J. Stern, 280–323. Madison: University of Wisconsin Press, 1987.

———. "Calendarios tributarios e intervención mercantil. La articulación estacional de los ayllus de Lipez con el mercado minero potosino (siglo XIX)." In *La participación indígena en los mercados surandinos estrategias y reproducción social siglos XVI a XX*, edited by Olivia Harris, Brooke Larson, and Enrique Tandeter. La Paz, Bolivia: Centro de Estudios de la Realidad Económica y Social, 1987.

———. *Estado boliviano y ayllu andino: tierra y tributo en el norte de Potosí*. Historia andina 9. Lima: Instituto de Estudios Peruanos, 1982.

———. "The Janus State: Indian Sovereignty and Patrician Democracy in Republican Bolivia." Paper presented at the annual meeting of the Latin American Studies Association, 1999.

———. "Liberalism and Ethnocide in the Southern Andes." *History Workshop* 17 (Spring 1984): 3–18.

Pólit Laso, Manuel M. *Escritos y discursos de Gabriel García Moreno*. Quito: Imprenta del Clero, 1988.

Postero, Nancy. "Articulations and Fragmentations: Indigenous Politics in Bolivia." In *The Struggle for Indigenous Rights in Latin America*, edited by Nancy Grey Postero and Leon Zamosc, 189–216. Brighton: Sussex Academic Press, 2004.

———. *Now We Are Citizens: Indigenous Politics in Postmulticultural Bolivia*. Stanford: Stanford University Press, 2007.

Powers, Karen Vieira. *Andean Journeys: Migration, Ethnogenesis, and the State in Colonial Quito*. Albuquerque: University of New Mexico Press, 1995.

Prieto, Mercedes. "Haciendas estatales: un caso de ofensiva campesina: 1926–1948." In *Ecuador: cambios en el agro serraño*, edited by Miguel Murmis et al., 101–30. Quito: Facultad Latinoamericana de Ciencias Sociales (FLACSO)–Centro de Planificación y Estudios Sociales (CEPLAES), 1980.

———. *Liberalismo y temor: imaginando los sujetos indígenas en el Ecuador postcolonial, 1895–1950*. Quito: FLACSO, 2004.

Quintero, Rafael, and Erika Silva. *Ecuador: una nación en ciernes*. 3 vols. Colección Estudios 1. Quito: FLACSO–Abya-Yala, 1991.

Quispe Huanca, Felipe. *El indio en escena*. La Paz: Pachakuti, 1999.

Radcliffe, Sarah A., and Sallie Westwood. *Remaking the Nation: Identity and Politics in Latin America*. London and New York: Routledge, 1996.

Ramón Valarezo, Galo. *El regreso de los runas: la potencialidad del proyecto indio en el Ecuador contemporánea*. Quito: COMUNIDEC-Fundación Interamericana, 1993.

———. *La resistencia andina: Cayambe, 1500–1800*. Cuaderno de discusión Popular 14. Quito: Centro Andino de Acción Popular, 1987.

———. "La visión andina sobre el estado colonial." *Ecuador Debate* 12 (December 1986).

Rasnake, Roger. *Domination and Cultural Resistance: Authority and Power among an Andean People*. Durham: Duke University Press, 1988.

Redclift, Michael R., and David A. Preston. "Agrarian Reform and Rural Change in Ecuador." In *Environment, Society, and Rural Change in Latin America: The Past, Present, and Future in the Countryside*, edited by David A. Preston, 53–63. New York: J. Wiley, 1980.

Remy, María Isabel. "The Indigenous Population and the Construction of Democracy in Peru." In *Indigenous Peoples and Democracy in Latin America*, edited by Donna Lee Van Cott, 107–30. New York: St. Martin's Press in association with the Inter-American Dialogue, 1994.

Rénique C., José Luis. *La batalla por Puno conflicto agrario y nación en los Andes peruanos, 1866–1995*. Serie Estudios históricos, 39. Lima: IEP Ediciones. SUR. CEPES, 2004.

———. *Los sueños de la sierra: Cusco en el siglo XX*. Lima: CEPES, 1991.

República del Ecuador. *Anales de diputados*. September 7, 1910.

Ribadeneira, Juan Carlos, ed. *Derecho, pueblos indígenas y reforma del estado*. Biblioteca Abya-Yala 2. Quito: Ediciones Abya-Yala, 1993.

Rival, Laura M. *Trekking Through History: The Huaorani of Amazonian Ecuador*. New York: Columbia University Press, 2002.

Rivera, Silvia. "Liberal Democracy and Ayllu Democracy in Bolivia: The Case of Northern Potosí." In *The Challenge of Rural Democratisation: Perspectives from Latin America and the Philippines*, edited by Jonathan Fox. London: F. Cass, 1990.

———. *Oprimidos pero no vencidos. Luchas del campesino aymara-qheshwa, 1900–1980*. La Paz: CSUTCB-HISBOL, 1984.

Robalino Dávila, Luis. *Orígenes del Ecuador de hoy*. Vol. 1, *García Moreno*. Quito: Talleres Gráficos Nacionales, 1948.

Robinson, William I. *Promoting Polyarchy: Globalization, US Intervention, and Hegemony*. Cambridge: Cambridge University Press, 1996.

Rodas, Raquel. *Dolores Cacuango: Gran líder del pueblo indio*. Quito: Banco Central del Ecuador, 2006.

———. *Nosotras que del amor hicimos*. Quito: Raquel Rodas, 1992.

Rodríguez, Linda Alexander. *The Search for Public Policy: Regional Politics and Government Finances in Ecuador, 1830–1940*. Berkeley: University of California Press, 1985.

Rodríguez O., Jaime E., ed. *The Divine Charter: Constitutionalism and liberalism in nineteenth-century Mexico*. Latin American Silhouettes. Lanham, MD: Rowman and Littlefield Publishers, 2005.

Rogers, Elizabeth Marberry. "Ethnicity, Property, and the State: Legal Rhetoric and the Politics of Community in Otavalo, Ecuador." *Research in Economic Anthropology* 19 (1998): 69–113.

Rogers, Mark. "Spectacular Bodies: Folklorization and the Politics of Identity in Ecuadorian Beauty Pageants." *Journal of Latin American Anthropology* 3, no. 2 (1998): 54–85.

Rojas, Isaías. *The Push for Zero Coca: Democratic Transition and Counternarcotics Policy in Peru*. Washington, DC: WOLA, 2003.

Roseberry, William. *Anthropologies and Histories: Essays in Culture, History, and Political Economy*. New Brunswick, NJ: Rutgers University Press, 1989.

———. "Hegemony and the Language of Contention." In *Everyday Forms of State Formation: Revolution and Negotiation of Rule in Modern Mexico*, edited by Gilbert M. Joseph and Daniel Nugent, 355–66. Durham: Duke University Press, 1994.

———. "Images of the Peasant in the Consciousness of the Venezuelan Proletarian." In *Proletarians and Protest: The Roots of Class Formation in an Industrializing World*, edited by Michael P. Hanagan and Charles Stephenson, 149–69. New York: Greenwood Press, 1986.

Rosero, Fernando. *Levantamiento indígena: tierra y precios*. Serie Movimiento Indígena en el Ecuador Contemporáneo 1. Quito: Centro de Estudios y Difusión Social, 1990.

Rubenstein, Steven L. *Alejandro Tsakimp: A Shuar Healer in the Margins of History*. Fourth World Rising. Lincoln: University of Nebraska Press, 2002.

———. "Colonialism, the Shuar Federation, and the Ecuadorian State." *Environment and Planning D: Society and Space* 19, no. 3 (2001): 263–93.

Rubin, Jeffrey W. *Decentering the Regime: Ethnicity, Radicalism, and Democracy in Juchitán, Mexico*. Durham: Duke University Press, 1997.

———. "Meanings and Mobilizations: A Cultural Politics Approach to Social Movements and States." *Latin American Research Review* 39, no. 3 (October 2004): 106–42.

Rubio Orbe, Alfredo, ed. *Legislación indigenista del Ecuador*. Ediciones especiales del Instituto Indigenista Interamericano 17. Mexico City: Instituto Indigenista Interamericano, 1954.

Rubio Orbe, Gonzalo. *Los indios ecuatorianos: Evolución histórica y políticas indigenistas*. Quito: Corporación Editora Nacional, 1987.

Rudel, Thomas K., Diane Bates, and Rafael Machínguiashi. "Ecologically Noble Amerindians? Cattle Ranching and Cash Cropping among Shuar and Colonists in Ecuador." *Latin American Research Review* 37, no. 1 (2002): 144–59.

Rueda Novoa, Rocío. "La ruta a la Mar del Sur: un proyecto de las élites serranas en Esmeraldas (s. XVIII)." *Procesos: Revista Ecuatoriana de Historia* 3, II semestre (1992): 33–54.

Rueschemeyer, Dietrich, Evelyne Huber Stephens, and John D. Stephens. *Capitalist Development and Democracy*. Chicago: University of Chicago Press, 1992.

Saad, Pedro. "Acerca de la unidad nacional y los gobiernos seccionales." In *Los comunistas en la historia nacional*, edited by Domingo Paredes, 81–121. Guayaquil: Editorial Claridad, S.A., 1987.

Sáenz, Moisés. *Sobre el indio ecuatoriano y su incorporación al medio nacional*. Mexico City: Publicaciones de la Secretaría de Educación Pública, 1933.

Salazar, Ernesto. "The Federación Shuar and the Colonization Frontier." In *Cultural Transformations and Ethnicity in Modern Ecuador*, edited by Norman E. Whitten Jr., 589–613. Urbana: University of Illinois Press, 1981.

Salgado, Judith, ed. *Justicia indígena. Aportes para un debate*. Quito: Ediciones Abya-Yala; Universidad Andina Simón Bolívar, 2002.

Salomon, Frank. *Native Lords of Quito in the Age of the Incas: The Political Economy of North Andean Chiefdoms*. Cambridge Studies in Social Anthropology 59. Cambridge: Cambridge University Press, 1986.

Salomon, Frank, and Stuart B. Schwartz, eds. *The Cambridge History of the Native Peoples of the Americas*. Cambridge: Cambridge University Press, 1999.

Sánchez-Parga, José. "Comunidad indígena y estado nacional." In *Pueblos indios, estado y derecho*, edited by Enrique Ayala Mora et al., 61–78. Quito: Corporación Editora Nacional, 1993.

Santana, Roberto. *Ciudadanos en la etnicidad? Los indios en la política o la política de los indios*. Colección Biblioteca Abya-Yala 19. Quito: Ediciones Abya-Yala, 1995.

———. "La cuestión étnica y la democracia en el Ecuador." *Ecuador Debate* 12 (December 1986): 101–24.

Sattar, Aleezé. "An Unresolved Inheritance: Postcolonial State Formation and Indigenous Communities in Chimborazo, Ecuador, 1820–1875." PhD diss., New School University, 2001.

Saunders, J. V. D. "Man-Land Relations in Ecuador." *Rural Sociology* 26, no. 1 (March 1961): 57–69.

Sawyer, Suzana. *Crude Chronicles: Indigenous Politics, Multinational Oil, and Neoliberalism in Ecuador*. American Encounters/Global Interactions. Durham: Duke University Press, 2004.

———. "Fictions of Sovereignty: Of Prosthetic Petro-Capitalism, Neoliberal States, and Phantom-Like Citizens in Ecuador." *Journal of Latin American Anthropology* 6, no. 1 (2001): 156–97.

———. "The 1992 Indian Mobilization in Lowland Ecuador." *Latin American Perspectives* 24, no. 3 (94) (May 1997): 65–82.

Schodt, David. *Ecuador: An Andean Enigma*. Westview Profiles: Nations of Contemporary Latin America. Boulder, CO: Westview Press, 1987.

Selmeski, Brian R. "Blurred Lines Between Defense, Development and Institutional Enrichment: The Ecuadorian Army's Apoyo al Desarrollo Program." Paper presented at the Primer Encuentro de LASA Sobre Estudios Ecuatorianos, July 18–20, 2002.

———. *Remarkable Images: Ecuador's Military-Indigenous Uprising*. New York: Latin American Video Archive (LAVA), 2000. Videocassette.

Selverston, Melina H. "The Politics of Culture: Indigenous Peoples and the State in Ecuador." In *Indigenous Peoples and Democracy in Latin America*, edited by Donna Lee Van Cott, 131–52. New York: St. Martin's Press, in association with the Inter-American Dialogue, 1994.

Selverston-Scher, Melina. *Ethnopolitics in Ecuador: Indigenous Rights and the Strengthening of Democracy*. Coral Gables, FL: North-South Center Press at the University of Miami, 2001.

Smith, Richard Chase. "The Dialectics of Domination in Peru: Native Communities and the Myth of the Vast Amazonian Emptiness." Occasional paper 8. Cambridge, MA: Cultural Survival, Inc., October 1982.

———. "A Search for Unity Within Diversity: Peasant Unions, Ethnic Federations, and Indianist Movements in the Andean Republics." In *Native Peoples and Economic Development: Six Case Studies from Latin America*, edited by Theodore MacDonald, 5–38. Cambridge, MA: Cultural Survival, Inc., 1985.

Spindler, Frank MacDonald, and Nancy Cooks Brooks, eds. *Selections from Juan Montalvo*. Special Studies 23. Tempe: Center for Latin American Studies, Arizona State University, 1984.

Starn, Orin. *Nightwatch: The Politics of Protest in the Andes*. Latin America Otherwise. Durham: Duke University Press, 1999.

———. "Villagers at Arms: War and Counterrevolution in the Central-South Andes." In *Shining and Other Paths: War and Society in Peru, 1980–1995*, edited by Steve J. Stern, 224–57. Durham: Duke University Press, 1998.

Stern, Steve J. *The Secret History of Gender: Women, Men, and Power in Late Colonial Mexico*. Chapel Hill: University of North Carolina Press, 1995.

———. "The Social Significance of Judicial Institutions in an Exploitative Society: Huamanga, Peru, 1570–1640." In *The Inca and Aztec States, 1400–1800: Anthropology and History*, edited by George A. Collier, Renato I. Rosaldo, and John D. Wirth, 289–320. New York: Academic Press, 1982.

Stern, Steve J., ed. *Resistance, Rebellion, and Consciousness in the Andean Peasant World: 18th to 20th Centuries*. Madison: University of Wisconsin Press, 1987.

Stevenson, William Bennet. *Historical and Descriptive Narrative of Twenty Years' Residence in South America: containing travels in Arauco, Chile, Peru and Columbia: with Account of the Revolution, its Rise, Progress, and Results*. London: Longman, Rees, Orme, Brown and Green, 1825.

Steward, Julian H., and Alfred Métraux. "Tribes of the Peruvian and Ecuadorian Montana." In *Handbook of South American Indians*. Vol. 3, *Tropical Forest Tribes*, edited by Julian H. Steward, 535–657. Washington, DC: U.S. Government Printing Office, 1948.

Stirling, M. W. *Historical and Ethnographical Material on the Jivaro Indians*, Smithsonian Institution, Bureau of American Ethnology Bulletin 117. Washington, DC: American Ethnological Society, 1939.

Stoll, David. *Fishers of Men or Founders of Empire? The Wycliffe Bible Translators in Latin America*. London: Zed Press, 1982.

Striffler, Steve. *In the Shadows of State and Capital: The United Fruit Company, Popular Struggle, and Agrarian Restructuring in Ecuador, 1900–1995*. American Encounters/Global Interactions. Durham: Duke University Press, 2002.

Stutzman, Ronald. "*El Mestizaje*: An All-Inclusive Ideology of Exclusion." In *Cultural Transformations and Ethnicity in Modern Ecuador*, edited by Norman E. Whitten Jr., 45–94. Urbana: University of Illinois, 1981.

Sylva Charvet, Paola. *Gamonalismo y lucha campesina*. Quito: Ediciones Abya Yala, 1986.

Taylor, Anne-Christine. "God-Wealth: The Achuar and the Missions." In *Cultural Transformations and Ethnicity in Modern Ecuador*, edited by Norman E. Whitten Jr., 647–76. Urbana: University of Illinois Press, 1981.

———. "El Oriente ecuatoriano en el siglo XIX: 'el otro litoral.'" In *Historia y región en el Ecuador 1830–1930*, edited by Juan Maiguashca, 17–67. Quito: Corporación Editora Nacional, 1994.

———. "The Western Margins of Amazonia from the Early Sixteenth to the Early Nineteenth Century." In *The Cambridge History of the Native Peoples of the Americas*. Vol. 3, *South America, part 2*, edited by Frank Salomon and Stuart B. Schwartz, 188–256. Cambridge: Cambridge University Press, 1999.

Taylor, William B. *Drinking, Homicide and Rebellion in Colonial Mexican Villages*. Stanford: Stanford University Press, 1979.

Thompson, E. P. "Eighteenth-Century English Society: Class Struggle without Class?" *Social History* 3, no. 2 (1978): 133–65.

Thrupp, Lori Ann, Gilles Bergeron, and William F Waters. *Bittersweet Harvests for Global Supermarkets: Challenges in Latin America's Agricultural Export Boom*. Washington, DC: U.S.A: World Resources Institute, 1995.

Thurner, Mark. *From Two Republics to One Divided: Contradictions of Postcolonial Nationmaking in Andean Peru*. Durham: Duke University Press, 1997.

Tibán, Lourdes. "Justicia Indígena: procedimientos y prácticas." Paper presented at the Panel: Interculturalidad y justicia indígena, Universidad Andina Simón Bolívar, Quito, July 19, 2002.

Tibán, Lourdes, Raúl Llaquiche, and Eloy Alfaro. *Historia y proceso organizativo*. Latacunga, Ecuador: Movimiento Indígena y Campesino de Cotopaxi "MICC," 2003.

Ticona Alejo, Esteban, Gonzalo Rojas Ortuste, and Xavier Albó. *Votos y Wiphalas: Campesinos y pueblos originarios en democracia*. Serie Temas de la modernización: Cuadernos de investigación 43. La Paz: Fundación Milenio. Centro de Investigación y Promoción del Campesinado, 1995.

Tilly, Charles. *Social Movements, 1768–2004*. Boulder, CO: Paradigm Publishers, 2004.

Torre Araúz, Patricia de la. *La Junta de Beneficencia de Guayaquil: lo privado-local en el estado ecuatoriano*. Quito: Ediciones Abya-Yala, 1999.

Torres Galarza, Ramón, ed. *Derechos de los pueblos indígenas: Situación jurídica y políticas de estado*. Quito: CONAIE/CEPLAES–Abya-Yala, 1995.

Trabucco, Federico E. *Constituciones de la República del Ecuador*. Quito: Universidad Central, Editorial Universitaria, 1975.

Tresierra, Julio C. "Mexico: Indigenous Peoples and the Nation-State." In *Indigenous Peoples and Democracy in Latin America*, edited by Donna Lee Van Cott, 187–210. New York: St. Martin's Press, in association with the Inter-American Dialogue, 1994.

Tribunal Supremo Electoral (TSE). *Elecciones y democracia en el Ecuador*. Vol. 3, *Legislación electoral ecuatoriana*. Quito: Tribunal Supremo Electoral. Corporación Editora Nacional, 1990.

Trujillo, Jorge. *La hacienda serrana, 1900–1930*. Quito: Instituto de Estudios Ecuatorianos (IEE)–Ediciones Abya-Yala, 1986.

Uggen, John F. *Tenencia de la tierra y movilizaciones campesinas: zona de Milagro*. Ecuador 1. Quito: Andean Center for Latin American Studies, 1993.

Universidad de Guayaquil. *El 28 de mayo de 1944: testimonio*. Colección Universidad de Guayaquil 8. [Guayaquil]: Litografía e Impr. de la Universidad de Guayaquil, 1984.

Urban, Greg, and Joel Sherzer, eds. *Nation-States and Indians in Latin America*. Austin: University of Texas Press, 1991.

Uzendoski, Michael. *The Napo Runa of Amazonian Ecuador*. Urbana: University of Illinois Press, 2005.

Vallejo, Raúl. *Crónica mestiza del nuevo Pachakutik (Ecuador: del levantamiento indígena de 1990 al Ministerio Étnico de 1996)*. Latin American Studies Center Working Papers 2. College Park: University of Maryland, 1996.

Vallejo Larrea, Rafael. "Instituto Indigenista del Ecuador." *Previsión Social: Boletín del Ministerio de Previsión Social y Trabajo* 14 (1943): 8.

Van Aken, Mark. "The Lingering Death of Indian Tribute in Ecuador." *Hispanic American Historical Review* 61, no. 3 (August 1981): 429–59.

Van Cott, Donna Lee. "Broadening Democracy: Latin America's Indigenous Peoples' Movements." *Current History* 103, no. 670 (February 2004): 80–85.

———. *The Friendly Liquidation of the Past: The Politics of Diversity in Latin America*. Pittsburgh: University of Pittsburgh Press, 2000.

———. "From Exclusion to Inclusion: Bolivia's 2002 Elections." *Journal of Latin American Studies* 35, no. 4 (November 2003): 751–75.

Van Cott, Donna Lee, ed. *Indigenous Peoples and Democracy in Latin America*. New York: St. Martin's Press, in association with the Inter-American Dialogue, 1994.

Vega Ugalde, Silvia. *La Gloriosa: de la revolución del 28 de mayo de 1944 a la contrarrevolución velasquista*. Colección Ecuador/Historia. Quito: Editorial El Conejo, 1987.

Velasco Abad, Fernando. *Reforma agraria y movimiento campesino indígena de la sierra*. 2d ed. Quito: Editorial El Conejo, 1983.

Velasco, Juan de. *Historia del Reyno de Quito en la América Meridional*. Edición de la Comisión Nacional Permanante de Conmemoraciones Cívicas. Quito: Casa de la Cultura Ecuatoriana "Benjamín Carrión," 1998.

Vickers, William T. "The Modern Political Transformaton of the Secoya." In *Millennial Ecuador: Critical Essays on Cultural Transformations and Social Dynamics*, edited by Norman E. Whitten Jr., 46–74. Iowa City: University of Iowa Press, 2003.

Villavicencio, Manuel. *Geografía de la república del Ecuador*. New York: Impr. de R. Craighead, 1858.

Wade, Peter. *Race and Ethnicity in Latin America*. Critical Studies on Latin America. London. Chicago: Pluto Press, 1997.

Walsh, Catherine. "The Ecuadorian Political Irruption. Uprisings, Coups, Rebellions, and Democracy." *Nepantla: Views From South* 2, no. 1 (Spring 2001): 173–204.

Waltz, Kenneth Neal. *Theory of International Politics*. Reading, MA: Addison-Wesley, 1979.

Warren, Kay B. "Indigenous Movements as a Challenge to the Unified Social Movement Paradigm for Guatemala." In *Cultures of Politics/Politics of Cultures: Re-visioning Latin American Social Movements*, edited by Sonia E Alvarez, Evelina Dagnino, and Arturo Escobar, 165–95. Boulder, CO: Westview Press, 1998.

Warren, Kay B., and Jean E. Jackson, eds. *Indigenous Movements, Self-Representation, and the State in Latin America*. Austin: University of Texas Press, 2003.

Waters, William F. "The Road of Many Returns: Rural Bases of the Informal Urban Economy in Ecuador." *Latin American Perspectives* 24, no. 3 (94) (May 1996): 50–64.

Waters, William F., and Frederick H. Buttel. "Diferenciación sin descampesinización: acceso a la tierra y persistencia del campesinado andino ecuatoriano." *Estudios Rurales Latinoamericanos* 10, no. 3 (1987): 355–81.

Weismantel, Mary J. *Food, Gender, and Poverty in the Ecuadorian Andes*. Philadelphia: University of Pennsylvania Press, 1988.

Weismantel, Mary, and Stephen F. Eisenman. "Race in the Andes: Global Movements and Popular Ontologies." *Bulletin of Latin American Research* 17, no. 2 (May 1998): 121–42.

Whitehead, Laurence. "Bolivia and the Viability of Democracy." *Journal of Democracy* 12, no. 2 (2001): 6–16.

Whitten, Norman E., Jr. *Sacha Runa: Ethnicity and Adaptation of Ecuadorian Jungle Quichua*. Urbana: University of Illinois Press, 1976.

———. *Sicuanga Runa: The Other Side of Development in Amazonian Ecuador*. Urbana: University of Illinois Press, 1985.

Whitten, Norman E., Jr., ed. *Cultural Transformations and Ethnicity in Modern Ecuador*. Urbana: University of Illinois Press, 1981.

———. *Millennial Ecuador: Critical Essays on Cultural Transformations and Social Dynamics*. Iowa City: University of Iowa Press, 2003.

Williams, Derek. "Assembling the 'Empire of Morality': State Building Strategies in Catholic Ecuador, 1861–1875." *Journal of Historical Sociology* 14, no. 2 (June 2001): 149–74.

———. "The Making of Ecuador's *Pueblo Católico*, 1861–1875." In *Political Cultures in the Andes, 1750–1950*, edited by Nils Jacobsen and Cristóbal Aljovín de Losada. Durham: Duke University Press, 2005.

———. "Popular Liberalism and Indian Servitude: The Making and Unmaking of Ecuador's Antilandlord State, 1845–1868." *Hispanic American Historical Review* 83, no. 4 (November 2003): 697–733.

Williams, Raymond. *Marxism and Literature*. Oxford: Oxford University Press, 1977.

Willingham, Eileen. "Creating the Kingdom of Quito: Patria, History, Language and Utopia in Juan de Velasco's *Historia del Reino de Quito* (1789)." PhD diss., University of Wisconsin, Madison, 2001.

Yashar, Deborah J. "Contesting Citizenship: Indigenous Movements and Democracy in Latin America." *Comparative Politics* 31, no. 3 (October 1998): 23–42.

Ycaza, Patricio. *Historia del movimiento obrero ecuatoriana: De la influencia de la táctica del frente popular a las luchas del FUT*, segunda parte. Quito: Centro de Documentación e Información Sociales del Ecuador (CEDIME), 1991.

Yost, James A. "Twenty Years of Contact: The Mechanisms of Change in Wao ('Auca') Culture." In *Cultural Transformations and Ethnicity in Modern Ecuador*, edited by Norman E. Whitten Jr., 677–704. Urbana: University of Illinois Press, 1981.

Young, Iris Marion. "Polity and Group Difference: A Critique of the Ideal of Universal Citizenship." *Ethics* 99, no. 2 (January 1989): 250–74.

Zamosc, Leon. "Agrarian Protest and the Indian Movement in the Ecuadorian Highlands." *Latin American Research Review* 29, no. 3 (1994): 37–68.

———. *Estadística de las áreas de predominio étnico de la sierra ecuatoriana: Población rural, indicadores cantonales y organizaciones de base*. Quito: Abya Yala, 1995.

———. "The Indian Movement in Ecuador: from Politics of Influence to Politics of Power." In *The Struggle for Indigenous Rights in Latin America*, edited by Nancy Grey Postero and Leon Zamosc, 131–57. Brighton: Sussex Academic Press, 2004.

———. *Peasant Struggles and Agrarian Reform: The Ecuadorian Sierra and the Colombian Atlantic Coast in Comparative Perspective*. Latin American Issues Monograph 8. Meadville, PA: Allegheny College, 1990.

Zavaleta Mercado, René. *50 años de historia*. Colección obras completas. Cochabamba, Bolivia: Editorial "Los Amigos del Libro," 1998.

Ziegler-Otero, Lawrence. *Resistance in an Amazonian Community: Huaorani Organizing Against the Global Economy*. New York: Berghahn, 2004.

Contributors

MICHIEL BAUD is director of the Centre for Latin American Research and Documentation (CEDLA) in Amsterdam and professor of Latin American Studies at the University of Amsterdam. His current research interests are *indigenista* ideologies and their influence on present-day academic interpretations of the Andes, the role of ethnic movements in Latin American politics, and the construction of collective memories in present-day Latin America. His publications include *Peasants and Tobacco in the Dominican Republic, 1870–1930* (1995), *Etnicidad como estrategía en América Latina y el Caribe* (1996), and *Intelectuales y sus utopías: Indigenismo y la imaginación de América Latina* (2003). He recently coedited *Popular Intellectuals and Social Movements: Framing Protest in Asia, Africa, and Latin America* (2004).

MARC BECKER is associate professor of history at Truman State University in Kirksville, Missouri, where he teaches courses on ethnic identities, revolutions, and peasants. He has published *Mariátegui and Latin American Marxist Theory* (1993) and has a forthcoming book, *Indians and Leftists in the Making of Ecuador's Modern Indigenous Movements*. He is a founding member of the Ecuadorian Studies section of the Latin American Studies Association (LASA) and works with NativeWeb to help indigenous organizations establish a presence on the Internet.

A. KIM CLARK is associate professor of anthropology at the University of Western Ontario. Her book *The Redemptive Work: Railway and Nation in Ecuador, 1895–1930* (1998) won a Choice Outstanding Academic Book Award; she has also published in the *Journal of Latin American Studies*, the *Journal of Historical Sociology*, *Anthropologica*, and various Ecuadorian publications. Her ongoing research deals with relations between subordinate groups and the state in Ecuador in the first half of the twentieth century, as well as with the historical construction of racial, gender, and national ideologies during this period. Most recently, this has taken the form of a wide-ranging study of public health and Ecuadorian state formation.

JULIET S. ERAZO is assistant professor of anthropology at Florida International University and recently completed a two-year S. V. Ciriacy-Wantrup Postdoctoral Fellowship at the University of California, Berkeley. She is revising her work entitled "Constructing Autonomy: Indigenous Organizations, Governance, and Land Use in the Ecuadorian Amazon," which traces the forty-year history of an indigenous agricultural cooperative. She has contributed to group-authored articles in *Conservation Biology* and the *Journal of Political Ecology*, and has under review various articles addressing changing understandings of property and space in the cooperative.

MARÍA ELENA GARCÍA is a Mellon Postdoctoral Fellow at Tufts University. Her primary research interests include racial and ethnic politics, social movements, the anthropology of colonialism and development, and Andean cultural politics. Her book *Making Indigenous Citizens: Identities, Education, and Multicultural Activism in Peru* (2005) is a multisited ethnography of the articulation of indigenous identity, development practices, and citizenship in the Andes.

JOSÉ ANTONIO LUCERO is assistant professor of political science at Temple University. His research on indigenous politics in Bolivia, Ecuador, and Peru has been supported by the National Science Foundation, the Fulbright Institute for International Education, the MacArthur Foundation, and various sources at Princeton University and Temple University. His work on social movement theory, indigenous politics, and political crises in the Andes has appeared in *Comparative Politics, Latin American Perspectives,* and the *Journal of Democracy*. He is currently completing a book entitled *Voices of Struggle/Struggles of Voice: Indigenous Movements and Representation in Bolivia and Ecuador.*

SHANNAN MATTIACE is associate professor of political science at Allegheny College in Meadville, Pennsylvania, where she teaches courses on Latin American politics, U.S.-Latin American relations, social movements, and the politics of memory. Her work focuses on indigenous organization and politics in Chiapas, Mexico. She is the author of *To See with Two Eyes: Peasant Activism and Indian Autonomy in Chiapas, Mexico* (2003) and coeditor of *Mayan Lives, Mayan Utopias: The Indigenous Peoples of Chiapas and the Zapatista Rebellion* (2003).

ERIN O'CONNOR is assistant professor of history at Bridgewater State College in Massachusetts. Her work examines the ways that gender affected interethnic and intraethnic relations during the processes of nineteenth-century state formation. Her book *Gender, Indian, Nation: The Contradictions of Making*

Ecuador, 1830–1925 will be published in 2007. Her essays have also been published in the journal *The Americas* and in the edited collection *Contemporary Indigenous Movements in Latin America* (2003). Her ongoing research focuses on the intersection of social history and gender analysis, and she is particularly interested in urban indigenous experiences and middle-class women's engagements with the nation.

AMALIA PALLARES is associate professor of political science and Latin American and Latino studies at the University of Illinois at Chicago. Her book *From Peasant Struggles to Indian Resistance: The Ecuadorian Andes in the Late Twentieth Century* (2002) analyzes the shifts in political identity and mobilization strategy that shaped the contemporary indigenous movement. More recently, she has researched the regional autonomy movement in the Ecuadorian coast and Ecuadorian immigrant communities in the United States. She is currently working with Shannan Mattiace on a project analyzing the role played by Latin American social movements in local democratic governance and decentralization.

ALEEZÉ SATTAR has a PhD in anthropology from the New School University. Her work entitled "Postcolonial State Formation and the Reconfiguration of Indian Communities in Chimborazo, Ecuador, till 1875," based on archival research conducted in local archives in Riobamba between 1997 and 1998, examines one of the most famous indigenous uprisings of nineteenth-century Ecuador (the 1871 Rebellion of Daquilema) within the context of the shifting relationship between the state and highland Indian communities. It concludes that the 1871 rebellion was both rooted in the contradictions of Ecuador's colonial legacy and a response to the accelerated changes in state-Indian relations.

BRIAN R. SELMESKI is an anthropologist and research associate at the Royal Military College of Canada's Centre for Security, Armed Forces, and Society. From 1999 to 2001 he carried out ethnographic fieldwork on Ecuadorian military garrisons with funding from SSRC and Fulbright. His research examines how the armed forces have constructed a shared cultural framework with Indians to promote national unity, development, and security through conscription and civic action programs. In addition to written publications, Brian produced a documentary video on the January 2000 indigenous-military uprising. He has taught at FLACSO and the Pontifia Universidad Católica del Ecuador, and twice served as chair of LASA's Ecuadorian Studies Section.

WILLIAM F. WATERS was a founding professor at the Universidad San Francisco de Quito between 1988 and 1994 and returned to USFQ in 2005. In the intervening eleven years, he taught and conducted research at the George Washington University. His major professional interest is in transnational health, particularly regarding how globalization is shaped at the local level by communities and households. Working in the general area of health and development, his research interests include microenterprise development and the informal sector, health inequalities and access to health care, and the epidemiologic transition in the United States and Latin America. His applied work primarily focuses on barriers to care and the design, implementation, monitoring, and evaluation of community-based programs.

DEREK WILLIAMS teaches Latin American history at the University of Toronto. He is currently completing a book on Ecuadorian nation building under President García Moreno, *A Truly Catholic Nation: Religion and Modernity in Nineteenth-Century Ecuador.* His research on postindependence Ecuador has appeared in the *Hispanic American Historical Review,* the *Journal of Historical Sociology,* and *Procesos: Revista ecuatoriana de historia*. His current research studies nineteenth-century Catholic engagements with modernity in Latin America, focusing on initiatives in schooling, print capitalism, and civil society organizations.

Index